THE BOOK
VOLUME II

THE AMERICAN ADVERTISING AWARDS
REGIONAL AND NATIONAL
ADDY WINNERS

Quark**Immedia**™

gratification.

It's what you can expect from QuarkImmedia.

Building on the familiar **power** and **precision** of QuarkXPress™, the QuarkImmedia Design Tool lets you quickly and easily add **interactivity** to your existing print content — or create **compelling multimedia** projects from scratch. A companion to the design tool, the royalty-free QuarkImmedia Viewer, makes **Internet** distribution a snap.

Oh, sure, your ego wants to brag about scaling some monstrous learning curve. And your superego tells you that writing a dozen lines of code just to establish a hot link builds character. But your id wants to make amazing stuff, and it wants it to be painless. It wants **speed**. It wants **control**. And it wants it **now**. In short, it wants to make you look as good on screen as QuarkXPress makes you look on paper.

So let it.

www.quark.com/immedia.htm
1.800.788.7835

QUARK™

1800 Grant Street
Denver, CO 80203

THE BOOK
VOLUME II

60,000+ LOCAL ADDY ENTRIES

6,000 LOCAL WINNERS
ADVANCE TO THE REGIONAL ADDY COMPETITIONS

1350 REGIONAL WINNERS
ADVANCE TO THE AMERICAN ADVERTISING AWARDS

71 NATIONAL ADDY WINNERS

112 NATIONAL CITATIONS OF EXCELLENCE

THE AMERICAN ADVERTISING AWARDS
ADDY BOOK
IS AN ANNUAL PUBLICATION OF

ACC PUBLISHING, INC.
One East Chase Street • Suite 1129-30
Baltimore, MD 21202

ACC PUBLISHING, INC.

ANDERSON HUMPHREYS
Vice President

CHIC DAVIS
President and Publisher

CHIP WEINMAN
Secretary/Treasurer

EDITORS:
CHIC DAVIS
KIT TIPPETT
CHIP WEINMAN

BOOK DESIGN:
ANDERSON HUMPHREYS
JIM WASSERMAN

DESIGN & LAYOUT:
JIM WASSERMAN
STUDIO 31, INC.
NEW YORK, NY

MAPS:
BILLY RILEY

PRODUCTION PHOTOGRAPHY:
GLENWOOD JACKSON
GLENWOOD JACKSON STUDIOS
BALTIMORE, MD

THE BOOK IS LICENSED BY:
THE AMERICAN ADVERTISING FEDERATION
1101 VERMONT AVENUE, SUITE 500
WASHINGTON, DC 20005
202-898-0089

SPONSOR:
QUARK XPRESS

ISBN: 2-88046-255-X

DISTRIBUTED TO THE TRADE BY
ROTOVISION SA
Route de Suisse 9 CH-1295 Mies/VD Switzerland
Tel: 41-22-755-3055 • Fax: 41-22-755-4072

ROTOVISION SA, SALES & PRODUTION OFFICE
Sheridan House 112/116A Western Road
HOVE BN3 2AA/England
Tel : 44-1273-7272-68 • Fax : 44-1273-7272-69

PRODUCTION AND SEPARATION IN SINGAPORE BY
PROVISION PTE LTD
Tel: 65-334-7720 • Fax: 65-334-7721
Printed in Singapore

CONTENTS

*A NOTE ON CATEGORIES

Winners shown in each category represent the 1995 District ADDY winners;
of these winners, those that received a 1995 National ADDY Award
(black background) and a National Citation of Excellence
(grey background) preface each category.

Message from the Publisher

Welcome to Volume Two of the American Advertising Awards (ADDY) Annual — second generation of *The Book*. It seems like only yesterday when we were working feverishly to complete our first AAF Awards Annual, and we here are on number two. Thank you for your continued support for the ADDY process.

We believe that you will find this Awards Annual rewarding, informative, and useful. Its pages are a great place for recalling those special satisfying moments of your own achievement; enjoying the creative artistry and daring of others; looking for the seed or spark of a new idea; or searching for the name of a hot new creative prospect. If you respect the creative process and its processors, then this book is for you.

Publishing a book of this size, weight and variety — dependent on thousands of specifics from hundreds of places — is a tough task. Sometimes the work spurts are all-day, every-day. Always the toil is uphill, high-hill. Someone has to stay late and work hard. That "someone" this time was Kit Tippett, a young, old ADDY friend. It would have been difficult to have made it without her, and we are grateful for her efforts.

The expressed goal of the AAF American Advertising Awards (ADDYs) is to recognize and reward creative excellence in the art of advertising. The ensuing mission of this Awards Annual is to record and preserve forever the creators of advertising excellence and the creations for which they have been cited. We salute all those makers of the magic in our business.

Should you have any questions or comments, or if I can be of service in any way, please call me. I would very much like to hear from you.

Thank you.

Sincerely,

Chic

Chic Davis

From the President of the
American Advertising Federation

Congratulations to all the finalists in the American Advertising Awards Competition (*formerly the National ADDY Awards*). Your journey, that began as one of the 60,000 entries in our local awards competitions, demonstrates the uniqueness of the most representative and challenging advertising competition in the country.

I especially want to congratulate our national winners. Your work truly exemplifies **the best in American advertising**. At each level, the toughest critics of advertising in the world . . . other creatives . . . judged your work. You have competed and won against the best in American advertising.

The American Advertising Awards acknowledge and recognize creative excellence in all media of local, regional and national advertising. And that's exactly what you will see in this publication.

Thanks to your participation, proceeds from the competitions will be reinvested in the industry to support advertising education and public service advertising.

We value your support and look forward to witnessing your creative excellence in coming year's competitions.

Sincerely,

Wally Snyder

Wally Snyder

1995 AMERICAN ADVERTISING AWARD JUDGES

FRANK DeVITO
Chairman
American Advertising Awards

TED CHIN
President/Creative Director
Ted Chin & Company

STEVE SIMPSON
Associate Creative Director
Goodby, Silverstein & Partners

PHIL GANT
Executive Vice President/
Chief Creative Officer
BBDO Chicago

1995 AMERICAN ADVERTISING AWARD JUDGES

NINA DISESA
Executive Vice President/
Executive Creative Director
McCann-Erickson New York

CAROLINE R. JONES
President/Executive Creative Director
Caroline Jones Advertising

ANITA SANTIAGO
President/Creative Director
Anita Santiago Advertising

RONALD J. GORDON
President
ZGS Communications

DISTRICT ADDY JUDGES

DAVID AYRISS
Creative Director
Cole & Weber

MAUREEN BONO
*Manager of Marketing/Advertising and
Consumer Relations*
Domino Sugar Corporation

MARK BRADLEY
Senior Art Director
Young & Laramore

BOB BRIHN
Creative Director
Cole & Weber

PAT BURNHAM
Creative Director
Campbell-Mithum-Esty

REBECCA CAIN
Graphic Designer
Cain & Associates

JORGE CANTO
Creative Director
The Bravo Group

TED CHIN
President/Creative Director
Ted Chin & Company

FRANK DEVITO

TOM DIJULIO
Vice President/Creative Director
TCB

NINA DISESA
*Executive Vice President/
Executive Creative Director*
McCann-Erickson New York

DWIGHT DOUTHIT
President
Dwight Douthit Design, Inc.

LEE EPSTEIN
President/Creative Director
Epstein & Walker

JIM GARAVENTI
VP/Group Creative Director
Ingalls Quinn & Johnson

JERRY GENTILE
Chiat/Day

MICHAEL GERICKE
Partner
Pentagram Design

FRANK GINSBERG
Creative Director
Avrett Free & Ginsberg

LINDA GOLDBERG
Senior Design Director
Leo Burnett USA

ROZ GREENE
Senior Vice President/Creative Director
Altschiller Reitzfeld

ROLAND GRYBAUSKAS

DION HUGHES
Freelance Creative
Hughes & Windley

NANCY PERRY JOHNSON
Executive Vice President
Market Force, Inc.

DISTRICT ADDY JUDGES

MIKE KRIENIK
President & Creative Director
Krienik Advertising

EDWARD I. LAYTON
Director of Print Services
Temerlin McClain

JANE MAAS
Chairman Emeritus
Earle Palmer Brown/NY

LUIS MIGUEL MESSIANU
Creative Director
Del Rivero Messianu Advertising

TY MONTAGUE
Creative Director
Montague & Associates

JOE NAGY
Senior Copywriter
The Martin Agency

JARL OLSEN
Dublin Productions

KEVIN O'NEILL
EVP/Group Creative Director
Lintas NY

SUSAN READ
Consultant

MIKE RENFORD
Creative Group Head
The Richards Group

AMY KRAUSE ROSENTHAL
Boy & Girl Advertising

STEVE SILVER
Hal Riney & Partners

STEVE SIMPSON
Associate Creative Director
Goodby, Silverstein & Partners

TERI SLOSS
Partner
Take Two Productions

GENE SULIGA
Nobel Steed & Associates

LESLIE SWEET
No Bullshit Advertising

FEDERICO TRAEGER
Creative Director
Sosa, Bromley, Aguilar and Associates

SCOTT VINCENT
Fallon McElligott

BILLY WHITELAW
Senior Vice President
Y&R Detroit

JAY WILLIAMS
Creative Director
Arnold Advertising

LLOYD WOLFE
Creative Director
TBWA Switzer-Wolfe

AMERICAN ADVERTISING FEDERATION
CLUBS AND FEDERATIONS

District 1
Ad Club of Greater Boston

District 2
Advertising Association of Baltimore
Advertising Club of Metro Washington
Advertising Club of New York
Advertising Club of Central Pennsylvania
Advertising Women of New York
Frederick County Advertising Federation
New Jersey C.A.M.A.
Northeast Pennsylvania Advertising Club
Philadelphia Advertising Club
Pittsburgh Advertising Club
Professional Communicators of Western New York
Rochester Advertising Federation

District 3
Ad 2 of the Roanoke Valley
Ad 2 Richmond
Ad 2 Triangle
Ad 2 Upstate
Advertising Club of Richmond
Advertising Federation of Western North Carolina
Advertising Federation of Charleston
Advertising Federation of Spartanburg
Advertising Federation of the Roanoke Valley
Advertising Federation of Greater Hampton Roads
Cape Fear Advertising Federation
Charlotte Advertising Club
Coastal Advertising & Marketing Professionals
Columbia Advertising & Marketing Federation
Fayetteville Area Advertising Federation
Greenville Advertising Club
Hilton Head Advertising Club, Inc.
Pee Dee Advertising Federation
Piedmont Triad Advertising Federation
Triangle Advertising Federation
Triangle East Advertising & Marketing Association

District 4
Ad 2 Greater Orlando
Ad 2 Tampa Bay
Advertising Club of the Palm Beaches
Advertising Club of The Virgin Islands
Advertising Federation of Greater Ft. Lauderdale, Inc.
Advertising Federation of Southwest Florida
Advertising Federation of Greater Miami
Asociacion de Agencias Publicitarias de Puerto Rico
Daytona Beach Advertising Federation
Emerald Coast Advertising Federation
Gainesville Advertising Federation
Greater Ocala Advertising Federation
Greater Tallahassee Advertising Federation
Jacksonville Advertising Federation
Orlando Area Advertising Federation
Polk Advertising Federation
Sarasota/Bradenton/Venice Advertising Federation
Space Coast Advertising Federation
Tampa Bay Advertising Federation
Treasure Coast Advertising Federation
West Florida Advertising Council

District 5
Ad 2 Louisville
Advertising Club of Louisville
Advertising Club of Cincinnati
Advertising Club of Toledo
Advertising Club of Charleston
Advertising Club of Huntington
Advertising Federation of Columbus
Canton Advertising Club
Cleveland Advertising Club
Dayton Advertising Club
Lexington Advertising Club
The Advertising Federation of Greater Akron

District 6
Adcraft Club of Detroit
Advertising Association of Fort Wayne
Advertising Club of Evansville
Advertising Club of Lafayette
Advertising Club of Indianapolis
Advertising Federation of Saginaw Valley
Ann Arbor Advertising Club
Central Illinois Advertising Association
Chicago Advertising Federation
Flint Area Advertising Federation
Grand Rapids Area Advertising Federation
M.A.R.T.
Muncie Advertising Club
Northern Illinois Advertising Council
The Art Directors Club of Detroit
The Lansing Advertising Club, Inc.
Women's Advertising Club of Chicago

District 7
Acadiana Advertising Federation
Ad 2 Atlanta
Ad Federation of South Mississippi
Advertising Club of Central Georgia
Advertising Club of Columbus
Advertising Club of New Orleans
Advertising Federation of Greater Mobile
Advertising Federation of Greater Baton Rouge
Athens Advertising Club
Atlanta Advertising Club
Birmingham Advertising Club
Central Louisiana Advertising Club
Chattanooga Advertising Federation
Dothan Advertising Federation
Golden Triangle Advertising Federation
Greater Augusta Advertising Club
Greater Knoxville Advertising Federation
Jackson Advertising Federation
Memphis Advertising Federation
Mississippi Delta Advertising Club
Mississippi Gulf Coast Advertising Club
Montgomery Advertising Federation
Nashville Advertising Federation
North Mississippi Advertising Federation
Northeast Georgia Advertising Federation
Savannah Advertising Club
Shoals Advertising Federation
The Huntsville Advertising Federation

AMERICAN ADVERTISING FEDERATION CLUBS AND FEDERATIONS

Tri-City Metro Advertising Federation
Tuscaloosa Advertising Federation

District 8
Ad 2 Milwaukee
Advertising Association of Fox River Valley
Advertising Club of Mid Wisconsin
Advertising Club of Racine
Advertising Federation of Minnesota
Advertising Federation of Bismarck-Mandan
Advertising Federation of Fargo-Moorhead
Advertising/Marketing Federation of Central Minn.
Black Hills Advertising Federation
Great River Avertising Federation
Green Bay Advertising Federation
Lake Superior Advertising Club
Madison Advertising Federation
Milwaukee Advertising Club
South Dakota Advertising Federation
Valley Advertising and Marketing Federation

District 9
Advertisers of Dubuque
Advertising Club of Greater St. Louis
Advertising Club of Kansas City
Advertising Federation of Sioux City
Advertising Federation of Cedar Rapids
Advertising Federation of Wichita
Advertising Federation of Lincoln
Advertising Federation of Southeast Missouri
Advertising Professionals of Des Moines
Joplin Area Advertising Club
Mid Missouri Advertising Federation
Omaha Federation of Advertising
Quad City Advertising Federation
Springfield Advertising Association
St. Joseph Advertising Marketing Federation
Topeka Advertising Federation

District 10
Abilene Texas Advertising Club
Ad 2 Arkansas
Ad 2 Dallas
Ad 2 Houston
Advertising Club of Fort Worth
Advertising Club of Waco
Amarillo Advertising Federation
Arkansas Advertising Federation
Austin Advertising Federation
Central Texas Advertising League
Corpus Christi Advertising Federation
Dallas Advertising League
East Texas Advertising Federation
Greater Ft. Smith Ad Club
Houston Advertising Federation
Lake Charles Advertising Federation
Lubbock Advertising Federation
Northeast Louisiana Advertising Federation
Northwest Arkansas Advertising Federation
Oklahoma City Advertising Club
Permian Basin Advertising Federation
San Antonio Advertising Federation

Shreveport-Bossier Advertising Federation
Southeast Texas Advertising Federation
Tulsa Advertising Federation
Valley Advertising Federation
Wichita Falls Advertising Federation

District 11
Ad 2 Portland
Ad 2 Seattle
Advertising Club of Central Oregon
Advertising Federation of Alaska
American Advertising Museum
Boise Advertising Federation
Idaho Falls Advertising Federation
Mid Oregon Advertising Club
Montana Advertising Federation
Pocatello Advertising Federation
Portland Advertising Federation
Seattle Advertising Federation
Southern Oregon Advertising Professionals
Spokane Advertising Federation
Tacoma Advertising Club
The Lewis Clark Valley Ad Club
Yakima Advertising Federation

District 12
Ad 2 Phoenix
Advertising Federation of El Paso
Denver Advertising Federation
New Mexico Advertising Federation
Phoenix Advertising Club
Pikes Peak Advertising Federation, Inc.
Santa Fe Advertising Club
Tucson Advertising Club
Utah Advertising Federation

District 13
Ad 2 Honolulu
Honolulu Advertising Federation

District 14
Ad 2 San Francisco
AdMark! The East Bay Advertising Club
Bay Area S.T.A.R.
Chico Advertising Club
Fresno Advertising Federation
Greater San Jose Advertising Association
Reno Advertising Club
Sacramento Advertising Club
San Francisco Advertising Club

District 15
Advertising Club of Los Angeles
Advertising Club of San Diego
Desert Advertising Federation
Inland Empire Ad Club
Kern County Advertising Club
Las Vegas Ad Club
Los Angeles Advertising Women
The Santa Barbara Advertising Club
Ventura County Advertising Club, Inc.

AMERICAN ADVERTISING AWARDS
BEST OF SHOW TELEVISON

District 2

CLIENT
Little Caesars Pizza

AGENCY
Cliff Freeman &
Partners
New York, NY

CREATIVE DIRECTORS
Cliff Freeman
Arthur Bijur
Donna Weinheim

ART DIRECTORS
John Leu
Greg Bell
Donna Weinheim

COPYWRITERS
Greg Bell
John Leu
Cliff Freeman
Arthur Bijur
Michelle Roufa

PRODUCERS
Anne Kurtzman
MaryEllen Duggan

PRODUCTION
Crossroads Films
Harmony Pictures

Magic Fingers

SFX: *Romantic music on the radio*

WOMAN: We should've gotten the pizza.

SUPER: $1

ANNCR (VO): Pizza for a Buck! Now when you buy two pizzas with two toppings for $8.98, you get a third pizza for a buck!

LITTLE CAESAR: Pizza! Pizza!

Singing Baby

GRANNY: Have you ever seen anything more amazing than Little Caesars Italian Sausage pizza?

FATHER: ...No.

ANNCR: Italian Sausage pizza! Loaded with sausage, peppers and onions. The newest from a whole menu of Little Caesars Pleasers. Any two for $9.98!

LITTLE CAESAR: Pizza! Pizza!

ANNCR: Or get one for $5.99!

LITTLE CAESAR: Pizza!

Focus Group

SFX: *Heroic Music starts low and builds throughout.*

MODERATOR: O.K ... how many of you would like more cheese on your pizza?

MODERATOR: O.K ...

MODERATOR: How many of you would like more toppings on your pizza?

MODERATOR: ... O.K. more cheese?

MODERATOR: ... O.K ... more toppings?

MODERATOR: ... O.K ... more cheese? ... More toppings? ... More? ... More? More toppings?

MODERATOR: Cheese? ... Toppings? ... More?

SFX: *Music reaches crescendo.*

RESEARCHER: Well ... that's every man, woman, and child.

ANNCR VO: By popular demand, it's the new Little Caesars Pleasers Menu. More meat ... more cheese ... more pepperoni ... more toppings.

ANNCR VO: Any two for one low price. Satisfaction guaranteed or your money back.

LITTLE CAESAR: Pizza! Pizza!

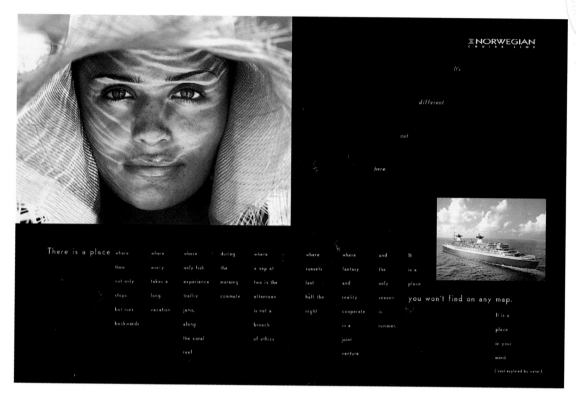

District 14

CLIENT
Norwegian Cruise Lines

AGENCY
Goodby, Silverstein & Partners
San Francisco, CA

CREATIVE DIRECTORS
Jeffrey Goodby
Rich Silverstein

ART DIRECTOR
Steve Luker

COPYWRITER
Steve Simpson

PHOTOGRAPHERS
Herb Ritts
Jim Erickson

DESIGNER
Steve Luker

PRODUCER
Laurie Lambert

ACCOUNT EXECUTIVE
Marty Wenzell

National ADDY Award

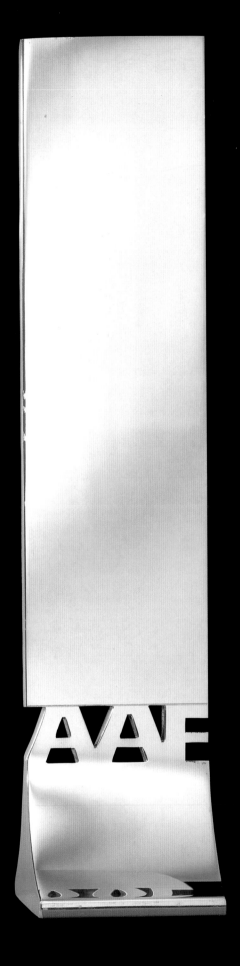

CONSUMER MAGAZINE

1
District 2

CLIENT
House of Seagrams

AGENCY
TBWA
New York, NY

CREATIVE DIRECTORS
Arnie Arlow
Peter Lubalin

ART DIRECTORS
Dan Braun
Bart Slomkowski

COPYWRITERS
Dan Braun
Bart Slomkowski

PHOTOGRAPHER
Steve Bronstein

ABSOLUT BROOKLYN.

CLIENT
Utah Symphony

AGENCY
Williams & Rockwood
Salt Lake City, UT

CREATIVE DIRECTOR
Scott Rockwood

ART DIRECTOR
David Carter

COPYWRITER
Harold Einstein

ILLUSTRATOR
Clint Hansen

Mozart. The man. The music. The wigs.

There comes a point when we realize it's time to stop partying and get down to business. For Mozart, it was age four.

Wolfgang Amadeus Mozart, the greatest child prodigy music has ever known, was pretty much like any other kid his first few years. He cried, spit up food and smelled up his diapers. Then one day he decided what the heck, plopped down and composed his first piano concerto.

Mom fainted. Dad had a more capitalistic response. No sooner was Mozart out of diapers then his father, Leopold, had him on the road, touring Europe. People came in droves to see the little boy who could play a piano sonata while blindfolded, improvise a lively tune on the violin or name any note the audience sang out. Yes, Mozart even had perfect pitch, the little bugger.

He was also the youngest musician to have groupies. Among them was little Marie Antoinette, whom Mozart proposed to at the tender age of seven. Being only seven herself, she declined of course. Marie wasn't one to lose her head until much later.

Leaving Marie behind, Mozart returned to Salzburg where he continued to make progress. He became a virtuoso on the piano and organ, composed his first symphony at seven and his first opera at twelve. The opera would have come sooner but he took some time out to hunt frogs.

Mozart did it during the Classical Period. He started young, lived young, died young. There'll never be another like him.

While he matured physically and musically, he remained forever the boy in his view of life. This singular trait is the reason he had such a tough time finding work. Oh, sure, everyone loved Mozart's music. They just didn't care for the mouth that accompanied it.

Having been fired from his post as court organist to the Archbishop of Salzburg, Mozart decided it was time to relocate. He moved to Vienna and landed the position of Court Composer for the Emperor Joseph II, a silly man, really. He was the one responsible for nearly squelching the most popular opera of all time. Mozart's Marriage of Figaro.

The Emperor banned the opera because he feared it made fools of the aristocracy. He finally aquiesced, but still would show up to a rehearsel and say things like, "Ah, yes, Mozart!, now I know what the problem is. There are far too many notes." It seems Mozart wasn't the only one capable of making a fool of the Emperor.

Eventually, Mozart decided it was probably best to work for himself. He didn't care about the money. In fact, he had no business

> **SOMETHING to IMPRESS YOUR FRIENDS WITH at a PARTY.**
> *Mozart has the distinct honor of being the only composer who could write out one piece of music while composing another in his head. He is also credited with relaxing after these tremendous displays of concentration and aptitude by turning somersaults on a table.*

sense at all. He composed music for fun. And when fun didn't pay the bills, he was more than happy to accept a commission.

The weirdest occurred just before he died. A mysterious stranger appeared at Mozart's door one evening and commissioned him to write a "mass for the dead" for an anonymous third party. Mozart set out to consume the challenge laid before him. As fate would have it, the piece wound

When listening to the 3rd movement melody of Mozart's Seranade for Winds, K. 361, one can't help but wonder if he was merely taking dictation from God.

up consuming him. Mozart took ill during this time and died, at 36, before the composition could be completed. Yet not even that could keep the Requiem Mass from becoming his greatest work of all.

Perhaps the reason Mozart's music stands apart from the rest is because he continued to approach it with a child's naivete. Music was something to play with like a good toy. Ahh, to remain a child forever. If only the rest of us were so blessed.

Title page

Symphony No. 25 in G minor

The Abduction from the Seraglio

The Marriage of Figaro

> *Upcoming Concerts*
>
> November 27 & 28
> Messiah Sing-in
> Ed Thompson, Conductor
> The Utah Symphony Chorus and soloists
>
> December 2 & 3
> Classical Series - Emerald
> Joseph Silverstein, Conductor
> Misha Dichter, Piano
> DVORAK My Home: Overture
> "MOZART Piano Concerto No. 21
> STRAVINSKY "The Firebird" Suite
>
> December 8
> Chamber Series
> Joseph Silverstein, Conductor and Violin
> VIVALDI The Four Seasons
>
> December 16 & 17
> Entertainment Series
> Joseph Silverstein, Conductor
> Featuring local high school choirs

UTAH SYMPHONY
JOSEPH SILVERSTEIN, MUSIC CONDUCTOR
Call 533-NOTE for tickets

For every vehicle there is one

perfect fuel. For performance

horses, it's Omolene 200. That's

because we start with all the

nutrients horses need, then add

our exclusive Athlete Pellet–all

the extras your performance

horse demands. In other words,

there's nothing regular about it.

Formula Ones don't run on regular.

5

District 9

CLIENT
Purina Mills Inc.

AGENCY
Simmons, Durham
St. Louis, MO

CREATIVE DIRECTOR
Ted Smmons

ART DIRECTOR
Eric Tilford

COPYWRITER
Brad Fels

For every vehicle there is one perfect fuel. For performance horses, it's Omolene 200. That's because we start with all the nutrients horses need, then add our exclusive Athlete Pellet—all the extras your performance horse demands. In other words, there's nothing regular about it.

Formula Ones don't run on regular.

Okay. Maybe Omolene 200 won't turn your horse into an instant champion. But no other feed lets your horse perform better. That's because we start with all of the nutrients horses need, then add our exclusive Athlete Pellet—all the extras your performance horse demands. Something for you to remember next trip to the feed store.

Remember what spinach did for Popeye?

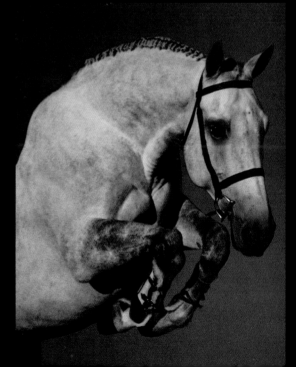

CLIENT
Norwegian Cruise Lines

AGENCY
Goodby, Silverstein & Partners
San Francisco, CA

CREATIVE DIRECTORS
Jeffrey Goodby
Rich Silverstein

ART DIRECTOR
Steve Luker

COPYWRITER
Steve Simpson

PHOTOGRAPHERS
Herb Ritts
Jim Erickson

DESIGNER
Steve Luker

PRODUCER
Laurie Lambert

ACCOUNT EXECUTIVE
Marty Wenzell

≅ NORWEGIAN
CRUISE LINE

It's

different

out

here

There is a place where ... where ... where ... during ... where ... where ... where ... and ... It
time ... worry ... only fish ... the ... a map of ... sunsets ... fantasy ... the ... is a
not only ... takes a ... experience ... morning ... two in the ... last ... and ... only ... place
stops ... long ... traffic ... commute ... afternoon ... half the ... reality ... reason ... you won't find on any map.
but runs ... vacation ... jams ... is not a ... night ... cooperate ... is ... It is a
backwards ... along ... breach ... in a ... place
the coral ... of others ... point ... in your
reef ... venture ... mind

There is no law that says you
can't make love at 4 in the afternoon on a Tuesday
shall not study a sunset or train butterflies ... must pay tax on itemized moments of pleasure
may not have extra mushrooms with your steak ... can't disembark in Tortola and stay there
must park every along with your luggage ... can't learn about life from a turtle
must contribute to the GNP every single solitary day of your life
absolutely must act your chronological age not your shoesize ... shall maintain strict economies of emotion
can't make love again at 5 in the afternoon on the Tuesday we spoke of earlier
because the laws of the land do not apply ... the laws are different out here

It's

different

out

here

≅ NORWEGIAN
CRUISE LINE

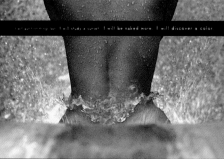

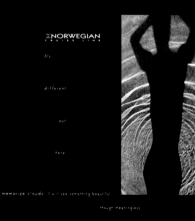

≅ NORWEGIAN
CRUISE LINE

It's

different

out

here

7

Clockwise from top left, that's Jack Daniel, Jess Motlow, Lem Tolley, Frank Bobo and Jess Gamble. (Jimmy's in the middle).

JACK DANIEL'S HEAD DISTILLER, Jimmy Bedford, has lots of folks looking over his shoulder.

Since 1866, we've had only six head distillers. (Every one a Tennessee boy, starting with Mr. Jack Daniel himself.) Like those before him, Jimmy's mindful of our traditions, such as the oldtime way we smooth our whiskey through 10 feet of hard maple charcoal. He knows Jack Daniel's drinkers will judge him with every sip. So he's not about to change a thing. The five gentlemen on his wall surely must be pleased about that.

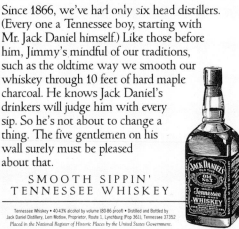

SMOOTH SIPPIN'
TENNESSEE WHISKEY

Tennessee Whiskey • 40-43% alcohol by volume (80-86 proof) • Distilled and Bottled by
Jack Daniel Distillery, Lem Motlow, Proprietor, Route 1, Lynchburg (Pop 361), Tennessee 37352
Placed in the National Register of Historic Places by the United States Government.

8

Now that you've narrowed down your college financial aid options, we can help.
We offer a pile of loan programs. And something even better: people who can tell you about them
in plain English. Just stop by any National City Bank office. Or call 1-800-622-5097.

National City Bank ℠

Going the distance for you

9

9
District 5

CLIENT
National City
Corporation

AGENCY
Marcus Advertising
Beachwood, OH

ART DIRECTOR
Brian Roach

COPYWRITER
Jim Sollisch

10
District 5

CLIENT
Jewish Hospital

AGENCY
Doe-Anderson
Advertising & PR
Louisville, KY

CREATIVE DIRECTOR
Gary Sloboda

ART DIRECTORS
Scott Troutman
Stefanie Becker

COPYWRITER
Russ Cashon

PHOTOGRAPHER
John Lair

10

11
District 2

CLIENT
General Motors
Corporation

AGENCY
N.W. Ayer & Partners
New York, NY

CREATIVE DIRECTOR
Stephen Feinberg

ART DIRECTOR
Jochen Oster

COPYWRITER
Bob Waldner

PHOTOGRAPHER
Robert Riggs

12
District 10

CLIENT
Tracy-Locke, Inc.

AGENCY
DDB Needham
Worldwide Dallas
Group
Dallas, TX

CREATIVE DIRECTOR
Mary Knight

ART DIRECTOR
Greg Gerhard

COPYWRITER
Hal Reeves

PHOTOGRAPHER
John Katz

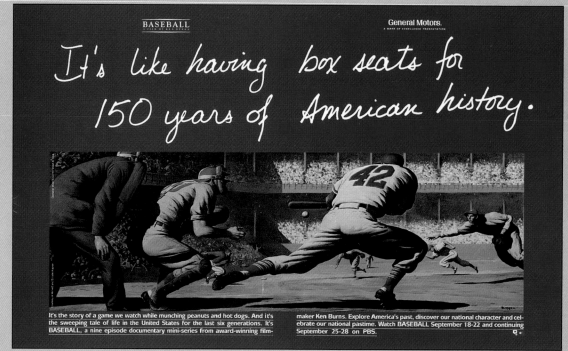

11

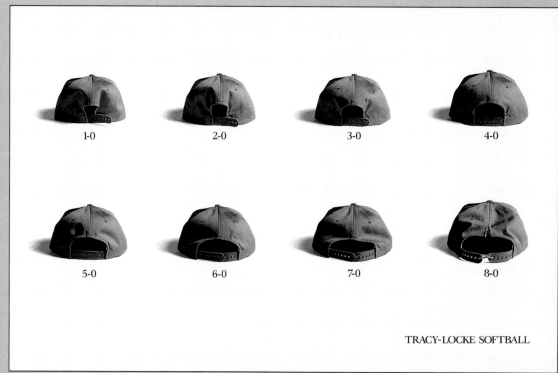

12

SOMEWHERE BETWEEN HOME AND WORK
IS A VACATION.

RALEIGH

13
District 11
CLIENT
Raleigh
AGENCY
Hammerquist & Saffel
Seattle, WA
ART DIRECTOR
Fred Hammerquist
COPYWRITER
Hugh Saffel
PRODUCTION
Norm Hansen
ACCOUNT EXECUTIVE
Sally Bjornsen

EXERCISE YOUR RIGHT TO LEAVE
YOUR CAR AT HOME.

RALEIGH

YOU WON'T HAVE TO PUT CARDS IN THE SPOKES
TO MAKE IT FEEL FAST.

RALEIGH

CONSUMER MAGAZINE

14

District 12

CLIENT
Utah Symphony

AGENCY
Williams & Rockwood
Salt Lake City, UT

CREATIVE DIRECTOR
Scott Rockwood

ART DIRECTOR
David Carter

COPYWRITER
Harold Einstein

ILLUSTRATOR
Clint Hansen

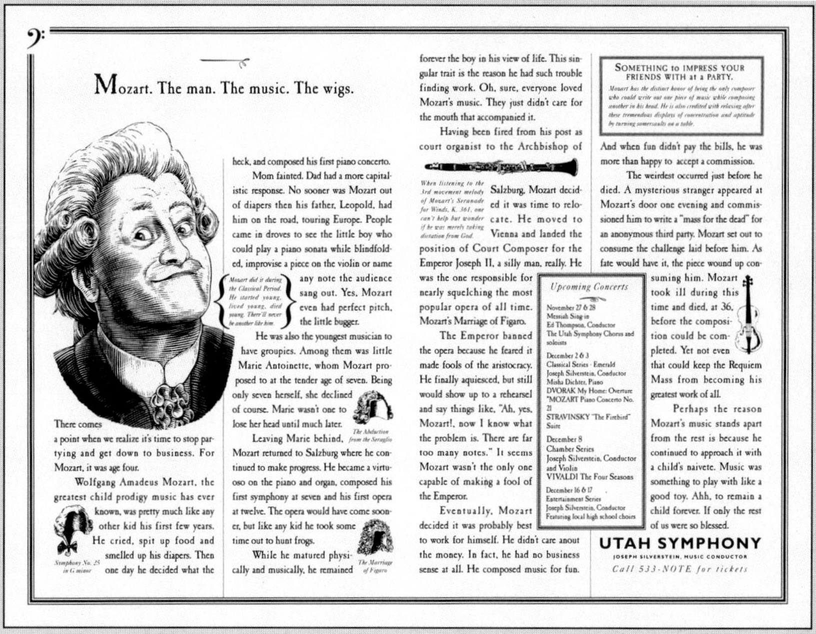
Mozart. The man. The music. The wigs.
There comes a point when we realize it's time to stop partying and get down to business. For Mozart, it was age four.
Wolfgang Amadeus Mozart, the greatest child prodigy music has ever known, was pretty much like any other kid his first few years. He cried, spit up food and smelled up his diapers. Then one day he decided what the heck, and composed his first piano concerto.
Symphony No. 25 in G minor
Mom fainted. Dad had a more capitalistic response. No sooner was Mozart out of diapers then his father, Leopold, had him on the road, touring Europe. People came in droves to see the little boy who could play a piano sonata while blindfolded, improvise a piece on the violin or name any note the audience sang out. Yes, Mozart even had perfect pitch, the little bugger.
Mozart did it during the Classical Period. He started young, lived young, died young. There'll never be another like him.
He was also the youngest musician to have groupies. Among them was little Marie Antoinette, whom Mozart proposed to at the tender age of seven. Being only seven herself, she declined of course. Marie wasn't one to lose her head until much later.
The Abduction from the Seraglio
Leaving Marie behind, Mozart returned to Salzburg where he continued to make progress. He became a virtuoso on the piano and organ, composed his first symphony at seven and his first opera at twelve. The opera would have come sooner, but like any kid he took some time out to hunt frogs.
While he matured physically and musically, he remained forever the boy in his view of life. This singular trait is the reason he had such trouble finding work. Oh, sure, everyone loved Mozart's music. They just didn't care for the mouth that accompanied it.
The Marriage of Figaro
Having been fired from his post as court organist to the Archbishop of Salzburg, Mozart decided it was time to relocate. He moved to Vienna and landed the position of Court Composer for the Emperor Joseph II, a silly man, really. He was the one responsible for nearly squelching the most popular opera of all time. Mozart's Marriage of Figaro.
When listening to the 3rd movement melody of Mozart's Serenade for Winds, K. 361, one can't help but wonder if he was merely taking dictation from God.
The Emperor banned the opera because he feared it made fools of the aristocracy. He finally aquiesced, but still would show up to a rehearsel and say things like, "Ah, yes, Mozart!, now I know what the problem is. There are far too many notes." It seems Mozart wasn't the only one capable of making a fool of the Emperor.
Eventually, Mozart decided it was probably best to work for himself. He didn't care anout the money. In fact, he had no business sense at all. He composed music for fun.
Upcoming Concerts
November 27 & 28
Messiah Sing-in
Ed Thompson, Conductor
The Utah Symphony Chorus and soloists
December 2 & 3
Classical Series · Emerald
Joseph Silverstein, Conductor
Misha Dichter, Piano
DVORAK My Home: Overture
*MOZART Piano Concerto No. 21
STRAVINSKY "The Firebird" Suite
December 8
Chamber Series
Joseph Silverstein, Conductor and Violin
VIVALDI The Four Seasons
December 16 & 17
Entertainment Series
Joseph Silverstein, Conductor
Featuring local high school choirs
SOMETHING to IMPRESS YOUR FRIENDS WITH at a PARTY.
Mozart has the distinct honor of being the only composer who could write out one piece of music while composing another in his head. He is also credited with relaxing after these tremendous displays of concentration and aptitude by turning somersaults on a table.
And when fun didn't pay the bills, he was more than happy to accept a commission.
The weirdest occurred just before he died. A mysterious stranger appeared at Mozart's door one evening and commissioned him to write a "mass for the dead" for an anonymous third party. Mozart set out to consume the challenge laid before him. As fate would have it, the piece wound up consuming him. Mozart took ill during this time and died, at 36, before the composition could be completed. Yet not even that could keep the Requiem Mass from becoming his greatest work of all.
Perhaps the reason Mozart's music stands apart from the rest is because he continued to approach it with a child's naivete. Music was something to play with like a good toy. Ahh, to remain a child forever. If only the rest of us were so blessed.
UTAH SYMPHONY
JOSEPH SILVERSTEIN, MUSIC CONDUCTOR
Call 533-NOTE for tickets

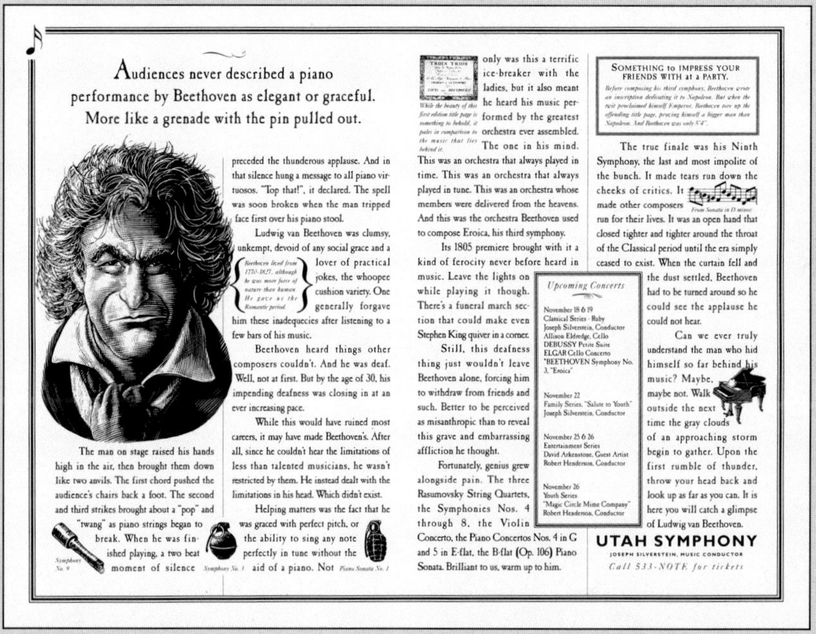
Audiences never described a piano performance by Beethoven as elegant or graceful. More like a grenade with the pin pulled out.
The man on stage raised his hands high in the air, then brought them down like two anvils. The first chord pushed the audience's chairs back a foot. The second and third strikes brought about a "pop" and "twang" as piano strings began to break. When he was finished playing, a two beat moment of silence preceded the thunderous applause. And in that silence hung a message to all piano virtuosos. "Top that!", it declared. The spell was soon broken when the man tripped face first over his piano stool.
Symphony No. 9
Ludwig van Beethoven was clumsy, unkempt, devoid of any social grace and a lover of practical jokes, the whoopee cushion variety. One generally forgave him these inadequecies after listening to a few bars of his music.
Beethoven lived from 1770-1827, although he was more force of nature than human. He gave us the Romantic period.
Beethoven heard things other composers couldn't. And he was deaf. Well, not at first. But by the age of 30, his impending deafness was closing in at an ever increasing pace.
While this would have ruined most careers, it may have made Beethoven's. After all, since he couldn't hear the limitations of less than talented musicians, he wasn't restricted by them. He instead dealt with the limitations in his head. Which didn't exist.
Helping matters was the fact that he was graced with perfect pitch, or the ability to sing any note perfectly in tune without the aid of a piano. Not only was this a terrific ice-breaker with the ladies, but it also meant he heard his music performed by the greatest orchestra ever assembled. The one in his mind. This was an orchestra that always played in time. This was an orchestra that always played in tune. This was an orchestra whose members were delivered from the heavens. And this was the orchestra Beethoven used to compose Eroica, his third symphony.
Symphony No. 3
Piano Sonata No. 1
While the beauty of this first edition title page is something to behold, it pales in comparison to the music that lies behind it.
Its 1805 premiere brought with it a kind of ferocity never before heard in music. Leave the lights on while playing it though. There's a funeral march section that could make even Stephen King quiver in a corner.
Still, this deafness thing just wouldn't leave Beethoven alone, forcing him to withdraw from friends and such. Better to be perceived as misanthropic than to reveal this grave and embarrassing affliction he thought.
Fortunately, genius grew alongside pain. The three Rasumovsky String Quartets, the Symphonies Nos. 4 through 8, the Violin Concerto, the Piano Concertos Nos. 4 in G and 5 in E-flat, the B-flat (Op. 106) Piano Sonata. Brilliant to us, warm up to him.
Upcoming Concerts
November 18 & 19
Classical Series · Ruby
Joseph Silverstein, Conductor
Allison Eldredge, Cello
DEBUSSY Petite Suite
ELGAR Cello Concerto
*BEETHOVEN Symphony No. 3, "Eroica"
November 22
Family Series, "Salute to Youth"
Joseph Silverstein, Conductor
November 25 & 26
Entertainment Series
David Arkenstone, Guest Artist
Robert Henderson, Conductor
November 26
Youth Series
"Magic Circle Mime Company"
Robert Henderson, Conductor
SOMETHING to IMPRESS YOUR FRIENDS WITH at a PARTY.
Before composing his third symphony, Beethoven wrote an inscription dedicating it to Napoleon. But when the twit proclaimed himself Emperor, Beethoven tore up the offending title page, proving himself a bigger man than Napoleon. And Beethoven was only 5'4".
The true finale was his Ninth Symphony, the last and most impolite of the bunch. It made tears run down the cheeks of critics. It made other composers run for their lives. It was an open hand that closed tighter and tighter around the throat of the Classical period until the era simply ceased to exist. When the curtain fell and the dust settled, Beethoven had to be turned around so he could see the applause he could not hear.
From Sonata in D minor
Can we ever truly understand the man who hid himself so far behind his music? Maybe, maybe not. Walk outside the next time the gray clouds of an approaching storm begin to gather. Upon the first rumble of thunder, throw your head back and look up as far as you can. It is here you will catch a glimpse of Ludwig van Beethoven.
UTAH SYMPHONY
JOSEPH SILVERSTEIN, MUSIC CONDUCTOR
Call 533-NOTE for tickets

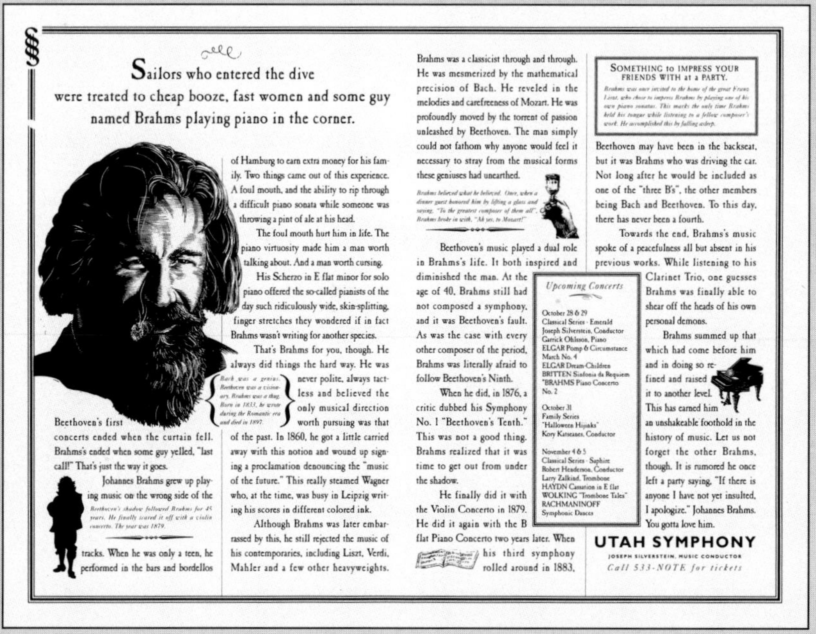
Sailors who entered the dive were treated to cheap booze, fast women and some guy named Brahms playing piano in the corner.
Beethoven's first concerts ended when the curtain fell. Brahms's ended when some guy yelled, "last call!" That's just the way it goes.
Johannes Brahms grew up playing music on the wrong side of the tracks. When he was only a teen, he performed in the bars and bordellos of Hamburg to earn extra money for his family. Two things came out of this experience. A foul mouth, and the ability to rip through a difficult piano sonata while someone was throwing a pint of ale at his head.
Beethoven's shadow followed Brahms for 45 years. He finally scared it off with a violin concerto. The year was 1879.
The foul mouth hurt him in life. The piano virtuosity made him a man worth talking about. And a man worth cursing.
His Scherzo in E flat minor for solo piano offered the so-called pianists of the day such ridiculously wide, skin-splitting, finger stretches they wondered if in fact Brahms wasn't writing for another species.
That's Brahms for you, though. He always did things the hard way. He was never polite, always tactless and believed the only musical direction worth pursuing was that of the past. In 1860, he got a little carried away with this notion and wound up signing a proclamation denouncing the "music of the future." This really steamed Wagner who, at the time, was busy in Leipzig writing his scores in different colored ink.
Bach was a genius. Beethoven was a visionary. Brahms was a thug. Born in 1833, he wrote during the Romantic era and died in 1897.
Although Brahms was later embarrassed by this, he still rejected the music of his contemporaries, including Liszt, Verdi, Mahler and a few other heavyweights. Brahms was a classicist through and through. He was mesmerized by the mathematical precision of Bach. He reveled in the melodies and carefreeness of Mozart. He was profoundly moved by the torrent of passion unleashed by Beethoven. The man simply could not fathom why anyone would feel it necessary to stray from the musical forms these geniuses had unearthed.
Brahms believed what he believed. Once, when a dinner guest honored him by lifting a glass and saying, "To the greatest composer of them all", Brahms broke in with, "Ah yes, to Mozart!"
Beethoven's music played a dual role in Brahms's life. It both inspired and diminished the man. At the age of 40, Brahms still had not composed a symphony, and it was Beethoven's fault. As was the case with every other composer of the period, Brahms was literally afraid to follow Beethoven's Ninth.
When he did, in 1876, a critic dubbed his Symphony No. 1 "Beethoven's Tenth." This was not a good thing. Brahms realized that it was time to get out from under the shadow.
He finally did it with the Violin Concerto in 1879. He did it again with the B flat Piano Concerto two years later. When his third symphony rolled around in 1883,
Upcoming Concerts
October 28 & 29
Classical Series · Emerald
Joseph Silverstein, Conductor
Garrick Ohlsson, Piano
ELGAR Pomp & Circumstance March No. 4
ELGAR Dream-Children
BRITTEN Sinfonia da Requiem
*BRAHMS Piano Concerto No. 2
October 31
Family Series
"Halloween Hijinks"
Kory Katseanes, Conductor
November 4 & 5
Classical Series · Saphire
Robert Henderson, Conductor
Larry Zalkind, Trombone
HAYDN Cassation in E flat
WOLKING "Trombone Tales"
RACHMANINOFF Symphonic Dances
SOMETHING to IMPRESS YOUR FRIENDS WITH at a PARTY.
Brahms was once invited to the home of the great Franz Liszt, who chose to impress Brahms by playing one of his own piano sonatas. This marks the only time Brahms held his tongue while listening to a fellow composer's work. He accomplished this by falling asleep.
Beethoven may have been in the backseat, but it was Brahms who was driving the car. Not long after he would be included as one of the "three B's", the other members being Bach and Beethoven. To this day, there has never been a fourth.
Towards the end, Brahms's music spoke of a peacefulness all but absent in his previous works. While listening to his Clarinet Trio, one guesses Brahms was finally able to shear off the heads of his own personal demons.
Brahms summed up that which had come before him and in doing so refined and raised it to another level. This has earned him an unshakeable foothold in the history of music. Let us not forget the other Brahms, though. It is rumored he once left a party saying, "If there is anyone I have not yet insulted, I apologize." Johannes Brahms. You gotta love him.
UTAH SYMPHONY
JOSEPH SILVERSTEIN, MUSIC CONDUCTOR
Call 533-NOTE for tickets

We've just received conclusive evidence that proper wining and dining can win you votes.

The readers of Condé Nast Traveler recently voted us as "One of the Top 5 Restaurants in Hawaii." For reservations, call 922-6611.

Located in the Hawaiian Regent, 2552 Kalakaua Avenue. Open nightly. Free validated parking.

15

Your body is 70% water, so the majority of you will love this.

THE FLORIDA AQUARIUM
OPENING MARCH 31

16

This is one of Franco Galli's secret recipes. Good thing most Italian chefs in California can't read Italian.

As a young boy growing up in Carpenedolo, Italy, Franco Galli learned from some of the world's finest chefs. Aunts, uncles, cousins. Some recipes he even wrote down (in Italian of course). Now, as Il Fornaio's Maestro (teacher), Franco embodies the difference between an interpretation and true Cucina Italiana. Authenticity recognized by the readers of San Francisco Focus Magazine (who voted us the Bay Area's Best Italian Restaurant four years running). And that's it. In plain English.

Il Fornaio

17

CONSUMER MAGAZINE

18
District 13

CLIENT
Ihilani Resort and Spa

AGENCY
Milici Valenti Ng Pack
Honolulu, HI

CREATIVE DIRECTOR
Mike Wagner

ART DIRECTOR
Mike Wagner

COPYWRITER
George Chalekian

19
District 14

CLIENT
American Isuzu
Motors, Inc.

AGENCY
Goodby, Silverstein
& Partners
San Francisco, CA

CREATIVE DIRECTORS
Jeffrey Goodby
Rich Silverstein

ART DIRECTOR
Tom Routson

COPYWRITER
Scott Aal

PHOTOGRAPHER
Harry DeZitter

PRODUCER
Suzee Barrabee

ACCOUNT EXECUTIVE
Robert Riccardi

20
District 4

CLIENT
Florida Division
of Tourism

AGENCY
Fahlgren-Benito
Tampa, FL

CREATIVE DIRECTORS
John Stertz
Rebecca Flora
Jim Noble

ART DIRECTOR
Rich Wakefiled

COPYWRITER
Jim Noble

There's nothing like stimulating apricot aromatherapy to get a lineman fired up for the big game.

*R*eceivers, on the other hand, tend to be somewhat more excitable. For them, our Spa Director recommends a soothing regimen of herbal wraps and Lomi Lomi massage. For the coaching staff, reflexology and Roman Pools. Vichy showers and Shiatsu. Seawater workouts and salt scrubs. Thalasso therapy. And long, lingering walks on the beach.

All of which is why, we're quite proud to say, the 1994 NFL Pro Bowl teams have chosen to stay on Oahu, at Ihilani Resort & Spa.

Then again, they may have come for the food. (We do have a rather impressive array of restaurants.)

Not to mention a 6,867-yard Ted Robinson-designed golf course, recently named one of the most outstanding resort courses in America by *Golf Digest*.

In fact, we may never know whether they came for the golf, the restaurants or the spa. But one thing is absolutely certain. None of the players will complain if they're sent to the showers.

For reservations or more information call your travel agent or Ihilani at (808)679-0079.

Ihilani
RESORT & SPA
Ko'Olina Resort · Oahu, Hawaii

18

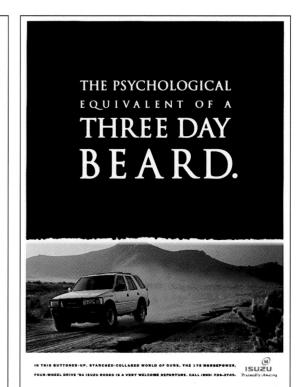

19

20

21

22

23

24

21
District 12

CLIENT
Utah Symphony

AGENCY
Williams & Rockwood
Salt Lake City, UT

CREATIVE DIRECTOR
Scott Rockwood

ART DIRECTOR
David Carter

COPYWRITER
Harold Einstein

ILLUSTRATOR
Clint Hansen

22
District 2

CLIENT
House of Seagrams

AGENCY
TBWA Advertising
New York, NY

ART DIRECTOR
Alix Botwin
Brennan Dailey

COPYWRITER
David Oakley

PHOTOGRAPHER
Steve Bronstein

23
District 4

CLIENT
The Orlando Sentinel

AGENCY
Fry Hammond Barr
Orlando, FL

CREATIVE DIRECTOR
Tim Fisher

ART DIRECTOR
Cathy Casbourne

COPYWRITER
Tony Pucca

24
District 2

CLIENT
House of Seagrams

AGENCY
TBWA Advertising
New York, NY

CREATIVE DIRECTORS
Arnie Arlow
Peter Lubalin

ART DIRECTORS
Dan Braun
Bart Slomkowski

COPYWRITERS
Dan Braun
Bart Slomkowski

PHOTOGRAPHER
Steve Bronstein

25

26

The Difference Between Love And Hate Is Just One Finger.

These days, the line between love and hate isn't just thin — it's invisible. Our children are having a harder time than ever understanding and controlling their emotions. That's where you come in. At Freeport-McMoRan, we're helping to fund conflict resolution programs in New Orleans schools. But we need your help. These programs are teaching kids how to deal with conflict peacefully with creative, non-violent solutions. By training teachers and parents and encouraging role play, our kids are learning that the solution lies somewhere between passivity and aggression. They are learning to give peace a chance. Lend a hand. To make a donation, call the Twomey Center at 861-5830.

FREEPORT-McMoRan
Giving Something Back ®

27

27
District 7

CLIENT
Freeport-McMoran

AGENCY
Peter A. Mayer
Advertising
New Orleans, LA

CREATIVE DIRECTOR
Dee Smith

ART DIRECTOR
Michael Meadows

COPYWRITER
Lori Archer Lundquist
Michael Meadows

PHOTO ILLUSTRATION
Michael Meadows

28
District 5

CLIENT
Hillerich & Bradsby
of Canada

AGENCY
Doe-Anderson
Advertising Agency
Louisville, KY

CREATIVE DIRECTOR
Gary Sloboda

ART DIRECTOR
Ron Livingston

COPYWRITER
Ed Neary

PHOTOGRAPHER
John Lair

ON THE ICE EVERYONE IS OUT TO GET
STEVE YZERMAN.
MAYBE THEY SHOULD JUST GET HIS
EQUIPMENT.

The extreme comfort, feel and maneuverability of Louisville forward equipment makes darting through defenders a walk in the park for players like Steve Yzerman.

Maybe that's why so many other NHL players are switching to Louisville Hockey gloves and pads. Because if you can't beat Steve Yzerman, you may as well join him.

HOW WINNERS PLAY THE GAME.

28

CONSUMER MAGAZINE

29
District 12
CLIENT
Jackson Hole
AGENCY
FJCandN
Salt Lake City, UT
CREATIVE DIRECTOR
Dave Newbold
ART DIRECTOR
Jeff Olsen
COPYWRITER
Dave Newbold
PHOTOGRAPHER
Michael Schoenfeld
ACCOUNT EXECUTIVES
B. Fother
Peggy Lander

30
District 2
CLIENT
Mellon Bank
AGENCY
Werner Chepelsky
and Partners
Pittsburgh, PA
CREATIVE DIRECTORS
Ray Werner
John Chepelsky
ART DIRECTOR
David Hughes
COPYWRITER
Matt Shevin
PHOTOGRAPHER
Tom Gigliotti
PRODUCTION
Greg Hope

31
District 12
CLIENT
Utah Symphony
AGENCY
Williams & Rockwood
Salt Lake City, UT
CREATIVE DIRECTOR
Scott Rockwood
ART DIRECTOR
David Carter
COPYWRITER
Harold Einstein
ILLUSTRATOR
Clint Hansen

32
District 5
CLIENT
Hillerich & Bradsby
of Canada
AGENCY
Doe-Anderson
Advertising Agency
Louisville, KY
CREATIVE DIRECTOR
Gary Sloboda
ART DIRECTOR
Ron Livingston
COPYWRITER
Ed Neary
PHOTOGRAPHER
John Lair

29

30

31

32

CONSUMER MAGAZINE

WITH OUR SAME-DAY SERVICE FROM OVER A DOZEN CONVENIENT LOCATIONS, IT SHOULD NEVER COME DOWN TO THIS.

Klinke Cleaners

In By Eleven, Ready At Four, Monday Through Saturday. Always.

33

YOUR MAMA WEARS ARMY BOOTS.

COOL.

NORTHPARK

Dillard's, Gayfers, JCPenney, McRae's, plus more than 130 dazzling stores.
Open Monday-Saturday 10:00 a.m.-9:00 p.m.; Sunday 12:30 p.m.-6:00 p.m. Exit I-55 at County Line, Ridgeland.

34

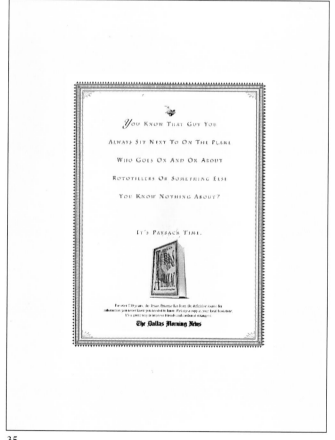

35

36

District 14

CLIENT
Norwegian Cruise Line

AGENCY
Goodby, Silverstein & Partners
San Francisco, CA

CREATIVE DIRECTORS
Jeffrey Goodby
Rich Silverstein

ART DIRECTOR
Steve Luker

COPYWRITER
Steve Simpson

PHOTOGRAPHERS
Herb Ritts
Pete Seaward
Doug Perrine

DESIGNER
Steve Luker

PRODUCER
Laurie Lambert

ACCOUNT EXECUTIVE
Marty Wenzell

37

District 12

CLIENT
Utah Symphony

AGENCY
Williams & Rockwood
Salt Lake City, UT

CREATIVE DIRECTOR
Scott Rockwood

ART DIRECTOR
David Carter

COPYWRITER
Harold Einstein

ILLUSTRATOR
Clint Hansen

38

District 12

CLIENT
Utah Symphony

AGENCY
Williams & Rockwood
Salt Lake City, UT

CREATIVE DIRECTOR
Scott Rockwood

ART DIRECTOR
David Carter

COPYWRITER
Harold Einstein

ILLUSTRATOR
Clint Hansen

36

37

38

39

39
District 4
CLIENT
Designing Eye
AGENCY
Turkel Advertising
Miami, FL
CREATIVE DIRECTOR
Bruce Turkel
ART DIRECTOR
Sally Ann Field
COPYWRITER
David Evans

40

40
District 12
CLIENT
Utah Symphony
AGENCY
Williams & Rockwood
Salt Lake City, UT
CREATIVE DIRECTOR
Scott Rockwood
ART DIRECTOR
David Carter
COPYWRITER
Harold Einstein
ILLUSTRATOR
Clint Hansen

41
District 4
CLIENT
Gametek
AGENCY
Crispin & Porter
Advertising
Miami, FL
CREATIVE DIRECTOR
Alex Bogusky
ART DIRECTORS
Markham Cronin
Steve Mapp
COPYWRITER
Pieter Blikslager

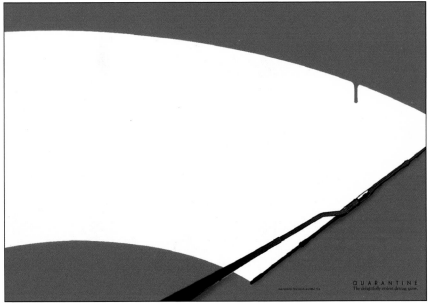

41

42
District 12

CLIENT
Utah Symphony

AGENCY
Williams & Rockwood
Salt Lake City, UT

CREATIVE DIRECTOR
Scott Rockwood

ART DIRECTOR
David Carter

COPYWRITER
Harold Einstein

ILLUSTRATOR
Clint Hansen

43
District 15

CLIENT
Nissan Motor
Corporation

AGENCY
Chiat/Day Inc.
Advertising
Venice, CA

ART DIRECTOR
Craig Tanimoto

COPYWRITER
Eric Grunbaum

DESIGNER
Charles Anderson

PRODUCTION
Madeline Bailey

44
District 6

CLIENT
Hatteras Yachts

AGENCY
BK&M Advertising
Ann Arbor, MI

CREATIVE DIRECTOR
Jon Gustafson

ART DIRECTOR
Debra Pregler

COPYWRITER
Jon Gustafson

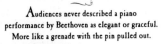

42

43

44

After hearing Bach's music, fellow composers often wondered if it was too late to enroll in law school.

As a violinist he was pretty fair. As an organist he was second to none. It was perhaps this more than anything that contributed to his ingenious and diabolical style of composition. Bach didn't just write pieces to challenge musicians, but often to taunt them.

Johann Sebastian Bach was born in 1685, composed during the Baroque era and died in 1750. But there's more to it than that. If you happened to be walking around Germany in the early 1700's, it was not uncommon to hear the hissing of egos being deflated.

One of the chief causes of this was the Toccata and Fugue in D minor. One would often find the top ranked organists pounding their fists onto the keys during a particularly difficult passage, even though Bach never indicated this on his score.

Fortunately, if you were alive during the Baroque era and in the mood for Bach,

IF GOD IS IN THE DETAILS, BACH KNEW WHAT HE LOOKED LIKE BETTER THAN ANYONE.

you didn't have to settle for mere replicas of the master. Bach performed just about everywhere. You could catch his act at the church of Saint Bonifacius in Arnstadt, the

"Why me?", the unfortunate chap would babble into his cup of weak tea. "Why did I choose to become a composer during an era graced with the talent of one Johann Sebastian Bach?" Life's funny that way.

Bach, or Bach to his friends, was a stern, humorless man and without question the most famous descendant of a musical family that spans the better part of five generations.

court of Prince Leopold of Anhalt-Cothen, or at Zimmerman's coffee house in Leipzig, on Friday nights from 8 to 10. Although, no one knows for sure whether or not Zimmerman thought enough of Bach to name a sandwich after him.

Of course, the depth of Bach's talent doesn't end with the Toccata and Fugue in D

Bach's employers would often hand him a musical theme on which to compose a fugue around. No pressure, though. They usually gave him ten to fifteen seconds.

minor. Or the Unaccompanied Partitas and Suites for solo violin and cello. Or the 48 preludes and fugues that of The Well-Tempered Clavier.

Bach was good enough to leave us with one of the most valued treasures of Western Civilization. The Art of Fugue. Never has there been another piece of music that can match its degree of ingenuity and cunning. Trying to fathom its complex sequence of notes would make even the most dedicated software designer faint from exhaustion.

The Art of Fugue shows us how far a mortal can stretch the techniques of musical counterpoint, meaning single voices played simultaneously against one another.

The melody, or subject, is first presented forward, then backwards, upside

SOMETHING to IMPRESS YOUR FRIENDS WITH at a PARTY.
When Bach played the organ he would occasionally use a stick in his mouth to reach the keys that his hands could not. Some historians believe this came about because of his love for full harmony. Others believe he simply didn't get enough attention as a child.

down, inside-out and, in measure 234, can be seen executing a reverse 3-and-a-half somersault with two twists.

Oh, sure, all this mumbo-jumbo suggests that only a true intellectual could appreciate The Art of Fugue. And it would be just like one to agree. The fool.

All said and done, this is both heady and gut wrenching stuff. The Art of Fugue is a piece of music, yes. It is a piece of history, yes. It makes the other seven natural wonders of the

Bach was a very prolific composer. 212 concertos. 69 sacred songs. 95 preludes and fugues. 29 cantatas. 6 English suites. 6 French suites. 20 children.

world resemble something akin to a child's sand castle, yes. And to cap it off, Bach didn't even live long enough to finish his masterpiece. Well, there you have it.

"Why me?!", the desperate soul wailed into his tea. Can you blame him?

Upcoming Concerts

September 22 Chamber Series
Joseph Silverstein, Conductor & Violin
Eugene Watanabe, Violin & Piano
Erich Graf, Flute
*BACH Concerto for two violins.
*BACH Violin Concerto No. 2
*BACH Piano Concerto No. 5
*BACH Brandenburg Concerto No. 5

September 30, October 1
Classical Series - Sapphire
Joseph Silverstein, Conductor
Elmar Oliveira, Violin
BERLIOZ Le Corsaire: Overture
MENDELSSOHN Violin Concerto
BEETHOVEN Syphony No. 7

October 7 & 8
Cinema Series
"The General"
Donald Hunsberger, Conductor

UTAH SYMPHONY
JOSEPH SILVERSTEIN, MUSIC CONDUCTOR
Call 533-NOTE for tickets

45

Our bodies are her living voice.

MARTHA GRAHAM
DANCE COMPANY
THE FIRST HUNDRED YEARS

PHILIP MORRIS COMPANIES INC
Supporting the spirit of innovation

46

For pie in the sky, mud in your eye, sagging socks, plunging stocks, chances missed, frogs kissed, climbing each rung. This is your day in the sun.

South Carolina
Smiling faces. Beautiful places.

Find your day in the sun with our free 128-page travel guide. Call 1-800-346-3634. Hearing impaired call 1-800-635-9800.

47

CONSUMER MAGAZINE

48
District 12

CLIENT
Zions Bank

AGENCY
Williams & Rockwood
Salt Lake City, UT

CREATIVE DIRECTOR
Scott Rockwood

ART DIRECTOR
Scott Rockwood

COPYWRITER
Rod Miller

ILLUSTRATOR
CF Payne

49
District 13

CLIENT
Kauai-Hawaii Visitors
Bureau

AGENCY
The Schiller Group
Honolulu, HI

ART DIRECTOR
James Ford

COPYWRITER
Trent Farr

PHOTOGRAPHER
Mark Segal

DESIGNER
James Ford

50
District 2

CLIENT
General Motors
Company

AGENCY
N.W. Ayer & Partners
New York, NY

CREATIVE DIRECTOR
Stephen Feinberg

ART DIRECTOR
Jochen Oster

COPYWRITER
Bob Waldner

48

49

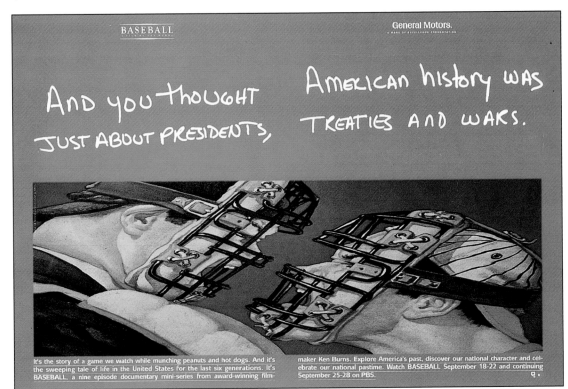

50

ON THE ICE EVERYONE IS OUT TO GET
STEVE YZERMAN.
MAYBE THEY SHOULD JUST GET HIS
EQUIPMENT.

The extreme comfort, feel and maneuverability of Louisville forward equipment makes darting through defenders a walk in the park for players like Steve Yzerman.

Maybe that's why so many other NHL players are switching to Louisville Hockey gloves and pads. Because if you can't beat Steve Yzerman, you may as well join him.

HOW WINNERS PLAY THE GAME.

51
District 5

CLIENT
Hillerich & Bradsby
of Canada

AGENCY
Doe-Anderson
Advertising Agency
Louisville, KY

CREATIVE DIRECTOR
Gary Sloboda

ART DIRECTOR
Ron Livingston

COPYWRITER
Ed Neary

SINCE WE'VE BEEN MAKING
GOALIE
EQUIPMENT, NHL SCORING IS DOWN.
JUST A COINCIDENCE?

If forwards are having a harder time scoring, they may have Louisville Hockey to blame. Louisville goalie equipment is helping net minders like NHL

great Curtis Joseph and every goalie in the CHL stop rubber with astonishing frequency. Try our goalie equipment and you'll be blanking the competition as well.

HOW WINNERS PLAY THE GAME.

IF WINNING IS 90%
DESIRE,
THEN THE OTHER 10% IS
GRAPHITE.

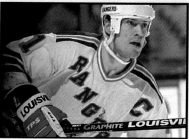

The superior balance and feel of the Louisville Graphite sticks rival the finest wood sticks made, yet it's 15% lighter than aluminum. The graphite composite shaft stores energy more efficiently. Then, during

power shots, the shaft releases energy faster, giving you increased shot velocity. Try the Louisville Graphite stick soon. If it can raise Mark Messier's game, imagine what it can do for yours.

HOW WINNERS PLAY THE GAME.

52

District 2

CLIENT
Greater Wildwood
Tourism Improvement
Development
Authority

AGENCY
The Lunar Group
Whippany, NJ

CREATIVE DIRECTORS
Jeff Propper
Jon Harcharek

ART DIRECTOR
Jeff Propper

COPYWRITER
Jon Harcharek

53
District 13

CLIENT
Kong Lung Company

AGENCY
Gonzalez Design
Company
Honlulu, HI

CREATIVE DIRECTOR
Patricia Ewing

ART DIRECTOR
Leo Gonzalez

COPYWRITER
Sam Malvancy

DESIGNER
Fred Bechlen

54
District 4

CLIENT
Gametek

AGENCY
Crispin & Porter
Miami, FL

CREATIVE DIRECTOR
Alex Bogusky

ART DIRECTORS
Markham Cronin
Sharon Harms
Steve Mapp

COPYWRITERS
Pieter Blikslager
Katherine Patterson

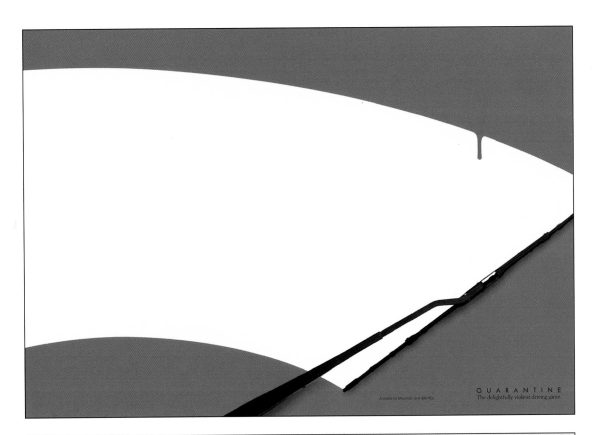

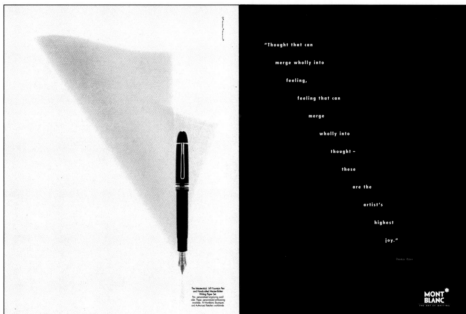

55
District 2

CLIENT
Montblanc

AGENCY
Waring & LaRosa Inc.
New York, NY

CREATIVE DIRECTOR
James Caporimo

ART DIRECTOR
James Caporimo

COPYWRITER
Larry Vine

PHOTOGRAPHER
Shu Akashi

PRODUCTION
Vito Lomenzo

56
District 10

CLIENT
BRSG, Inc.

AGENCY
BRSG, Inc.
Houston, TX

CREATIVE DIRECTORS
Bill Large
Lee Wheat

ART DIRECTORS
Cuqui Rodriguez
Bart Darling

COPYWRITERS
Lee Gonzalez
Jimmy Armogida

PRODUCTION
Linda Lipton

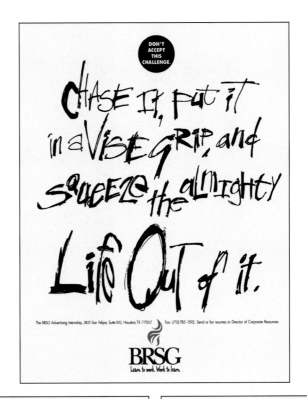

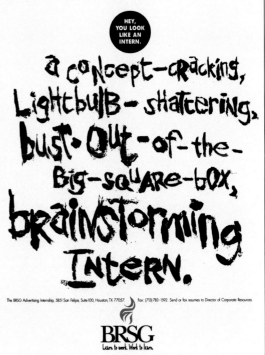

57

District 10

CLIENT
Subaru

AGENCY
Temerlin McClain
Irving, TX

CREATIVE DIRECTOR
Artie Megibben

ART DIRECTORS
Artie Megibben
Donna Lempert
Mike Martin

COPYWRITERS
Dee Leone
Vinny Minchillo
Diane Seimetz

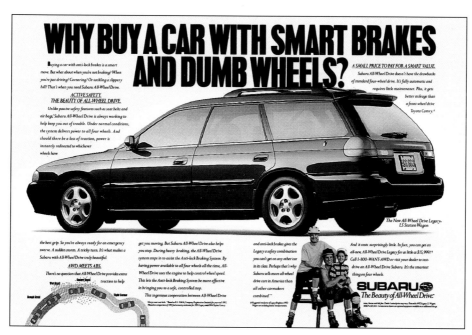

58
District 12

CLIENT
Jackson Hole

AGENCY
FJCandN
Salt Lake City, UT

CREATIVE DIRECTOR
Dave Newbold

ART DIRECTOR
Jeff Olsen

COPYWRITER
Dave Newbold

PHOTOGRAPHER
Michael Schoenfeld

ACCOUNT EXECUTIVES
Peggy Lander
B. Fother

FOR THOSE WHO TAKE THE ROAD LESS TRAVELED.

When others vacationed at the beach, you trekked through the Outback. When others read bestsellers, you perused Proust. When others towed the corporate line, you followed your dreams. When others bought homes in all the usual places, you took the road less traveled.

HAIG POINT
Your Island Retreat

FOR THOSE WHO HAVE MET THE CHALLENGES OF LIFE AND PREVAILED.

When others played the usual courses, you journeyed to St. Andrews. When others rode in carts, you chose to walk. When others took the easy route, you risked it all. When others settled for life in ordinary places, you searched for something unique. Welcome to Haig Point.

HAIG POINT
Your Island Retreat

When others followed the crowd, you went your own way. When others followed convention, you broke the mold. When others listened to those around them, you listened to your heart. When others settled for the commonplace, you searched for something better.

HAIG POINT
Your Island Retreat

59
District 7

CLIENT
International Paper Realty Corp.

AGENCY
The Anderson Group
Hilton Head Island, SC

CREATIVE DIRECTOR
David Anderson

ART DIRECTORS
Renee Hatton
Allyson Abbott

COPYWRITER
Carolyn Fleming

ACCOUNT PLANNER
Joel Constantz

60
District 4

CLIENT
WKCF-TV Channel 18

AGENCY
Anson-Stoner
Orlando, FL

CREATIVE DIRECTOR
Joe Anson

ART DIRECTOR
Brett Stiles

COPYWRITERS
Tom Kane
Joe Anson

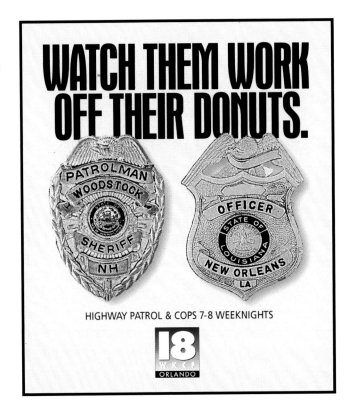

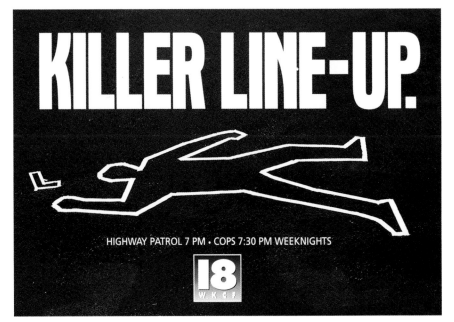

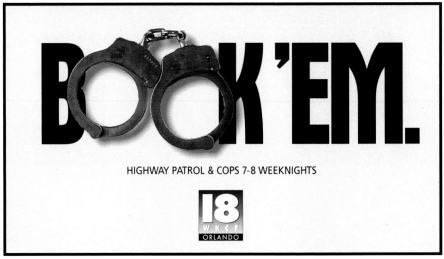

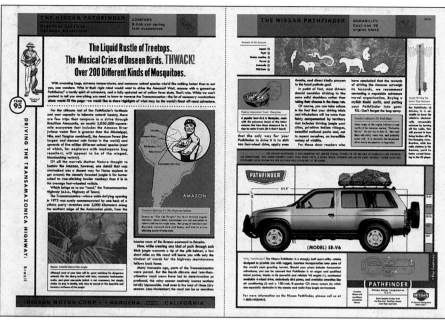

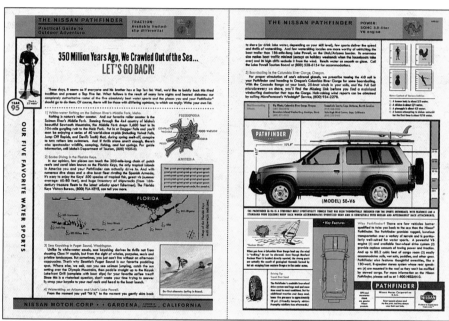

61

District 15

CLIENT
Nissan Motor
Corporation

AGENCY
Chiat/Day Inc.
Advertising
Venice, CA

ART DIRECTOR
Craig Tanimoto

COPYWRITER
Eric Grunbaum

DESIGNER
Charles Anderson

PRODUCTION
Madeline Bailey

62
District 8

CLIENT
Berkley Outdoor
Technologies

AGENCY
Nelson Graphic
Design
Baxter, MN

ART DIRECTOR
Chuck Nelson

COPYWRITER
Dave Skyberg

PHOTOGRAPHER
Rick Hammer

THE LONGER YOU LOOK AT NEON, THE BRIGHTER IT GETS.

Hi. To see what kind of bright thinking went into *Automobile Magazine's* "Automobile of the Year," start in front.

The new Neon's headlights are more than cute. They're halogen. With specially-designed reflectors. Their lenses are made up of dozens of tiny prisms designed to concentrate and better direct the light. And they're made of a durable polycarbonate material like you'll find in motorcycle helmets.

Keep looking and you'll see lots of other things that make Neon shine. From its six-layer paint job that resists fading and stone chips, to its 132 horsepower multi-valve engine. From its standard driver and front passenger airbags to its available integrated child safety seat. And with its cab-forward design, you get more interior room than you'd ever expect in a car like this.

Neon. We think the more you know about what went into it, the more you'll want to get into one yourself.

neon

$8,975 FOR STARTERS. $12,500 NICELY LOADED.
ONLY FROM PLYMOUTH AND DODGE
1-800-NEW NEON

MSRPs exclude tax & destination charge   Always wear your seat belt

---

IT'S ONE OF THE FRIENDLIEST CARS ON EARTH.

It's the nature of the new Neon to keep nature in mind. So, if using an innovative waterborne paint is easier on the environment, Neon is all for it. If using an electrically-charged powdered primer can help reduce factory emissions, Neon is only too happy to oblige. And if using a CFC-free air conditioning refrigerant will help keep the ozone intact, then Neon wouldn't have it any other way.

The fact is, with its specially-designed exhaust system, asbestos-free brakes, and clean burning 2.0 liter, four-cylinder engine, Neon is one of the more environmentally conscious activists on four wheels.

Hi.

It even goes so far as to have many of its plastic parts coded for the day when they can be recycled.

Neon. *Automobile Magazine's* "Automobile of the Year." No matter what color you choose, you can be sure we did our darndest to make it green.

neon

$8,975 FOR STARTERS. $12,500 NICELY LOADED.
ONLY FROM DODGE AND PLYMOUTH
1-800-NEW NEON

MSRPs exclude tax & destination charge   Always wear your seat belt

---

WE USED A 132 HORSEPOWER ENGINE TO PROVE NEON IS A GAS.

Hi. In trying to squeeze 132 horses out of a four-cylinder engine, we made a startling discovery. It's possible to have a great time in an economical car.

Of course, we're not talking about just any car. We're talking about the new Neon...*Automobile Magazine's* "Automobile of the Year."

We're also talking about a 2.0 liter, sixteen-valve, single overhead cam engine that's far from ordinary.

Its race car-inspired intake manifold is made of a composite material for exceptionally good airflow. And that power plant is teamed with a four-wheel independent suspension and specially designed tires that benefit from Formula One racing technology.

Now, there are still those who think it takes more than that to have a car that's fun to drive. So for them, we came up with a great sounding stereo, too.

neon

$8,975 FOR STARTERS. $12,500 NICELY LOADED.
ONLY FROM PLYMOUTH AND DODGE
1-800-NEW NEON

MSRPs exclude tax & destination charge   Always wear your seat belt

---

63
District 6

CLIENT
Chrysler/Dodge

AGENCY
BBDO-Detroit
Southfield, MI

CREATIVE DIRECTOR
Dick Johnson

ART DIRECTORS
Dave Carnegie
Beth Farley
Gene Turner

COPYWRITER
Craig MacIntosh

64
District 14

CLIENT
Isuzu

AGENCY
Goodby, Silverstein
& Partners
San Francisco,CA

CREATIVE DIRECTORS
Jeffrey Goodby
Rich Silverstein
Mike Mazza

ART DIRECTOR
Mike Mazza

COPYWRITER
Dave O'Hare

PHOTOGRAPHER
Graham
Westmoreland

ILLUSTRATOR
Alan Daniels

PRODUCER
Suzee Barrabee

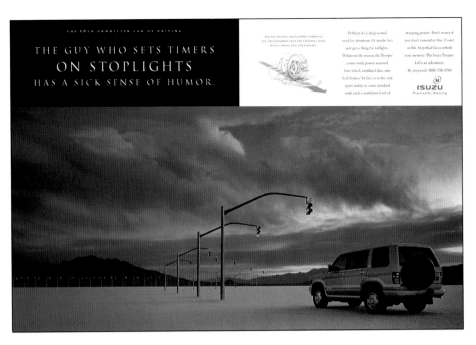

NEWSPAPER

65
District 7

CLIENT
Sky Dive North
Carolina

AGENCY
Pringle Dixon Pringle
Atlanta, GA

CREATIVE DIRECTOR
Jim Pringle

ART DIRECTOR
Jeff Goss

COPYWRITER
Bob Morrison

ACCOUNT EXECUTIVE
Jeff Goss

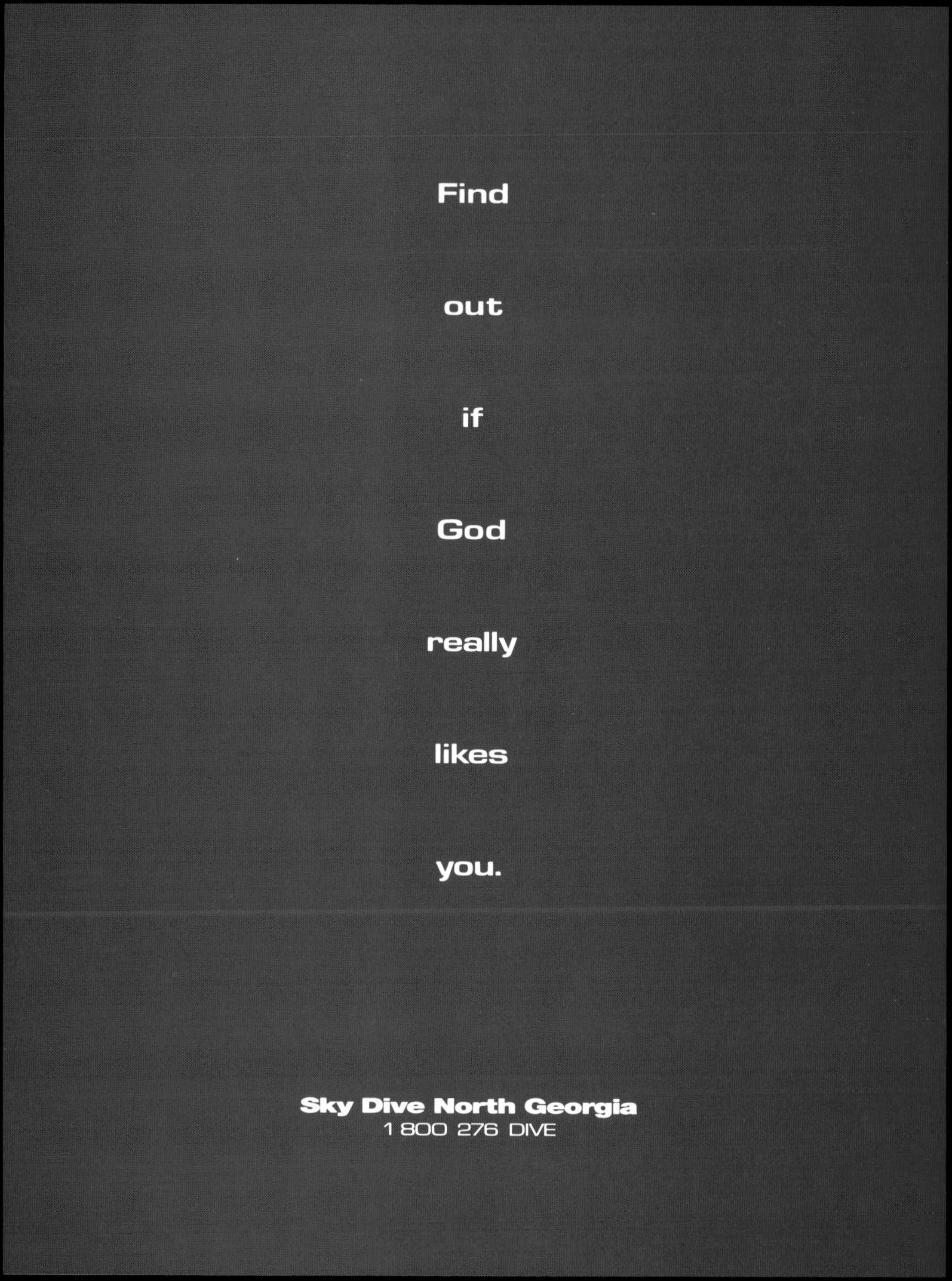

Find

out

if

God

really

likes

you.

Sky Dive North Georgia
1 800 276 DIVE

Iffisnot Germann Wie Dönfekset.

If you own a Porche, BMW, Audi or Mercedes, we speak your language. From routine maintenance to major repairs, we'll give your car all the care it'll ever need. For an appointment, call Ken Hunt at 540-0712. **German Technology, Inc.** Where the accent is on quality.

Wië Feks Germannkars Aldätyme.

If your German car is acting up, we have ways of making it run. Whether you drive a Porche, BMW, Audi or Mercedes, we'll give your car all the care it'll ever need. For an appointment, call Ken Hunt at 540-0712. **German Technology, Inc.** Where the accent is on quality.

Germannkars Es Alwiedö.

If your German car is sounding funny, try having a few words with us. We'll put your Audi, BMW, Porche, or Mercedes in top shape and help you keep it that way. For an appointment, call Ken Hunt at 540-0712. **German Technology, Inc.** Where the accent is on quality.

CRA

AGENCY
Rhodes Stafford
Wines
Dallas, TX

CREATIVE DIRECTORS
Steve Stafford
Brad Wines

ART DIRECTORS
Pete Sockwell
Brad Wines

COPYWRITER
Steve Stafford

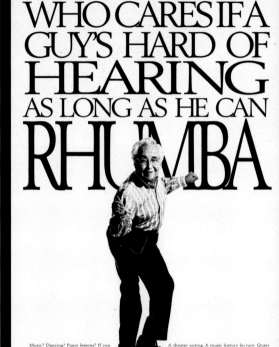

Now there's an Emergency Department just for kids, too.

At Orlando Regional Medical Center, we've designed our new Children's Emergency Department around the belief that there are many ways to make a child feel better, and sometimes, they have little to do with medicine. So we decorated the walls with colorful sealife murals and dinosaur paintings, to make it feel more like a child's room than an emergency room. To ensure this friendly environment is the only one your child sees, we now have private treatment rooms and a special waiting area just for kids. We'll even park your car so you and your child can stay close. Plus, you'll find a staff of specially trained doctors and nurses, all experienced in turning pouts into smiles, and supported by the expertise of the Arnold Palmer Hospital for Children & Women. At ORMC, we've always offered you the best healthcare in the area. But when it comes to your child, we thought you'd like a little more. The new Children's Emergency Department at Orlando Regional Medical Center. Where kids feel better. For details and free child safety information, please call HealthLine at 648-7899.

ORLANDO REGIONAL MEDICAL CENTER
Part of Orlando Regional Healthcare System

The new Children's Emergency Department.

68

**Your grandmother wore it on her wedding day.
Then your mother.
Then you.
Spare your daughter.**

WHITMIRE'S FINE JEWELRY

We turn bad memories into good money.

237-2948

69

68
District 4
CLIENT
ORHS
AGENCY
Gouchenour Advertising
Orlando, FL
CREATIVE DIRECTORS
Chris Robb
Bob Gottron
ART DIRECTOR
Matt Mowat
COPYWRITER
Mark Ronquillo
PHOTOGRAPHER
John Petrey

69
District 2
CLIENT
Whitmire's Fine Jewelry
AGENCY
Lord, Dentsu & Partners
New York, NY
CREATIVE DIRECTOR
Mark Hughes
ART DIRECTOR
Mark Hughes
COPYWRITERS
Andrew Payton
Sims Boulware
PHOTOGRAPHER
Nicholas Eveleigh

70
District 7

CLIENT
Great Financial Bank

AGENCY
The Buntin Group
Nashville, TN

CREATIVE DIRECTOR
Steve Fechtor

ART DIRECTOR
Bob Jensen

COPYWRITER
Steve Fechtor

71
District 2

CLIENT
Great Brands of
Europe

AGENCY
TBWA Advertising
New York, NY

CREATIVE DIRECTORS
Arnie Arlow
Peter Lubalin

ART DIRECTORS
Maria Kostyk-Petro
Lisa Lipkin

COPYWRITERS
Lisa Lipkin
Maria Kostyk-Petro

PHOTOGRAPHER
Steve Bronstein

ILLUSTRATOR
Maria Kostyk-Petro

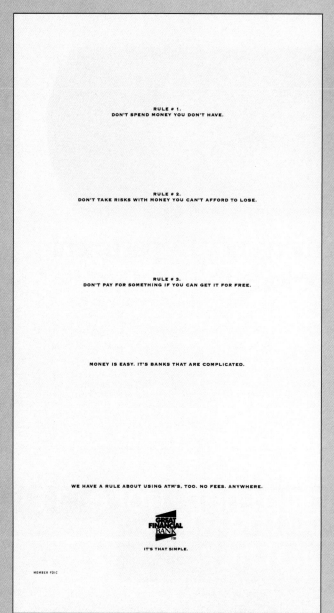

70

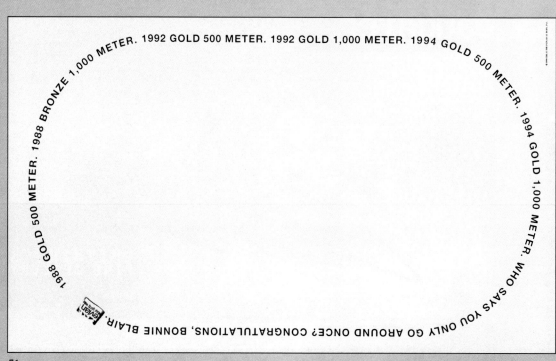

71

Audiences never described a piano
performance by Beethoven as elegant or graceful.
More like a grenade with the pin pulled out.

UTAH SYMPHONY
JOSEPH SILVERSTEIN, MUSIC CONDUCTOR
Call 533-NOTE for tickets

Mozart. The man. The music. The wigs.

UTAH SYMPHONY
JOSEPH SILVERSTEIN, MUSIC CONDUCTOR
Call 533-NOTE for tickets

Sailors who entered the dive
were treated to cheap booze, fast women and some guy
named Brahms playing piano in the corner.

UTAH SYMPHONY
JOSEPH SILVERSTEIN, MUSIC CONDUCTOR
Call 533-NOTE for tickets

73
District 7

CLIENT
Great Financial Bank

AGENCY
The Buntin Group
Nashville, TN

CREATIVE DIRECTOR
Steve Fechtor

ART DIRECTOR
Bob Jensen

COPYWRITER
Steve Fechtor

YOU WORK, YOU MAKE MONEY.

YOU DON'T WORK, YOU DON'T MAKE MONEY.

YOUR MONEY WORKS, IT MAKES MONEY.

YOUR MONEY DOESN'T WORK, IT DOESN'T MAKE MONEY.

MONEY IS EASY. IT'S BANKS THAT ARE COMPLICATED.

GREAT
FINANCIAL
BANK

IT'S THAT SIMPLE.

EVERY BANK COMES WITH A MONEY-BACK GUARANTEE.

IF YOU DON'T LIKE WHAT THEY'RE DOING WITH YOUR MONEY,

YOU CAN TAKE IT RIGHT BACK.

SIMPLE AS THAT. NO QUESTIONS ASKED.

IT'S SURPRISING THAT MORE PEOPLE

DON'T TAKE ADVANTAGE OF THAT GUARANTEE.

MONEY IS EASY. IT'S BANKS THAT ARE COMPLICATED.

IT'S THAT SIMPLE.

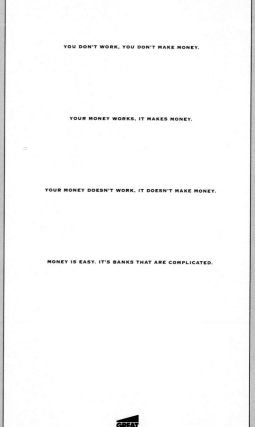

YOU DON'T WORK, YOU DON'T MAKE MONEY.

YOUR MONEY WORKS, IT MAKES MONEY.

YOUR MONEY DOESN'T WORK, IT DOESN'T MAKE MONEY.

MONEY IS EASY. IT'S BANKS THAT ARE COMPLICATED.

IT'S THAT SIMPLE.

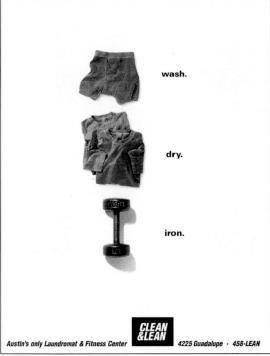

wash.

dry.

iron.

CLEAN &LEAN

Austin's only Laundromat & Fitness Center   4225 Guadalupe · 458-LEAN

74

Whenever you wear it, you think of him.

(Falling off a cliff, drowning, burning in hell etc.)

WHITMIRE'S
FINE JEWELRY

We turn bad memories into good money.

237-2948

75

You haven't taken it off since your wedding day.

(Considering he married someone else 12 years ago, you might want to drop by and see us.)

WHITMIRE'S
FINE JEWELRY

We turn bad memories into good money.

237-2948

76

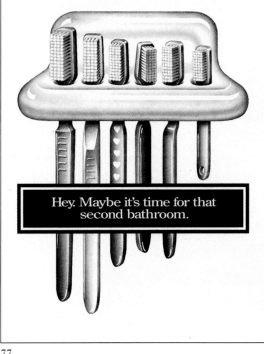

Hey. Maybe it's time for that second bathroom.

77

78

79

80

Maybe He Just Had A Bad Hair Day.

Traffic jams, rude people, slow service – it's enough to make you crazy. Which is exactly what happens to Michael Douglas in "Falling Down," a shocking tale of urban reality playing on HBO during the month of March. Only on Warner Cable. Call 633-9044 in Akron. Unless, of course, you had a bad day yourself.

Ask Us About Free Installation.

WARNER CABLE
Great Performances. Every Day.

81

Thanks a latte.

This season, give and keep on living.

URBAN
stampede

gift store ▼ coffee bar

Grand Forks ▼ North Dakota

82

Museum? Don't touch. Be quiet. No fun. That's a museum. But not here. We're The Children's Do-seum. A hands-on, touchy-feely place where kids and their grown-ups can have fun and–pssst– maybe even learn just a little. It's a place where dinosaurs still roam the earth, mummies come to life, and the stars are open for visitation. It's also an inexpensive place where admission for a family of four is less than $20! Come enjoy five full floors of fantastic family fun!

The Children's Museum ~~do~~

THE CHILDREN'S MUSEUM OF INDIANAPOLIS

Call 924-KIDS For more information.

83

Get an airbag in a new car. Not in a loan officer.

❈ United Southern Bank Auto Loans

84

81
District 5

CLIENT
Warner Cable
Communications

AGENCY
Hitchcock Fleming
& Associates
Akron, OH

ART DIRECTOR
Kim Stein

COPYWRITER
Greg Bukosky

COMPUTER GRAPHICS
Bruce Hodor

82
District 8

CLIENT
Urban Stampede

AGENCY
Ink, Inc.
Grand Forks, ND

CREATIVE DIRECTION
Kelly Thompson
Urban Stampede

83
District 6

CLIENT
The Children's
Museum of
Indianapolis

AGENCY
McCaffrey & McCall
Advertising
Indianapolis, IN

CREATIVE DIRECTOR
Bernie Stanich

COPYWRITER
Mark LeClerc

DESIGNER
Gary Burriss

84
District 7

CLIENT
United Southern
Bank

AGENCY
Thompson
& Company
Memphis, TN

CREATIVE DIRECTORS
Trace Hallowell
Michael H. Thompson

ART DIRECTOR
Trace Hallowell

COPYWRITER
Jimmy Hamiter

TYPOGRAPHER
Great Faces

PRODUCTION
Helen McLain

ACCOUNT EXECUTIVE
Jim Simkins

85

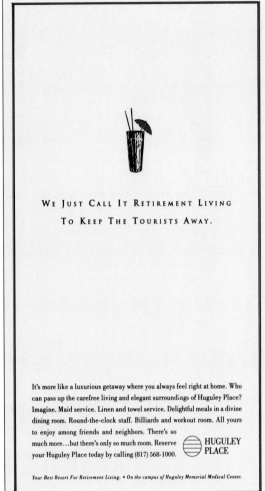

86

87

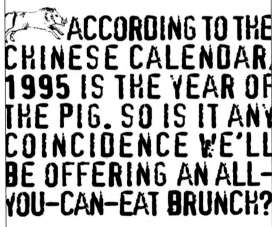

88

89

one more sunset, one more birthday, another anniversary, one more baby's birth, one more walk in the sand, another party, one more romantic dinner, one more ballgame, another hug, one more kiss, one more handshake, another grandchild's giggle, one more round of golf, one more Christmas pageant, one more sunrise, one more smile, another whisper in the dark, another morning listening to rain tapping on the roof, one more welcome home, another night of star gazing, one more candle on the birthday cake, more vacations, more dinners with friends, another love song, one more touch, more cookies to bake, one more stroll to take, more secrets, more novels to read, one more sigh of relief, more letters to write, one more crisp, clear morning, another morning paper to read over coffee, more Thanksgiving dinners to share, more elegant evening gowns to wear, more decorations to get for the Christmas tree, one more shopping spree, one more mother-daughter talk, another Super Bowl, one more John Wayne movie, one more toast to make, another child to teach to ride a bike, one more fish to catch, once more around the lake, one more crackling fire to sit around, more tulip bulbs to plant, one more tango, more sweet perfume to smell, another Valentine's Day with flowers and candy, one more first snow, another walk with the dog, one more dark movie to hold hands through, one more knowing look, one more wink, one more prayer, one more swim in crystal, blue water, once more sipping tea on the porch, one more afternoon of reminiscing, another perfect tomato to grow, ...

one more.

One more year, more years to come. The Open Heart Surgery Program of Cape Fear Valley's Heart Center is one year old. During our first year, with the community's support, we've helped many people add more time and more memories to their lives. Because at The Heart Center, we know it isn't just about adding years to your life, it's about adding *life* to your years.

The Heart Center
of Cape Fear Valley Medical Center

90

91

92

89
District 9

CLIENT
First National Bank of Omaha

AGENCY
Bozell
Omaha, NE

CREATIVE DIRECTOR
Ellen Moran

ART DIRECTOR
Michael Stodola

COPYWRITER
Michael Exner

90
District 3

CLIENT
Cape Fear Balley Medical Center

AGENCY
The Ad Works Agency, Inc.
Fayetteville, NC

CREATIVE DIRECTOR
Bruce Cotton

COPYWRITER
Lisa Nance

GRAPHIC ARTIST
Julia Geissinger

91
District 4

CLIENT
Enzian

AGENCY
Gouchenour Advertising
Orlando, FL

CREATIVE DIRECTOR
Chris Robb

ART DIRECTOR
Chris Robb

COPYWRITER
Mark Ronquillo

PRODUCTION
Craig Gouchenour

92
District 2

CLIENT
New York Botanical Garden

AGENCY
Kaprielian/O'Leary Advertisiing
New York, NY

CREATIVE DIRECTOR
Walter Kaprielian

ART DIRECTORS
James Clarke
Joe Phair

COPYWRITER
Diana Bosniack

PHOTOGRAPHER
Bob Deschamps

PRODUCTION
Master Eagle

93
District 4

CLIENT
Orlando Business
Journal

AGENCY
Cramer-Krasselt
Orlando, FL

CREATIVE DIRECTORS
Bill Nosan
Mitch Boyd

ART DIRECTORS
Bill Nosan
Mitch Boyd

COPYWRITER
Tom Woodward

PHOTOGRAPHER
John Bateman

DESIGNER
Bill Olivari

94
District 7

CLIENT
The Vortex

AGENCY
Cole Henderson
Drake
Atlanta, GA

CREATIVE DIRECTOR
Denzil Strickland

ART DIRECTOR
Dick Henderson

PHOTOGRAPHER
Mark Gooch

95
District 6

CLIENT
AC-Delco

AGENCY
Lintas Campbell-
Ewald
Warren, MI

CREATIVE DIRECTION
Debbie Karnowsky
Cindy Sikorski
Ron Petroff
Gil Clough

96
District 10

CLIENT
Better Kids. Better
Dallas

AGENCY
DDB Needham
Worldwide Dallas
Group
Dallas, TX

CREATIVE DIRECTOR
David Fowler

ART DIRECTOR
John Farris

COPYWRITER
David Parson

93

94

95

96

We've been doing this long enough.

Jacobson's

We're finally open. Today, 10 a.m. Oxmoor Center.

97

98

Come see what's playing at the Garden.

Dancing leaves of gold and copper. Blooming chrysanthemums ripe with color. Hayrides and pumpkins. Apples and acorns. They're all part of the harvest of activities waiting for you this fall at The New York Botanical Garden in the Bronx.
We invite you to visit us for our special events listed below. Or simply spend the day strolling about our 250 acres of gardens and meadows, wood lands and wetlands, forests and waterfalls—all bursting with the vibrant color and aroma of fall.
We're just 20 minutes from midtown and easy to get to by car, subway, bus or Metro North. Remember, you don't have to travel upstate to experience the glory of autumn. Just take a ride uptown to The New York Botanical Garden.

DATE	EVENT
SEPTEMBER 10	CHILDREN'S HARVEST CELEBRATION
SEPTEMBER 10 & 11	BOOK AND PRINT SALE
SEPTEMBER 18	"PETER YARROW & FRIENDS" FAMILY CONCERT, 4:30PM
SEPTEMBER 24 & 25	GARDEN CRAFT FAIR
OCTOBER 1 & 2	GARDEN HARVEST FESTIVAL
OCTOBER 15 & 16	CHRYSANTHEMUM FESTIVAL
OCTOBER 15-16	BONSAI EXHIBITION
OCTOBER 30	GREAT PUMPKIN COSTUME PARADE, 3:00PM

Whether you visit for a special event or simply to take in nature at her peak of beauty, we invite you to come see what's playing at The New York Botanical Garden. For directions, garden hours and event information, call 718-817-8700, ext. 30. Hurry, performances are limited.

The New York Times Company Foundation Inc. is a leadership sponsor of the Garden's programming for children and families.

The New York Botanical Garden, Bronx, New York

99

Sailors who entered the dive were treated to cheap booze, fast women and some guy named Brahms playing piano in the corner.

Beethoven's first concerts ended when the curtain fell. Brahms's ended when some guy yelled, "last call!" That's just the way it goes.
Johannes Brahms grew up playing music on the wrong side of the tracks. When he was only a teen, he performed in the bars and bordellos of Hamburg to earn extra money for his family. Two things came out of this experience. A foul mouth, and the ability to rip through a difficult piano sonata while someone was throwing a pint of ale at his head.
The foul mouth hurt him in life. The piano virtuosity made him a man worth talking about. And a man worth cursing.
His Scherzo in E-flat minor for solo piano offered the so-called pianists of the day such ridiculously wide, skin-splitting finger stretches they wondered if in fact Brahms wasn't writing for another species.
That's Brahms for you, though. He always did things the hard way. He was never polite, always tactless and believed the only musical direction worth pursuing was that of the past. In 1860, he got a little carried away with this notion and wound up signing a proclamation denouncing the "music of the future." This really steamed Wagner who, at the time, was busy in Leipzig writing his scores in different colored ink.
Although Brahms was later embarrassed by this, he still rejected the music of his contemporaries, including Liszt, Verdi, Mahler and a few other heavyweights. Brahms was a classicist through and through. He was mesmerized by the mathematical precision of Bach. He reveled in the melodies and carefreeness of Mozart. He was profoundly moved by the torrent of passion unleashed by Beethoven. The man simply could not fathom why anyone would feel it necessary to stray from the musical forms these geniuses had unearthed.
Beethoven's music played a dual role in Brahms's life. It both inspired and diminished the man. At the age of 40, Brahms still had not composed a symphony, and it was Beethoven's fault. As was the case with every other composer of the period, Brahms was literally afraid to follow Beethoven's Ninth.
When he did, in 1876, a critic dubbed his Symphony No. 1 "Beethoven's Tenth." This was not a good thing. Brahms realized that it was time to get out from under the shadow.
He did it with the Violin Concerto in 1879. He did it again with the B-flat Piano Concerto two years later. When his third symphony rolled around in 1883, Beethoven may have been in the backseat, but it was Brahms who was driving the car. Not long after he realized he could be included as one of the "three B's", the other members being Bach and Beethoven. To this day, there has never been a fourth.
Towards the end, Brahms's music spoke of a peacefulness all but absent in his previous works. While listening to his Clarinet Trio, one guesses Brahms was finally able to shear off the heads of his own personal demons. Brahms summed up that which had come before him and in doing so refined and raised it to another level. This has earned him an unshakable foothold in the history of music. Let us not forget the other Brahms, though. It is rumored he once left a party saying, "If there is anyone I have not yet insulted, I apologize." Johannes Brahms. You gotta love him.

Upcoming Concerts

SOMETHING to IMPRESS YOUR FRIENDS WITH at a PARTY.

UTAH SYMPHONY
JOSEPH SILVERSTEIN, MUSIC CONDUCTOR
Call 533-NOTE for tickets

100

NEWSPAPER

101
District 6

CLIENT
Indianapolis Power and Light

AGENCY
Young & Laramore
Indianapolis, IN

CREATIVE DIRECTORS
David Young
Jeff Laramore

ART DIRECTOR
Carolyn Hadlock

COPYWRITER
Scott Montgomery

PHOTOGRAPHER
Greg Whitaker

ACCOUNT MANAGER
Ilene Schankerman

102
District 8

CLIENT
Lands' End

AGENCY
Waldbillig
& Besteman, Inc.
Madison, WI

CREATIVE DIRECTION
Waldbillig
& Besteman

103
District 14

CLIENT
Sunvalley Shopping Center

AGENCY
Goldberg, Moser O'Neill
San Francisco, CA

CREATIVE DIRECTOR
Brian O'Neil

ART DIRECTOR
Simon Chandler

COPYWRITER
Neville deSouza

ACCOUNT EXECUTIVES
Wayne Buder
Joe Silvestri

104
District 3

CLIENT
Fitness World

AGENCY
West & Vaughan
Durham, NC

CREATIVE DIRECTORS
Bill West
Tom Gardner

ART DIRECTOR
Scott Ballew

COPYWRITER
Cheryl Case

PHOTOGRAPHER
Duane Salstrand

DESIGNER
Dee Dee Wilkins

101

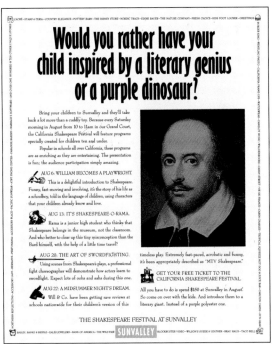

103

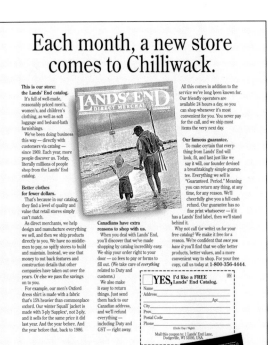

102

104

105

105
District 5

CLIENT
Workstyles, Inc.

AGENCY
Blasko, Sipos
& Courtney, Inc.
Cleveland, OH

ART DIRECTOR
Leonard Blasko

COPYWRITER
Phil Sipos

DESIGNER
Leonard Blasko

PRINTER
S.P. Mount

TYPOGRAPHER
Artists Studios

106
District 9

CLIENT
Hunan Garden
Restaurant

AGENCY
The Puckett Group
St. Louis, MO

ART DIRECTOR
David Nien-Li Yang

COPYWRITERS
David Nien-Li Yang
Eric Weltner

106

NEWSPAPER

107
District 9

CLIENT
Jack Daniel Distillery

AGENCY
Simons, Durham
& Associates
St. Louis, MO

CREATIVE DIRECTOR
Ted Simmons

ART DIRECTOR
Mike Eckhard

COPYWRITER
Tim Halpin

PHOTOGRAPHER
Jim Braddy

PRODUCTION
Karen Boes

Just one sip of Jack Daniel's will tell you why we haven't changed its oldtime taste since 1866. And why we never will.

SMOOTH SIPPIN'
TENNESSEE WHISKEY

Jimmy Bedford is only our sixth head distiller since 1866. His job is to make Jack Daniel's Whiskey in the oldtime way our founder prescribed. One sip will tell you, no one does it better.

SMOOTH SIPPIN'
TENNESSEE WHISKEY

Pure spring water and our charcoal mellowing method account for Jack Daniel's uncommon rareness. And, we believe, for its uncommon number of friends.

SMOOTH SIPPIN'
TENNESSEE WHISKEY

Yeah, well I bet I could kick some serious tail if I could just figure out where to pin my number

Examiner Bay to Breakers

Sunday, May 15.

Just a reminder that at this year's Examiner Bay to Breakers race, you're encouraged to dress as you see fit. In other words, giant canned hams, oversized pimentos and cocktail weenies are all perfectly welcome. As always, prizes will be awarded for the best costumes (remember, nudity is not a costume). If you missed the May 2nd registration deadline, you can still sign up to run at one of the Nordstrom/Breakers specialty stores located at One Embarcadero Center and the San Francisco Centre. Look for more information in today's San Francisco Examiner, or call (415) 512-5000 and enter category #2222. We'll be saving a number for you.

Crystal Geyser   Hyatt Regency   KGO AM 810   KIA   KPIX 5   Nordstrom   Southwest Airlines

108
District 14

CLIENT
San Francisco
Examiner Newspaper

AGENCY
Goodby, Silverstein
& Partners
San Francisco, CA

CREATIVE DIRECTORS
Jeffrey Goodby
Rich Silverstein

ART DIRECTOR
Dave Ayriss

COPYWRITER
Scott Aal

PRODUCER
Michael Stock

ACCOUNT EXECUTIVE
Lori Warren

Come on honey, we have to get moving before your father congeals.

Examiner Bay to Breakers

Sunday, May 15.

We're happy to announce that the registration deadline for the Examiner Bay to Breakers race has been extended to May 2. (important) Enter now by using the registration form in today's paper. For more information, call (415) 512-5000 and enter category #2222. And while you're at it, (shameless plug) order a subscription to the San Francisco Examiner. A daily reading can go a long way toward keeping you fresh.

Crystal Geyser   Hyatt Regency   KGO AM 810   KIA   KPIX 5   Nordstrom   Southwest Airlines

Hello mother ship. Do you read me? Yes we are still monitoring the Earth people. But we have no explanation for their behavior.

Examiner Bay To Breakers

Sunday, May 15.

You too can be part of this year's Examiner Bay to Breakers. Look for entry information in today's San Francisco Examiner.

109
District 2

CLIENT
Landmark Mall

AGENCY
Goldberg
Marchesano
Kohlman
Washington, DC

CREATIVE DIRECTOR
Bill Reple

ART DIRECTOR
Rich Park

COPYWRITER
Freddie McKenna
Bill Reple

PHOTOGRAPHER
Max Hirshfield

PRODUCTION
Mary Duncan

ACCOUNT EXECUTIVE
Stephanie Miller

110
District 7

CLIENT
United Southern
Bank

AGENCY
Thompson &
Company
Memphis, TN

CREATIVE DIRECTORS
Trace Hallowell
Michael H. Thompson

ART DIRECTOR
Trace Hallowell

COPYWRITER
Jimmy Hamiter

ILLUSTRATOR
Guy Stiefferman

TYPOGRAPHER
Great Faces

PRODUCTION
Helen McLain

ACCOUNT EXECUTIVE
Jim Simkins

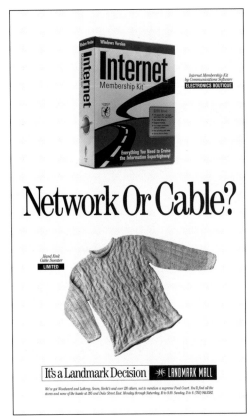

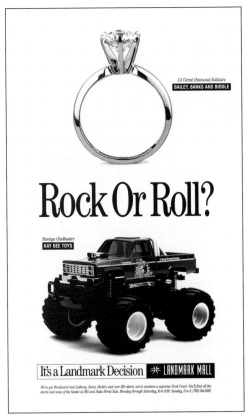

109

110

111

District 14

CLIENT

American Isuzu
Motors, Inc.

AGENCY

Goodby, Silverstein
& Partners
San Francisco, CA

CREATIVE DIRECTORS

Jeffrey Goodby
Rich Silverstein

ART DIRECTOR

Michael Mazza

COPYWRITER

Dave O'Hare

PHOTOGRAPHER

Michael Rupert

PRODUCER

Suzee Barrabee

ACCOUNT EXECUTIVE

Robert Riccardi

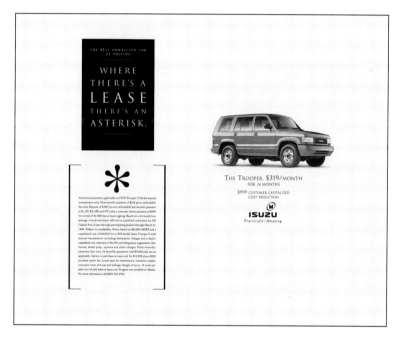

112
District 6

CLIENT
Body Basics

AGENCY
Cramer-Krasselt
Chicago, IL

ART DIRECTOR
Lisa Howard

COPYWRITER
Larry Lipson

PHOTOGRAPHER
Christopher Hawker

ILLUSTRATOR
Lisa Howard

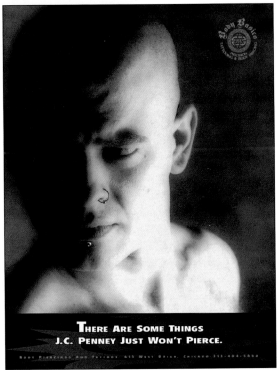

112

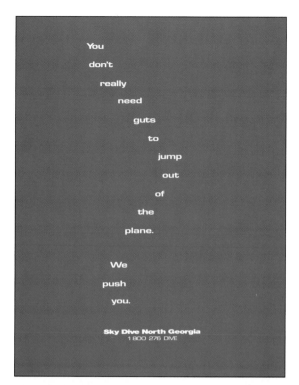

113
District 7

CLIENT
Sky Dive North
Georgia

AGENCY
Pringle Dixon Pringle
Atlanta, GA

CREATIVE DIRECTOR
Jim Pringle

ART DIRECTOR
Jeff Goss

COPYWRITER
Bob Morrison

PRINTER
Graphic Ads

PRODUCTION
Jeff Goss

ACCOUNT EXECUTIVE
Jeff Goss

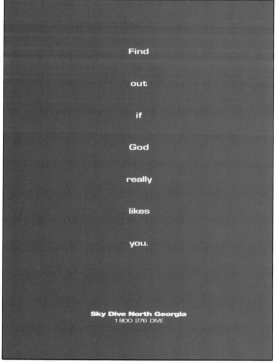

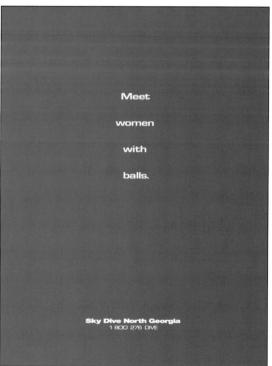

114
District 10

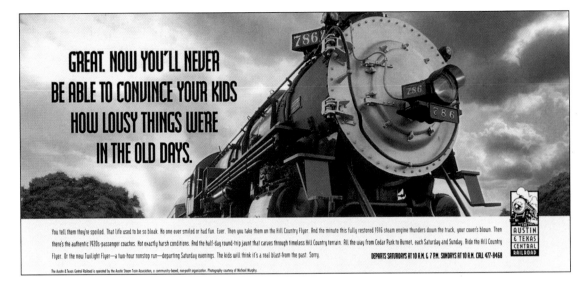

Reject.

Not just any product can wear a Publix label. While other stores may put their label on anything and everything, we don't. We put all of our Publix brands through rigorous quality assurance testing. If it doesn't meet up to our standards, we just don't carry it. Because we never cut quality, you can rest assured that if it has our name on it, the quality is always in it. Guaranteed.

If We're Not Sold On It, We Just Don't Sell It.

115
District 4

CLIENT
Publix Supermarkets

AGENCY
Publix Supermarkets

ART DIRECTORS
Susan Nobles
Kim Cook

COPYWRITER
Susan Nobles

Bread so fresh, anything else is for the birds.

Could you imagine anyone feeding birds with our bread, no way, it's just too fresh and delicious. While other stores sell their bread off day old bread racks, we don't. We put a priority on providing you with the freshest baked goods available. Before the day breaks each morning we're hard at work baking our breads fresh, right in our stores. We also offer a wide variety of other baked goods as well, such as pastries, donuts, cookies, pies, and of course our specially decorated cakes. So if you don't want to spend your hard-earned dough on bird feed, make sure you only shop at the Publix Bakery.

When It Comes To Fresh Baked Goods, Publix Soars Above The Rest.

This is the only side of beef they specialize in.

While other stores try to specialize in anything and everything under the sun, we don't. We put all of our effort into bringing you the freshest, finest selection of meats you can find. For years, Publix has specialized in quality foods, quality that is guaranteed to be enjoyed. From USDA Choice beef to fresh poultry, pork and seafood, we carry it all. And if you have any questions, just ask one of our fully trained experienced staff. They'll be able to help you with just about anything, anything that is, except how to find the shoe department.

Specializing In Quality Meats Since 1930.

116
District 6

CLIENT
Foot Place

AGENCY
Asher Agency, Inc.
Fort Wayne, IN

ART DIRECTOR
Kelly Gayer

COPYWRITER
Dan Schroeter

PHOTOGRAPHY
Galliher
Photographic
Illustration

DIGITAL IMAGING
Dan Mobley

ACCOUNT EXECUTIVE
Rob Cowin

We expect our customers to get up and walk out on us.

If they didn't, we wouldn't be satisfied. After all, they come to The Premier Footplace for the best in specialized foot care. Whether that means surgery, x-rays, therapy or treatment for arthritis and other injuries. So, hobble, hop or limp in today. We'll help you walk out too.

PREMIER footplace We specialize in repairing used feet.

1333 Maycrest Drive at 3030 Lake Avenue · Fort Wayne · 422-3214 · Fax: 423-6344

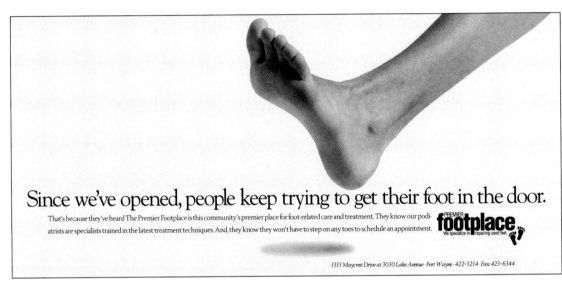

Since we've opened, people keep trying to get their foot in the door.

That's because they've heard The Premier Footplace is this community's premier place for foot-related care and treatment. They know our podiatrists are specialists trained in the latest treatment techniques. And, they know they won't have to step on any toes to schedule an appointment.

PREMIER footplace We specialize in repairing used feet.

1333 Maycrest Drive at 3030 Lake Avenue · Fort Wayne · 422-3214 · Fax: 423-6344

Most people just cover up their foot problems.

They're in denial. In fact, seven out of 10 people go through life thinking their feet are supposed to hurt. Then they buy all kinds of exotic shoes to try and cover up their problems. They could just go to The Premier Footplace for treatment. It's really the best solution.

PREMIER footplace We specialize in repairing used feet.

1333 Maycrest Drive at 3030 Lake Avenue · Fort Wayne · 422-3214 · Fax: 423-6344

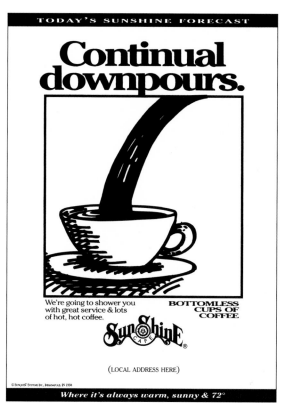

117
District 6

CLIENT
SunShine Cafe

AGENCY
Pearson, Crahan
& Fletcher
Indianapolis, IN

CREATIVE DIRECTOR
Ron Pearson

ART DIRECTOR
Carol Kappel

COPYWRITERS
Carol Kappel
Larry Fletcher

ILLUSTRATOR
Carol Kappel

118

District 4

CLIENT
Orlando Business
Journal

AGENCY
Cramer-Krasselt
Orlando, FL

CREATIVE DIRECTORS
Bill Nosan
Mitch Boyd

ART DIRECTORS
Bill Nosan
Mitch Boyd

COPYWRITER
Tom Woodward

PHOTOGRAPHER
John Bateman

The SECOND *most* IMPORTANT PAPER *in the* EXECUTIVE WASHROOM.

Subscribe to OBJ for all the facts your business needs, rolled into one. We promise the area's most complete coverage, and every week we deliver. Call 407-649-8470.

If YOU'RE GETTING IT ONCE *a week*, *you're* DOING SOMETHING RIGHT.

Subscribe to OBJ for all the facts your business needs, rolled into one. We promise the area's most complete coverage, and every week we deliver. Call 407-649-8470.

Put SOME MEAT *into* YOUR FRIDAYS.

Subscribe to OBJ for all the facts your business needs, rolled into one. We promise the area's most complete coverage, and every week we deliver. Call 407-649-8470.

GET *the* PAPER THAT'S *more* ABSORBING.

ORLANDO BUSINESS JOURNAL

Subscribe to OBJ for all the facts your business needs, rolled into one. We promise the area's most complete coverage, and every week we deliver. Call 407-649-8470.

119
District 5

CLIENT
KeyCorp

AGENCY
J. Walter Thompson
Cleveland, OH

CREATIVE DIRECTORS
Dan Cerullo
Jane Pritchard

120
District 13

CLIENT
Windward Mall

AGENCY
Craig Matsumoto
Honolulu, HI

CREATIVE DIRECTOR
Craig Matsumoto

ART DIRECTOR
Craig Matsumoto

PHOTOGRAPHER
Carl Saniff

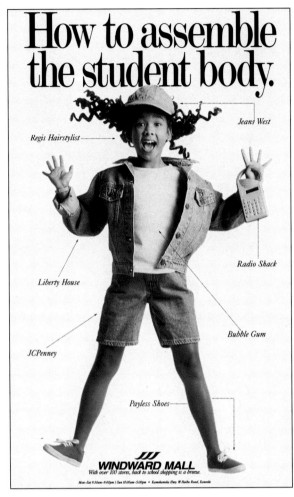

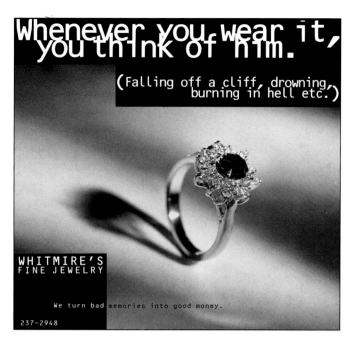

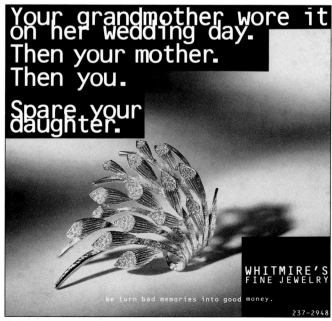

121
District 2

CLIENT
Whitmire's Fine
Jewelry

AGENCY
Lord, Dentsu
& Partners
New York, NY

CREATIVE DIRECTOR
Mark Hughes

ART DIRECTOR
Mark Hughes

COPYWRITERS
Andrew Payton
Sims Boulware

PHOTOGRAPHER
Nicholas Eveleigh

122
District 8

CLIENT
Dean Foundation

AGENCY
The Hiebing Group
Madison, WI

CREATIVE DIRECTOR
Barry Callen

ART DIRECTOR
Bob Martin

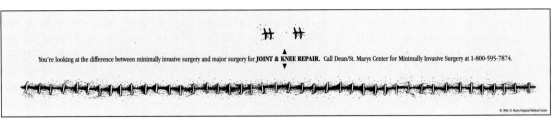

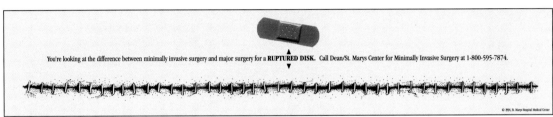

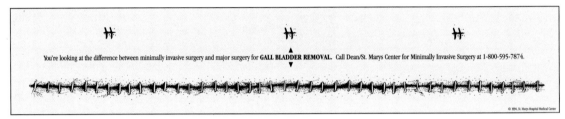

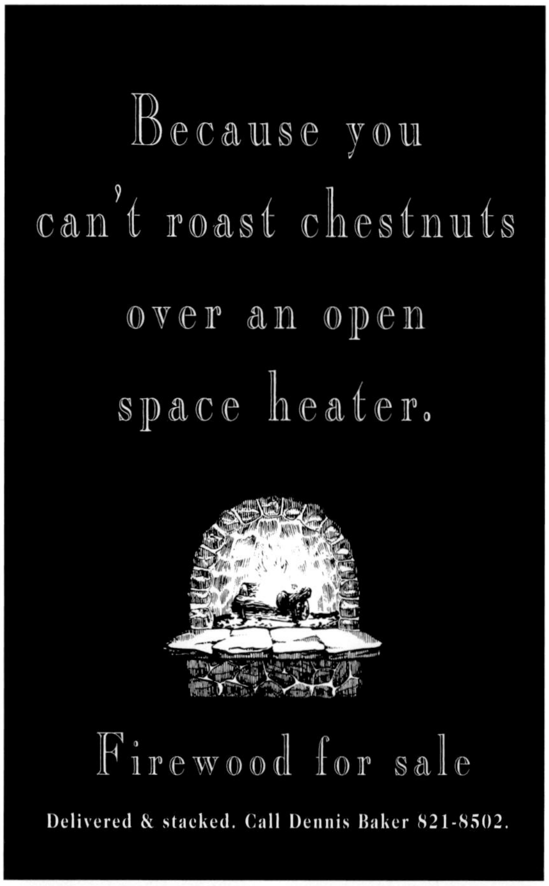

Because you can't roast chestnuts over an open space heater.

Firewood for sale

Delivered & stacked. Call Dennis Baker 821-8502.

123
District 9

CLIENT
Dennis Baker

AGENCY
Bar Napkin Creative
St. Peters, MO

ART DIRECTOR
Eric Revels

COPYWRITER
Christopher J. Torba

ILLUSTRATOR
Richard Heroldt

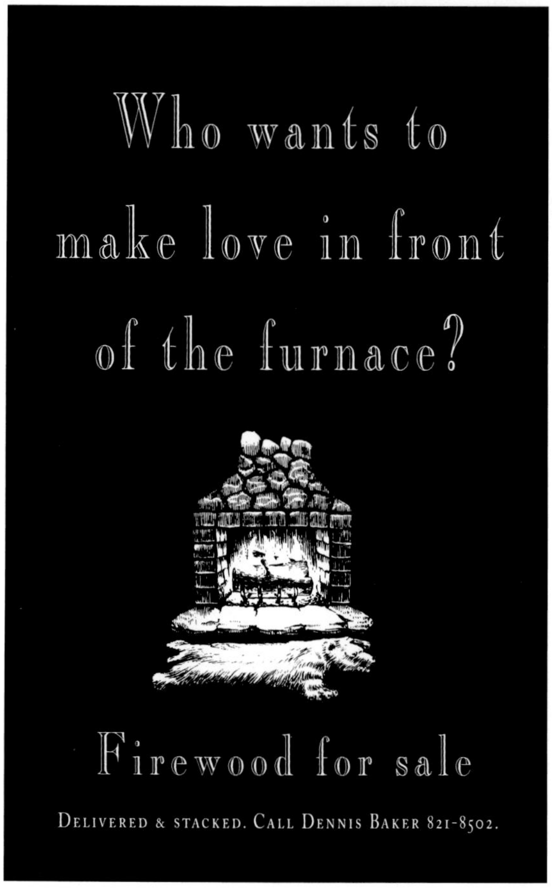

Who wants to make love in front of the furnace?

Firewood for sale

DELIVERED & STACKED. CALL DENNIS BAKER 821-8502.

Who ever heard of curling up with a good book in front of the hot air vent.

Firewood for sale

Delivered & stacked. Call Dennis Baker 821-8502.

124

District 7

CLIENT
Palisades

AGENCY
The Ramey Agency
Jackson, MS

CREATIVE DIRECTOR
Alan Goodson

ART DIRECTOR
Alan Goodson

PHOTOGRAPHER
Harold Head

DESIGNER
Mark Moore

ENGRAVER
K&W Prepress

PRODUCERER
Jim Garrison

HOMES FROM THE 300'S.
VALUES FROM THE 50'S.

✈ Remember when you were young? When you and your wide-eyed buddies practically grew up outdoors. When all the neighbors truly knew each other. When the sound of the doorbell made you happy, not nervous. ✈ For too many people, those days are gone. ✈ Things are different at Palisades. Here, property values are exceeded only by human values. The folks in our private community enjoy friendship and peace of mind uncommon in today's society. You could say our security is, well, secure. Indeed, much of Palisades is embraced by the Reservoir, with rolling woods and abundant wetlands offering sanctuary for wildlife, and family life as well. It is no less than an ideal place to grow up. And grow old. ✈ If you value our values, call 829-9080. Or visit our small piece of paradise by taking Northshore Parkway from Spillway Road, then follow the signs (our guardhouse is hard to miss). You'll soon see why other families thought moving here was such a swell idea.

IF YOUR CHILDREN SPEND MORE TIME
IN OUTER SPACE THAN OUT-OF-DOORS, MAYBE
IT'S TIME TO BRING THEM BACK TO EARTH.

🦌 When was the last time your kids were actually outside when you called them "in" for dinner? 🦌 Indeed, these days many children need to be put in their place – where Mother Nature can drop kick any kung-fu warrior or disintegrate any alien invader. 🦌 Palisades is such a place. Nestled comfortably along the Reservoir between dense woodlands and geese-guarded marshes, our private paradise offers something quite rare to children these days: a childhood. 🦌 Kids here know the fine art of skipping rocks. They're adept at climbing trees. They play kick-the-can. They build forts. They catch fish. They discover. They imagine. And with custom homes, private docks and unsurpassed security, Palisades is quite a place for big kids, too. 🦌 For more information, call 829-9080. Or visit us by taking Northshore Parkway from Spillway Road, then follow the signs to our guardhouse. 🦌 You'll love the gorgeous homesites inside our gates. And there's more than an outside chance your kids will, too.

"HONEY, I'M HOME."

🎣 Despite what you may have heard, not all Palisades residents arrive home from the office in a leather-appointed luxury sedan. 🎣 After all, the people here are unlike those of other communities. They are inhabitants of a quiet oasis, surrounded by cool waters and calm wetlands teeming with wildlife. It is in this setting that security, tranquility and peace of mind not only survive, but thrive. 🎣 Here, children leave their bicycles overnight in their front yards. Families take long walks. Couples share stunning sunsets, peaceful picnics and enchanted evenings. Neighbors are friends, not strangers. 🎣 And you? Simply relax and savor what you've earned. 🎣 For more information, call 829-9080. Or take Northshore Parkway from Spillway Road, then follow the signs to our guardhouse. 🎣 Inside, you'll find an oasis known for its sparkling blue waters. And loved for the lifestyle it affords.

BUSINESS/
TRADE
PUBLICATION

Daddy fought in the war.

The Motorola MicroTAC Ultra Lite™ comes from a long line of heroes. Like the original SCR 536 hand-held wireless radio, which cut our boys loose from the wires of war. Lives depended on us then. Busy lives depend on us now. Motorola. The best-selling, most-preferred cellular phones in the world.

 MOTOROLA

125
District 6

CLIENT
Motorola Cellular

AGENCY
J. Walter Thompson
Chicago, IL

CREATIVE DIRECTOR
Dave Moore

ART DIRECTOR
Paul Behnen

...etn...
Jurassic desert some
years ago—now lie etched by wind
and water into delicate swirls of
geologic time. Rococo formations
and cool, deep, narrow slot canyons
characterize the Paria Canyon
...on Cli...

WE SEND THEIR MINDS.

THEIR BODIES SOON FOLLOW.

NATIONAL GEOGRAPHIC
Traveler

Photographer: Tom Bean

I believe

light

is the ornament

OF darkness.

That

shadows

are the
messengers
of

perspective.

And passion

the element

that pounds each

into
delicate

submission.

H
i
r
o
s
h
i

N
o
n
a
m
i

Inside Mr. Nonami's camera there is a film with ideal color balance.
It is Kodak Ektachrome 100 Plus professional film. And you can get it in whatever format you shoot.

CLIENT
National Geographic

AGENCY
Arnold Advertising
McLean, VA

CREATIVE DIRECTOR
Jim Kinsley

ART DIRECTOR
Nora Jaster

COPYWRITER
Francis Sullivan

PRODUCTION
Myles Marlow

Ah, the inimitable dolce vita of Positano—sunshine, warm spirits, cool wine, and the fruits of local orchards and the sea. Who would not linger on the celebrated Amalfi coast

WE SEND THEIR MINDS.

THEIR BODIES SOON FOLLOW.

NATIONAL GEOGRAPHIC
Traveler

For more than a century, the National Geographic Society has inspired people to see the world.
For more than a decade, National Geographic Traveler has shown them how.

etr... Jurassic desert some years ago—now lie etched by wind and water into delicate swirls of geologic time. Rococo formations and cool, deep, narrow slot canyons characterize the Paria Canyon ...on Cl...

WE SEND THEIR MINDS.

THEIR BODIES SOON FOLLOW.

NATIONAL GEOGRAPHIC
Traveler

For more than a century, the National Geographic Society has inspired people to see the world.
For more than a decade, National Geographic Traveler has shown them how.

BUSINESS/TRADE

129
District 14

CLIENT
Norwegian Cruise
Line

AGENCY
Goodby, Silverstein
& Partners
San Francisco, CA

CREATIVE DIRECTORS
Jeffrey Goodby
Rich Silverstein

ART DIRECTORS
Steve Luker
Rachel Gorenstein

COPYWRITERS
Steve Simpson
Blake Daley

PHOTOGRAPHERS
Tom Tracy
RJ Muna

DESIGNER
Steve Luker

PRODUCER
Laurie Lambert

ACCOUNT EXECUTIVE
Marty Wenzell

130
District 14

CLIENT
Clark Candy
Company

AGENCY
McCann-Erickson,
Inc.
San Francisco, CA

CREATIVE DIRECTORS
Pat Marcoccia
John Migliaccio

ART DIRECTOR
Mark Wenneker

COPYWRITER
Derrick Ogilvie

PHOTOGRAPHER
Jamie Biondo

PRODUCER
Marie Fox

ACCOUNT EXECUTIVE
Kate Lillard

131
District 2

CLIENT
Ingersoll-Rand

AGENCY
Anderson
& Lembke, Inc.
New York, NY

CREATIVE DIRECTOR
John Athorn

ART DIRECTOR
Erik Granlund

COPYWRITER
Joe Sweet

PHOTOGRAPHER
Fred Collins

PRODUCTION
Maria Bogaenko

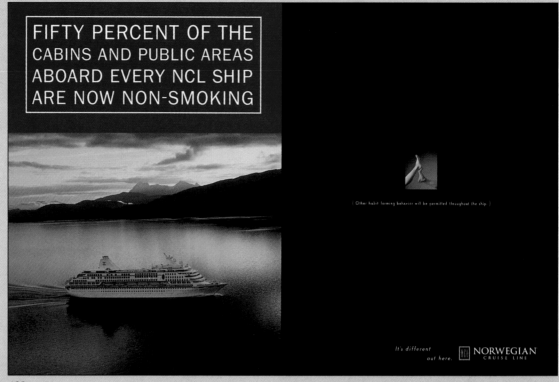

129

130

131

BUSINESS/TRADE

It's hard to

believe that

people could be

so *devoted*

to something

that merely goes

back and forth

over and over again.

We, however.

understand

perfectly.

AmericanAirlines

132

YOUR BELOVED CAMPAIGN GETS KILLED

CLIENT ADDS SNIPE TO AD

CLIENT'S WIFE CHANGES BACKGROUND COLOR

ACCOUNT EXECUTIVE CUTS PRODUCTION SCHEDULE IN HALF TO IMPRESS CLIENT

GETTING SNUBBED BY MODELS DURING SHOOT

ATTENDING TRADE SHOW TO BOND WITH CLIENTS

BREATHING TOXIC MARKER FUMES

BREATHING SECOND-HAND SMOKE IN PRODUCTION MANAGER'S OFFICE

WORKING WITH EMOTIONALLY FRAGILE GRAPHIC DESIGNER

WORKING FOR CREATIVE DIRECTOR WHO THINKS HE'S GOD

WORKING FOR CREATIVE DIRECTOR WHO THINKS HE'S PYTKA

HEADHUNTER SPILLS A DECAF LATTE INTO YOUR BOOK

YOU SEND YOUR ADS TO THE LAMINATOR—HE SENDS YOU BACK CHUCK E. CHEESE PLACEMATS

REPEATED EXPOSURE TO PHRASE "THE BIG IDEA"

PULLING ALL-NIGHTERS FOR NEW BUSINESS PITCH

PULLING ALL-NIGHTERS FOR NEW BUSINESS PITCH AND LOSING

IRS SAYS $30,000 HOME ENTERTAINMENT SYSTEM WASN'T A PROFESSIONAL EXPENSE

YOUR 24-YEAR-OLD ASSISTANT BECOMES YOUR CREATIVE DIRECTOR

FACE IT. YOU'RE NOT GETTING ANY YOUNGER. SO MAYBE YOU SHOULD CALL STAN MUSILEK. MANY ART DIRECTORS FIND THAT SHOOTING WITH STAN ACTUALLY REVERSES THE AGING PROCESS BY AN AVERAGE OF TWO YEARS PER SHOOT. BUT EVEN IF YOU DON'T WANT TO SHOOT WITH STAN, CALL HIM ANYWAY AT 800-669-5330 OR 415-621-5336. HE'LL SEND YOU A FREE PORTFOLIO.

HOW OLD ARE YOU IN AD YEARS?

133

134
District 5

CLIENT
Procter & Gamble
Professional Crisco

AGENCY
Northlich Stolley
LaWarre
Cincinnati, OH

ART DIRECTOR
Richard Westendorf

COPYWRITER
Neill Rodgers

PRODUCTION
Lynn Studer

135
District 11

CLIENT
Raleigh

AGENCY
Hammerquist
& Saffel
Seattle, WA

ART DIRECTOR
Fred Hammerquist

COPYWRITER
Hugh Saffel

PRODUCTION
Norm Hansen

ACCOUNT EXECUTIVE
Sally Bjornsen

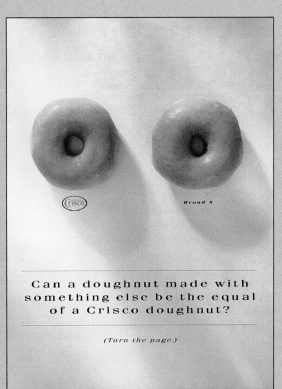

Can a doughnut made with something else be the equal of a Crisco doughnut?

(Turn the page.)

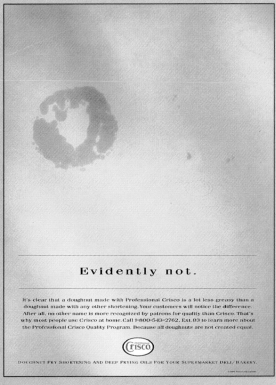

Evidently not.

It's clear that a doughnut made with Professional Crisco is a lot less greasy than a doughnut made with any other shortening. Your customers will notice the difference. After all, no other name is more recognized by patrons for quality than Crisco. That's why most people use Crisco at home. Call 1-800-543-2762, Ext. 83 to learn more about the Professional Crisco Quality Program. Because all doughnuts are not created equal.

DOUGHNUT FRY SHORTENING AND DEEP FRYING OILS FOR YOUR SUPERMARKET DELI/BAKERY.

134

SOMEWHERE BETWEEN HOME AND WORK
IS A VACATION.

RALEIGH

135

An inaccurate summary can change the whole picture.

Introducing DepoLab™. It's a whole new way to get your depositions summarized with unvarying standards of accuracy, speed and confidentiality. You can use DepoLab services instantly via modem or via overnight express. Either way, it's probably more cost-effective than the way you're doing it now. Call us at 1-800-DepoLab or call your local Interim® Legal Personnel office. We'll change the way you look at depositions.

136

Most Valuable Players
Spend Time On The Bench.

THAT'S WHERE THEY
GAIN THE CONFIDENCE,
THE COORDINATION AND
THE CONCENTRATION
THAT HELPS MAKE
THEM WINNERS.
ON THE PLAYING FIELD.
AT SCHOOL.
IN LIFE.
GIVE A CHILD
THE GIFT OF MUSIC.
IT IS VALUABLE
BEYOND WORDS.

WURLITZER

137

136
District 4

CLIENT
Interim Personnel
Services

AGENCY
Chrispin & Porter
Advertising
Miami, FL

CREATIVE DIRECTOR
Alex Bogusky

ART DIRECTOR
Alex Bogusky

COPYWRITER
Steve Horowitz

137
District 7

CLIENT
The Wurlitzer
Company

AGENCY
Sossaman Bateman
McCuddy
Memphis, TN

CREATIVE DIRECTORS
Rikki Boyce
Eric Melkent

ART DIRECTOR
Billy Riley

COPYWRITER
Rikki Boyce

PHOTOGRAPHER
Nick Vedros

ENGRAVING
Memphis Engraving

TYPOGRAPHY
Billy Riley

PRODUCTION
Randall Hartzog

ACCOUNT EXECUTIVE
Ken Sossaman

138
District 2

CLIENT
Parenting Magazine

AGENCY
Altschiller
& Company
New York, NY

CREATIVE DIRECTOR
Rosalind Greene

ART DIRECTOR
Steve Mitsch

COPYWRITER
Rosalind Greene

PHOTOGRAPHER
April Saul

PRINTER
Parenting Magazine

PRODUCTION
Bobbie Howard
Steve Mitsch

HOW YOU see THE WORLD *depends* ON YOUR POINT OF VIEW.

Perhaps it was inevitable that sooner or later a magazine would come along with a point of view that would appeal to parents who are better educated and more aware than any group of parents before them. But until PARENTING, no such publication existed.

We cover issues that are *their* issues, with the kind of journalism that is both sophisticated and substantive. We offer our readers unconventional wisdom along with the tried and true. We understand their skepticism and their humor.

What we share with them is more than pretty baby pictures. It is an informed and thoughtful approach to children and how to bring them up.

KIDS HAVE *minds* OF THEIR OWN. SHOULDN'T YOU?

There are always people who prefer to think for themselves. Like the readers of PARENTING. They are the parents who buy books as well as rent videos. They still play ball. They put on sneakers and mascara. They might browse through an issue of *Fortune*. They use pc's, and cd's. They take vacations with their kids. And without them.

With their energy and independence of mind it is these individuals who invariably set the pace and influence others. So shouldn't you have a mind of your own when it comes to reaching the very parents who think more, and act more, and buy more?

Just WHAT YOU'VE ALWAYS WANTED. MORE MOTHERS AND FATHERS.

With a circulation that's just reached 1,000,000, that's right, one million, PARENTING is now the best way to get the focused attention of unstintingly active and influential people who happen to be mothers and fathers.

PARENTING
MAGAZINE
The *thinking* PERSON'S GUIDE TO RAISING CHILDREN.

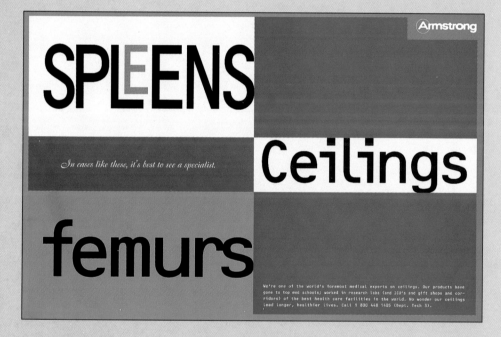

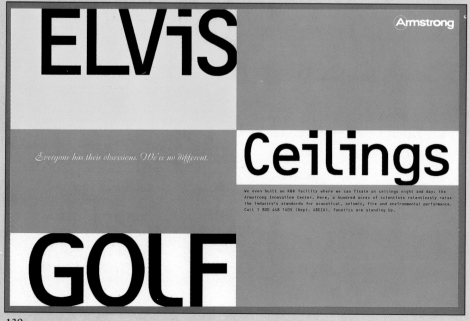

139
District 2

CLIENT
Armstrong

AGENCY
Lord, Dentsu
& Partners
New York, NY

CREATIVE DIRECTOR
Mark Hughes

ART DIRECTOR
Mark Hughes

COPYWRITERS
Tom Cunniff
Mark Hughes

PRODUCTION
Diane Vialard

COMPUTER GRAPHICS
Joseph Pavia

140
District 10

CLIENT
Subaru

AGENCY
Temerlin McClain
Irving, TX

CREATIVE DIRECTOR
Artie Megibben

ART DIRECTORS
Artie Megibben
Donna Lampert
Mike Martin

COPYWRITERS
Dee Leone
Vinny Minchillo
Diane Seimetz

BUSINESS/TRADE

141

142

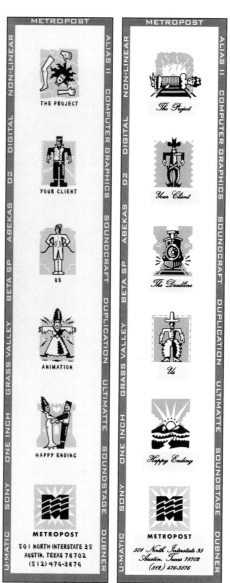

143

144
District 3

CLIENT
Instell

AGENCY
The Holt Group
Greensboro, NC

CREATIVE DIRECTOR
Vickie Canada

COPYWRITER
Mary Giunca

PHOTOGRAPHER
Ron Rovtar

145
District 4

CLIENT
Action Lane

AGENCY
The Zimmerman
Agency
Tallahassee, FL

CREATIVE DIRECTOR
Daniel Russ

ART DIRECTOR
Fernando Lecca

COPYWRITER
Kathy Salomon

146
District 7

CLIENT
The Ritz-Carlton

AGENCY
Cole Henderson
Drake
Atlanta, GA

CREATIVE DIRECTOR
Denzill Strickland

ART DIRECTOR
Debbie Kron

COPYWRITER
Chase Clausser

ACCOUNT EXECUTIVE
Lisa Barber

147
District 2

CLIENT
Elan-Monark

AGENCY
Richardson, Myers
& Donofrio, Inc.
Baltimore, MD

CREATIVE DIRECTOR
Ken Majka

ART DIRECTOR
Dave Curtis

COPYWRITER
Ken Majka

PHOTOGRAPHER
Michael Furman

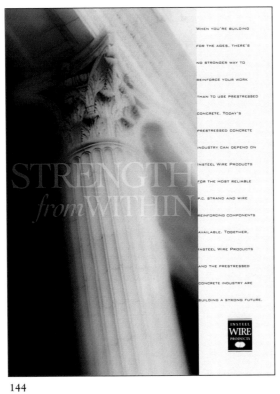

144

145

146

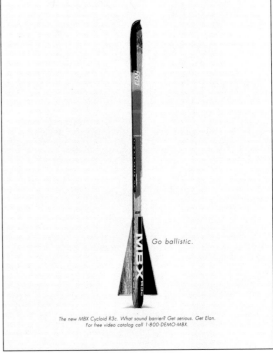

147

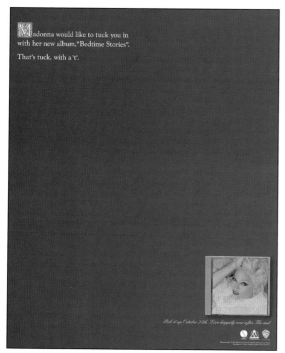

148

150

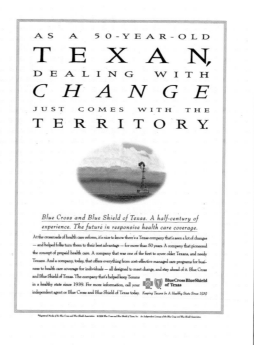

149

151

BUSINESS/TRADE

152

153

154

155

Adjoining our spa is a lovely 600 square-mile workout area.

OAHU does offer a rather expansive range of recreational possibilities. The best of which can be found on the island's western shore, where (not coincidentally) Ihilani Resort & Spa happens to be located.

For one thing, this is the sunniest place on the island. It offers some of the most untrammeled beaches in all of Hawaii. And the purest seawater available, just off the soft, white-sand beach that rings our private lagoon. (An observation that won't be lost on those who visit our multi-tiered spa for a session of Thalasso therapy, a warm seawater massage administered by 160 computer-controlled jets).

In short, Ihilani is situated amid a pristine environment. One equipped with a Ted Robinson-designed, championship golf course. Six Kramer-surfaced tennis courts. As well as the aforementioned spa, which, given its catalog of treatments, is virtually a destination itself.

Of course, satisfying one set of appetites only gives rise to another. Which is why, in addition to everything else, we offer five restaurants. *Azul*, which unites the flavors of the Mediterranean. *Kyuan*, for traditional Japanese cuisine. The *Naupaka*, specializing in continental fare. *Niblick*, for a quick bite between rounds. And for a lighter touch, the *Spa Cafe*, which proffers a menu of sensible delicacies that limit fat, not flavor.

So next time you're looking for the ideal place to book your clients, consider Ihilani Resort & Spa. With the entire island of Oahu as a playground, we can work out something to satisfy virtually anyone. For more information call 800-626-4446 from the U.S. and Canada. Worldwide, call 808-679-0079, or FAX us at 808-679-0295.

Ihilani
RESORT & SPA

156

156
District 13

CLIENT
Ihilani Resort and Spa

AGENCY
Milici Valenti Ng Pack
Honolulu, HI

CREATIVE DIRECTOR
Mike Wagner

ART DIRECTOR
Mike Wagner

COPYWRITER
George Chalekian

PHOTOGRAPHERS
Bob Mizono
John DeMello

157
District 4

CLIENT
Designing Eye

AGENCY
Turkel Advertising
Miami, FL

CREATIVE DIRECTOR
Bruce Turkel

ART DIRECTOR
Sally Ann Field

COPYWRITER
David Evans

Flamenco with a heavy metal twist.

Designing Eye

Andrés Eduardo Martín custom designs for the New World. Call 305-576-8925.

157

158
District 2

CLIENT
Armstrong

AGENCY
Lord, Dentsu
& Partners
New York, NY

CREATIVE DIRECTOR
Mark Hughes

ART DIRECTOR
Mark Hughes

COPYWRITERS
Tom Cunniff
Mark Hughes

COMPUTER GRAPHICS
Joseph Pavia

PRODUCTION
Diane Vialard

159
District 2

CLIENT
Armstrong

AGENCY
Lord, Dentsu
& Partners
New York, NY

CREATIVE DIRECTOR
Mark Hughes

ART DIRECTOR
Mark Hughes

COPYWRITERS
Tom Cunniff
Mark Hughes

COMPUTER GRAPHICS
Joseph Pavia

PRODUCTION
Diane Vialard

160
District 2

CLIENT
Armstrong

AGENCY
Lord, Dentsu
& Partners
New York, NY

CREATIVE DIRECTOR
Mark Hughes

ART DIRECTOR
Mark Hughes

COPYWRITER
Tom Cunniff

COMPUTER GRAPHICS
Joseph Pavia

PRODUCTION
Diane Vialard

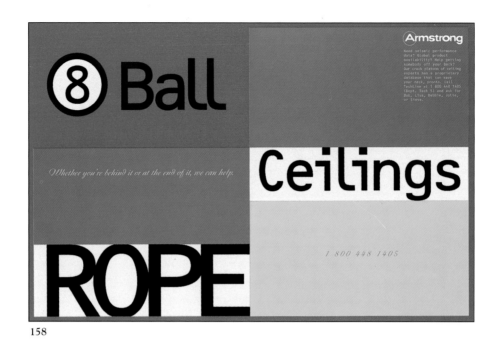

158

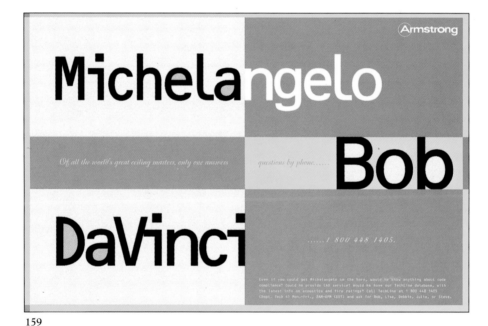

159

160

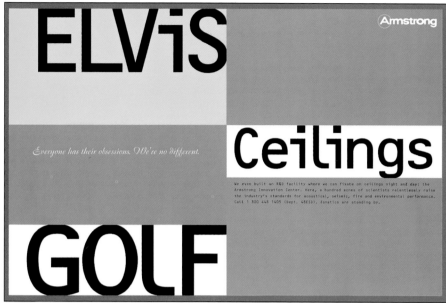

161

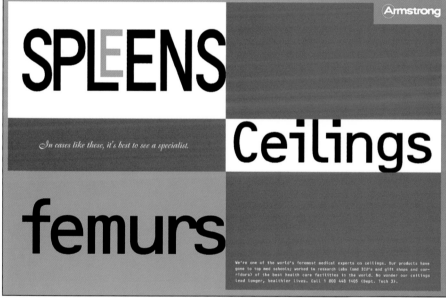

162

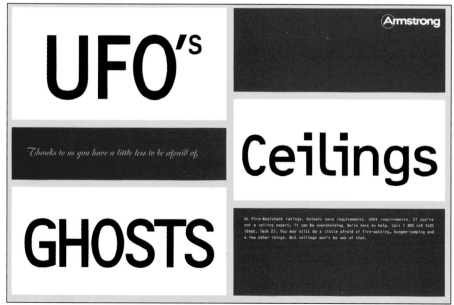

163

161
District 2

CLIENT
Armstrong

AGENCY
Lord, Dentsu
& Partners
New York, NY

CREATIVE DIRECTOR
Mark Hughes

ART DIRECTOR
Mark Hughes

COPYWRITERS
Tom Cunniff
Mark Hughes

COMPUTER GRAPHICS
Joseph Pavia

PRODUCTION
Diane Vialard

162
District 2

CLIENT
Armstrong

AGENCY
Lord, Dentsu
& Partners
New York, NY

CREATIVE DIRECTOR
Mark Hughes

ART DIRECTORS
Mark Hughes
Ron Arnold

COPYWRITERS
Tom Cunniff
Mark Hughes

COMPUTER GRAPHICS
Joseph Pavia

PRODUCTION
Diane Vialard

163
District 2

CLIENT
Armstrong

AGENCY
Lord, Dentsu
& Partners
New York, NY

CREATIVE DIRECTOR
Mark Hughes

ART DIRECTOR
Mark Hughes

COPYWRITERS
Tom Cunniff
Mark Hughes

COMPUTER GRAPHICS
Joseph Pavia

PRODUCTION
Diane Vialard

164
District 13

CLIENT
Ihilani Resort and Spa

AGENCY
Milici Valenti Ng Pack
Honolulu, HI

CREATIVE DIRECTOR
Mike Wagner

ART DIRECTOR
Mike Wagner

COPYWRITER
George Chalekian

165
District 6

CLIENT
Delco Electronics

AGENCY
Young & Laramore
Indianapolis, IN

CREATIVE DIRECTORS
David Young
Jeff Laramore

ART DIRECTOR
Mark Bradley

COPYWRITER
Scott Montgomery

ACCOUNT MANAGERS
David Clifton
Mel Humbert

164

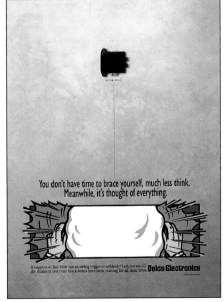

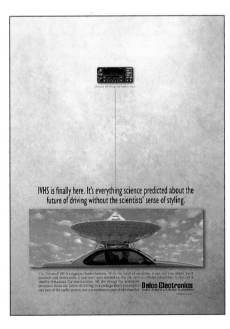

165

BUSINESS/TRADE

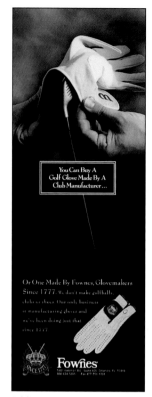

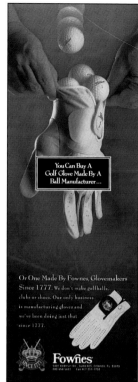

166

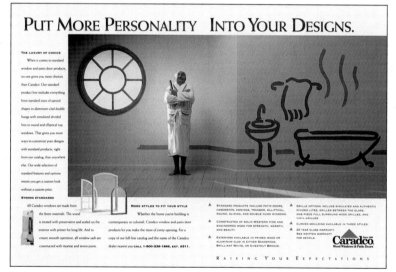

167

168
District 12

CLIENT
Lorraine Press

AGENCY
Dahlin Smith White
Salt Lake City, UT

CREATIVE DIRECTOR
Jon White

ART DIRECTOR
Connie Caldwell

COPYWRITER
Chris Drysdale

PHOTOGRAPHER
Michael McRae

DIGITAL
Dennis Millard

You know the routine. You see a painting, you take a few steps back. You see a press proof, you reach for your magnifying loupe.

That's because a painting can look weird up close and still be great. But if a printed piece looks weird through the loupe, you're toast.

Meanwhile, getting a project to look right through a loupe is about as easy as finding a drinking fountain in the Louvre (or anywhere else in France for that matter).

And finding a printer who cares as much about perfection as the average art director is even more difficult.

Except at Lorraine Press. We specialize in pleasing art directors who are way above average, you know, the kind most printers

call prima donnas.

Now, we admit, pleasing perfectionists is not easy (Just ask the spouse of the fine artist of your choice). That's why we got into electronic pre-press—to give picky people more control.

For example, did you ever wonder why you spend

On canvas, genius is apparent from a distance. On paper, the opposite is true.

time correcting MatchPrints™ from your color house if no printer can match them? It's a darn good question. And we have a darn good answer.

Most color houses use an industry standard to calculate dot gain on press. Which would be fine if all presses

were the same. But some presses are worn and sloppy, while others are well-maintained and crisp (like ours). The sad part is, most separators have adjusted their equipment to match a press somewhere in the middle.

By doing our own scans, we can regularly calculate the dot gain on our presses and create custom separations, and match prints, for your approval. So at Lorraine, what you see in pre-press is a lot closer to what you get on press.

So you see, finding a printer who's as picky as you are isn't so impossible after all.

Just come to Lorraine Press. And don't forget your loupe.

◆ LORRAINE PRESS
(801) 972-5626

Remember art class? Your first experience with pointillism probably involved a bunch of No. 2 pencil dots in the shape of a kerosene lantern. Or was it an egg? No matter. The important thing is, now that you're a big time art director, you're still making pictures with dots.

It's just that now there are several vendors and an impatient press operator between what you have in your head and what actually appears on paper. Unless, of course, your printer is Lorraine Press.

We cater to art directors who believe communication is an art. That's why our electronic pre-press and stochastic printing techniques insure your projects will be just that: art.

If you haven't discovered

stochastic printing yet, you might want to read this next part sitting down.

You know morays? Forget about them. Want better contrast? It's yours. Detail? No problem. Now, please, before your false advertising meter shrills too loudly, allow us to explain.

French Impressionists made art with dots of many colors. We only need four.

You see, stochastic printing is a new process that uses very small spots (20 microns, if you want to get technical about it) in a random fashion. More spots where the colors are darker. Fewer spots where the colors are lighter. There are no angled screens.

No morays. No rosette on the individual spots.

Picture this: you can't even see a dot pattern with the naked eye.

We could go on and on about how stochastic printing makes screen-created PMS colors look smooth and solid like a fifth color, even for fine type, but this is obviously something you're just going to have to see to believe.

Naturally, we'd be happy to arrange a personal demonstration at your request.

Just dial (801) 972-5626.

Our dots may not be as visible as the ones in those fancy French paintings. Of course, the way we look at it, that's a darn good thing.

◆ LORRAINE PRESS
(801) 972-5626

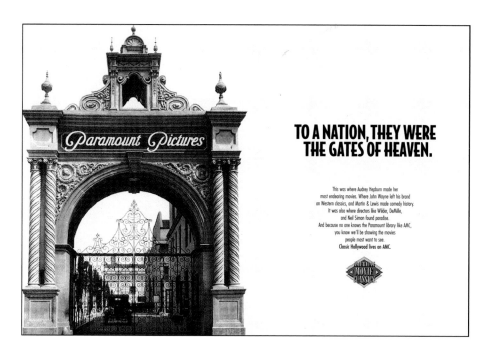

TO A NATION, THEY WERE THE GATES OF HEAVEN.

This was where Audrey Hepburn made her
most endearing movies. Where John Wayne left his brand
on Western classics, and Martin & Lewis made comedy history.
It was also where directors like Wilder, DeMille,
and Neil Simon found paradise.
And because no one knows the Paramount library like AMC,
you know we'll be showing the movies
people most want to see.
Classic Hollywood lives on AMC.

169
District 2

CLIENT
American Movie
Classics

AGENCY
Waring & LaRosa
New York, NY

CREATIVE DIRECTOR
James Caporimo

ART DIRECTOR
Howard Title

COPYWRITER
Larry Vine

PRODUCTION
Vito Lomenzo

EVERY FEW YEARS, FOX DROPPED A BOMBSHELL ON AMERICA.

All eyes were on Twentieth Century Fox.
Alice Faye's costumes, Grable's legs,
Marilyn's pout, and Mansfield's sweaters.
Fox definitely had the ladies, as well
as westerns, epics, musicals, comedies,
mysteries, and even science fiction.
And because no one knows the Fox library
like AMC, you know we'll be showing
the movies people most want to see.
Classic Hollywood lives on AMC.

**THEY SAID GOLDWYN
DIDN'T HAVE A HEART.**

**THAT'S BECAUSE HE LEFT
A PIECE OF IT IN EVERY
MOVIE HE MADE.**

Goldwyn was the producers' producer.
He was involved in every aspect of movie making.
And it showed on the screen. He produced Hollywood's first feature film
and followed it with Rodgers and Hammerstein musicals,
classic dramas, Bogart, Cooper, Brando, and much more. And because
no one knows the Goldwyn library like AMC,
you know we'll be showing the movies people most want to see.
Classic Hollywood lives on AMC.

170
District 7

CLIENT
AmSouth

AGENCY
SlaughterHanson
Advertising
Birmingham, AL

CREATIVE DIRECTOR
Terry Slaughter

ART DIRECTOR
Marion English

COPYWRITER
David Williams

SEPARATOR
Techtron

TYPOGRAPHER
Great Faces

ACCOUNT EXECUTIVE
Ruth Bean

PRETEND YOU'RE GOING IN FOR MAJOR SURGERY TOMORROW, AND JUST FOUND OUT THAT ONLY ONE PERSON WILL BE HANDLING THE WHOLE OPERATION.

The Relationship Team approach to banking.

CORPORATE BANKING IS, IN MANY WAYS, A LOT LIKE MAJOR SURGERY. COMPARATIVELY SPEAKING, THERE'S JUST NOT A WHOLE LOT OF ROOM FOR ERROR. AND, WHILE ONE DOCTOR IS GOOD, A TEAM OF SPECIALISTS IS MUCH MORE COMFORTING. BESIDES, IT IMPROVES THE ODDS. NOW LET'S WORK UNDER THE PREMISE THAT YOUR BUSINESS IS YOUR LIFE. THE CONCEPT OF JUST ONE BANKER SERVICING YOUR OPERATION JUST DOESN'T

MEMBER OF THE TEAM HAS A FINGER ON THE PULSE OF YOUR COMPANY, YOU HAVE ACCESS TO THE WHOLE TEAM, ALL UNDER THE GUIDANCE OF THE RELATIONSHIP MANAGER. CONSEQUENTLY, YOUR LOAN NEEDS ARE MET. FOR TIES OVERSEAS, WE'LL GIVE YOU AN INTERNATIONAL BANKER FOR THINGS LIKE EMPLOYEE BENEFITS, CASH MANAGEMENT, COMMERCIAL REAL ESTATE AND LEASING—YOU'RE COVERED THERE, TOO.

HOW DO YOU FEEL?

MAKE SENSE. ONE BANKER CAN'T POSSIBLY REMEDY EVERY EMERGENCY. WHICH IS PRECISELY WHY AT AMSOUTH BANK WE PRESCRIBE A WHOLE TEAM TO YOUR ACCOUNT. IT'S CALLED THE RELATIONSHIP TEAM APPROACH TO BANKING, AND WE FEEL IT'S A WAY OF DOING BUSINESS YOU'LL FIND A LOT MORE COMFORTABLE. TO BEGIN WITH, A RELATIONSHIP MANAGER WRAPS HIS HANDS AROUND YOUR CORPORATION. THE DIFFERENCE BETWEEN OUR APPROACH AND OTHER BANKS IS THAT THERE'S A WHOLE TEAM WORKING WITH HIM TO SERVE YOUR NEEDS. EVERY

IN SHORT, THEY CAN BE REAL LIFE-SAVERS. WE BELIEVE THIS TEAM APPROACH FOSTERS FASTER, MORE INNOVATIVE SOLUTIONS, AND LONG, HEALTHY RELATIONSHIPS WITH OUR CLIENTS. WHICH SHOULD MAKE EVEN THE QUEASIEST STOMACH FEEL BETTER. SO CALL AMSOUTH AND SCHEDULE AN APPOINTMENT. TODAY. BECAUSE TAKING CARE OF YOUR CORPORATE RELATIONSHIP IS ONE OPERATION IT PAYS TO FEEL GOOD ABOUT.

AmSouth BANK
THE RELATIONSHIP PEOPLE

LET'S SAY YOU JUST GOT ON A FULL 747 FOR HONG KONG. WHILE FINDING YOUR SEAT, YOU FIND OUT THERE'S ONLY ONE PILOT. AND HE'S FLYING THE ENTIRE 18 HOUR FLIGHT.

The Relationship Team approach to banking.

BELIEVE IT OR NOT, CORPORATE BANKING IS A LOT LIKE FLYING ONE OF THOSE HUGE, COMMERCIAL AIRPLANES. IN EITHER CASE, EVEN THE TINIEST LITTLE MISTAKE COULD RESULT IN A BIG DISASTER. AND, WHILE HAVING ONE PILOT IS NICE, YOU'D PROBABLY FEEL A WHOLE LOT BETTER KNOWING THAT A TEAM OF QUALIFIED SPECIALISTS WERE MAKING THIS EXPERIENCE A SAFE AND PLEASANT ONE. NOW, IF YOUR BUSINESS IS LIKE A 747, THE IDEA OF JUST ONE PERSON

WORKING TO SERVE YOUR NEEDS, YOUR RELATIONSHIP MANAGER CAN HELP STEER YOU THROUGH ALL KINDS OF CONDITIONS, AND ON TO WHAT YOU MIGHT CALL SUNNIER SPREAD SHEETS. WITH FINANCIAL SPECIALISTS ON YOUR TEAM IN EVERY AREA UNDER THE SUN, FROM CORPORATE LENDING, INTERNATIONAL BANKING, EMPLOYEE BENEFITS, CASH MANAGEMENT, COMMERCIAL REAL ESTATE AND LEASING, REST ASSURED YOUR BUSINESS WILL NEVER FLY OUT OF CONTROL. YOU HAVE IMMEDIATE

STILL WANT TO FLY?

PILOTING THE ENTIRE THING IS PRETTY FRIGHTENING. MOST CORPORATE RELATIONSHIPS ARE SIMPLY TOO BIG TO NAVIGATE ALONE. WHICH IS WHY AT AMSOUTH BANK WE INSIST ON A WHOLE TEAM TO SERVICE YOUR ACCOUNT. WE CALL IT THE RELATIONSHIP TEAM APPROACH TO BANKING. A WAY OF DOING BUSINESS WE THINK YOU'LL FIND A LOT MORE COMFORTING. FROM THE MOMENT YOU'RE ON BOARD WITH AMSOUTH, A RELATIONSHIP MANAGER TAKES COMMAND OF YOUR RELATIONSHIP, BECOMING INTIMATELY INVOLVED WITH IT. BACKED BY THE ENTIRE TEAM

ACCESS TO ANY AND EVERY ONE OF THEM, ANY TIME YOU NEED THEM. WE BELIEVE THIS TEAM APPROACH TO BANKING LEADS TO QUICKER, MORE INNOVATIVE SOLUTIONS, AND AIR-TIGHT RELATIONSHIPS WITH OUR CLIENTS. TO SEE HOW WE CAN HELP YOUR BUSINESS REALLY TAKE OFF, CALL AMSOUTH TODAY. BECAUSE THE STATE OF YOUR CORPORATE BANKING RELATIONSHIP IS THE LAST THING YOU WANT TO BE UP IN THE AIR ABOUT.

AmSouth BANK
THE RELATIONSHIP PEOPLE

IT'S LIKE YOU'RE THE QUARTERBACK. AND DURING THE GAME AGAINST THE TOUGHEST TEAM IN THE LEAGUE, YOUR ENTIRE FRONT LINE WALKS OFF THE FIELD.

The Relationship Team approach to banking.

STRANGELY ENOUGH, THE GAME OF FOOTBALL AND CORPORATE BANKING ARE ALIKE IN MORE WAYS THAN ONE. FOR STARTERS, THE CHANCES OF GETTING HURT DEPEND GREATLY ON THE TEAM YOU HAVE AROUND YOU. AND, WHILE HAVING THE BALL IS GOOD, HAVING IT WITH A TEAM OF SPECIALISTS TO PROTECT YOU IS BETTER. HEALTHIER, TOO. IF YOU THINK OF THE PLAYING FIELD AS THE BUSINESS WORLD, THE IDEA

DIFFERENCE BETWEEN OUR APPROACH AND OTHERS IS, THERE'S A WHOLE TEAM WORKING WITH HIM TO SERVE YOUR NEEDS. EVERY MEMBER WORKING TO PUSH YOU TOWARDS YOUR GOAL. CONSEQUENTLY, HOWEVER YOU DECIDE TO PLAY IT, YOU'LL FIND THERE'S A CORPORATE LOAN OFFICER, AN INTERNATIONAL BANKER, EMPLOYEE BENEFITS AND CASH MANAGEMENT SPECIALISTS, AND OTHERS ON THE SIDELINE TO LEND A HAND. UNDER THE GUIDANCE OF THE

STILL WANT THE BALL?

OF FACING THE COMPETITION ALONE DOESN'T MAKE A LOT OF SENSE. ALONE, IT'S PRACTICALLY IMPOSSIBLE TO WIN, AND YOU'RE ASSURED A BEATING YOU MAY NOT RECOVER FROM. THAT'S WHY AT AMSOUTH BANK WE LIKE TO SEE A WHOLE TEAM RUN WITH YOUR ACCOUNT. A FORMATION CALLED THE RELATIONSHIP TEAM APPROACH TO BANKING. IT BEGINS WITH A RELATIONSHIP MANAGER TAKING SIGNALS FROM YOU. AND GETTING DEEPLY ENTRENCHED IN YOUR NEEDS. TO BETTER MANAGE YOUR BUSINESS RELATIONSHIP. THE MAIN

RELATIONSHIP MANAGER, YOU HAVE ACCESS TO ANY AND EVERY ONE OF THEM. AT ANY POINT IN THE GAME. WE'VE FOUND THAT OUR TEAM APPROACH LEADS TO FASTER, MORE INNOVATIVE SOLUTIONS, AND MANY SAY, UNBEATABLE RELATIONSHIPS WITH OUR CLIENTS. SO CALL AMSOUTH TODAY, AND LET US DRAW UP A GAME PLAN FOR YOU. BECAUSE WHEN IT COMES TO CORPORATE BANKING RELATIONSHIPS, WE WON'T DROP THE BALL.

AmSouth BANK
THE RELATIONSHIP PEOPLE

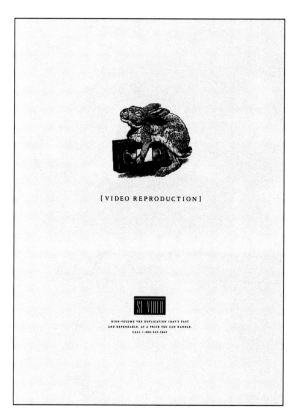

171
District 14

CLIENT
SF Video

AGENCY
Odiorne Wilde
Narraway Groome
San Francisco, CA

CREATIVE DIRECTORS
Michael Wilde
Jeff Odiorne

ART DIRECTOR
Mike Lewis

COPYWRITER
Oliver Albrecht

ILLUSTRATOR
Carl Buell

ACCOUNT EXECUTIVE
Harry Groome

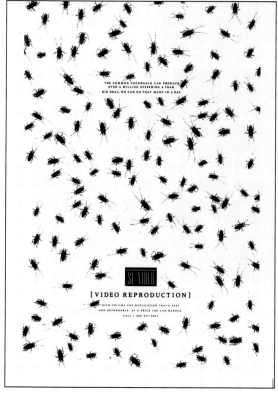

172
District 3

CLIENT
Louisville Bedding

AGENCY
Easterby &
Associates, Inc.
Asheville, NC

CREATIVE DIRECTOR
Sam Easterby

ART DIRECTORS
Ken Fulford
Dana Irwin

COPYWRITER
Matthew O'Connell

172

173
District 5

CLIENT
The Kelly-Springfield
Tire Company

AGENCY
Marcus Advertising
Beachwood, OH

ART DIRECTOR
Bryan Nimeth

COPYWRITER
Jim Sollisch

PHOTOGRAPHERS
Charlie Coppins
Andy Russeti

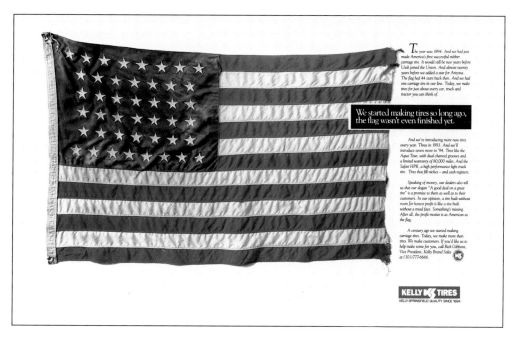

174
District 7

CLIENT
Economic
Development
Partnership of
Alabama

AGENCY
Lewis Advertising/
Birmingham
Birmingham, AL

CREATIVE DIRECTOR
Spencer Till

ART DIRECTOR
Robert Froedge

COPYWRITERS
Carey Moore
Dave Reyburn

ILLUSTRATOR
Greg Dearth

SEPARATOR
Precision Color

TYPOGRAPHER
Communications Arts

PRODUCER
Giannina Stephens

ACCOUNT EXECUTIVE
Larry Norris

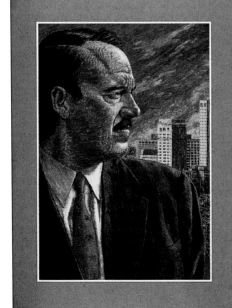

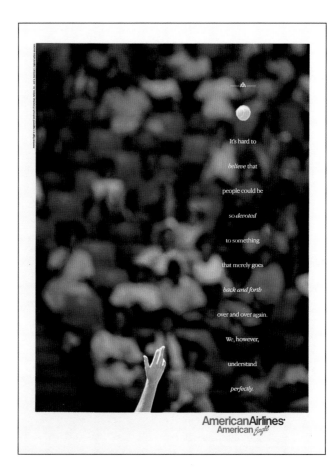

175
District 10

CLIENT
American Airlines

AGENCY
Temerlin McClain
Irving, TX

CREATIVE DIRECTOR
Bill Oakley

ART DIRECTOR
Brad White

COPYWRITER
Melvin Strobbe

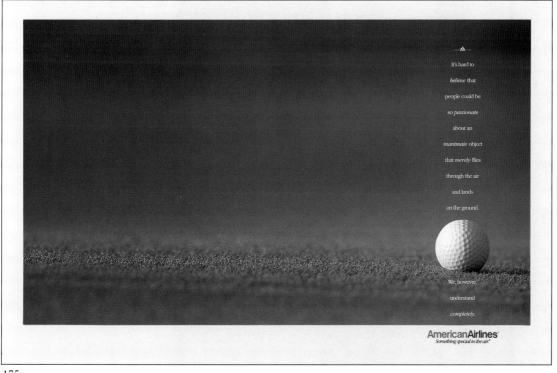

176
District 2

CLIENT
Mannington Mills

AGENCY
The Weightman
Group
Philadelphia, PA

CREATIVE DIRECTOR
Bill Lunsford

ART DIRECTORS
Ed Huber
Andrew Ferrence

COPYWRITERS
Jeff Lonoff
Margaret Myers

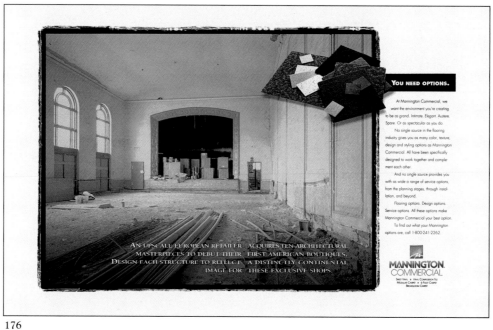

OUTDOOR

CLIENT
Pacific Science
Center

AGENCY
CF2GS
Seattle, WA

CREATIVE DIRECTOR
Cynthia Hartwig

ART DIRECTOR
Tom Scherer

COPYWRITER
Cheryl Van Ooyen

PRODUCTION MANAGER
Tom Scherer

PRODUCTION
Cheryl Van Ooyen

got milk?

178
District 14

CLIENT
California Fluid Milk
Processors Advisory
Board

AGENCY
Goodby, Silverstein
& Partners
San Francisco, CA

CREATIVE DIRECTORS
Jeffrey Goodby
Rich Silverstein

ART DIRECTOR
Chris Hooper

COPYWRITER
Chuck McBride

PHOTOGRAPHER
Terry Heffernan

PRODUCER
Michael Stock

CLIENT
California Fluid Milk
Processors Advisory
Board

AGENCY
Goodby, Silverstein
& Partners
San Francisco, CA

CREATIVE DIRECTORS
Jeffrey Goodby
Rich Silverstein

ART DIRECTOR
Chris Hooper

COPYWRITER
Chuck McBride

PHOTOGRAPHER
Terry Heffernan

PRODUCER
Michael Stock

ACCOUNT EXECUTIVE
Tom Hollerbach

180

181

180
District 10

CLIENT
Austin Gym

AGENCY
DDB Needham
Worldwide Dallas
Group
Dallas, TX

ART DIRECTOR
Christopher Gyorgy

COPYWRITER
Pat Mendelson

PHOTOGRAPHER
Michael Haskins

181
District 10

CLIENT
Kelsey-Seybold

AGENCY
Stan & Lou
Houston, TX

CREATIVE DIRECTORS
Lou Congelio
Jim Harris

ART DIRECTOR
August Kovach

COPYWRITER
Greg Giles

182
District 9

CLIENT
Brian Bohr Karate,
Inc.

AGENCY
The Puckett Group
St. Louis, MO

ART DIRECTOR
David Nien-Li Yang

COPYWRITER
Barton Corley

183
District 11

CLIENT
Darigold

AGENCY
McCann-Erickson
Seattle
Seattle, WA

CREATIVE DIRECTOR
Jim Walker

ART DIRECTOR
Kristy Willson

COPYWRITER
John Schofield

PRODUCTION
Alice Isackson

182

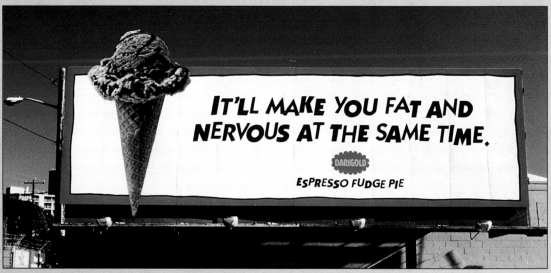

183

184
District 7

CLIENT
Bronx Bagel Bar

AGENCY
Patterson Design
Works
Memphis, TN

CREATIVE DIRECTOR
Pat Patterson

ART DIRECTOR
Greg Hastings

COPYWRITERS
Greg Hastings
Dan Conaway

ILLUSTRATOR
Greg Hastings

PRINTER
Mid South Color Lab

PRODUCTION
Greg Hastings

ACCOUNT EXECUTIVE
Pat Patterson

185
District 14

CLIENT
NIKE

AGENCY
Imagic
San Francisco, CA

ART DIRECTOR
Eric King

PHOTOGRAPHER
Ross Elmi

ILLUSTRATOR
Michael Kerbow

DESIGNER
Michael Kerbow

PRODUCTION
Imagic

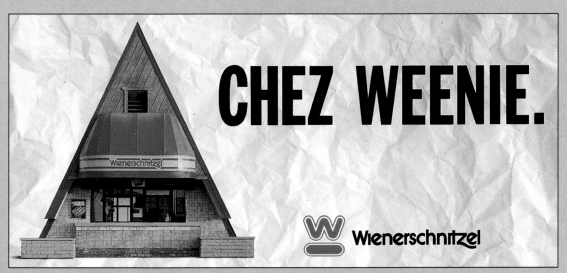

186
District 15

CLIENT
Wienerschnitzel

AGENCY
Stein Robaire Helm
Los Angeles, CA

CREATIVE DIRECTORS
John Stein
Jean Robaire

ART DIRECTOR
Check Bennett

COPYWRITER
Clay Williams

PHOTOGRAPHER
John Kelly

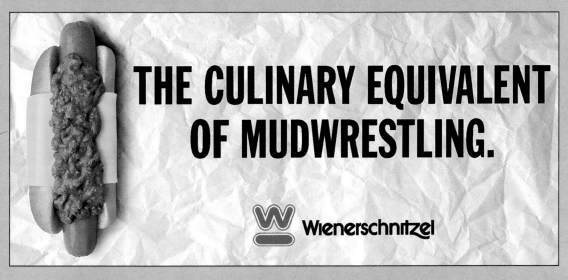

187
District 5

CLIENT
Louisville Zoo

AGENCY
Doe-Anderson
Advertising Agency
Louisville, KY

CREATIVE DIRECTOR
Gary Sloboda

ART DIRECTOR
Kevin Lippy

COPYWRITER
Rankin Mapother

188
District 7

CLIENT
Shallowford
Vascectomy Clinic

AGENCY
Turner & Turner
Communications
Atlanta, GA

CREATIVE DIRECTOR
Jamie Turner

ART DIRECTORS
Marilee Fogeltanz
Richard Link
Tom Sapp

COPYWRITER
Richard Link

ACCOUNT EXECUTIVE
Monica Ross

189
District 3

CLIENT
Greenville Ballet

AGENCY
The Creative Market
Greenville, SC

CREATIVE DIRECTOR
James Gibbons

ART DIRECTOR
Anne Peck

COPYWRITER
James Gibbons

PHOTOGRAPHER
George Lee

187

188

189

190

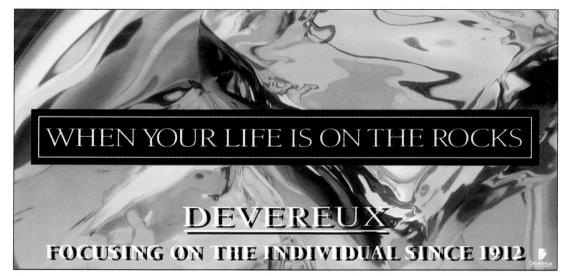

191

192

190
District 8

CLIENT
Jiffy Lubes of Wisconsin

AGENCY
Carl Ames Communications
Madison, WI

CREATIVE DIRECTOR
Carl Ames

COPYWRITER
Carl Ames

ILLUSTRATOR
Mara Scheckler

191
District 10

CLIENT
Devereux

AGENCY
The Hively Agency
Houston, TX

CREATIVE DIRECTOR
Charles Hively

ART DIRECTOR
Laura Tolar

COPYWRITER
Charles Hively

PHOTOGRAPHER
Michael Pruzan

PRODUCTION
Fred Harveat

192
District 5

CLIENT
McDonald's

AGENCY
Fahlgren
Parkersburg, WV

ART DIRECTOR
Anne Johnson

COPYWRITER
Heath Honaker

193
District 6

CLIENT
Indiana State Fair

AGENCY
MZD
Indianapolis, IN

CREATIVE DIRECTOR
Mike Soper

ART DIRECTOR
Scott Davis

COPYWRITER
Tim Abare

194
District 10

CLIENT
Hi/LO

AGENCY
Fogarty Klein &
Partners
Houston, TX

CREATIVE DIRECTORS
Tom Monroe
Nancy Self

ART DIRECTOR
Tom Gates

COPYWRITER
Julie Finch

195
District 6

CLIENT
Welborn Mulberry

AGENCY
Keller Crescent
Advertising Company
Evansville, IN

CREATIVE DIRECTOR
Dick Thomas

COPYWRITER
Nancy Kirkpatrick

PRODUCER
Mike Niles

ACCOUNT EXECUTIVE
Ann Stegall

193

194

195

196

197

198

196
District 9
CLIENT
The Advertising Club
of Greater St. Louis
AGENCY
Kupper Parker
Communications, Inc.
St. Louis, MO
CREATIVE DIRECTOR
Peter A.M. Charlton
ART DIRECTOR
Bill Tuttle
COPYWRITER
Peter A.M. Charlton

197
District 4
CLIENT
Sunglass Hut
AGENCY
Crispin & Porter
Advertising
Miami, FL
CREATIVE DIRECTOR
Alex Bogusky
ART DIRECTOR
Diane Durban
COPYWRITER
Richard Bloom

198
District 4
CLIENT
Valencia Community
College
AGENCY
Gouchenour
Advertising
Orlando, FL
CREATIVE DIRECTOR
Chris Robb
ART DIRECTOR
Chris Robb
COPYWRITERS
Jeff Nicosia
Julio Lima
PHOTOGRAPHER
Don Burlinson
PRODUCTION
Craig Gouchenour

199
District 7

CLIENT
Buffalo Rock Bottling
Co. - Diet Pepsi

AGENCY
Claude Dorsey
Tuscaloosa, AL

CREATIVE DIRECTOR
David Chandler

200
District 5

CLIENT
Jacobson's

AGENCY
Doe-Anderson
Advertising Agency
Louisville, KY

CREATIVE DIRECTOR
Gary Sloboda

ART DIRECTOR
Stefanie Becker

COPYWRITER
Ed Neary

201
District 10

CLIENT
Columbia Doctors
Hospital

AGENCY
Stone & Ward
Little Rock, AR

CREATIVE DIRECTORS
Larry Stone
Jean Romano

ART DIRECTOR
John Barnard

COPYWRITER
Trent Patterson

ILLUSTRATOR
Brent Bennette

PRODUCTION
Mitzi Miller

ACCOUNT EXECUTIVES
Fran Webb
Mimi San Pedro

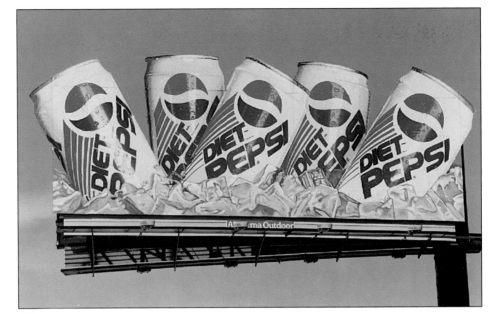

199

200

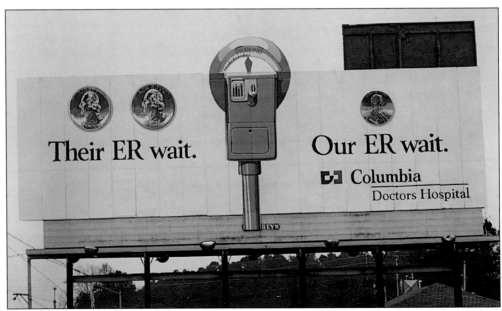

201

202

203

204

202
District 7

CLIENT
The Kroger Company

AGENCY
The Buntin Group
Nashville, TN

CREATIVE DIRECTOR
Stephen Fechtor

ART DIRECTOR
Bob Jensen

COPYWRITER
Tom Cocke

ENGRAVER
Spectra National

PRODUCTION
Chris Carroll

203
District 9

CLIENT
Bum Steer

AGENCY
Bailey Lauerman
& Associates
Lincoln, NE

CREATIVE DIRECTOR
Rich Bailey

ART DIRECTOR
Carter Weitz

COPYWRITER
Laura Crawford

ACCOUNT EXECUTIVES
Rich Bailey
Dan Levy

204
District 10

CLIENT
The Collection

AGENCY
The Bradford Lawton
Design Group
San Antonio, TX

CREATIVE DIRECTOR
Brad Lawton

ART DIRECTOR
Jennifer Griffith-
Garcia

ILLUSTRATOR
Jody Laney

DESIGNERS
Brad Lawton
Jody Laney

CONSTRUCTION
Advanced Signing

205
District 9

CLIENT
Mill Creek Brewery

AGENCY
Barkley & Evergreen
Fairway, KS

CREATIVE DIRECTOR
Jim Aylward

ART DIRECTORS
Edd Timmons
Craig Neuman

ILLUSTRATOR
Nancy Stahl

DESIGNERS
Edd Timmons
Craig Neuman

206
District 14

CLIENT
Medicine Bow Guest
Ranch

AGENCY
Odiorne Wilde
Narraway Groome
San Francisco, CA

CREATIVE DIRECTORS
Michael Wilde
Jeff Odiorne

ART DIRECTORS
Michael Wilde
Brad Webb

COPYWRITERS
Eric Weltner
Jeff Odiorne

PHOTOGRAPHER
Terry Husebye

205

206

207
District 4

CLIENT
Sunglass Hut

AGENCY
Crispin & Porter
Advertising
Miami, FL

CREATIVE DIRECTOR
Alex Bogusky

ART DIRECTORS
Diane Durban
Steve Mapp

COPYWRITERS
Richard Bloom
Alex Bogusky
Katherine Patterson

208
District 7

CLIENT
Mr. Pride Car Wash

AGENCY
Thompson & Company
Memphis, TN

CREATIVE DIRECTORS
Trace Hallowell
Michael H. Thompson

ART DIRECTOR
Trace Hallowell

COPYWRITER
Sheperd Simmons

PHOTOGRAPHER
Woody Woodliff

ILLUSTRATOR
Kelly Brother

PRINTER
Naegele

TYPOGRAPHY
Great Faces

PRODUCTION
Helen McLain

ACCOUNT EXECUTIVE
Barb Drabowicz

209
District 9

CLIENT
President Riverboat
Casino

AGENCY
The Puckett Group
St. Louis, MO

CREATIVE DIRECTOR
Steve Puckett

ART DIRECTOR
David Yang

COPYWRITERS
Rich Wolchock
Bart Corley

ACCOUNT SUPERVISOR
Matt Andrew

210
District 10

CLIENT
Devereux

AGENCY
The Hively Agency
Houston, TX

CREATIVE DIRECTOR
Charles Hively

ART DIRECTOR
Laura Tolar

COPYWRITER
Charles Hively

PRODUCTION
Fred Harveat

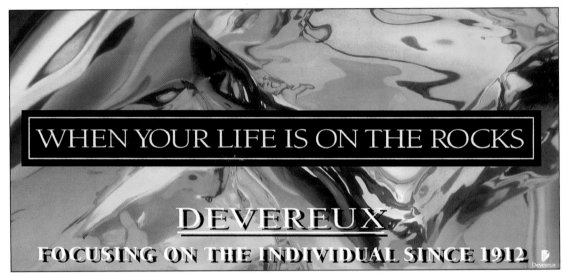

211
District 9

CLIENT
Ellerbe Becket
Architects

AGENCY
Kiku Obata
& Company
St. Louis, MO

CREATIVE DIRECTOR
Kiku Obata

DESIGNERS
Tim McGinty
Kay Pangraze
Heather Testa
Theresa Henrekin
Amy Knopf

212
District 9

CLIENT
Library Ltd.
Bookstore

AGENCY
Cube Advertising
& Design
Clayton, MO

DESIGNER
David Chiow

ARCHITECT
Howard Koblenz

212

TELEVISION

213
District 2

CLIENT
The Baltimore Zoo

AGENCY
Eisner & Associates
Baltimore, MD

CREATIVE DIRECTORS
Bill Mitchell
Chuck Thompson

ART DIRECTOR
Bill Mitchell

COPYWRITER
Chuck Thompson

PRODUCER
David Berger

ACCOUNT EXECUTIVE
Pauline Danielweski

213
Monkey Boy
MIKE: If I could be any animal in the whole entire zoo I would be a... a monkey. I would go crazy and I would jump all over the place, run up the trees and just act funny. And, ah, make faces and swing on the vine like Tarzan. But if my Mom & Dad were at the Zoo I would probably act on my best behavior.
LOGO: THE BALTIMORE ZOO. I-83 EXIT 7

Elephant's Trout
ZACH: An elephant has a nose. Not really a nose, it's like a tube actually
MIKE: It hangs down real long and low. And it...
ZACH: It's like a straw connected to a nose.
MIKE: It's like a hand or something.
ZACH: It's like a gigantic hose kind of thing.
MIKE: It's a snout.
ZACH: Horn. (Horn SFX)
MIKE: A trout. An elephant has a trout.
LOGO: THE BALTIMORE ZOO I-83 EXIT 7

Talking Penguin
ANGELA: When I come to the Zoo, the first thing I want to see is the penguins. I really like the way they talk. And they sound really funny. If you listen really careful you can hear what they're saying. One time, they said "I like you. You're very nice. You're my best friend." And I think they said it to me!

i dumped matthew

buying jelly donuts

can live with one less

a soft

poor elvis

accountant

214

District 2

CLIENT
WMMR 93.3 FM

AGENCY
Earle Palmer Brown/
Philadelphia
Philadelphia, PA

CREATIVE DIRECTOR
Mike Drazen

ART DIRECTOR
Robert Shaw West

COPYWRITERS
Kelly Simmons
Ken Cillis

PRODUCER
Joe Mosca

214

Dumped

VO: People think I dump all my
boyfriends for petty reasons not true I
dumped Michael because he had a soft
mattress I dumped Matthew because
he had a soft stomach and Martin?
how embarrassing he had a soft rock
album

Elvis

VO: Last night I dreamt I saw Elvis
buying jelly donuts at the mini-mart I
asked him what it was like to be dead
he said it was great big cadillacs fatty
foods and angels playing nothing but
country western music poor Elvis I
thought for sure he'd make it to
heaven

Accountant

VO: Doctors have this theory that if
you play classical music to infants
they'll grow up with a better
understanding of complex
relationships like math they don't
know what effect rock and roll will
have but I play this stuff for him
anyway I figure the world can live with
one less accountant

215
District 10
CLIENT
Houston Rockets
AGENCY
GSD&M
Austin, TX
CREATIVE DIRECTORS
Bryan Jessee
Guy Bommarito
ART DIRECTOR
Bryan Jessee
COPYWRITERS
Oscar Casares
Felipe Bascope
PRODUCER
Kenny Grant
DIRECTOR
John Zurick

216
District 2
CLIENT
Little Caesars Pizza
AGENCY
Cliff Freeman &
Partners
New York, NY
CREATIVE DIRECTOR
Cliff Freeman
ART DIRECTORS
John Leu
Greg Bell
COPYWRITERS
Greg Bell
John Leu
Cliff Freeman
PRODUCER
MaryEllen Duggan
PRODUCTION
Crossroads Films

215
SFX: *Rockets game on the radio*
RADIO ANNCR: (Peterson) Just four seconds left on the clock, the Rockets are trailing by one. Vernon Maxwell takes it left to right over the circle goes down to the dream underneath. Olajuwon has it - shake n' bake right. Goes up for the shot-no good.
FAN: That's it! I just can't take it anymore!
SFX: *Anvil being thrown over ledge.*
VO: The Houston Rockets would like to thank you for your support this season.
RADIO ANNCR: (Peterson) But wait...fouled.
VO: Because everyone knows, it's not easy being a sports fan in Houston.
LOGO: HOUSTON ROCKETS.
RADIO ANNCR: (Peterson) Just one more chance, folks! Do you believe in miracles?!

216
SFX: *Heroic music starts low and builds throughout.*
MODERATOR: O.K...how many of you would like more cheese on your pizza?
MODERATOR: O.K...
MODERATOR: How many of you would like more toppings on your pizza?
MODERATOR:...O.K. more cheese?
MODERATOR:...O.K...more toppings?
MODERATOR:...O.K...more cheese?...More toppings?..More?..More? More toppings?
MODERATOR: Cheese?...Toppings?...More?
SFX: *Music reaches crescendo.*
RESEARCHER: Well...that's every man, woman, and child.
ANNCR VO: By popular demand, it's the new Little Caesars Pleasers Menu. More meat...more cheese...more pepperoni...more toppings.
ANNCR VO: Any two for one low price. Satisfaction guaranteed or your money back.
Little Caesar: Pizza! Pizza!

217

District 14

CLIENT
Norwegian Cruise Line

AGENCY
Goodby, Silverstein & Partners
San Francisco, CA

CREATIVE DIRECTORS
Jeffrey Goodby
Rich Silverstein

ART DIRECTOR
Steve Luker

COPYWRITER
Steve Simpson

PHOTOGRAPHERS
Ritts/Hayden

PRODUCER
Elizabeth O'Toole

218

District 2

CLIENT
Visa

AGENCY
BBDO New York
New York, NY

CREATIVE DIRECTOR
Jimmy Siegel

ART DIRECTOR
Rich Hanson

COPYWRITER
Jimmy Siegel

PRODUCER
David Frankel

PRODUCTION
Gartner-Grasso

217

SFX: BLUE MOON by The Cowboy Junkies in background
Text: Out Here (Remains on screen throughout) The Memory Factory
VO: Out here the memory factory...
TEXT: Works Overtime
VO: Works overtime
TEXT: Worry desolves in salt water. Fantasy and reality trade places.
VO: Worry desolves in salt water. Fantasy and reality trade places.
TEXT: The muscles in your neck
VO: And the muscles in your neck...
TEXT: Relax
VO: Relax
TEXT: It's different out here. Norwegian Cruise Line. Ships Registry Bahamas
VO: It's different out here. Norwegian Cruise Line.

218

WOMAN: Oh it's so cute.
MAN: Ahh excusi, could you take a picture of us with the Burro over there?
BOYS: Oh, camera - burro, burro, - camera!
TITLE: Unbelievable!
VO: If you take off to the Italian town of Todi.
TITLE: They traded us this camera for that stupid donkey?
VO: But your camera just takes off.
MAN: Where'd they go?
VO: You better have Visa Gold. Because there's not a camera store there that takes American Express.
MAN: There's a great shot.
VO: Visa Gold. It's everywhere you want to be.

219

District 4

CLIENT
Nokia Mobile Phones

AGENCY
Peak Barr Petralia
Biety, Inc.
Tampa, FL

CREATIVE DIRECTORS
Joe Petralia
Jim Barr

PRODUCER
Jim Barr

DIRECTOR
Arnie Lerner

220

District 14

CLIENT
California Fluid Milk
Processor Advisory
Board

AGENCY
Goodby, Silverstein
& Partners
San Francisco, CA

CREATIVE DIRECTORS
Jeffrey Goodby
Rich Silverstein

ART DIRECTOR
Sean Ehringer

COPYWRITER
Harry Cocciolo

PRODUCER
Cindy Epps

PRODUCTION
Propaganda Films

The California Fluid Milk Processor Advisory Board

219
MICHAEL DAVIS: Enter with me into the world of the unusual, where the commonplace is considered ordinary.
ANNCR: One Touch Dialing. With a NOKIA cellular phone, you can dial important numbers or emergency services with one push of one button.
SFX: PHONE RINGS
WOMAN ON PHONE: Hello?
MICHAEL: Hello.
WOMAN ON PHONE: Michael!
MICHAEL: Amazing...and now the even more unusual: conference calling.
SUPER: NOKIA logo...Connecting People
ANNCR: NOKIA...largest European cellular phone manufacturer, now in America.

220
MAN: (Calmly) Tom, can I make a suggestion?...(Loud) You're fired!!!
SFX: *Truck horn wailing*
MAN: Aaaaaaaah!!!
SFX: *Chimes*
SFX: *Bird flapping wings*
WOMAN: Welcome to eternity.
MUSIC: Slow, rolling piano intro. Slow, easy, swing jazz with alto lead.
SFX: *Door shutting.*
SFX: *Tick, tick, tick.*
SFX: *Cat purring.*
MAN: Heaven!...
MAN: Yes!
MAN: Hmmm...
MAN: Milk!...
MAN: Wait a minute. Where am I?
SUPER: California Fluid Milk Processor Advisory Board.
CARD: Got milk?

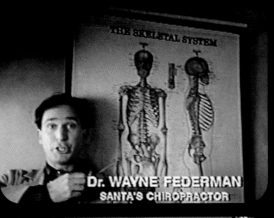

Apple

221

District 2

CLIENT
Maryland State Lottery

AGENCY
TBC Advertising
Baltimore, MD

CREATIVE DIRECTOR
Allan Charles

ART DIRECTOR
Amy Yarnot

COPYWRITERS
Jane King
Jeff Alphin

PRODUCER
Dana Cole

ACCOUNT EXECUTIVE
Ann Nicolaides

222

District 2

CLIENT
Apple Computer

AGENCY
BBDO West
Los Angeles, CA

CREATIVE DIRECTOR
David Lubars

ART DIRECTOR
Denise Crandall

COPYWRITER
Greg Ketchum

PRODUCER
Shelley Eisner

PRODUCTION
Bedford Falls
Sarah Caplan

DIRECTOR
Ed Zwick

EDITORS
John Murray
Jim Haygood

221
TITLE: DR. WAYNE FEDERMAN, SANTA'S CHIROPRACTOR
DR. FEDERMAN: This is a normal human spine. That's the Santa spine. He's gotta lift this bike onto the roof, into the chimney, under the tree, without making any noise. He's a master. Heavy gifts cause curvature. ...mmmm...94 pounds...16 pounds...12 pounds, but cumbersome. This year ask for lightweight Holiday Scratch-Off tickets. Your chances of winning are one in three. He's not Hercules. He's just a man with a bad back.

222
TEACHER: Now it's time for Show & Tell..Who's ready with their report
DAD: Drop in the title
GAVIN: Like this Dad?
TITLE (on computer screen): Summer Vacation
GIRL: This is my star fish, it kind of smells real icky
DAD: Do you like this bit?
GAVIN: Yeah, I like that
BOY: I really like snorkeling, but the water still went up my nose

223
District 10
CLIENT
Farah, Inc.
AGENCY
GSD&M
Austin, TX
CREATIVE DIRECTORS
Bryan Jessee
Hillary Jordon
ART DIRECTOR
Gene Brenek
COPYWRITER
Peter Berta
PRODUCERS
Sandy Mislang
Jeff Johnson
DIRECTOR
Matthew Harris
EDITOR
Jeff Wishergrad

224
District 9
CLIENT
Anheuser Busch -
Budweiser
AGENCY
DMB&B St. Louis
St. Louis, MO
CREATIVE DIRECTORS
Ric Anello
Michael Hutchinson
ART DIRECTOR
Michael Smith
COPYWRITER
Dave Swaine
PRODUCER
Chan Hatcher

223
WOMAN: You jerk! I never want to see you again!
VO: Savane soft 100 percent cotton pants. They're the only pants made with Process 2000. So they don't wrinkle. Which means you'll always come off looking good. No matter what you've done.
CUT TO LOGO AND SUPER: The Original No Wrinkle Pants.

224
SFX: *Crickets, night sounds*
Open on one frog who croaks the word
'BUD'
Cut to two frogs...second frog croaks the word
'WEIS'
Now both frogs work together to say
'BUD...WEIS...'
Cut to third frog who now enters the group and croaks the word
'ER'
Now all three work together to say
'BUD...WEIS...ER'
Over and over
Camera pulls back to reveal a neon sign reflecting in a pool of water at night... continues to move up and reveal a

225
District 2
CLIENT
Staples Office
Supplies
AGENCY
Cliff Freeman &
Partners
New York, NY
CREATIVE DIRECTOR
Arthur Bijur
ART DIRECTORS
Greg Bell
Matt Vescovo
COPYWRITER
Steve Dildarian
PRODUCERS
Ann Kurtzman
MaryEllen Duggan
PRODUCTION
Industrial Artists

225
MUSIC: "THE MOST WONDERFUL TIME OF THE
YEAR."
VO: It's that time of year again.
VO: They're going back!
VO: It's back to school time at Staples!
VO: Over 5,000 school supplies at the guaranteed low
price.
STAPLES LOGO ANIMATION (A huge stapler spelling
out the word STAPLES).
VO: Staples, Yeah, we've got that.

226
District 2

CLIENT
Little Caesars Pizza

AGENCY
Cliff Freeman &
Partners
New York, NY

CREATIVE DIRECTORS
Cliff Freeman
Arthur Bijur
Donna Weinheim

ART DIRECTORS
John Leu
Greg Bell
Donna Weinheim

COPYWRITERS
Greg Bell
John Leu
Cliff Freeman
Arthur Bijur
Michelle Roufa

PRODUCERS
Anne Kurtzman
Mary Ellen Duggan

PRODUCTION
Crossroads Films
Harmony Pictures

226

Magic Fingers
SFX: *Romantic music on the radio*
WOMAN: We should've gotten the
pizza.
SUPER: $1
ANNCR (VO): Pizza for a Buck! Now
when you buy two pizzas with two
toppings for $8.98, you get a third pizza
for a buck!
LITTLE CAESAR: Pizza! Pizza!

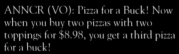

Singing Baby
GRANNY: Have you ever seen
anything more amazing than Little
Caesars Italian Sausage pizza?
FATHER: ...No.
ANNCR: Italian Sausage pizza!
Loaded with sausage, peppers and
onions. The newest from a whole
menu of Little Caesars Pleasers. Any
two for $9.98!
LITTLE CAESAR: Pizza! Pizza!
ANNCR: Or get one for $5.99!
LITTLE CAESAR: Pizza!

Focus Group
SFX: *Heroic music starts low and builds
throughout.*
MODERATOR: O.K...how many of
you would like more cheese on your
pizza?
MODERATOR: O.K...
MODERATOR: How many of you
would like more toppings on your
pizza?
MODERATOR:...O.K. more cheese?
MODERATOR:...O.K...more
toppings?
MODERATOR:...O.K...more
cheese?...More toppings?.. More?..
More? More toppings?
MODERATOR: Cheese?...
Toppings?... More?
SFX: *Music reaches crescendo.*
RESEARCHER: Well...that's every
man, woman, and child.
ANNCR VO: By popular demand, it's
the new Little Caesars Pleasers Menu.
More meat...more cheese...more
pepperoni...more toppings.
ANNCR VO: Any two for one low
price. Satisfaction guaranteed or your
money back.

227
District 2

CLIENT
Staples Office
Supplies

AGENCY
Cliff Freeman &
Partners
New York, NY

CREATIVE DIRECTOR
Arthur Bijur

ART DIRECTORS
Greg Bell
John Leu
Matt Vescovo

COPYWRITER
Steve Dildarian

PRODUCERS
Ann Kurtzman
MaryEllen Duggan

PRODUCTION
Industrial Artists
Crossroads Films

227
Most Wonderful Time
MUSIC: "THE MOST
WONDERFUL TIME OF THE
YEAR."
VO: It's that time of year again.
VO: They're going back!
VO: It's back to school time at
Staples!
VO: Over 5,000 school supplies at the
guaranteed low price.
STAPLES LOGO ANIMATION
(A huge stapler spelling out the word
STAPLES).
VO: Staples, Yeah, we've got that.

Mailman
WOMAN: Working in the city can
get to you after a while. I commuted
for 20 years until one day I just
snapped and said 'enough is enough.'
So I gave it all up and started working
out of my house. I thought it would be
nice change of pace.
WOMAN: (Hollering) Hey...you! Get
off my lawn!
VO: Staples has everything you need
to work out of your home. Over 5,000
office supplies at the guaranteed low
price.
STAPLES LOGO ANIMATION
(A huge stapler spelling out the word
STAPLES).
VO: Staples. Yeah, we've got that.

No Surprises
VO: It's hard to surprise people during
the holidays.
SFX: *Paper crinkling*
VO: So shop at Staples and give them
something different.
VO: Like a laser printer, electronic
organizer or cordless phone.
SFX: Panting and wagging.
VO: Over 5,000 great gift ideas at the
guaranteed low price.
STAPLES LOGO ANIMATION
(A huge staples spelling out the word
STAPLES).
VO: Staples. Yeah, we've got that.

228

District 2

CLIENT
Pepsi

AGENCY
BBDO New York
New York, NY

CREATIVE DIRECTORS
Don Schneider
Ted Sann
Michael Patti

ART DIRECTOR
Don Schneider

COPYWRITERS
Michael Patti
Ted Sann

PRODUCER
Regina Ebel

PRODUCTION
Gartner-Grasso
Pytka

228

Chimps

SUPER: Institute For Beverage Research

AVO: In order to discover the real difference between the world's two leading soft drinks, we're implementing the fail safe scientific, anthropological study. Chimp A will be allowed nothing but Coca Cola. Chimp B will be allowed nothing but Pepsi.

SUPER: Six Weeks Later

AVO: The results are astounding. The chimp that drank Coca-Cola showed remarkable improvement in motor skills. The chimp that drank Pepsi however, quickly lost interest and disappeared.

WOMAN: Hello, it's him!

SUPER: Be Young, Have Fun Drink Pepsi.

PEPSI LOGO

Summer Love

GUY1 TO GUY 2: Here comes those hippies again.

GUY ON LOUD SPEAKER: Testing...1, 2...1..., check, check, OK. Stay away from the green pesto sauce.

MAN: Is that you Sunflower?

WOMAN: Pigpen!

GUY2: Place hasn't changed in twenty five years.

GUY1: Yeah, it's a shame you know they should have put in some condos by now.

GUY2: I'm on a low sodium, low fat diet.

GUY3: Well, how do you feel?

GUY2: Terrible.

GUY: Green marble goes in the upstairs bathroom!

KID1: This is the anniversary of a historical event.

KID2: Which one?

KID1: Watergate

GUY ON LOUDSPEAKER: Let's have a warm welcome for "Country Joe MacDonald."

JOHN: Joe, remember when we did this twenty five years ago?

JOE: No.

AVO: Wouldn't it be nice if your youth was as easy to hold on to as an ice cold Pepsi?

KID1: Do you think he'll go skinny dippin' again?

GUY: Yaaah!!!!

KID2: I hope not.

SUPER: Be Young Have Fun Drink

A Day in the Life

AVO: Most things in this world aren't big enough to handle 7 feet 2 inches, 3 hundred and 10 pounds.

SHAQ: And I ordered the big breakfast.

TAILOR: How does that feel?

BELLBOY: Oh, watch your head Mr. O'Neal.

AVO: There is one notable exception, the big slam from Pepsi. One ice cold... liter of Pepsi big enough to handle the biggest thirst.

SHAQ: Ain't life grand.

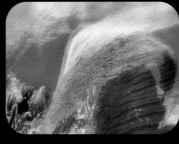

229
District 2

CLIENT
Mexico Tourism

AGENCY
Saatchi & Saatchi Advertising
New York, NY

CREATIVE DIRECTOR
John Morrison

ART DIRECTOR
Dabni Harvey

COPYWRITER
Cheryl Chapman

PRODUCER
Liz Graves

PRODUCTION
GMS

DIRECTOR
Peter Nydrle

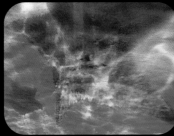

229

Colors

VO: Come up for air now you come upon a red so big the building can not hold it can not keep it from clashing horribly perfectly flawless into your eyes wiggle with green purple magenta they scream they scream how they must have screamed off the brush quiet! be quiet! no, do not be quiet.
SUPER: You are very close to far away.

Underwater

VO: Yes I will come I will come with you waves into the world the swaying world below the world that dances slowly dances as I move as I feel as I drift I drift through time, through cultures and it is now right now it is a zillion years of nows.
SUPER: You are very close to far away. Mexico.

Day of the Dead

They are not sad they do not cry they do not wear black or dark or veil or glove they do not whisper they will not mourn no tissues no grief no hearts weigh heavy not a tear they will surrender they will not surrender they will celebrate I love you grandmother.
SUPER: You are very close to far away. Mexico.

230
District 14

CLIENT
California Fluid Milk
Processor Advisory
Board

AGENCY
Goodby, Silverstein
& Partners
San Francisco, CA

CREATIVE DIRECTORS
Jeffrey Goodby
Rich Silverstein

ART DIRECTORS
Sean Ehringer
Joe Shands

COPYWRITERS
Harry Cocciolo
Chuck McBride

PRODUCER
Cindy Epps

PRODUCTION
Propaganda Films

230

Heaven
MAN: (Calmly) Tom, can I make a
suggestion?...(Loud) You're fired!!!
SFX: *Truck horn wailing*
MAN: Aaaaaaaah!!!
SFX: *Chimes*
SFX: *Bird flapping wings*
WOMAN: Welcome to eternity.
MUSIC: Slow, rolling piano intro.
Slow, easy, swing jazz with alto lead.
SFX: *Door shutting.*
SFX: *Tick, tick, tick.*
SFX: *Cat purring.*
MAN: Heaven!...
MAN: Yes!
MAN: Hmmm...
MAN: Milk!...
MAN: Wait a minute. Where am I?
SUPER: California Fluid Milk
Processor Advisory Board.
CARD: Got milk?
VO: Got Milk?

Diner
MUSIC UNDER THROUGHOUT:
GROOVE ME
YOUNG MAN: (With mouth full of
pancake looking up at cook): Could I
get some milk, please?
COOK: She got the last one.
WOMAN (TO COOK): Excuse me.
I'll be right back, O.K.?
COOK VO: I need two specials!
MAN: Mmmmmohhhh!
WOMAN: Hi, Sweet.
SFX: *PLATES BREAKING*
SUPER: GOT MILK
YOUNG MAN: (VO): Check Please.

Vending Machine
MUSIC UNDER THROUGHOUT:
CHORAL, HYMNAL CHANTING
PRIEST: Mmmmm. Hmmm! Hmmm!
Mmmmm. Hmmm! Hmmm! Hmmm!
Mmmm...Mlllkkk!
SFX: *Strained vending machine motor
revving.*
SUPER: The California Fluid Milk
Processor Advisory Board.
SFX: *Slam! (echoed)*
SFX: *Repeated slams (echoed).*
TITLE: Got Milk?
VO: *Got milk?*

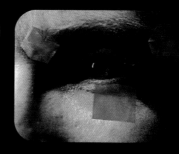

231
District 2

CLIENT
DuPont Corporation

AGENCY
Rumrill Hoyt, Inc.
Rochester, NY

CREATIVE DIRECTOR
Ann Hayden

ART DIRECTOR
Ron Sullivan

COPYWRITERS
Tony Caccamo
Clark Moss

PRODUCER
Donna Farrington

PRODUCTION
Morton Jankel
Zender

231

Kevlar

WOMAN: I'm an inventor of one of the world's strongest fibers. Kevlar. I started the work in 1964. It proved to be a time of great joy, of frustration. We called it Fiber B. Kevlar is five times as strong as steel. It's used in skis, racing boats, in helmets, golf clubs, tennis racquets, bullet-resistant vests. I'm still working for DuPont. Every day is a new learning experience.

Roads

MAN: I was driving down a road, and to my right there was a rather deep pothole. Pow! I survived. That's a problem. You want to prevent potholes. DuPont's technology can make a road that will last longer. The chemistry that we use to modify asphalt......is similar to the chemistry that we use to make other products. We change the molecule so that...it can be used in perfume bottles...roller skates, bowling pins. We can make golf balls that spin better...that changed the game of golf. It was my idea. I feel like I have accomplished something...I guess.

Holography

WOMAN: A hologram captures all the information about light. You can see different things from different angles. Depth. The 3-D effect. Help me. Obi-Wan. DuPont makes film that makes holography possible. Everything you can imagine doing with a hologram is sort of fun. In the future, holography could be used in book illustrations that pop to life. Heads-up displays is a way for motorists to save their eyes from fatigue. That kind of everyday problem is really what we do at DuPont. I never thought anything was impossible.

232
District 2
CLIENT
WMMR 93.3 FM
AGENCY
Earle Palmer Brown/
Philadelphia
Philadelphia, PA
CREATIVE DIRECTOR
Mike Drazen
ART DIRECTOR
Robert Shaw West
COPYWRITER
Ken Cillis
PRODUCER
Joe Mosca

233
District 2
CLIENT
The Baltimore Zoo
AGENCY
Eisner & Associates
Baltimore, MD
CREATIVE DIRECTOR
Bill Mitchell
COPYWRITER
Chuck Thompson
PRODUCER
David Berger
ACCOUNT EXECUTIVE
Pauline Danielweski

232
VO: Doctors have this theory that if you play classical music to infants they'll grow up with a better understanding of complex relationships like math they don't know what effect rock and roll will have but I play this stuff for him anyway I figure the world can live with one less accountant

233
SFX: *Polaroid camera motor.*
BOY 1 VO: My favorite thing at the Zoo is the Polaroid bear.
LITTLE GIRL VO: Camel drinks water and the humps grow. The most humps I've seen on a camel was...seven.
BOY 2 VO: This is a sun bear. This is a sun bear. And this is a sun bear. There is no daughter bears.
LOGO: The Baltimore Zoo I-83 Exit 7

234
District 2
CLIENT
Baltimore Opera
AGENCY
Gray Kirk/VanSant
Advertising
Baltimore, MD
CREATIVE DIRECTOR
Jeff Millman
COPYWRITER
Scharpf
PRODUCER
Noble
DIRECTOR
Mark Tiedeman
ACCOUNT EXECUTIVE
Nagle

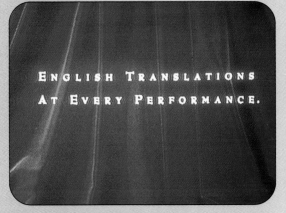

235
District 2
CLIENT
Mexico Tourism
AGENCY
Saatchi & Saatchi
Advertising
New York, NY
CREATIVE DIRECTOR
John Morrison
ART DIRECTOR
Dabni Harvey
COPYWRITER
Cheryl Chapman
PRODUCER
Liz Graves
PRODUCTION
GMS
DIRECTOR
Peter Nydrle

234
MUSIC: A tenor singing a love song
INTERPRETER: (Italian accent) I cannot hide my feelings for you any longer. (More singing) A fire is burning in my heart and in my loins. (More singing) I yearn for the taste of your ruby red lips.
CARD: English Translations at Every Performance. The Baltimore Opera

235
VO: They are not sad they do not cry they do not wear black or dark or veil or glove they do not whisper they will not mourn no tissues no grief no hearts weigh heavy not a tear they will not surrender they will not surrender they will celebrate I love you grandmother.
SUPER: You are very close to far away. Mexico.

236
District 10

CLIENT
Concorde School

AGENCY
Beanmeister
Unlimited
San Antonio, TX

ART DIRECTOR
James Howe

COPYWRITER
Kevin Paetzel

PRODUCTION
Shootz

POST PRODUCTION
Maverick Video
Production

TALENT
Jesse

"F" word

a loaded

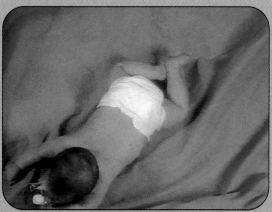

fart.

236

F' Word
SUPER: Isn't it
SUPER: nice
SUPER: to know
SUPER: there is a place
SUPER: where the
SUPER: "F" word
SUPER: is
SFX: *Fart sound*
SUPER: fart.
SUPER: CONCORDE SCHOOL LOGO
SUPER: Downtown at Gray and Louisiana
SFX: *Child's laugh*

Loaded Diaper
SUPER: The
SUPER: most lethal
SUPER: thing
SUPER: we confiscate
SUPER: from students
SUPER: is
SUPER: a loaded
SFX: *Fart sound*
SUPER: diaper.
SUPER: CONCORDE SCHOOL LOGO
SUPER: downtown at Gray and Louisiana
SFX: *Child's laugh*

TELEVISION

Video Cameras

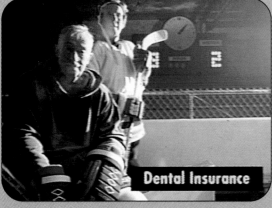

Dental Insurance

Southwestern Bell Yellow Pages

237
District 14

CLIENT
Southwestern Bell
Yellow Pages

AGENCY
Ketchum,
Advertising/
San Francisco
San Francisco, CA

CREATIVE DIRECTOR
Bruce Campbell

ART DIRECTOR
Bruce Campbell

COPYWRITER
Bruce Campbell

PRODUCERS
Bruce Campbell
James Horner

PRODUCTION
Gartner/Grasso

ACCOUNT EXECUTIVE
John Faville

238
District 2

CLIENT
Federal Express

AGENCY
BBDO New York
New York, NY

CREATIVE DIRECTORS
Dennis Berger
Mike Campbell

ART DIRECTOR
Kevin Moehlenkamp

COPYWRITERS
Dennis Berger
Mike Campbell
Tom Giovagnoli

PRODUCER
Bob Emerson

PRODUCTION
Gartner-Grasso

237
SUPER: Florist
SUPER: Class rings and pins
SUPER: Video cameras
SUPER: Smoke alarms
SUPER: Agents-Theatrical
SUPER: Photographers portrait
SUPER: Dental insurance
SUPER: Vacuum cleaner repair
SUPER: Stress management
SUPER: Southwestern Bell Yellow Pages
SUPER: Where people get what they want
SUPER: SWBYP's

238
MR. C: What's the matter, son?
JIM: I'm kinda worried about a package I sent out for Mr. Jones.
MR. C: Cup of coffee? Well, sending out that package is a big responsibility. Jones knows you'll come through. Hard work, faith, trust in each other, that's what it's all about. Besides, in over 20 years, FedEx has never let me down...
JIM: What if I didn't use FedEx?
MR. C: Well then, your dead!!
ANNCR: Next time, use FedEx.
MR. C: Get the lights on your way out.

239
District 2

CLIENT
Little Caesars Pizza

AGENCY
Cliff Freeman &
Partners
New York, NY

CREATIVE DIRECTOR
Arthur Bijur

ART DIRECTOR
Bruce Hurwit

COPYWRITER
Arthur Bijur

PRODUCER
MaryEllen Duggan

PRODUCTION
Crossroads Films

240
District 10

CLIENT
Southwestern Bell
Telephone

AGENCY
Inventiva
San Antonio, TX

CREATIVE DIRECTOR
Jesus Ramirez

ART DIRECTOR
Rafael Serrano

COPYWRITER
Adriana Ramos

PRODUCER
Victoria Varela
Hudson

PRODUCTION
Sean Salas

ACCOUNT EXECUTIVE
Heberto Gutierrez

239
VOICE THROUGH SPEAKER: One banana?... Or two bananas?
SFX: (Buzzz)
ANNCR: One female orangutan?... Or two female orangutans?
SFX: (Buzzzzz!)
ANNCR: One pizza for $9.98... Or two for $9.98?
ANNCR: He seems to prefer two.
ANNCR: Two is better than one, so why settle for one supreme pizza when you can get two at Little Caesars for just 9.98!

240
BACHELOR: Elena? or Adriana? Let's see what the cards say. Don't answer it. Elena or Adriana? Elena? Adriana?
ANNCR: If he had Caller ID he would know the name and number of the caller, before answering the phone.
BACHELOR: Elena? ...Adriana!!!
ANNCR: Order Caller ID from Southwestern Bell Telephone.
BACHELOR: I was waiting for your call... Elena? Oh...Elena is my dog's name...

TELEVISION

241
District 2
CLIENT
Frito-Lay/Tostitos
AGENCY
BBDO New York
New York, NY
CREATIVE DIRECTOR
Al Merrin
ART DIRECTOR
Matt Fischer
COPYWRITER
Don Austen
PRODUCER
David Frankel
PRODUCTION
Steifel/Jon Francis
Films

242
District 2
CLIENT
Clairol, Inc.
AGENCY
J. Walter Thompson
New York, NY
CREATIVE DIRECTORS
Charlie Gennarelli
Linda Kaplan
ART DIRECTOR
Marty Muller
COPYWRITER
Laurie Garnier
PRODUCER
Judi Nierman
PRODUCTION
Kektor Higgins

241
AUDITOR: So you claimed $84,000 in entertainment expenses?
CHRIS: Yes I did.
AUDITOR: Do you have any receipts to back this up?
CHRIS: No I don't.
AUDITOR: Well, what's in the bag then?
CHRIS: Tostitos Chips and Salsa. People really love 'em. Everytime I open a bag, I mean, one thing...
AVO: Tostitos Tortilla Chips, So deliciously perfect with Tostitos Salsa...Next thing you know, it's a party.
AUDITOR: I smell refund.
CHRIS: Really?
AUDITOR: No... Not really.
AVO: You Got Tostitos. You Got a Party.

242
J: You know, you'd look great as a blond.
W: Do I know you?
J: Nice n Easy 104, it's you.
W: Well, I've never colored my hair.
J: Oh, trust me. See, Nice n Easy works with your hair's own tones and highlights. Look at mine. Doesn't that look natural? Time to rinse.
M: She looks fabulous.
J: She's gonna stop traffic.
VO: It's Nice n Easy, only from Clairol.

243
District 2

CLIENT
Eastman Kodak

AGENCY
J. Walter Thompson
New York, NY

CREATIVE DIRECTORS
Charlie Gennarelli
Linda Kaplan

ART DIRECTOR
Terri Meyer

COPYWRITER
Sandy Greenberg

PRODUCER
Bruce Davidson

PRODUCTION
Dektor Higgins

244
District 2

CLIENT
Pepsi

AGENCY
BBDO New York
New York, NY

CREATIVE DIRECTOR
Don Schneider

ART DIRECTOR
Don Schneider

COPYWRITER
Michael Patti

PRODUCER
Regina Ebel

PRODUCTION
Gartner-Grasso

243

CHEERS: Tommy! Tommy! Tommy!

ANNCR DAN: Man oh man Joanne, on this great Olympic morning all eyes are on Tommy Higgins.

ANNCR JOANNE: You know, you're right Dan and I love this athlete's piercing concentration.

DAN: I agree. But will Tommy achieve maximum wing span? Let's find out.

JOANNE: What a snow angel!

VO: Just a reminder from Kodak that some of the greatest winter games take place right in your own backyard. Why trust these moments to anything less than Kodak film?

244

AVO: Most things in this world aren't big enough to handle 7 feet 2 inches, 3 hundred and 10 pounds.

SHAQ: And I ordered the big breakfast.

TAILOR: How does that feel?

BELLBOY: Oh, watch your head Mr. O'Neal.

AVO: There is one notable exception, the big slam from Pepsi. One ice cold... liter of Pepsi big enough to handle the biggest thirst.

SHAQ: Ain't life grand.

245
District 14
CLIENT
Saturn Corporation
AGENCY
Hal Riney & Partners
San Francisco, CA
CREATIVE DIRECTORS
James Dalthorp
Steve Baer
ART DIRECTOR
Stephanie Halverson
COPYWRITERS
Annie Kinscherff
Dave Swaine
Mark Choate
Larry Harris
PRODUCER
Kevin VanFleet
PRODUCTION
Propaganda

246
District 14
CLIENT
Levi Strauss & Co.
AGENCY
Foote, Cone &
Belding
San Francisco, CA
CREATIVE DIRECTORS
George Chadwick
Geoff Thompson
ART DIRECTOR
George Chadwick
COPYWRITER
Mimi Cook
PRODUCER
Iliani Matisse
PRODUCTION
Will Vinton Studios
DIRECTOR
Mark Gustafson
ACCOUNT EXECUTIVE
Laura Haber

245

VO (ERIN): I.. thought the days of women... being treated differently than men were long gone...
SALESMAN 1: Hey, how ya doin'? What was your name again? Karen, right?
ERIN: Erin.
SALESMAN 2: Aerial, let me show you... Erin, I'm sorry.
VO (ERIN): Then I tried to buy... a car. Something reliable...
SALESMAN 3: You, uh, want to buy a car, huh?
VO (ERIN): ...sporty...
SALESMAN 2: What a great day to buy... a car.
VO (ERIN): With lots of... standard features.
SALESMAN 4: This is the vanity mirror so you can check your make-up.
SALESMAN 5: You're gonna love it.
ERIN (Off camera): Tell me about the mileage.
SALESMAN 3: It has no miles on it yet.
ERIN: Okay, what about safety features?
SALESMAN 4: You feel safe. It's safe.
SALESMAN 1: How much... you lookin' to spend?
ERIN (Off camera): I want to spend about... twelve thousand dollars.
SALESMAN 1: Rich! Rich can help you out. I'll be back to you.
VO (ERIN): When I got to Saturn, I didn't know what... to expect. But Dave... Pierce actually... took the time to answer... all my questions. Not only did I buy... a Saturn. I thought.. it might be fun... to sell them. You know what I like... best about working... here? Showing... guys the vanity mirror.

246

247
District 2

CLIENT
Radio Shack

AGENCY
Lord, Dentsu &
Partners
New York, NY

CREATIVE DIRECTOR
Mike Scardino

ART DIRECTORS
Steve St. Clair
Mike Scardino

COPYWRITERS
Andrew Payton
Mike Scardino

PRODUCER
Elise Baruch

PRODUCTION
Eric Young

DIRECTOR
Eric Young

248
District 4

CLIENT
McDonald's
Corporation

AGENCY
del Rivero, Messianu
Advertising
Coral Gables, FL

CREATIVE DIRECTORS
Luis Miguel
Messiano
Daniel Marrero
Pablo Mayoral

ART DIRECTOR
Pablo Mayoral

COPYWRITER
Daniel Marrero

PRODUCER
Michelle Headley

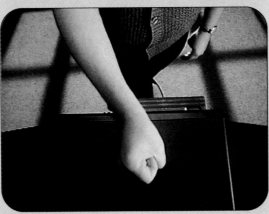

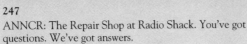

247
ANNCR: The Repair Shop at Radio Shack. You've got
questions. We've got answers.

248
First Word (Translated from Spanish)
DAD: Hi Dear, I brought McDonald's.
MOM: Guess who's waiting for you?
DAD: Tommy! Let's see if you say it this time. You will,
right Champ? Say Pa...pa.. Pa..pa... Pa...pa... OK, breath
in... Papa...
TOMMY: Pa..pa...
DAD: He said Papa!
(Tommy laughs)

249
District 14

CLIENT
First Interstate
Bankcorp

AGENCY
Hal Riney & Partners
San Francisco, CA

CREATIVE DIRECTOR
Steve Silver

ART DIRECTOR
Curtis Melville

COPYWRITER
Steve Silver

PRODUCER
Ann Storm

PRODUCTION
Sonzero/Pugliese

ACCOUNT EXECUTIVE
Pat Madden

250
District 2

CLIENT
Little Caesars Pizza

AGENCY
Cliff Freeman &
Partners
New York, NY

CREATIVE DIRECTORS
Arthur Bijur
Donna Weinheim

ART DIRECTOR
Donna Weinheim

COPYWRITER
Arthur Bijur

PRODUCER
Anne Kurtzman

PRODUCTION
Harmony Pictures

249
MALE VOICE: ...Our special tonight...
TITLE: Fiscal Year 1995 22 empty tables.
TITLE: Fiscal Year 1999 Reservations highly recommended.
FEMALE VOICE: How's everything tonight?
TITLE: Small Business Loans SBA Equipment financing Lines of credit.
FEMALE VOICE: ...are you enjoying yourself?
LOGO: YOU & I First Interstate.
MALE VOICE:...would you like another glass of wine?...

250
GRANNY: Have you ever seen anything more amazing than Little Caesars Italian Sausage pizza?
FATHER: ...No.
ANNCR: Italian Sausage pizza! Loaded with sausage, peppers and onions. The newest from a whole menu of Little Caesars Pleasers. Any two for $9.98!
L.C.: Pizza! Pizza!
ANNCR: Or get one for $5.99!
L.C.: Pizza!

251

District 2

CLIENT
Apple

AGENCY
BBDO West
Los Angeles, CA

CREATIVE DIRECTORS
Chris Wall
Susan Westre

ART DIRECTOR
Susan Westre

COPYWRITER
Chris Wall

PRODUCERS
Kathy McGoff
Shelley Eisner
Adrienne Cummins

PRODUCTION
Smilie Films

DIRECTOR
Bob Grigg

EDITOR
Dan Swietlik

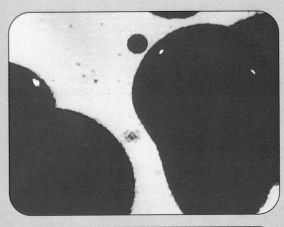

251

Highway of the Future
VO: The highway of the future will have no speed limit.
Shouldn't you be driving the fastest machine on the road?
SUPER: Power Macintosh.

VO: Power Macintosh is here and the future is better than
you expected.
APPLE COLOR LOGO

Lava Lamp
VO: The future... Where breakthroughs in biochemistry
and genetics increase life expectancy and the quality of our
existence. Leaving us more time to contemplate the things
in life that are truly important. Like built-in sound. Power
Macintosh is here. And the future is better than you
expected.
APPLE COLOR LOGO

252

District 2

CLIENT
Federal Express

AGENCY
BBDO New York
New York, NY

CREATIVE DIRECTORS
Dennis Berer
Mike Campbell

ART DIRECTORS
Rich Midler
Steve Rutter
Kevin Moehlenkamp

COPYWRITERS
Steve Anacker
Mike Campbell
Susan Credle
Tom Giovagnoli
Dennis Berger

PRODUCER
Bob Emerson

PRODUCTION
Gartner-Grasso

252

Larry

BILL: Oh, Boss meet Larry. He's new.

BOSS: Say, Larry, hypothetical question. How would you send a big important package to a big important client in say... Hong Kong?

LARRY: FedEx

BOSS: Right. Say someone didn't use FedEx, and that big important package never got there. What would you call that someone Larry?

LARRY: A dope?

BOSS: Right, a dope.

VO: Big or small, around the world, next time use FedEx.

LARRY: If I would have known you were the dope, I wouldn't...

Mr. Omatsu

JACK: Oh hello, Mr. Omatsu? You know your shipment is ready.

MR. OMATSU: Hello. How are you?

JACK: Fine Sir. I just have a question about custom regulations for your country. Do I need an import license, a certificate of origin, 525V or, or what?

MR. OMATSU: Hello? How are you?

JACK: Fine. Could you hold?

ANNCR: All you got to do to simplify international shipping...

FEDEX AGENT: That's all you need

ANNCR: Is us FedEx.

JACK: Mr. Omatsu?

JACK: Yes sir. I'm fine. We're all fine.

Mr. Calm

MR. C: What's the matter, son?

JIM: I'm kinda worried about a package I sent out for Mr. Jones.

MR. C: Cup of coffee? Well, sending out that package is a big responsibility. Jones knows you'll come through. Hard work, faith, trust in each other, that's what it's all about. Besides, in over 20 years, FedEx has never let me down...

JIM: What if I didn't use FedEx?

MR. C: Well then, your dead!!

ANNCR: Next time, use FedEx.

MR. C: Get the lights on your way out.

253

District 9

CLIENT
Anheuser-Busch/
Budweiser

AGENCY
DMB&B St. Louis
St. Louis, MO

CREATIVE DIRECTORS
Mark Choate
Michael Hutchinson

ART DIRECTOR
Michael Smith

COPYWRITER
Dave Swaine

PRODUCER
John Seaton

  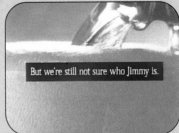

253
1876
CARD: Sure, in 1876,
CARD: we were a microbrewery too.
CARD: And then we got better.
CARD: And better.
CARD: And, yeah, a little bigger.
SUPER: BUD CLASSIC NEON.

Brewmaster
CARD: To achieve perfection at every
stage of brewing,
CARD: Our brewmasters taste the
beer...
CARD: over...
CARD: and over...
CARD: and over.
CARD: Is that a great job or what?
SUPER: BUD CLASSIC NEON.

Jimmy
CARD: Grandpa was a Bud drinker,
CARD: he used to say,
CARD: "Jimmy, you get what you pay
for."
CARD: or "Jimmy, some things are
just worth it."
CARD: And ya know, he was always
right.
CARD: But we're still not sure who
Jimmy is.
SUPER: BUD CLASSIC NEON.

254
District 7
CLIENT
NBAF
AGENCY
Fitzgerald &
Company
Atlanta, GA
CREATIVE DIRECTOR
Jim Paddock
ART DIRECTOR
Eddie Snyder
COPYWRITER
Jim Paddock
ACCOUNT EXECUTIVE
Katherine Way

254

Animated World

ANNCR: It took seven days to create the world... But we can change the way you look at it, in nine. Be a part of the National Black Arts Festival...
SUPER: The National Black Arts Festival Atlanta July 29-August 7
ANNCR: In Atlanta, July 29th through August 8th.
SUPER: 1-800-BLACK ART
ANNCR: Call 1-800-BLACK ART

Color Wheel

ANNCR: Our jazz is red hot in Paris. On the Emerald Isle...they can't get enough of our blues. Our dance has been embraced across the spectrum. Out truth, in black and white, has received Sweden's Nobel Prize for literature. And you wonder why we're called people of color. Come celebrate the National Black Arts Festival, in Atlanta, July 29th through August 7th.

Walls

ANNCR: In 1963 the writing was on the wall...By '73 it was also in the jungle... and at the top of the charts. By '83 it was in living rooms across America. And by '93 that writing on the wall had spread to the presidential inauguration... and the ceremonies for the Nobel prize. This year... don't miss the National Black Arts Festival.
CARD: The National Black Arts Festival Atlanta — July 29-Aug 7.
ANNCR: Because over time... perhaps only art can make the walls come tumbling down.
CARD: 1-800-BLACK ARTS

255
District 10

CLIENT
Southwestern Bell
Messaging Services

AGENCY
GSD&M
Austin, TX

CREATIVE DIRECTORS
Wally Williams
Tom Gilmore

ART DIRECTOR
Marty McDonald

COPYWRITER
Oscar Casares

PRODUCER
Joanne
Michels-Bennett

PRODUCTION
Jon Francis Films

DIRECTOR
Jon Francis

256
District 9

CLIENT
Security National
Bank

AGENCY
Rochester Rossiter &
Wall
Sioux City, IA

CREATIVE DIRECTOR
Tim Poppen

COPYWRITER
Ron Dobbs

PRODUCER
Greg Wall

DIRECTOR
Greg Wall

VIDEOGRAPHY
Greg Wall

OFF LINE EDITING
Steve Ford
Editech

255

SFX: *Romantic music.*
GUY: Do you mind if I...
SFX: *Phone ringing.*
GUY: The machine will get it...
ANSWERING MACHINE (DEREK): Hey, this is Derek.
Please leave a message.
SFX: *Answering machine beep.*
ANSWERING MACHINE (ELAINE): Listen, Derek, if
you think you can just walk right in like you did this
afternoon and try to get back together, you're wrong.
VO: To listen to your messages in private get CallNotes,
from Southwestern Bell Messaging Services. All you need is
a touch-tone phone.
SFX: *Noise from television.*

256

MAN: I think we can get that to you by the 22nd. We'd be
pushing it otherwise. I can personally guarantee it. No, no,
not a problem, let me check on that first and get back to
you. Just a moment please.
JOE: We've got a meeting in 5, remember?
MAN: Thanks Joe, be right there. Mr. Banks can I look
over the document and call you later this afternoon. Great.
TAG: Most days there's barely time to do all that needs
doing. So when it comes to managing your investments, let
us do the work for you.
LOGO: Security investment management and trust
services, we're working for your best interest.

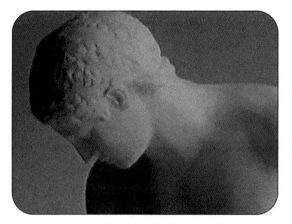

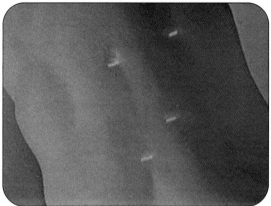

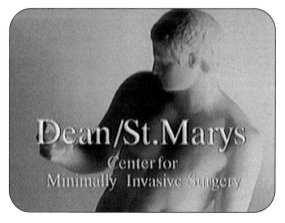

257
District 8

CLIENT
Dean/St. Marys

AGENCY
The Hiebing Group
Madison, WI

CREATIVE DIRECTORS
Michael Kelly
Dick Kallstrom

ART DIRECTOR
Dick Kallstrom

COPYWRITER
Michael Kelly

258
District 6

CLIENT
Chicago Film Festival

AGENCY
DDB Needham
Chicago, IL

ART DIRECTOR
Corey Ciszek

COPYWRITER
Dan Fietsam

PRODUCER
Liat Ebersohl

DIRECTOR
Kevin Smith

PRODUCTION
Backyard
Productions

257
ANNCR VO: There's a whole new way to do surgery. And Dean/St. Mary's has the edge. This new surgery is minimally invasive - a few very small incisions - minimal pain - minimal scarring - minimal time off work. Maximum results. The Dean/St. Mary's Center for Minimally Invasive Surgery. It just may be the kindest cut of all.

258
(Music from foreign film soundtrack throughout. Cuts of romantic scenes from many featured films.)
SUPER: Catch up on foreign affairs. The Chicago International Film Festival. October 6-23.

259
District 2
CLIENT
The Baltimore Zoo
AGENCY
Eisner & Associates
Baltimore, MD
CREATIVE DIRECTORS
Bill Mitchell
Chuck Thompson
ART DIRECTOR
Bill Mitchell
COPYWRITER
Chuck Thompson
ANIMATION
Big Shot
PRODUCER
David Berger
MUSIC
Clean Cuts
DIRECTOR
Charles Vanderpool
AUDIO DIRECTOR
Bob Schwartz

260
District 12
CLIENT
Crossroads Plaza
AGENCY
Williams and
Rockwood
Salt Lake City, UT
ART DIRECTOR
David Carter
COPYWRITER
Kurtis Glade
DIRECTOR
Laurie Rubins
PRODUCTION
Crossroads Film

259
ZACH: An elephant has a nose. Not really a nose, it's like a tube actually
MIKE: It hangs down real long and low. And it...
ZACH: It's like a straw connected to a nose.
MIKE: It's like a hand or something.
ZACH: It's like a gigantic hose kind of thing.
MIKE: It's a snout.
ZACH: Horn. (Horn SFX)
MIKE: A trout. An elephant has a trout.
LOGO: THE BALTIMORE ZOO I-83 EXIT 7

260
MUSIC: Gregorian chant
TYPE ON FOOT: A Black Leather shoe.
AROUND NECK: A silver necklace.
ON BACK: A black evening gown.
ON LIPS: A shade of red.
BEHIND EAR: The smell of fresh flowers.
ON CURTAIN: Crossroads Plaza. For what you have in mind.

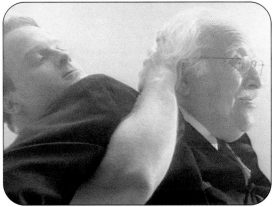

261
District 7
CLIENT
Audubon Institute
AGENCY
Peter A. Mayer
Advertising
New Orleans, LA
CREATIVE DIRECTOR
Dee Smith
COPYWRITER
Josh Mayer
PRODUCER
Marylyn Cahill
DIRECTOR
Brian Bain
PRODUCTION
Buckholtz
Production
MUSIC
Pelican Pictures

262
District 6
CLIENT
Great Lakes Bancorp
AGENCY
Perich & Partners
Ann Arbor, MI
CREATIVE DIRECTOR
Ernie Perich
ART DIRECTOR
Ernie Perich
COPYWRITER
Ernie Perich

261

MUSIC: Light and lively
VO: What lurks behind the smile of a stingray? Are they really happy, or is it all an act? Do they sting all fish... or only fish named Ray? Come to the Aquarium of the Americas and find out. Gee. I hope none of you guys are named Ray.

262

BANKER: A lot of twirps come in here when they want a home. I mean look at me. I am money. You're really giggly about this home huh? Means a lot to you huh Frank?
CUSTOMER: It's Tom.
BANKER: Whatever. Point is, you've gotta like me. I don't like you. You're not listening are you? Go ahead, knock yourself out. I ain't no dummy.
VO: Stop wrestling with your mortgage. Call Great Lakes Bancorp.

263
District 3
CLIENT
CDI-W - Raleigh and
NC Museum of Art
AGENCY
Rockett, Burkhead,
Lewis & Winslow
Raleigh, NC
CREATIVE DIRECTOR
Michael Winslow
ART DIRECTOR
Michael Winslow
COPYWRITER
Michael Winslow
PRODUCER
Herb Campbell
DIRECTOR
Michael Winslow

264
District 4
CLIENT
Huffman Koos
AGENCY
Lance Benefield
Fort Myers, FL
EXECUTIVE PRODUCER
Lance G. Hanish
DIRECTOR
Sean Hanish
POST PRODUCTION
Bridget Richards
Joe Ban

263

264

BOB: You know... this is becoming so tiresome
CARD: Bob Becomes an Adult - Step Four - The Coffee Table
BOB: so I'll say it just one more time I am not an adult
CARD: But you bought a coffee table, Bob
BOB: Yeah, I'll admit it I bought a coffee table from Huffman Koos - Is that a crime?
CARD: Your parents would be proud
BOB: First of all I don't even drink coffee, I don't need coffee, my father drinks coffee. I put my feet on the coffee table, I put a pizza on the coffee table, but no coffee.
CARD: So it's a cocktail table
BOB: Oh Yeah, cocktails... like I gotta full set of glassware
CARD: So why'd you buy it, Bob?
BOB: My couch, um was lonely... no, no wait ah...
LOGO with Nice Try.

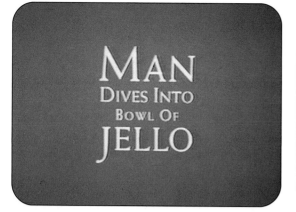

265
District 10

CLIENT
Toad Hall Children's
Bookstore

AGENCY
BRSG, Inc.
Houston, TX

CREATIVE DIRECTOR
Kerry Hilton

266
District 10

CLIENT
Arkansas
Department of Parks

AGENCY
Cranford Johnson
Robinson Woods
Little Rock, AR

CREATIVE DIRECTOR
Boyd Blackwood

ART DIRECTOR
Chuck Robertson

COPYWRITERS
Tracy Munro
Patterson Walz & Fox

PRODUCER
Debbie Wilson

PRODUCTION
Jones Productions

ACCOUNT EXECUTIVES
Rick Nall
Kelley Nichols
Shelby Woods

265

266

267
District 9

CLIENT
National Bank of
Commerce

AGENCY
Bailey Lauerman
& Associates
Lincoln, NE

CREATIVE DIRECTOR
Rich Bailey

ART DIRECTOR
Ron Sack

COPYWRITER
Laura Crawford

PRODUCER
Laura Crawford

PRODUCTION
Great Plains

ACCOUNT EXECUTIVE
Pam Hunzeker

268
District 3

CLIENT
Charleston
Symphony Orchestra

AGENCY
King Fisher
Productions
Charleston, SC

PRODUCER
Bryan Elsom

DIRECTOR
Bryan Elsom

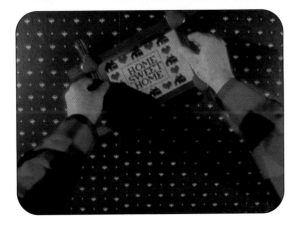

267

268

SFX: *Building noises, hammering, sawing, nailing, etc.*
SFX: *Three hammers.*
SUPER: Fast Home Loans.
SUPER: National Bank of Commerce Your Bank For Life.

269
District 9
CLIENT
Crown Cable
AGENCY
Kupper Parker
Communications
St. Louis, MO
CREATIVE DIRECTOR
Peter Charlton
ART DIRECTOR
Erik Koelle
COPYWRITER
Mike Scaletta
ACCOUNT EXECUTIVE
Ed Musen

270
District 9
CLIENT
Southeast
Missourian
Newspaper
AGENCY
KFVS 12
Cape Girardo, MO
CREATIVE DIRECTOR
Tom Emmendorfer

269

SFX: *Man wading over deep snow.*
SFX: *Man falls through ice.*
SUPER: THEN WHAT HAPPENED?
SUPER: 1-800-CABLE ME.

270

(FULL SING JINGLE): Early in the morning, as dawn
starts breaking through the world begins right outside your
doors. There's the stories and the faces, all the people and
the places, that tell you all the news and so much more.
The world begins right outside your door, The Southeast
Missourian is where you day begins. In every headline all
the news brings you the local attitude and leaves it on the
doorstep of your mind. The world begins right outside your
door. The Southeast Missourian it's where your world
begins.

271
District 9

CLIENT
The Nebraska State Fair

AGENCY
Bailey Lauerman & Associates
Lincoln, NE

CREATIVE DIRECTOR
Rich Bailey

ART DIRECTOR
Carter Weitz

COPYWRITER
Laura Crawford

PRODUCER
Laura Crawford

PRODUCTION
Great Plains

ACCOUNT EXECUTIVE
Pam Hunzeker

272
District 10

CLIENT
Justin Boot Company

AGENCY
Siboney USA
Dallas, TX

CREATIVE DIRECTOR
Tory Syvrud

ART DIRECTOR
Carlos Cardoza

COPYWRITER
Ezequiel Cuevas

PRODUCTION
Haberman Creative

PRODUCER
Danene Horsfall

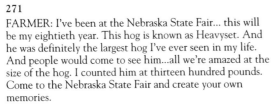

271
FARMER: I've been at the Nebraska State Fair... this will be my eightieth year. This hog is known as Heavyset. And he was definitely the largest hog I've ever seen in my life. And people would come to see him...all we're amazed at the size of the hog. I counted him at thirteen hundred pounds. Come to the Nebraska State Fair and create your own memories.

272
SFX: David Lee Garza music under voices
WM 2: I feel like dancing with someone.
WM 1: Here comes one!
MAN 1: Come on baby, let's dance.
WM 2: Uh...no thanks.
WM 3: Here comes another one!
MAN 2 (boyish): Hi, want to dance with me?
WM 2: Uh, just finished one... (pause) thanks.
WM 1: Oh my!
WM 3: Irene, Look!
WM 2: He's coming over here!
MAN 3: Would you honor me with a dance?
WM 1: You bet!
WM 2: Did you see his face?
WM 3: Did you see those boots?
ANNCR: Justin Boots. Only the best at your feet.

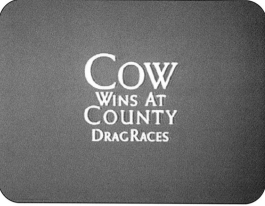

273
District 5
CLIENT
Jacobson's
AGENCY
Doe-Anderson
Advertising Agency
Louisville, KY
CREATIVE DIRECTOR
Gary Sloboda
ART DIRECTOR
Stefanie Becker
COPYWRITER
Ed Neary
PRODUCER
Liz Jackson

274
District 10
CLIENT
Toad Hall Children's
Bookstore
AGENCY
BRSG, Inc.
Houston, TX
CREATIVE DIRECTOR
Kerry Hilton

273

VO: The clothing you've always dreamed of. Without the usual sacrifice.

SUPER: Jacobson's logo

VO: By now you must be ready for something new.
Jacobson's. Coming November 3rd.

274

275
District 4

CLIENT
Squint Design

AGENCY
BBC Marketing, Inc.
Winter Park, FL

CREATIVE DIRECTOR
Loyd Boldman

COPYWRITER
Loyd Boldman

PRODUCER
David Clement

EDITOR
Joseph Bouch

276
District 8

CLIENT
Milwaukee Admirals

AGENCY
Reinke/Clement
& Associates
Milwaukee, WI

CREATIVE DIRECTOR
Charlie Clement

COPYWRITER
Charlie Clement

DIRECTOR
Steve Steigman

275

ANNCR VO: Attention Lonely Guys and the people who love them, support them and listen to them whine! According to the US Bureau of Unsupportable Statistics, there are 1.3 Lonely Guys for every live birth in North America. That's why we created Heartburn Theater, The video companion for the Lonely Guy. Take the Lonely Quiz to see if you qualify... See rare footage of The Lonely Guy in his natural habitat. It's just like a National Geographic special, except completely different. See your TV transform into a fireplace, a fish tank, a washing machine, and more. It will improve you SAT scores, rotate your tires, whiten your teeth - it may even help you find the woman of your dreams. But probably not. It's good, clean fun. Great for parties. Ladies, buy one for your hapless boyfriend to show him how lucky he is. Buy one to keep your husband occupied while you're away overhauling the National Health Care System. You might expect this tape to cost $1,000 or more. But wait! It's available now for the almost non-existent price of only $19.95. See that number at the bottom of the screen? Call now! Call as if your life depended on it! 1-800-6-LONELY. C'mon, do it now! I'm done.

276

UKE: You know, team apparel is getting to be big business these days. And I'll tell ya, Lloyd and Jane are some smart marketers. So I wasn't surprised when they called the staff together during the offseason to say...

LLOYD: We've decided we want to redesign the Admirals' uniforms.

UKE: And today's the day the guys get to model my new creation. Pretty sharp, huh Chief?

ANNCR: Admirals Hockey. Wednesday night at The Bradley Center.

LLOYD: (to Jane) Maybe we can get one more year out of the old ones, after all.

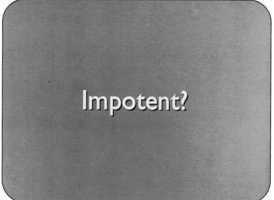

277
District 14
CLIENT
Eldorado Hotel
Casino
AGENCY
Bayer/Brown
Advertising
Reno, NV
CREATIVE DIRECTOR
Ken Bud Millman
ART DIRECTORS
Craig Mitchell
Dan Thompson
COPYWRITER
Scott Mortimore
PRODUCER
Scott Mortimore
DIRECTOR
Mark Herzig

278
District 7
CLIENT
The Shallowford
Center
AGENCY
Turner & Turner
Communications
Atlanta, GA
CREATIVE DIRECTOR
Jamie Turner
COPYWRITER
Richard Link
ACCOUNT EXECUTIVE
Monica Ross

277
MUSIC: Soothing instrumental, almost lullaby-like
MAN VO: (40-ish, soft-spoken, reference Jack Handy of "Deep Thoughts") If I won 50 thou... I'd buy 40 acres in the wild. So I could dance naked with the wind.
ANNCR: (male, smart-alecky) The Eldorado Fifty Thousand dollar pay-day give-away. It's free money. Do what you want with it.

278
Music up then abruptly stops.
SFX: *Crashing sounds.*
CARD: Impotent?
SFX: *Final crashing noises.*
CARD: Call the Shallowford Center 458-2827.

279

District 10

CLIENT
Tulsa State Fair

AGENCY
Littlefield Marketing
& Advertising
Tusla, OK

CREATIVE DIRECTORS
Doug Johnston
Rick Horney
Donna Williams

ART DIRECTOR
Rich Horney

PRODUCER
Donna Williams

PRODUCTION
Haley Films
Winner
Communications
Cloud 9

EDITOR
Mark Coffey

ACCOUNT EXECUTIVES
Teresa Slagle
John Crouch

280

District 3

CLIENT
Presbyterian-
Orthopaedic
Hospital

AGENCY
The Reimler Agency
Charlotte, NC

CREATIVE DIRECTOR
Bill Owens

ART DIRECTOR
Bill Owens

COPYWRITER
Kay Reimler

PRODUCTION
Boulevard Films

DIRECTOR
Mark Claywell

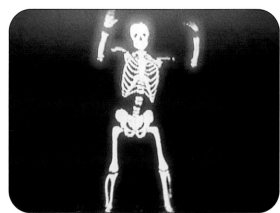

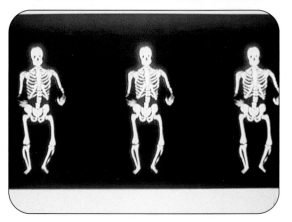

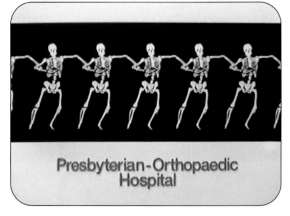

279

MALE VO: If you could have any one wish, what would it be?
FEMALE VO: I'd wish for world peace everyone lives in perfect harmony and farmers with warm hands.
SUPER: The World's Purtiest Cow Contest
ANNCR: The World's Purtiest Cow Contest...
SFX: *APPLAUSE*
FEMALE VO: Thank you....thank you...
ANNCR: Just one of the 1951 fun things to do at the Tulsa State Fair. September 29th through October 9...if we packed in anymore fun, we couldn't fit in anymore people.
MALE VO: And now, the swimsuit competition.
FEMALE VO: Uh oh.
FEMALE VO: Eeeeeeek!
SFX: *Catcalls, whistles*

280

VO (With "ALL OF ME" behind): No matter what your orthopaedic problem - from back and joints, to hands and feet, to sports injuries - you need the people who do orthopaedics and only orthopaedics. The specialists at Presbyteriam-Orthopaedic Hospital. The largest, most sophisticated orthopaedic hospital and staff in the Southeast. No bones about it.

281

District 10

CLIENT
Wendy's of Little Rock

AGENCY
Stone & Ward
Little Rock, AR

CREATIVE DIRECTOR
Larry Stone

ART DIRECTOR
Long

COPYWRITER
Patterson

PRODUCER
David Scharff

PRODUCTION
Soundscapes

EDITOR
David Scharff/
Jones Productions

ACCOUNT EXECUTIVE
Allison Jacuzzi

282

District 4

CLIENT
U.S. Legal Services

AGENCY
Beber Silverstein & Partners
Miami, FL

CREATIVE DIRECTOR
Joe Perz

COPYWRITER
Rob Stewart

PRODUCER
Sherri Fritzson

281
ANNCR: Life has its ups and downs. And since you've been missing some of the better ones, Wendy's will donate 5 cents from every Biggie Drink sold during July to help restore "Over the Jumps," The Arkansas Carousel.
LOGOS: FOTC, Wendy's, KTHV
ANNCR: Yippee Ky Yi Yea.

282
MUSIC: Beautiful instrumental rendition of "THAT'S AMORE"
SUPER: Statistics show 50% of all marriages end in divorce.
SUPER: We predict this number will soon increase.
SUPER: $29.95 Divorces.
SUPER: US Legal Services, Inc. 1-800-29-LEGAL.

283

District 9

CLIENT
The Nebraska State Fair

AGENCY
Bailey Lauerman & Associates
Lincoln, NE

CREATIVE DIRECTOR
Rich Bailey

ART DIRECTOR
Carter Weitz

COPYWRITER
Laura Crawford

PRODUCER
Laura Crawford

PRODUCTION
Great Plains

ACCOUNT EXECUTIVE
Pam Hunzeker

283

Lotta Hog
FARMER: I've been at the Nebraska State Fair... this will be my eightieth year. This hog is known as Heavyset. And he was definitely the largest hog I've ever seen in my life. And people would come to see him...all we're amazed at the size of the hog. I counted him at thirteen hundred pounds. Come to the Nebraska State Fair and create your own memories.

Fast Talker
BOY: Well, my dad won the auctioneer's contest back in 1986 when I was six years old there at the Nebraska State Fair. Usually, most kids want to be like their dads and I want to be in the contest too, myself, once I get old enough, of course. Eight dollar, here comes nine, nine, nine, nine, here comes nine dollars, here comes ten, and ten, ten, ten, ten.
NEBRASKA STATE FAIR LOGO
BOY: Use it as a back-scratcher, and ten, now eleven and twelve dollars, here comes twelve, twelve, twelve...

Pumpkin Patch
FATHER: About six years ago, we started a family tradition. Coming out every spring and planting pumpkins in the pumpkin patch.
BOY: We grow them every year.
GIRL: So we can take them to the State Fair.
BOY: We see what prize we win.
BOY: Yeah and then after awhile at Halloween we make Jack-O-Lantern out of them.
KIDS: Create your own memories at the Nebraska State Fair.
BOY: Oh, there's one dad.

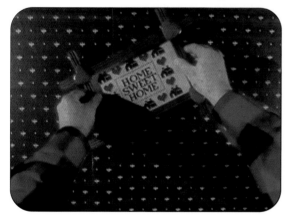

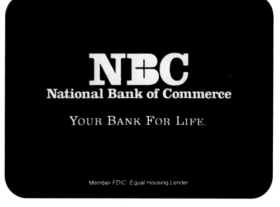

284
District 9

CLIENT
National Bank of Commerce

AGENCY
Bailey Lauerman
& Associates
Lincoln, NE

CREATIVE DIRECTOR
Rich Bailey

ART DIRECTOR
Ron Sack

COPYWRITER
Laura Crawford

PRODUCER
Laura Crawford

PRODUCTION
Great Plains

ACCOUNT EXECUTIVE
Pam Hunzeker

284

Fast Home
SFX: *Building noises, hammering, sawing, nailing, etc.*
SFX: *Three hammers.*
SUPER: Fast Home Loans.
SUPER: National Bank of Commerce Your Bank For Life.

Fast Car
SFX: *Car engine, sounds of cars passing, gears shifting.*
SUPER: Fast Car Loans.
SUPER: National Bank of Commerce Your Bank For Life.

285

District 5

CLIENT
Finast

AGENCY
Wyse Advertising
Cleveland, OH

ART DIRECTOR
Bob Calmer

COPYWRITER
Mike Smith

PRODUCER
Kristin Yamane

DIRECTOR
Martin Reuben

285

Choice Cookie

SUPER: Decadent

ANNCR: Looking for a truly decadent cookie? Finast was too, and they found President's Choice making cookies with real butter, real chocolate chips, and lots of um so they're 39% of the cookie.

SUPER: Real Butter

ANNCR: Which explains the decadent name.

SUPER: Decadent

ANNCR: Same with all the other President's Choice cookies. The names say it all.

SUPER: Lemon Temptations.

ANNCR: And the prices, even those will make your mouth water.

SUPER: Eat the middle first.

ANNCR: Along with all the other President's Choice products here at Finast. And they're only found at Finast.

LOGO: Finast

ANNCR: Another reason we're now the Finast store for all your shopping needs.

Pasta

SUPER: Decadent

ANNCR: Finast found you a decadent cookie, but you can't have cookies for dinner.

SUPER: Rotini

ANNCR: So President's Choice says, use your noodle. Well really these noodles.

SUPER: Radiatore

ANNCR: There's 5 kinds in all.

SUPER: Spaghetti

SUPER: Splendido

ANNCR: And the sauce - Splendido. It's thick, tangy and rich. Choose original, mushroom, beef or hot and spicy.

SUPER: Spaghetti

ANNCR: Any way you like it, it's a new spin on pasta. At a price that won't throw you for a loop. Just like all the other President's Choice products you can only find at Finast. Another reason we're now the Finast store for all your shopping needs.

LOGO: Finast

Snacks

SUPER: Splendido

ANNCR: Finast found you a great pasta dinner, but what about the other important meal of the day?

SUPER: Pepperoni

ANNCR: You know, snack time.

SUPER: Cheese

ANNCR: Well, try President's Choice Ultimate Pizzas

SUPER: 100% Real Cheese

ANNCR: topped with a 100% real cheese. Or how about popcorn

SUPER: 4 varieties

ANNCR: or crackers. There are 4 varieties.

SUPER: Cola

ANNCR: Whatever, all are perfect with a cool cola or soft drink. Oh yeah, the prices are cool too. Just like all the other President's Choice products you can only find at Finast. Another reason we're now the Finast store for all your shopping needs.

In this opera, a man has a drinking problem.

Her beauty knocks him off his feet.

286
District 4
CLIENT
Orlando Opera
AGENCY
Cramer-Krasselt
Orlando, FL
CREATIVE DIRECTORS
Bill Nosan
Mitch Boyd
ART DIRECTORS
Bill Nosan
Mitch Boyd
COPYWRITERS
Bill Nosan
Tom Woodward

Actually, a poison drinking problem.

On the other hand, it could be the poison.

Don't miss this story about first love and last rites.

Don't miss the original dead end romance.

286
Last Rites
MUSIC: ROMEO & JULIET theme music
SUPER: In this opera, a man has a drinking problem.
SUPER: Actually, a poison drinking problem.
SUPER: A girl falls for him anyway.
SUPER: Unfortunately, it's onto a knife.
SUPER: Cute couple.
SUPER: Romeo et Juliet November 18, 20, 22.
SUPER: Don't miss this story about first love and last rites.
SUPER: Orlando Opera Company
SUPER: Juicy stories, put to music

Dead End Romance
MUSIC: ROMEO & JULIET theme music
SUPER: Orlando Opera Company presents the story of a real Romeo.
SUPER: Who falls for a real Juliet.
SUPER: Her beauty knocks him off his feet.
SUPER: On the other hand, it could be the poison.
SUPER: Romeo et Juliet, November 18, 20 & 22.
SUPER: Don't miss the original dead end romance.
SUPER: For tickets, call 800-33-OPERA.
SUPER: Orlando Opera Company
SUPER: Juicy stories, put to music

287
District 8

CLIENT
Memorial Medical
Center

AGENCY
McDonald Davis
& Associates
Milwaukee, WI

CREATIVE DIRECTOR
Chuck Schiller

ART DIRECTOR
Joe Locher

COPYWRITER
Joe Locher

DIRECTOR
Roymond Bark

287

Children

YOUNG GIRL: Children have no concept of time. They don't know what lies ahead. That's okay, it's what makes them kids. But once you know what lies ahead, you act differently. That's why we should concentrate on the children now, to make sure they become healthy adults tomorrow. Because, it will be tomorrow before you know it.

Potential

YOUNG GIRL: Yesterday you were a child. And that child today is an adult tomorrow. Kids are more than charming little diversions. They are a resource we need to develop. But to see this we need to look past our abilities to our possibilities. Start with the children now, because it will be tomorrow before you know it.

Curiosity

YOUNG GIRL: Ever spend time watching kids? Ever wonder what goes on in their minds? If you want to understand people, you need to understand how their minds work. Their feelings, their senses. That's why it's worth it to study these things. Today it's impossible to know everything that goes on in the mind. But the more we know, the healthier we can keep people tomorrow. And you know, it will be tomorrow before you know it.

288
District 10

CLIENT
Oklahoma Natural
Gas

AGENCY
Larkin Meeder &
Schweidel
Tulsa, OK

CREATIVE DIRECTOR
Kim Schweidel

COPYWRITER
Terry Pair

PRODUCER
Dan Herrmann

ACCOUNT EXECUTIVE
Teresia Pool

289
District 3

CLIENT
Biltmore Estates

AGENCY
Price/McNabb
Asheville, NC

CREATIVE DIRECTOR
John Boone

ART DIRECTOR
John Boone

COPYWRITER
David Oakley

PRODUCER
Sarah Cherry

DIRECTOR
Amir Hamed

288
ANNCR VO: Abraham's Western Cafe is practically an institution in Oklahoma City. Abe swears by his gas griddle. It's so energy efficient, it's save him a bundle over the years. And it puts just the right amount of heat under the cheese burger that made him famous. And who can argue with success? No wonder more restaurants are warming up to natural gas. Oklahoma Natural Gas. Pure Oklahoma.

289
ANNCR VO: A century ago, George Vanderbilt acquired a rare painting by Claude Monet.
WIFE'S VO: George, did I tell you that Mother is coming to visit for the summer?
GEORGE'S VO: Same thing every year. There's not enough room in this house for the both of us...
GEORGE'S VO: ...she thinks she can move right in...
SUPER: The missing Monet.
ANNCR VO: The missing Monet. On display for the first time in nearly a century. At Biltmore Estate.

TELEVISION

290
District 6

CLIENT
Indiana State Fair

AGENCY
MZD
Indianapolis, IN

CREATIVE DIRECTOR
Mike Soper

ART DIRECTOR
Scott Davis

COPYWRITER
Tim Abare

291
District 7

CLIENT
Louisiana Lottery

AGENCY
Bauerlein
New Orleans, LA

CREATIVE DIRECTOR
Robbie Vitrano

ART DIRECTOR
Pat McGuinness

COPYWRITER
Jim Houck

PRODUCTION
Kurtz and Friends

PRODUCER
Debbie Koppman

DIRECTOR
Bob Kurtz

290

SFX: *Gobbling noises*
SFX: PHHHHLEEEOOP, BINK.
ANNCR: Ready for seed spittin' at the State Fair? Now through Sunday, August 10-21st.

291

HEART RATE CHUMP: Medical experts say to maintain good physical condition, we should raise the old heart rate for 20 minutes, three times a week. Now I thought about weightlifting and thigh mastering and cross-country skiing. Then it hit me, Lottery scratch games! Now, three times a week I pick up a different scratch game - there's lots to choose from - come home and stare at it for 19 minutes. Does my heart pound when I think about winning! Then, with a minute left, I start to scratch; up, down, left, down, right! Feeeel the burn!
ANNCR: Lottery scratch games. Ask you doctor if they're right for you.

292
District 3
CLIENT
Photovision
AGENCY
Corder Philips &
Associates
Charlotte, NC
CREATIVE DIRECTOR
Billy Wilson
ART DIRECTOR
Billy Wilson
COPYWRITER
Julie Marr
DIRECTOR
George Watkins
PRODUCTION
Bridge

293
District 3
CLIENT
Biltmore Estate
AGENCY
Price/McNabb
Asheville, NC
CREATIVE DIRECTOR
John Boone
ART DIRECTOR
John Boone
COPYWRITERS
Scott Corbett
David Oakley
DIRECTOR
Amir Hamed

292
MALE: My wife ordered one of those videos and I'm here to pick it up.
FEMALE: Yes sir. Your name please?
MALE: Bruiser.
FEMALE: Bruiser...oh, of course, Mr. Bruiser. Let me play it for you.
MALE: Oh, I'm in a hurry.
FEMALE: Oh, it will just take a minute.
VO: At Sears Portrait Studio, we'll create a video using thirty of you favorite photos, complete with opening title, music and special effects. All for just 29.95. Photovision at Sears Portrait Studios. It's Enough to Make a Grown Man Cry.
MALE: Yeah, not bad. I'll take it.

293
ANNCR: Long before baseball cards were invented, George Vanderbilt collected Royalty Cards.
GEORGE'S VO: Honey, have you seen my King Louis XIV?
SFX: *The sound a trading card makes when it is put into the spokes of a tricycle.*
SUPER: The Royalty Cards.
ANNCR: See the Royalty Cards. Revealed for the first time in nearly a century. At Biltmore Estate.

294
District 10
CLIENT
Royal Crown Cola
AGENCY
GSD&M Advertising
Austin, TX
CREATIVE DIRECTORS
Guy Bommarito
Scott Mackey
David Crawford
ART DIRECTOR
Doug Lyon
COPYWRITER
Tom Campion
PRODUCER
Jeff Johnson
DIRECTOR
David Wild
EDITOR
Hank Polonsky

295
District 7
CLIENT
Congressman
Charlie Rose
AGENCY
Lee Gipson
Jackson, MS
COPYWRITER
Lee Gipson
PRODUCER
Lee Gipson
PRODUCTION
Imageworks
DIRECTOR
John Stockwell

294
SFX: *Seagulls, harbor sounds*
ANNCR: For years you've been fed the same old line. That there are only two great-tasting colas to choose from.
FISHERMAN: Hook up. Fish on!
SFX: *Fishing reels spinning and cranking.*
ANNCR: Hey, you don't have to swallow that line. Drink RC and you'll look at colas in a whole new way. RC Cola. Shake Things Up.

295
MUSIC: Nostalgic big band
CHARLIE'S DAD VO: My son tells people it's named after me. But they know better. The farmers got together and named it after him. The Charlie Rose Agri-Expo Center. Of course, technically speaking, I was Charlie Rose before he was. But if they want to give him the credit, that's fine. It really doesn't matter. Long as they vote for Charlie Rose. Now that would definitely be him.

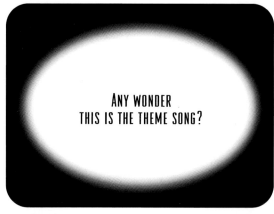

IN THIS OPERA,
A TAX COLLECTOR GOES TO PRISON

ANY WONDER
THIS IS THE THEME SONG?

ORLANDO OPERA COMPANY
JUICY STORIES, PUT TO MUSIC.

296
District 7
CLIENT
ABC Sports
AGENCY
Deaton Flanigen
Productions
Nashville, TN
CREATIVE DIRECTOR
Bob Toms
ART DIRECTOR
Greg Horne
COPYWRITER
Bob Toms
MUSIC
Scott Hendricks
EXECUTIVE PRODUCER
Tom Remiszewski
PRODUCER
Peter Zavadil
PRODUCTION
Deaton Flanigen
DIRECTORS
Robert Deaton
George J. Flanigen

297
District 4
CLIENT
Orlando Opera
Company
AGENCY
Cramer Krasselt/
AVID Inc.
Orlando, FL
CREATIVE DIRECTORS
Bill Nosan
Mitch Boyd
COPYWRITERS
Tom Woodward
Bill Nosan
EDITOR
Michael Speltz
ACCOUNT EXECUTIVE
Larry Muench

296

297
MUSIC: "IMPOSSIBLE DREAM" throughout
SUPER: On April 29, 30, and May 1
SUPER: Orlando Opera Company presents Man of La
Mancha
SUPER: In this opera, a tax collector goes to prison
SUPER: Any wonder this is the theme song?
SUPER: For tickets, call 800-33-OPERA.
SUPER: Get yours now.
SUPER: Then come see the tax man get his.
SUPER: Orlando Opera Company
SUPER: Juicy stories, put to music

298
District 4

CLIENT
Wegmans

AGENCY
Jay Incorporated
Tampa, FL

CREATIVE DIRECTOR
Ferdinand Jay Smith

COPYWRITER
Earl Repp

PRODUCER
Jeffrey Peyton Goff

ACCOUNT EXECUTIVE
Ferdinand Jay Smith

299
District 2

CLIENT
AT&T

AGENCY
NW Ayer & Partners
New York, NY

CREATIVE DIRECTORS
Keith Gould
Steve Feinberg

ART DIRECTOR
Kenny Evans

COPYWRITER
Jim Othmer

PRODUCER
Gaston Braun

PRODUCTION
HKM Productions

298
BILLY (CAPTAIN): Alright, first pick I got Munch...
CHARLIE (CAPTAIN): I want Tiny...
BILLY: I got little man...
CHARLIE: Al, Al!
2nd CAPTAIN: Okay, we got Norbert. You can have the other guy.
TOM: Oh man, we're stuck with the new guy!
CHARLIE: Okay. Tiny, I want you to play line and you (to Jim) what's your name again?
JIM: It's Jim.
CHARLIE: Okay Tim, I want you to play line, alright?
JIM (HOPEFULLY): Uh, I'm a pretty good quarterback though...
CHARLIE: Yeah, maybe next down, okay? Let's go!
SING: Share! What a feelin'! What a feelin'!
ANNCR: Cravin' something cool? Share a Wegman's WPOP!
SING: Wooo! Share! What a feelin'! Share the bubbles and the fizz, you won't believe how good the taste is! Share! What a feelin' What a feelin'
TOM: Whooo, with you on our team, we could win it all!
SING: Wooo!
JIM: Sooner or later, sooner or later...
ANNCR: Break the ice with someone nice...it'll make you feel dynamite!

299
AL: Right now,
SUPER: True Heroes D-Day - June 6, 1944 An AT&T Salute.
AL: for instance, I can't even find another guy that was with me there. Between the dead and growing old and.. and not wanting to remember...
SID: Got that... Hey, you're going to the 50th of course...
DICK (Chuckling): Yeah...
SFX: *Gunfire and bombs exploding*
AL: Out at the ocean all you could see was ships, ships, ships...
SFX: *Gunfire and men yelling*
DICK: I think of the men we lost here... I guess...I wonder...Why?
SID: Freedom.
HOWARD: Then you were born just two weeks after I left to come over here to England and...
WARREN: I go to a ball game... when they play The Star Spangled Banner, I think...think of my brother John.
ANNCR: AT&T invites you to join us in saluting the True Heroes of D-Day and all those who have fought for freedom.
AL: I was getting worried that nobody would know about it... That you wouldn't hear about it.

EVERYBODY KNOWS
THE BEST NUTS COME
FROM CALIFORNIA.

CALIFORNIA PISTACHIOS

300
District 2
CLIENT
Russell Athletic
AGENCY
BBDO
New York, NY
CREATIVE DIRECTORS
Ted Sann
Charlie Miesmer
Mike Campbell
Dennis Berger
ART DIRECTORS
Steve Rutter
Mike Campbell
COPYWRITER
Susan Credle
PRODUCTION
HKM Productions
PRODUCERS
J.D. Williams
Rani Vaz
DIRECTOR
Michael Karbelnikoff
EDITOR
Clayton Hemmert

301
District 15
CLIENT
California Sunkist
Pistachio
AGENCY
Chiat/Day Inc.
Advertising
Venice, CA
ART DIRECTOR
Jerry Gentile
COPYWRITER
Scott Vincent
PRODUCER
Michelle Burke
PRODUCTION
Johns & Gorman
Films

300
VO: Pros wear Russell Athletic 'cause it's made tough. It has to be.
PLAYER: Hey kid! Hey, you got my lucky jersey.
KID: Yeah?
PLAYER: I got kind of carried away. Can I have it back?
KID: You gotta be kidding.
PLAYER: Come here you little Pipsqueak!
KID: Give it!
PLAYER: Get off my back.
KID: No!
VO: You want athletic wear that can survive anything? Get Russell Athletic. Get touch.
COACH: Who was that kid?
PLAYER: I don't know, but sign him up.

301
SUPER: August Priest Sound Toner
INTERVIEWER: So what does sound toning do?
PRIEST: It opens you heart chakra, so you feel unconditional love just vibrating throughout all of you. Comfortably and easily. You can feel your guardian angel surrounding you. Creating balance and harmony.
SFX: *"SOUND TONING" noises*
SUPER: Everybody knows the best nuts come from California.
ANNCR VO: Sunkist California Pistachios. Now that's a nut.

302

District 6

CLIENT
Chrysler/Dodge

AGENCY
BBDO-Detroit
Southfield, MI

CREATIVE DIRECTOR
Dick Johnson

ART DIRECTORS
Gary Slomka
Gene Turner

COPYWRITER
Gene Turner

303

District 10

CLIENT
Southwest Airlines

AGENCY
GSD&M
Austin, TX

CREATIVE DIRECTORS
Wally Williams
Tom Gilmore

ART DIRECTOR
Tom Gilmore

COPYWRITER
Wally Williams

PRODUCER
Peggy Moore

EDITOR
Jack Waldrop

302

ANNCR VO: People don't really understand the idea that shaped it. It's capable of extrasensory communication. It contains platinum. Rhodium. And newly formed materials. It's shielded with a dry powder that was melted to a virtually impermeable finish. It's deeply concerned with our planet's environment. And no one has ever seen anything quite like it. Introducing Neon.
SUPER: Hi.
ANNCR VO: Eighty-nine seventy-five for starters, twelve-five nicely loaded.
TITLE: Neon. Only from Dodge and Plymouth.

303

METHYL: (COUNTING) One, two, three...
E&M: (SINGING) There's a quarter million miles around Texas Amarillo down to Lubbock to San Antone. From the Rio Grande Valley up to Houston on to Dallas, Austin to El Paso and then we'll fly you home. There's miles, and miles and miles and miles of Texas. From the beaches to the mountains to the plains. We'll get you there on time on Southwest Air...lines, I guess that's why we're called The Company Plane.

304
District 14

CLIENT
DHL

AGENCY
Goodby, Silverstein
& Partners
San Francisco, CA

CREATIVE DIRECTORS
Jeffrey Goodby
Rich Silverstein

ART DIRECTOR
Jeremy Postaer

COPYWRITER
Steven Johnston

PRODUCERS
Ed Galvez
Charles Stedwell

PRODUCTION
Straight Cut

305
District 7

CLIENT
Eastwood Mall

AGENCY
Cunningham, Black,
Slaton & Riley, Inc.
Montgomery, AL

CREATIVE DIRECTOR
Slats Slaton

COPYWRITER
Leon Barwick

PRODUCTION
Video One

DIRECTOR
Carey Golden

ACCOUNT EXECUTIVE
Nell Rankin

304

DELIVERY PERSON: I am bored today. I am filled with boredom. The bourgeois businessmen, waiting for their packages, they can wait.

ANNCR: Does you shipping company hire someone else to deliver your package overseas? Why take the chance? Especially when there's a company that uses it's own delivery people in more countries around the world. DHL or else.

305

WIFE: What do you think? This one or this one?

HUSBAND: The yellow one.

WIFE: You mean the mustard one. Me too. Oh Hon, would you toss me those shorts on the bed?

HUSBAND: You want the mayonnaise or thousand island?

ANNCR: Eastwood Mall. Fashioning your life!

306
District 15

CLIENT
California Sunkist
Pistachio

AGENCY
Chiat/Day Inc.
Advertising
Venice, CA

ART DIRECTOR
Jerry Gentile

COPYWRITER
Scott Vincent

PRODUCER
Michelle Burke

PRODUCTION
Johns & Gorman
Films

307
District 14

CLIENT
First Interstate
Bankcorp

AGENCY
Hal Riney & Partners
San Francisco, CA

CREATIVE DIRECTOR
Steve Silver

ART DIRECTOR
Curtis Melville

COPYWRITER
Steve Silver

PRODUCER
Ann Storm

PRODUCTION
Sonzero/Pugliese

ACCOUNT EXECUTIVE
Pat Madden

EVERYBODY KNOWS
THE BEST NUTS COME
FROM CALIFORNIA.

CALIFORNIA PISTACHIOS

306
BUDDY: My angel name is Sanfernandinaki. People call me Buddy.
SFX: *Man chanting: ROAH...MAAH...AAAH...*
SFX: *Chime sound.*
SFX: *Heavy breathing sounds from Sanfernandinaki.*
SFX: *Man chanting: EEEHEE...*
BUDDY: We have spiritual parties at our house...about once every month. If you're at all interested we'll invite you...
SUPER: Everybody knows the best nuts come from California.
ANNCR VO: Sunkist California Pistachios. Now that's a nut.

307
SFX: *Woman bathing her baby. Water splashing, baby giggling and gurgling, woman is humming...*
TITLE: Is: 2 bdr, 2 ba.
TITLE: Will Be: 3 brd, 3 ba.
TITLE: Home Improvement Loans Low rates Flexible terms Tax benefits.
LOGO: You & I First interstate Bank.

308
District 14
CLIENT
Isuzu
AGENCY
Goodby, Silverstein & Partners
San Francisco, CA
CREATIVE DIRECTORS
Jeffrey Goodby
Rich Silverstein
ART DIRECTOR
Mike Mazza
COPYWRITER
Dave O'Hare
PRODUCTION
Coppos Sata Thomas
PRODUCER
Cindy Fluitt
DIRECTOR
Brent Thomas

309
District 15
CLIENT
Kubota Tractor Company
AGENCY
Rubin Postaer & Associates
Santa Monica, CA
CREATIVE DIRECTOR
Larry Postaer
ART DIRECTOR
Richard Bess
COPYWRITER
Laura Juell
PRODUCER
Jack Epsteen

308
WEATHERMAN 1: Taking a look at the weather we've got a high pressure...
WEATHERMAN 2: ...high pressure...
WEATHERMAN 1: ...system...
WEATHERWOMAN 3: ...sitting right here...
WEATHERMAN 4: ...and that's bringing us...
WEATHERMAN 5: ...nothing but...
WEATHERMAN 6: ...clear skies...
WEATHERMAN 1: ...and old Mr. Sunshine...
ANNCR VO: The Isuzu Trooper...was designed around a simple fact of nature...
WEATHERMAN 7: But hold on...
WEATHERMAN 8: Hold on...
WEATHERWOMAN 3: It's gonna' get better...
WEATHERMAN 6: Clear as a bell...
WEATHERMAN 5: Not a cloud in the sky...
WEATHERMAN 1: Huh-huh...
WEATHERMAN 3: Soaring...
WEATHERMAN 8: Dry...
ANNCR VO: Weathermen are really only guessing. Hey, Life's an adventure. Be prepared.
WEATHERMAN 8: My prediction? It's gonna' rain. Trust me.
ANNCR VO: Isuzu. Practically/Amazing.

309
ANNCR VO: Yeah, but can they plow the back forty?
ANNCR VO: Introducing the new, more powerful Grand L Series from Kubota. With our smoothest, quietest...tractor engine yet.

310

District 14

CLIENT
The 3DO Company

AGENCY
Butler, Shine & Stern
Sausalito, CA

CREATIVE DIRECTORS
John Butler
Mike Shine

ART DIRECTOR
John Butler

COPYWRITER
Mike Shine

PRODUCER
Ben Latimer

PRODUCTION
Propaganda

DIRECTOR
Jonathon Kahn

311

District 4

CLIENT
Albany State College

AGENCY
JS Goodson &
Partners Advertising
Tallahassee, FL

COPYWRITER
John Goodson

PRODUCTION
J. Martin Production

POSTPRODUCTION
Catwalk

DIRECTOR
John Goodson

MUSIC
615 Productions

310
BOSS: You're working late tonight. (Spits at camera)
SFX: *SPLAT!*
SUPER: Response 1
EMPLOYEE 1: (wipes cigar chunk off forehead, opens briefcase.)
VO: The passive type. Probably plays Nintendo.
BOSS: (Bursts in) You're working late tonight. (Spits)
SFX: *SPLAT!*
SUPER: Response 2
EMPLOYEE 2: (Wipes cigar chunk off his nose) I can't, I got therapy!
VO: The aggressive type. Probably plays Sega.
BOSS: (Bursts in) You're working late tonight. (Spits)
SUPER: Response 3
EMPLOYEE 3: (Eating chinese food) Can we try that again with a knock?
VO: And the other type. Definitely plays 3DO, the most advanced home gaming system in the universe.
SUPER: 3DO. What are you playing with?
EMPLOYEE 3: Are you hitting on me?

311
SLATE: July 7, 1994
1ST ANNCR: Officials today ordered evacuation of areas along Georgia's Flint River after tropical storm Alberto dumped torrential rains on the Southeast...
SLATE: July 9, 1994
2nd ANNCR: As the Flint River burst out of its banks this morning, residents of Albany, Georgia began preparing for the worst...
SLATE: July 10, 1994
3rd ANNCR: ...are calling it the worst flood in Georgia's history. Especially hard hit is Albany State College, with most of its campus underwater. Elsewhere...
SLATE: July 20, 1994
4TH ANNCR: Today at Albany state college, a massive cleanup began even before flood waters completely receded. Recovery team director, retired Corps of Engineers General Bill Ray said...
SLATE: August 3, 1994
5TH NEWS ANNCR: Declaring Albany State College to be "Unsinkable," President Billy C. Black said today that summer classes have reopened and that fall classes will begin as scheduled on September 21st. He outlined a massive project to construct temporary facilities next to compus for use until all buildings are repaired. University system chancellor Steven Portch termed the attitude at Albany State "Remarkable."

312
District 5
CLIENT
Totes, Inc.
AGENCY
Sive/Young &
Rubicam
Cincinnati, OH
CREATIVE DIRECTORS
Mark Giambrone
Mike Kitei
ART DIRECTOR
Mark Giambrone
COPYWRITER
Melanie Marnich
PRODUCER
Trish Bugitzedes

313
District 10
CLIENT
Builders Square
AGENCY
Fogarty Klein &
Partners
Houston, TX
CREATIVE DIRECTORS
Tom Monroe
Nancy Self
ART DIRECTOR
Tom Gates
PRODUCER
Khrisana Mayfield

312

SFX: *Rumbling thunder and the ploop of a single drop of rain*

SFX: *The rhythmic tap-tap-tap of a tap shoe toe.*

SFX: *Click-pop! Of umbrella*

ANNCR: It's not news that totes is introducing an umbrella that's remarkably small.

SFX: *Click-pop!*

ANNCR: And it's not news that totes is introducing an umbrella that's remarkably big.

SFX: *Click-pop!*

ANNCR: But it is news that it's the same umbrella. Remarkably.

SFX: *Tap dancing.*

ANNCR: Totes' new golf-sized Big Top. Big enough to cover everyone. Small enough to carry everywhere.

SFX: *Tapping until end.*

313

MUSIC: Acoustic guitar

COACH: OK, Smiths, first base. Melinack, home plate. OK, Let's hit the field.

ANNCR: Where does the whole neighborhood go when it's time to fix up around the home?

ALL, GATHERED AT HOME PLATE: Builders Square.

COACH: They'll get you squared away.

TELEVISION

314
District 2
CLIENT
Tyson
AGENCY
Saatchi & Saatchi
Advertising
New York, NY
CREATIVE DIRECTORS
Craig Miller
Norm Weill
ART DIRECTOR
Melissa London
COPYWRITER
Gary Weintraub
PRODUCTION
Johns & Gorman Film

315
District 3
CLIENT
Denny's Inc.
AGENCY
DMB&B
Greenville, SC
CREATIVE DIRECTOR
Roger Lockwood
MANAGING DIRECTOR
Mark Wilmot

314

315
ANNCR: The Corlick sisters on Denny's new remodeling.
EDITH: Rose said we could get a complete makeover inside the restaurant
ROSE: I said the restaurant's getting a complete makeover.
EDITH: Ohh! Will they give it a mudpack?
ROSE: No. But they'll give it beautiful new colors, accents, lighting; a whole new look from top to bottom.
EDITH: I hope they do that to us. You could use it.
ROSE: They're doing it for us. We'll have a brand new dessert shop... with fresh Mother Butler pies, and Edith... hand-dipped Baskin-Robbins ice cream.
EDITH: They're going to dip our hands in Baskin-Robbins ice cream?
ROSE: They're going to put it in the restaurant.
EDITH: Everything is so beautiful. Come on, Rose. Let's get our makeover.
ROSE: We're not the ones being made over.
EDITH: Guess Rose just doesn't understand how things have changed so beautifully here at Lenny's.
ROSE: Denny's
EDITH: Denny's
ANNCR: Houston, come take a fresh look at an old friend. You won't believe the change.
SFX: *WORKER WHISTLES*
ROSE: I'm old enough to be your mother.

316
District 9

CLIENT
Anheuser-Busch/
Budweiser

AGENCY
DMB&B/St. Louis
St. Louis, MO

CREATIVE DIRECTORS
Mark Choate
James Borcherdt
Brad Ashton

ART DIRECTOR
Brad Ashton

COPYWRITER
Tom Remes

PRODUCER
Jane Liepshutz

317
District 2

CLIENT
Mexico Tourism

AGENCY
Saatchi & Saatchi
Advertising
New York, NY

CREATIVE DIRECTOR
John Morrison

ART DIRECTOR
Dabni Harvey

COPYWRITER
Cheryl Chapman

PRODUCER
Liz Graves

PRODUCTION
GMS

DIRECTOR
Peter Nydrle

316
MUSIC: THE STAR SPANGLED BANNER by Jimi
Hendrix
SUPER: For millions of people
SUPER: for hundreds of years.
SUPER: Getting to America
SUPER: has been the ultimate goal.
SUPER: It still is.
SUPER: Budweiser. Official beer of the 1994 World Cup.

317
ANNCR VO: The air. The air smells like it's just been
made like there's so much of it and when I breathe in it
feels good because the plants are big and full and they're
dripping big heavy drops ones they can't hold on to that
land on my face and ones that just hang in the misty air
that's making waves down my back all the way down my
back. You are very close to far away. Mexico

318

District 6

CLIENT
Cadbury Schweppes-Gingerale

AGENCY
Foote, Cone and Belding/Chicago
Chicago, IL

CREATIVE DIRECTOR
Chuck Rudnick

ART DIRECTOR
Scott Larson
Brad Berg

COPYWRITER
Scott Larson
Brad Berg

PRODUCER
Scott Mitchell

DIRECTOR
Scott Larson
Brad Berg

319

District 2

CLIENT
Toys R Us

AGENCY
J. Walter Thompson
New York, NY

CREATIVE DIRECTORS
Terri Meyer
Sandy Greenberg
Linda Kaplan

ART DIRECTOR
Stephen Krauss

COPYWRITER
John Nicholaides

TYPOGRAPHER
Rob Sutton

PRODUCER
Gary Bass

PRODUCTION
Jon Francis Films

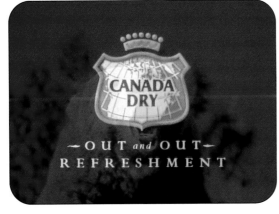

318

MUSIC: Big orchestral trak

SFX: *Ice cubes hitting bottom of glass.*

SFX: *Soda can popping open.*

SFX: *Soda pour.*

SFX: *Soda fizz.*

SFX: *Gulping.*

ANNCR: Crisp. Clean. Less sweet. With a golden tint and a sparkling flavor. Canada Dry Ginger Ale. Out and out refreshment.

SFX: *AHHH!*

319

BIKER: I was born to ride.

BIKER: It's like flying, only on the ground.

BIKER: Riding into town...big pack...everybody gets out of your way.

BIKER: We're showing off.

BIKER: The sun...wind...downhill...that's freedom.

VO: This May is bike month at Toys R Us. There's tons of bikes at incredible prices.

BIKER: I've got biking in my blood.

VO: There's bikes for kids, adults...

BIKER: Hi Mom.

VO: Even the most serious riders. In fact, Toys R Us has more bikes than anyone.

BIKER: Nice Chromali frame.

VO: You even get a free lock.

BIKER: I bike, therefore I am.

BIKER: Who brought the goat?

BIKER: We're just one big family.

VO: Bike month at Toys R Us.

320

District 9

CLIENT
Southwestern Bell Telephone

AGENCY
DMB&B/St. Louis
St. Louis, MO

CREATIVE DIRECTORS
Tom Gow
Greg Sullentrup
Michael Dukes

ART DIRECTOR
Kait Courlang
Greg Sullentrup

COPYWRITER
Michael Dukes

PRODUCER
Mary McCarthy

321

District 10

CLIENT
Luby's Cafeteria

AGENCY
Anderson Advertising
San Antonio, TX

CREATIVE DIRECTOR
Stan McElrath

ART DIRECTOR
Margaret Sandoz

COPYWRITER
Dirk Mitchell

PRODUCER
Mike Taylor

PRODUCTION
Johns & Gorman

POST PRODUCTION
Match Frame

DIRECTOR
Gary Johns

ACCOUNT EXECUTIVE
Loni Samet

320

ANNCR VO: Okay, here's 12 rubber alligators. And 12 yo-yos. Just to dramatize Southwestern Bell's best offer ever: 12 useful phone services, now at one great price. We call this package The works. 12 conveniences like Call Waiting, Call Return, even Caller ID. Best yet, you get our 12 most popular services for just 15 of these a month. And as you can clearly see, 12 is a lot. To order The Works at a full 45% discount, just dial 1-800-234-BELL. You could even ask...for operator 12. Heh heh. Southwestern Bell Telephone.

321

ETHEL: I do all the cooking.
HOWARD: I do the dishes.
ETHEL: I use all my mother's recipes.
HOWARD: I set the table.
ETHEL: One night a week my husband is responsible for dinner.
HOWARD: I drive.
ANNCR: If you want a freshly prepared meal without actually preparing it yourself, Luby's is where you want to be.
ETHEL: You look very handsome.
ANNCR: Luby's Cafeteria. It's your dinner place.

TELEVISION

322
District 14

CLIENT
Haggar

AGENCY
Goodby, Silverstein
& Partners
San Francisco, CA

CREATIVE DIRECTORS
Jeffrey Goodby
Rich Silverstein

ART DIRECTOR
Joe Shands

COPYWRITER
Ron Saltmarsh

PRODUCER
Cindy Epps

PRODUCTION
Smilie Films

323
District 2

CLIENT
P&G

AGENCY
Font & Vaamonde
New York, NY

CREATIVE DIRECTOR
Gustavo Asensi

ART DIRECTOR
Pedro Anlas

COPYWRITER
Gustavo Asensi

PRODUCTION
La Casa Films

PRODUCER
Betsy Collazo

322

SFX: Spanish guitar music.
SFX: Stomp of foot.
VO: Should a man be judged by what he wears? Are you really any less of a man because you don't wear the right shirt or pants? Should you have to wear a shirt or pants at all? Ask yourself, hasn't our society advanced to the point where a man... can feel comfortable... in a dress? Uhh...probably not.
ANNCR: Always appropriate, 100% cotton shirts and pants guys can feel comfortable in. Haggar, stuff you can wear.

323

SFX: Bolero music
SINGER VO: With you I learned what love and affection is in this life...with you I learned...
ANNCR: In the little details... In that touch of Downy... you'll find the softness in your home. In the little details... you'll find Temura. And only Downy gives your clothes...that maximum softness... and long lasting freshness that we call Temura. Use Downy...It's Temura.
SINGER VO: With you I learned...

324
District 2
CLIENT
Dannon
AGENCY
Font & Vaamonde
New York, NY
CREATIVE DIRECTOR
Gustavo Asensi
Peter Font
ART DIRECTOR
Pedro Anlas
COPYWRITERS
Gustavo Asensi
Peter Font
PRODUCTION
Concrete
Productions
PRODUCER
Betsy Collazo

325
District 2
CLIENT
Dominos
AGENCY
Font & Vaamonde
New York, NY
CREATIVE DIRECTORS
Gustavo Asensi
Xabier Gainza
ART DIRECTOR
Pedro Anlas
COPYWRITER
Xabier Gainza
PRODUCTION
El Coyote Pictures
PRODUCER
Betsy Collazo

324
FATHER: At home we used to have papayas, guavas and a Huge mango tree. My father used to throw one from behind me do that I believed... it had fallen... from the tree. I used to take it, peel it and... eat it. And those papayas... and pineapples. Tropifruta! What Flavor! It had to be Dannon!
ANNCR: New Dannon Tropifruta yogurt. Return to your roots.
FATHER VO: The bananas? We used to take them from the neighbor's tree.

325
PRESIDENT VO: People of maricusa, I promise you water... I promise you electricity... even food!
Domino's chant (crowd stomping and clapping)
PRESIDENT: Help me, what will we do?...
BODYGUARD: Domino's?
CROWD (Domino's chant): Gotta be...gotta be...Domino's
PRESIDENT VO: Gotta be...gotta be...Domino's

326
District 7

CLIENT
Touro Infirmary

AGENCY
McDonald Davis
& Associates
Milwaukee, WI

CREATIVE DIRECTOR
Joe Locher

DIRECTOR
Ken Morrison

326

Good Care
ANNCR: We've been in New Orleans for over 140 years.
And one thing is obvious. This city needs a good hospital.
SUPER: TOURO LOGO
THEME: Good Care for the Good Life.

Heart Beat
ANNCR: There are many things in New Orleans that
make your heart beat faster. Which is why, for over 140
years, we've been the place that keeps it beating right.
SUPER: TOURO LOGO
THEME: Good Care for the Good Life.

TELEVISION

Lunch TV

DON: Hey time for Brew Ha-Ha. Dis is my brodder Hank.

HANK: Hey!

DON: It's lunchtime here at The Bricktown Brewery...

HANK: Hey Don...You got Bricktown Quesadillas on your tie.

SFX: BOINK

DON: Hey, That's my nose.

HANK: Co...medy Don.

DON: OK. Let's go to the tables.

HANK: Excuse me miss. What kind of beer you got there?

HANK: Speak into the MIC.

FEMALE CUST: Oh...Ah, Copperhead Premium Amber Ale.

DON: Why do you like it so much?

FEMALE CUST: Oh I think it's the Fuggles and Willamette hops balance. The clean, smooth Malt finish...

HANK: Here. Have some Nachos...on us. Sorry about the chin. We'll get back with you.

DON: Hey. I'm kinda hungry now square head. How 'bout we break for lunch.

HANK: Sure. Let's grab a waiter...Hey we need some menus here now... Thanks. And some beers too "A".

DON: OK. Come down and see us at The Bricktown Brewery. OK? We'll have some handmade beer and some food and stuff.

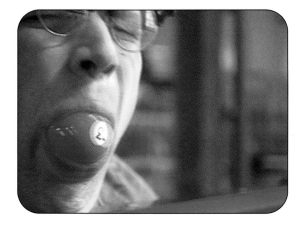

Sportz TV

DON: Time for Brew Ha-Ha at The Bricktown Brewery. Dis is Don and Hank Beogenschultz.

HANK: Hey!

DON: Hank's back there messin' around with the TV stuff... Hey get outta there cheddar head.

HANK: Hey Don... You watch baseball or stock car driving?

DON: Both. They like gots 29 screens or something.

HANK: I'm on that like a rat on a cheeto.

DON: OK. Let's go to the pool tables.

HANK: Hey come play darts over by the Moose head man.

DON: Wait... I'm golfing. Oh hey bring us some copperheads would yuh?

HANK: Hey. Don. Check this out.

DON: Hey you look like a ballet guy or something. Hey. I'm kinda thirsty now square head. How 'bout more beers.

HANK: Don. You gotta try that virtual reality. Supper cool.

DON: OK. Come down and see us at The Bricktown Brewery. OK? We'll have some handmade beer and play some games and stuff. "A."

Dinner TV

DON: Hey time for Brew Ha-Ha. Dis is Don and Hank Beogenschultz.

HANK: Hey!

DON: We're having dinner here at The Bricktown Brewery...

HANK: Hey Don...You done with those wings?

DON: Hey, get your hand out a my plate square head. Order your own.

HANK: Hey, I'm on that like a bum on a bologna sandwich

DON: OK. Let's go to the tables.

HANK: Excuse me sir. What kind of beer you got there?

HANK: Speak into the MIC.

MALE CUST: Oh...Bison Weizen.

DON: Why do you like the German beer so much?

MALE CUST: Its bold but light flavor.

HANK: Hey. I got some wings coming. Sorry about the chin. We'll get back with you.

DON: Hey. I'm kinda thirsty now square head. How 'bout we break for some beers.

HANK: Sure. Let's go sit up at the bar now. And let's get some Brisket and fries too "A."

DON: OK. Come down and see us at The Bricktown Brewery. OK? We'll have some handmade beer and some food and stuff.

327
District 10
CLIENT
Bricktown Brewery
AGENCY
Sizzlin' Brains'
Creative
Oklahoma City, OK
COPYWRITERS
Jef Fontana
Michelle De Long
PRODUCERS
Michelle De Long
Jef Fontana
DIRECTOR
Alan Atkins
EDITOR
Hays De Lisle

TELEVISION

328

District 14

CLIENT
First Interstate
Bankcorp

AGENCY
Hal Riney & Partners
San Francisco, CA

CREATIVE DIRECTOR
Steve Silver

ART DIRECTOR
Curtis Melville

COPYWRITER
Steve Silver

PRODUCER
Ann Storm

PRODUCTION
Sonzero/Pugliese

ACCOUNT EXECUTIVE
Pat Madden

328

Is/Will Be
SFX: *Woman bathing her baby. Water splashing, baby giggling and gurgling, woman is humming…*
TITLE: Is: 2 bdr, 2 ba.
TITLE: Will Be: 3 brd, 3 ba.
TITLE: Home Improvement Loans Low rates Flexible terms Tax benefits.
LOGO: You & I First interstate Bank.

Fiscal Year
MALE VOICE: …Our special tonight…
TITLE: Fiscal Year 1995 22 empty tables.
TITLE: Fiscal Year 1999 Reservations highly recommended.
FEMALE VOICE: How's everything tonight?
TITLE: Small Business Loans SBA Equipment financing Lines of credit.
FEMALE VOICE: …are you enjoying yourself?
LOGO: YOU & I First Interstate.
MALE VOICE:…would you like another glass of wine?…

Graduation
SFX: *Background noise of a crowd clapping.*
ANNCR'S VOICE: … Travis Carver…
ANNCR'S VOICE: …Chris Chaffin…
TITLE: Travis Carver Birthday: August 24, 1994.
ANNCR'S VOICE: …Debbie Chin…
ANNCR'S VOICE: …Kelli Cline…
TITLE: Graduation Day: June 4, 2016.
TITLE: College Savings Plans Mutual funds Tax-free bonds US Government Securities.
ANNCR'S VOICE: …David Cole…
LOGO: YOU & I First Interstate.
ANNCR'S VOICE: …Susan Conklin…

329

District 7

CLIENT
First Commerce
Corporation

AGENCY
Lawler Ballard Van
Durand
Birmingham, AL

CREATIVE DIRECTORS
Jeff Martin
Kevin Sutton

ART DIRECTORS
Jeff Martin
Katherine Petill

COPYWRITERS
Jack Becker
Kevin Sutton

PHOTOGRAPHER
Jon Perez

PRODUCERS
Jim Frame
Keith Brown

PRODUCTION
Truth Inc.

DIRECTOR
Eric McClellan

ACCOUNT EXECUTIVE
Darrell Daigre

329

Bank Failure

OFFICER: I'm afraid the committee has turned down your loan.

WIFE: What? Why?

OFFICER: I'm not exactly sure. Apparently they felt you weren't a very good risk.

HUSBAND: But didn't you tell them about our situation?

OFFICER: And what situation was that. Mr. Morgan.

HUSBAND: That's Martin.

SUPER: You've just witnessed a bank failure.

SUPER: Witness banking from a different point of view.

WIFE: So what do we do now?

HUSBAND: I don't know.

SUPER: Personal Banking from Rapides Bank

Bank Hold-Up

MAN: Excuse me - I've been waiting for 30 minutes to talk to someone.

OFFICER: I'm sure someone will be right with you.

SUPER: You've just witnessed a bank hold-up.

MAN: Excuse me...he...(sighs)

SUPER: Witness banking from a different point of view.

SUPER: Personal Banking from CNB

Bank Robbery

CUSTOMER: It's just that my statements seem to have an awful lot of extra charges on them.

OFFICER: Yeah, that's standard.

CUSTOMER: It seem kind of expensive.

OFFICER: Well, get a cheaper account then.

CUSTOMER: You have a cheaper account?

OFFICER: Of course.

CUSTOMER: You mean you had a cheaper account all this time and didn't tell me?

OFFICER: I didn't know that was what you wanted.

SUPER: You've just witnessed a bank robbery.

SUPER: Witness banking from a different point of view.

CUSTOMER: I can't believe this.

SUPER: Personal Banking from FirstNBC.

330
District 10

CLIENT
Coca Cola USA

AGENCY
Sosa, Bromley Aguilar
& Associates
San Antonio, TX

CREATIVE DIRECTORS
Mark Gonzalez
Jerry Benavidez

ART DIRECTOR
Santiago Garces

PRODUCER
Denise Melo

ACCOUNT EXECUTIVE
Luis Garcia

330

Truck-Balls

SFX: *Truck engine as it comes to a halt.*

SFX: *Engine turning off, and boots on the street.*

SFX: *Boots walking on the street.*

SFX: *Dolly being un-hooked from truck.*

SFX: *Bay being opened.*

SFX: *Soccer balls rushing out of truck and onto the street.*

SFX: *Sound of soccer balls flooding onto the street continues and then fades out.*

SUPER: Always Global, Always Coca-Cola.

Truck-Question

SFX: *Truck engine as it comes to a halt.*

SFX: *Engine turning off, and boots on the street.*

SFX: *Boots walking on the street.*

SFX: *Dolly being un-hooked from truck.*

SFX: *Bay being opened.*

SFX: *Bay door sliding open.*

DRIVER: What'd you expect?...Soccer balls?

SUPER: Always Global, Always Coca-Cola.

SFX: *Faint sounds of crowd and a soccer announcer.*

Truck-Stadium

SFX: *Truck engine as it comes to a halt.*

SFX: *Engine turning off, and boots on the street.*

SFX: *Boots walking on the street.*

SFX: *Dolly being un-hooked from truck.*

SFX: *Bay being opened.*

SFX: *Fans chanting their team's name loudly, and an announcer calling the game.*

SFX: *Sounds of fans and announcer continues and then fades out.*

SUPER: Always Global, Always Coca-Cola.

TELEVISION

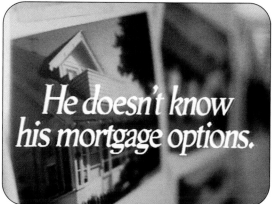

331
District 5
CLIENT
Long John Silver's
AGENCY
Temerlin McClain
Dallas, TX
CREATIVE DIRECTORS
Matt Munroe
Jobie Dixon

332
District 10
CLIENT
Fannie Mae
AGENCY
GSD&M
Austin, TX
CREATIVE DIRECTORS
Brent Ladd
Brian Brooker
ART DIRECTOR
Brent Ladd
COPYWRITERS
Brian Brooker
Rich Terry
PRODUCER
Jane Sircus
PRODUCTION
Propaganda Films

331
MUSIC: "DECK THE HALLS"
ELF: Santa?
SANTA: Yeah?
ELF: I've, uh, had another job offer.
SANTA: Oh no. How can we change your mind? How 'bout a raise? Company sled?
ANNCR: Everyone loves Long John Silver's batter-dipped fish. Now there's new Popcorn Fish. Tasty little bite-size fillets. With fries - just a dollar ninety-nine.
ELF: Maybe if you gave me your Popcorn Fish.
SANTA: Keep in touch, kid!
ANNCR: And get our Holiday Crystal for just ninety-nine cents.

332
LARRY: Early Saturday mornings, I like to play my jazz. But you see, I've got this condo...with real quiet neighbors.
SUPER: Larry wants a house.
LARRY: So I started looking into buying a house. I just hope I know what I'm doing.
SUPER: He doesn't know his mortgage options.
LARRY: Yeah, pretty soon I'll have my own place. Me and John Coltrane.
SUPER: Fannie Mae can help.
VO: At Fannie Mae, we're the nation's largest source of funds for mortgage lenders. Call us for a free guide to help you find the mortgage that's right for you.

333
District 3

CLIENT
Centura

AGENCY
Price/McNabb
Charlotte, NC

CREATIVE DIRECTOR
Robin Konieczny

ART DIRECTOR
Carol Holsinger

PRODUCER
Sandi Bachom

DIRECTOR
Kevin Donovan

333
Couch
SFX: *Subtle sighs of contentment, paper crackling*
MAN: (deadpan) I think my money could be doing more.
SUPER: Centura. The Money Managers.

Pool
SFX: *Sipping of a drink*
WOMAN: I think my money could be doing more.
SUPER: Centura. The Money Managers.

Adirondak
SFX: *Yawning and nature sounds.*
WOMAN: I think my money could be doing more.
SUPER: Centura. The Money Managers.

TELEVISION

334
District 2
CLIENT
Tyson
AGENCY
Saatchi & Saatchi
Advertising
New York, NY
CREATIVE DIRECTORS
Craig Miller
Norm Weill
ART DIRECTOR
Melissa London
COPYWRITER
Gary Weintraub
PRODUCTION
Johns & Gorman Film

335
District 10
CLIENT
Hat Brands, Inc.
AGENCY
Jordan Associates
Advertising
Communications
Oklahoma City, OK
CREATIVE DIRECTOR
Jim Atha
ART DIRECTORS
Steve Colton
Dan Birlew
Thomas Batista
PRODUCER
Dan Martel
DIRECTOR
Richard Black
EDITORS
West End Post
FILM
Mesita Films
ACCOUNT EXECUTIVE
Rhonda Hooper

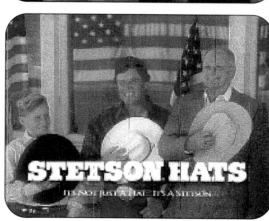

334

335
VO: It's not just a challenge... it's The challenge. It's not
just a kiss... it's The kiss. It's not just a song... it's The song.
It's not just a hat... it's a Stetson.

336

District 8

CLIENT
North Dakota
Tourism

AGENCY
G.L. Ness Agency,
Inc.
Fargo, ND

COPYWRITER
Guido

CINEMATOGRAPHER
David Savage

PRODUCTION
Dumb Luck
Productions
Snyder Films

POST PRODUCTION
Greg Mattern, HDMG

MUSIC
Hanson/Carvell

336

American Legacy Tour I

VO: It was a time when the west had not yet been won...and a place where America thinned and evaporated into England lands. When men harnessed the great Missouri to discover the destiny of the turbulent times at hand. And where you will travel along the American Legacy Tour...Where history rises like steam from the sacred land. And where men from the many nations met eye to eye for the first time and beheld their separate destinies. And from where you will return knowing for certain where the ghosts of America reside.

American Legacy Tour II

VO: It was a time of great wonder, at a place where America's western edge thinned and evaporated into an endless sea of prairie. Where the seeds of a new culture took root along the great rivers. And amidst the lives of those who came before. For here is where history rolls like thunder, and men from the many nations met eye to eye for the first time and beheld their separate destinies... And where you will travel backwards through time along North Dakota's America Legacy Tour.

Medora

If ever there was a town built solely on dreams, she was it. For to her they came, with dreams of a new life in the new West. Mostly, they were cowboys, dusty and gritty, men sandpapered by wind and rain...who some say still chase the mirage of golden cattle under an endless badlands sun and haunt the town of Medora. Who, on a dreamy summer night comes alive still...and sends her memories of the cowboys echoing from the stars.

337

Intro

RAY: I'm Ray Rally.
OKyourturnhurryup.
AL: And I'm Al Rally.
BOTH: We're the Rally Brothers/ers.
AL: We started Rally's 'cause I was tired of eating warmed-over fast food.
RAY: And I was tired of waiting for it.
AL: That's why Rally's burgers are made to order...hot, fresh
RAY: And fast. Fast is the key.
AL: No, Ray. Hot.
RAY: Quick.
AL: Good.
RAY: Well, of course it's good.
AL: Get a hot, fresh, delicious and fast Rallyburger, made to order for just 79 cents.
BOTH: Rally's.
AL: Twice as good.
RAY: Twice as Fast.
AL: How'd we do?
RAY: Fast.
AL: Good.

Big Buford

AL: We never knew anybody who loved cheeseburgers more than our Uncle Buford.
RAY: He ate 'em real fast.
AL: And when he was finished, he always wanted another one.
RAY: Right away. I remember one time...
AL: Well, Buford, this is your burger. It's got the second cheeseburger built in. Introducing the new Big Buford: Two all-beef patties covered in melted cheese, stacked high with your choice of fresh toppings. All for just $1.79.
AL: So c'mon in to Rally's.
RAY: Hurry.
AL: For the big taste of the new Big Buford.
BOTH: Rally's.
AL: Twice as Good.
RAY: Twice as Fast. Boy, Buford could really put 'em away, couldn't he? I remember one time Aunt Norma made a bunch of 'em...

Two Windows

AL: Al Rally here at Rally's, where we specialize in
RAY: Drive-thru—it's faster.
AL: Rally's is dedicated to the preparation of our hot, fresh, juicy and delicious burgers, fries and other great foods. We believe what the world needs is better fast food, prepared fresh, and delivered quickly.
RAY: Two drive-thrus—much faster.
AL: And if you really love hamburgers, but you didn't drive, walk.
RAY: Run, it's faster.
AL: Get the Rallyburger Combo with fries and regular drink for just $1.79.
BOTH: Rally's/s.
AL: Twice as Good.
RAY: Twice as Fast.

337
District 5
CLIENT
Rally's Hamburgers
AGENCY
Meldrum & Fewsmith
Cleveland, OH
CREATIVE DIRECTOR
Scott Crawford
ART DIRECTOR
Ted Kolosvary
COPYWRITER
Tom Millman
PRODUCER
Deanna Shenn

338
District 2
CLIENT
Painewebber
AGENCY
Saatchi & Saatchi
Advertising
New York, NY
CREATIVE DIRECTORS
Craig Miller
Norm Weill
ART DIRECTOR
Craig Miller
COPYWRITER
Norm Weill
PRODUCTION
Dektor Higgins
(No frames or scripts available)

339

District 15

CLIENT
California Sunkist
Pistachio

AGENCY
Chiat/Day Inc.
Advertising
Venice, CA

ART DIRECTOR
Jerry Gentile

COPYWRITER
Scott Vincent

PRODUCER
Michelle Burke

PRODUCTION
Johns & Gorman
Films

EVERYBODY KNOWS THE BEST NUTS COME FROM CALIFORNIA.

EVERYBODY KNOWS THE BEST NUTS COME FROM CALIFORNIA.

EVERYBODY KNOWS THE BEST NUTS COME FROM CALIFORNIA.

339

Sound Toner

SUPER: August Priest Sound Toner

INTERVIEWER: So what does sound toning do?

PRIEST: It opens you heart chakra, so you feel unconditional love just vibrating throughout all of you. Comfortably and easily. You can feel your guardian angel surrounding you. Creating balance and harmony.

SFX: *"Sound toning" noises*

SUPER: Everybody knows the best nuts come from California.

ANNCR VO: Sunkist California Pistachios. Now that's a nut.

Buddy

BUDDY: My angel name is Sanfernandinaki. People call me Buddy.

SFX: *Man chanting: ROAH...MAAH...AAAH...*

SFX: *Chime sound.*

SFX: *Heavy breathing sounds from Sanfernandinaki.*

SFX: *Man chanting: EEEHEE...*

BUDDY: We have spiritual parties at our house...about once every month. If you're at all interested we'll invite you...

SUPER: Everybody knows the best nuts come from California.

ANNCR VO: Sunkist California Pistachios. Now that's a nut.

Ping Pong Lady

SFX: *Bike Bell Rings*

MUSIC: From the song "Three Blind Mice"

SUPER: Everybody knows the best nuts come from California.

ANNCR VO: Sunkist California Pistachios. Now that's a nut.

340
District 4

CLIENT
Nokia Mobile Phones

AGENCY
Peak Barr Petralia
Biety, Inc.
Tampa, FL

CREATIVE DIRECTORS
Joe Petralia
Jim Barr

PRODUCER
Jim Barr

DIRECTOR
Arnie Lerner

340

Juggling

MICHAEL DAVIS: A bowling ball... a pineapple... a birthday cake... a Nokia cellular phone. One of these objects would make it easier for me to juggle my schedule.

ANNCR: He's a juggler...you're not... pick up a Nokia cellular phone... to help you juggle your schedule.

ANNCR: Nokia..largest European cellular phone manufacturer, now in America.

Baby Talk

MICHAEL DAVIS: Look what Daddy can juggle with his Nokia cellular phone... a rubber duck... and a teddy bear... a Nokia cellular phone, a rubber duck and a teddy bear...and... with my Nokia cellular phone I can juggle something even more amazing... my schedule.

ANNCR: One-touch dialing makes a Nokia cellular phone easy to use.

VOICE ON PHONE: Hello?

MD: Amazing.

ANNCR: Nokia...Cellular Phones

Ping Pong

MICHAEL DAVIS: Enter with me into the world of the unusual, where the commonplace is considered ordinary.

ANNCR: One Touch Dialing. With a NOKIA cellular phone, you can dial important numbers or emergency services with one push of one button.

SFX: Phone rings

WOMAN ON PHONE: Hello?

MICHAEL: Hello.

WOMAN ON PHONE: Michael!

MICHAEL: Amazing...and now the even more unusual: conference calling.

SUPER: NOKIA logo...Connecting People

ANNCR: NOKIA...largest European cellular phone manufacturer, now in America.

341

District 9

CLIENT
Anheuser-Busch/
Budweiser

AGENCY
DMB&B/St. Louis
St. Louis, MO

CREATIVE DIRECTORS
Ric Anello
Michael Hutchinson

ART DIRECTOR
Michael Smith

COPYWRITER
Dave Swaine

PRODUCER
Chan Hatcher

341

Frogs
SFX: Crickets, night sounds
Open on one frog who croaks the word
'BUD'
Cut to two frogs...
second frog croaks the word
'WEIS'
Now both frogs work together to say
'BUD...WEIS...'
Cut to third frog who now enters the
group and croaks the word
'ER'
Now all three work together to say
'BUD...WEIS...ER'
Over and over
Camera pulls back to reveal a neon sign reflecting in a pool
of water at night... continues to move up and reveal a New
Orleans Cajun style tavern with a large Budweiser neon
sign on top.

'94 Clydesdales
MUSIC: Rolling Stones song "WILD HORSES" performed
by the Sundays.
Super Bud Cassic Neon and "THIS BUD'S FOR YOU"

342
District 2

CLIENT
Apple Computers

AGENCY
BBDO New York
New York, NY

CREATIVE DIRECTORS
Chris Wall
Susan Westre

ART DIRECTOR
Gavin Milner

COPYWRITER
Maggie Powers

PRODUCER
Jackie Vidor

PRODUCTION
Pytka Productions

342

Mailbox

SFX: *Doorbell ringing*
MUSIC: Light, bubbly xylophone
DAD: This is our house
MOM: This is our Mac
DAD: This is our old mail box
MOM: This is our new mail box
DAD: This one is addressed to resident
MOM: This is a letter from Grandma
DAD: Occupant, occupant
SON: This is a letter to my friend in Pittsburgh
MOM: This is from Tom's office
DAUGHTER: I'm sending this to Grandma
DAD: You may have already won
MOM: This is from our daughter in college, she's on the internet
SON: This is my homework, I'm sending it in
MOM: Plane reservations, USA Today, banking, shopping
DAD: Look, a real letter, it's for the people next door.
SUPER: Performa The Family Macintosh

Learning

SFX: *Doorbell ringing*
MUSIC: Light, bubbly xylophone
DAD: This is our house
SON: This is my room
MOM: This is our kitchen
DAUGHTER: This is my homework
DAUGHTER: This is due tomorrow
SON: This is where I plug in my guitar
MOM: This is where you plug in the printer
DAD: This is a lawn mower I'm fixing
MOM: This is a proposal I'm faxing
DAD: Ties
MOM: Checks
DAD: Paints
MOM: Faxes
SON: This is my encyclopedia
DAD: Our taxes
SON: Astronauts, dinosaurs
DAD: Socks
SON: This is algebra, it's very hard
DAD: This is our Mac
DAUGHTER: It's easy
SUPER: Performa The Family Macintosh

Business at Home

SFX: *Doorbell ringing*
MUSIC: Light, bubbly xylophone
HUSBAND: This is where we live
WIFE: This is where we work
HUSBAND: The family room
WIFE: The marketing department
HUSBAND: The conference room table
WIFE: This is the finance department
HUSBAND: The executive wash room
WIFE: The mail room, administration, advertising, faxes, windows files
HUSBAND: Coffee?
WIFE: This is our Mac
WIFE: This is our whole company
SUPER: Performa The Family Macintosh
SFX: *Telephone ringing*
HUSBAND: Lawrence & Associates
SFX: *Shower water running*
HUSBAND: Uh, she's in a meeting.

343

District 4

CLIENT
The Florida Lottery

AGENCY
Earle Palmer Brown
St. Petersburg, FL

CREATIVE DIRECTOR
Ted Nelson

ART DIRECTOR
Taras Wayner

COPYWRITER
Ted Nelson

343

Dog House

MUSIC: Orchestral arrangement

ANNCR: The Lottery has a new scratch-off game with cash prizes big enough to buy a house like this... It's Lucky Dog! Each ticket could be worth up to $1,000! Lucky Dog, new from the Florida Lottery.

LOGO: Florida Lottery

The Wall

SFX: *Natural outdoor environment.*

NBR: (WHINY) That fence is 3 inches over on our property...

SFX: *DOG GROWL*

NBR: you're going to have to move it.

ANNCR: Ever feel like you just can't win? Play Florida Lottery's new Fantasy Five. Over 100 people a week win about $20,000... and with that many winners, it really does pay to be nice to people.

SFX: *Muffled sounds of party. Dog whines.*

344
District 4
CLIENT
Kash n' Karry
AGENCY
FKQ Advertising
Clearwater, FL
CREATIVE DIRECTION
The Creative Team
of FKQ

344
Fetch

JIM: HI, I'm Jim and this is Flash. He's a Kash n' Karry associate. Which means if you're having trouble finding any item, he'll take you right to it. or, if you're already in the checkout line... (ASIDE)...Pineapple...

SFX: *Zip, footsteps, zing.*

JIM: he'll even get it for you. Hmmm, uh, maple syrup.

SFX: *Zip, footsteps, zing.*

JIM: See, Flash just wants you to be happy. Hmm, watch this. Burpless cucumber.

SFX: *Zip, footsteps.*

JIM: Seedless! I think I got him stumped this time.

SFX: *Zing.*

JIM: Uh, what took you so long?

SUPER: LOGO

JIM: Kash n' Karry is working hard to keep you coming back. Identical twin?

Smart Lane

JIM: Hi, I'm Jim and this is Maria. And she's going to talk to us today about Kash n' Karry's Smart Lane checkout policy - It's another way Kash n' Karry just makes shopping a little easier for you. Maria, how does it work?

MARIA: Well, let's say we have a customer in line right over here. If three more customers show up, then we open another register up here, and so on.

JIM: Let me see if I got this, so three more customers show up, you know, they're shopping, and then you would open another register. Aha! But you left yourself open.

JIM: Kash n' Karry, we're working hard to keep you coming back. Ooh!

SUPER: LOGO

Jump

SFX: *Store ambiance.*

Jim: Hi. I'm Jim and this is Jo. But this is no ordinary Jo. No, no. This is a Jo who works at Kash n' Karry. Which means that she'll do anything to make your shopping experience just the very best it can be. In fact, with the new Kash n' Karry service commitment, when you say jump...

SFX: *Swoosh.*

JIM: See this is the kind of thing you'll see, not some mamby pamby little jump like at other stores. No sir, up in the air. Straight up like a rocket. You bet. Kash n' Karry is working hard to keep you coming back.

JIM: I can do that...

SUPER: LOGO

345
District 6

CLIENT
Indiana State Fair

AGENCY
MZD
Indianapolis, IN

CREATIVE DIRECTOR
Mike Soper

ART DIRECTOR
Scott Davis

COPYWRITER
Tim Abare

345

Watermelon Seed

SFX: *Gobbling noises*

SFX: *PHHHHLEEEOOP, BINK.*

ANNCR: Ready for seed spittin' at the State Fair? Now through Sunday, August 10-21st.

Chicken Man

SFX: *Guy mumbling statistics to the board*

E.G.: The fiduciary responsibility to the share holders...

E.G.: Buck Buck Buck Buckaaaaah.

ANNCR: Ready for the State Fair? It's comin'! Now through Sunday. August 10th through 21st.

Clothes Line

ANNCR: It's that time of year again.

ANNCR: And everybody's getting ready for the Indiana State Fair.

SFX: *ZIPPER*

ANNCR: Now through Sunday, August 10-21st.

346
District 10
CLIENT
Radio Shack
AGENCY
Lord, Dentsu &
Partners/Y&R
Fort Worth, TX
CREATIVE DIRECTOR
Mike Scardino
ART DIRECTOR
Steve St. Clair
COPYWRITER
Andrew Payton
DIRECTOR
Chuck Clemens

346

Instruction Manual

VO: The RF converter output of unit XLT-735B is pre-set to VHF channel 3 prior to shipment. The RF converter output of unit XLT-735B is pre-set to VHF channel 3 prior to shipment. The RF converter output of unit XLT-735B is pre-set to VHF channel 3 prior to shipment. Any questions?

ANNCR: Radio Shack has over 25,000 people with simple answers to complicated questions. Radio Shack. You've got questions. We've got answers.

Stereo

VO: Installation.

VO (Really fast): Jack and plugs of connecting cords are color coded as follows: red jacks and plugs for right channel of audio signals. White jacks and plugs for left channel of audio signals. Yellow jacks and plugs for video signals. To connect CD Player run white and red jacks from DAT and tape deck. This covers your basic hookup and except for AM/FM antenna front speakers rear speakers impedance selector AC power outlet auxiliary power and the remote commander you should be all set. Any questions?

ANNCR: Radio Shack has 6500 locations where you can find simple answers to all kinds of complicated questions. Radio Shack. You've got questions. We've got answers.

VCR Programming

VO: Programming.

VO (Really fast): To initiate on-screen programming four options will appear. First, clock. To set clock use Greenwich Mean Time. Set second minute hour AM PM day week month press time key. Second option daily program enter beginning and ending time of selected program enter channel. Third option weekly program same procedure applies. Fourth option program review to actually record refer to section K-9 pg. 67 paragraph 12 bottom left corner entitled: "It Even Records" Any questions.

ANNCR: For over 70 years Radio Shack has been finding simple answers to all kinds of complicated questions. Radio Shack. You've got questions. We've got answers.

347

District 2

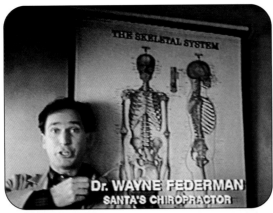

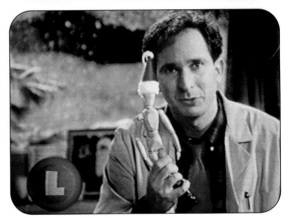

347

Santa's X-rays

TITLE: DR. WAYNE FEDERMAN, SANTA'S
CHIROPRACTOR

DR. FEDERMAN: This is a normal human spine. That's
the Santa spine.. He's gotta lift this bike onto the roof, into
the chimney, under the tree, without making any noise.
He's a master. Heavy gifts cause curvature. ...mmmm...94
pounds...16 pounds...12 pounds, but cumbersome. This year
ask for lightweight Holiday Scratch-Off tickets. Your
chances of winning are one in three. He's not Hercules.
He's just a man with a bad back.

Santa's Chiropractor

TITLE: DR. WAYNE FEDERMAN, SANTA'S
CHIROPRACTOR

DR. FEDERMAN: ...most people don't realize that the man
has to walk on a slanted roof. It's total re-alignment. ...So
the man lifts from his back and not his legs, How do we
expect him to get this down a chimney? ...I prescribed
physical therapy...he won't listen. Every year it's the same
thing... "People are counting on me, people need me." So,
ask for lightweight Holiday scratch-off tickets with a top
prize of $100,000. Do it for Nick.

348
District 14

CLIENT
The 3DO Company

AGENCY
Butler, Shine & Stern
Sausalito, CA

CREATIVE DIRECTORS
John Butler
Mike Shine

ART DIRECTOR
John Butler

COPYWRITER
Mike Shine

348

Date

DAD: (Harshly) And, what time will my daughter be home?
SUPER: Response 1
BOY 1: (Smiles nervously. He can't speak.)
VO: The passive type. Probably plays Nintendo.
DAD: (Harshly) And, what time will my daughter be home?
SUPER: Response 2
BOY 2: (Annoyed) Sometime between 10 and 2.
VO: The aggressive type. Probably plays Sega.
DAD: (Harshly) And, what time will my daughter be home?
SUPER: Response 3
BOY 3: You want her back?
VO: And the other type. Definitely plays 3DO, the most advanced home gaming system in the universe.
SUPER: 3DO. What are you playing with?

Boss

BOSS: You're working late tonight. (Spits at camera)
SFX: *SPLAT!*
SUPER: Response 1
EMPLOYEE 1: (wipes cigar chunk off forehead, opens briefcase.)
VO: The passive type. Probably plays Nintendo.
BOSS: (Bursts in) You're working late tonight. (Spits)
SFX: *SPLAT!*
SUPER: Response 2
EMPLOYEE 2: (Wipes cigar chunk off his nose) I can't, I got therapy!
VO: The aggressive type. Probably plays Sega.
BOSS: (Bursts in) You're working late tonight. (Spits)
SUPER: Response 3
EMPLOYEE 3: (Eating chinese food) Can we try that again with a knock?
VO: And the other type. Definitely plays 3DO, the most advanced home gaming system in the universe.
SUPER: 3DO. What are you playing with?
EMPLOYEE 3: Are you hitting on me?

Cop

COP: Do you have any idea how fast you were going?
SUPER: Response 1
DRIVER 1: (Sobbing, speechless)
VO: The passive type. Probably plays Nintendo.
COP: Do you have any idea how fast you were going?
SUPER: Response 2
DRIVER 2: (Annoyed). You're the guy with the radar.
VO: The aggressive type. Probably plays Sega.
COP: Do you have any idea how fast you were going?
SUPER: Response 3
DRIVER 3: I don't know. The little needle stops moving at a hundred.
VO: And the other type. Definitely plays 3DO, the most advanced home gaming system in the universe.
SUPER: 3DO. What are you playing with?

349

District 7

CLIENT
Charlie Rose

AGENCY
Lee Gipson
Jackson, MS

COPYWRITER
Lee Gipson

PRODUCER
Lee Gipson

PRODUCTION
Imageworks

DIRECTOR
John Stockwell

349

Two Charlies

MUSIC: Nostalgic Big Band

CHARLIE'S DAD VO: My son tells people it's named after
me. But they know better. The farmers got together and
named it after him. The Charlie Rose Agri-Expo Center.
Of course, technically speaking, I was Charlie Rose before
he was. But if they want to give him the credit, that's fine.
It really doesn't matter. Long as they vote for Charlie Rose.
Now that would definitely be him.

Beach

MUSIC: Nostalgic Big Band

CHARLIE'S DAD VO: Most people come here to relax.
But we never could get him to sit still. Charlie Rose
practically grew up on the beach. So when the sand down
here started washing away, well naturally some of the
mayors called Charlie. And of course, he rolled up his
sleeves and dug right in. Like I say, we've been coming here
since he was four years old. You can see it hasn't helped him
any.

350
District 10
CLIENT
Exxon
AGENCY
McCann-Erickson
Houston, TX
CREATIVE DIRECTORS
Brian Olesky
Mark Daspit
ART DIRECTOR
Mark Daspit
COPYWRITER
Brian Olesky

350

New Gasolines

DANIELLE GUEST: If I had one wish I would wish that the air would be clean air so everybody could be healthy.

ANNCR: For years, Exxon people have been working to help clear the air with a series of lower-emission gasolines.

KATIE PHILSON: Clean air looks like nothing, except sometimes it has rain in it.

ANNCR: Right now at Exxon, we're introducing reformulated gasolines to help reduce pollution in those cities with the most serious problems.

MATT GREGG: Well, clean air is important to us, and if we didn't have any we wouldn't have any plants to look at and cool trees to climb, and stuff.

ANNCR: At Exxon, we don't just design gasoline for what cars need. We also design it for what people need.

CHRISTINE RIGHETTI: If we don't take care of the air, our future generations are going to be very, very sad that we were so neglectful.

Mobile Bay

JEAN BURRELL: All things are connected, like the blood of a family...and that man did not build the web of life, he is merely a strand in it. But everything he does to the web, he does to himself.

ANNCR: It was here, in the fragile environment of Mobile Bay, Alabama, that Exxon came to develop one of America's largest reserves of clean-burning natural gas.

BUBBA: Really, a good healthy Bay is a good healthy economy, down here.

ANNCR: For the nearly 10 years they've been here, the people of Exxon have protected this environment.

BUBBA: Exxon made promises and commitments...and they've kept 'em.

ANNCR: At Exxon, we're helping our country meet its energy needs with fuels that burn cleaner than ever before.

JEAN: Mobile Bay is my home, and several hundred thousand other people's.

351

District 3

CLIENT
Biltmore Estate

AGENCY
Price/McNabb
Charlotte, NC

CREATIVE DIRECTOR
John Boone

ART DIRECTOR
John Boone

COPYWRITER
David Oakley

PRODUCER
Sarah Cherry

DIRECTOR
Amir Homed

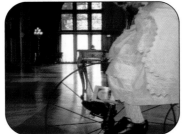  

351

Royalty Cards

ANNCR: Long before baseball cards were invented, George Vanderbilt collected Royalty Cards.

GEORGE'S VO: Honey, have you seen my King Louis XIV?

SFX: *The sound a trading card makes when it is put into the spokes of a tricycle.*

SUPER: The Royalty Cards.

ANNCR: See the Royalty Cards. Revealed for the first time in nearly a century. At Biltmore Estate.

Hair

ANNCR VO: In the late 1800's, George Vanderbilt returned from Europe with what he considered the purchase of a lifetime.

SFX: *FOOTSTEPS*

WIFE'S VO: You bought what? How much did you pay for that? Honestly George, all you do is spend, spend, spend...

SUPER: A lock of Lord Byron's hair.

ANNCR VO: See Lord Byron's hair. Revealed for the first time in nearly a century. At Biltmore Estate.

Monet

ANNCR VO: A century ago, George Vanderbilt acquired a rare painting by Claude Monet.

WIFE'S VO: George, did I tell you that Mother is coming to visit for the summer?

GEORGE'S VO: Same thing every year. There's not enough room in this house for the both of us...

GEORGE'S VO: ...she thinks she can move right in...

SUPER: The missing Monet.

ANNCR VO: The missing Monet. On display for the first time in nearly a century. At Biltmore Estate.

352
District 10
CLIENT
Royal Crown Cola
AGENCY
GSD&M Advertising
Austin, TX
CREATIVE DIRECTORS
Guy Bommarito
Bryan Jessee
ART DIRECTOR
Bryan Jessee
COPYWRITER
Peter Berta
PRODUCER
Kenny Grant
DIRECTOR
John Zurik
EDITOR
Paul Friedman

353
District 10
CLIENT
Arkansas
Department of Parks
AGENCY
Cranford Johnson
Robinson Woods
Little Rock, AR
CREATIVE DIRECTOR
Boyd Blackwood
ART DIRECTOR
Chuck Robertson
COPYWRITER
Tracy Munro
SCORE
Patterson Walz & Fox
PRODUCER
Debbie Wilson
PRODUCTION
Jones Productions
ACCOUNT EXECUTIVES
Rick Nall
Kelley Nichols
Shelby Woods

352

353

Refrigerator
SFX: *Sound of refrigerator door opening then closing*
SFX: *Muffled thumping and denting.*
VO: (Loud whisper) Shhhh! He's coming back!
VO: KICK. The new hardcore psycho nitro drink in a can.

Belch
SFX: *Can opening, FIZZZZZZZ.*
SFX: *Can opening followed by a very loud and long belch that is followed by a much smaller and shorter one.*
VO: KICK. The new hardcore psycho nitro drink in a can.

Straw Being Eaten
SFX: *Munch, munch, munch, belch.*
VO: KICK. The new hardcore psycho nitro drink in a can.

354

District 9

CLIENT
Southwestern Bell
Telephone

AGENCY
DMB&B/St. Louis
St. Louis, MO

CREATIVE DIRECTORS
Tom Gow
Greg Sullentrup

ART DIRECTORS
Greg Sullentrup
Kait Courland

COPYWRITER
Michael Dukes

PRODUCER
Mary McCarthy

354

Twelves/The Works

ANNCR VO: Okay, here's 12 rubber alligators. And 12 yo-yos. Just to dramatize Southwestern Bell's best offer ever: 12 useful phone services, now at one great price. We call this package The Works. 12 conveniences like Call Waiting, Call Return, even Caller ID. Best yet, you get our 12 most popular services for just 15 of these a month. And as you can clearly see, 12 is a lot. To order The Works at a full 45% discount, just dial 1-800-234-BELL. You could even ask...for operator 12. Heh heh. Southwestern Bell Telephone.

More Works

ANNCR VO: Okay, here's 10 rubber bats. And 10 cowboy hats. Just to dramatize Southwestern Bell's best offer ever: 10 useful phone services, now at one great price. We call this package The Works. 10 conveniences like, Call Return, Caller ID, and Call waiting for just $15.95 a month. To order The Works and save a full 40%, just dial 1-800-234-BELL. Hey...that's one plus ten numbers. Heh heh. Southwestern Bell Telephone. Hey, get The Works without Caller ID for even less.

Business Works

ANNCR VO: Okay, here's 12 bouncing bar codes. And 12 neon signs. Just to dramatize Southwestern Bell's best small business offer ever: 12 phone services, now at one great price. We call this package The Works. 12 conveniences like Call Waiting, Call Return, even Caller ID for just $17.95 a month.. To order The Works at a full 48% discount, just dial 1-800-234-BELL. Hey...ask for operator 12. Heh heh. Southwestern Bell Telephone.

DIRECT
MARKETING

355
District 7

CLIENT
Duck Head Apparel
Company

AGENCY
The Buntin Group
Nashville, TN

CREATIVE DIRECTOR
S.A. Habib

ART DIRECTOR
R.J. Lyons

COPYWRITERS
Tom Cocke
Karry Oliver

DESIGNER
Tonya Presley

ENGRAVER
GPI

PRINTER
Douglas Printing

PRODUCTION
Chris Carroll

355

356

District 9

CLIENT
James River
Corporation

AGENCY
Sayles Graphic
Design
Des Moines, IA

ART DIRECTOR
John Sayles

COPYWRITER
Wendy Lyons

PHOTOGRAPHER
Bill Nellans

ILLUSTRATOR
John Sayles

DESIGNER
John Sayles

PRINTERS
Columbia Printing
T-Shirt Graphics

DIRECT MARKETING

357
District 7

CLIENT
AmSouth Bank

AGENCY
SlaughterHanson
Advertising
Birmingham, AL

CREATIVE DIRECTOR
Terry Slaughter

ART DIRECTOR
Marion English

COPYWRITER
David Williams

PRINTER
American Printing

TYPOGRAPHY
Communication Arts

ACCOUNT EXECUTIVE
Ruth Bean

THE RELATIONSHIP TEAM

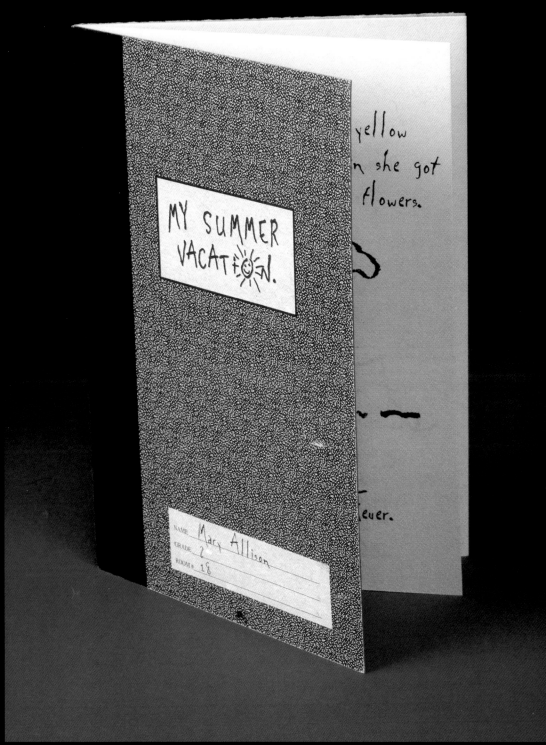

358
District 6
CLIENT
StatCare
AGENCY
Boyden & Youngblutt
Advertising and
Marketing
Fort Wayne, IN
ART DIRECTOR
Don Weaver
COPYWRITER
Don Weaver
ILLUSTRATOR
Don Weaver

359
District 10
CLIENT
Wilsonart
AGENCY
McKone & Company
Irving, TX
CREATIVE DIRECTOR
Steve Maxfield
ART DIRECTOR
Ric Delzell
COPYWRITER
John Gempel

360
District 7
CLIENT
Plain Clothes
AGENCY
SlaughterHanson
Advertising
Birmingham, AL
CREATIVE DIRECTOR
Terry Slaughter
ART DIRECTOR
Marion English
COPYWRITERS
Laura Holmes
Marion English
ILLUSTRATOR
Maya Metz
SEPARATOR
Techtron
PRINTER
American Printing
TYPOGRAPHY
Communication Arts
ACCOUNT EXECUTIVE
Terry Slaughter

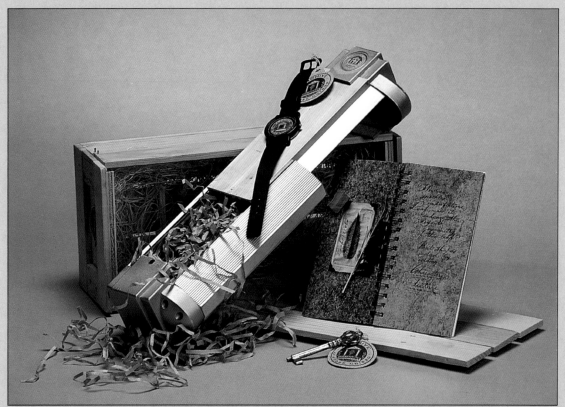

359

360

DIRECT MARKETING

Still Life

Action

Peter Caley Photography. An art director's best friend. 612-333-3090.

Still Life

Real Life

Peter Caley Photography. An art director's best friend. 612-333-3090.

Studio

Location

Peter Caley Photography. An art director's best friend. 612-333-3090.

361
District 3
CLIENT
Peter Caley
Photography
AGENCY
Price/McNabb
Charlotte, NC
ART DIRECTOR
Ed Schumacher
COPYWRITER
Jonathan Kaler
PHOTOGRAPHER
Peter Caley

362
District 9
CLIENT
Muller + Company
AGENCY
Muller + Company
Kansas City, MO
ART DIRECTORS
Jon Simonsen
Amy Dawson
DESIGNERS
Jon Simonsen
Amy Dawson
Angela Coleman

363
District 9
CLIENT
Doskocil Companies
AGENCY
Greteman Group
Wichita, KS
CREATIVE DIRECTOR
James Strange
ART DIRECTOR
James Strange
COPYWRITERS
Paul Hansen
Greg Menefee
DESIGNER
James Strange

364
District 4
CLIENT
Valencia Community
College
AGENCY
Gouchenour
Advertising
Orlando, FL
CREATIVE DIRECTOR
Chris Robb
ART DIRECTOR
Chris Robb
COPYWRITERS
Jeff Nicosia
Julio Lima
PRODUCTION
Craig Gouchenour

365
District 3
CLIENT
E/W Partners - Old
North State Club
AGENCY
Price/McNabb
Charlotte, NC
CREATIVE DIRECTOR
John Boone
ART DIRECTOR
Connie Hartman
COPYWRITER
Patrick McLean
DESIGNER
Connie Hartman
PRODUCTION
Pam Allen

362

363

365

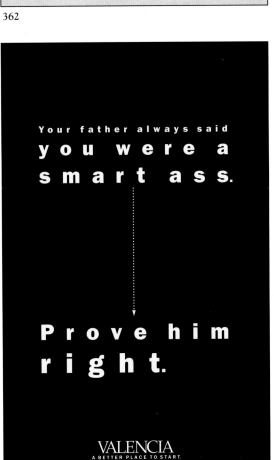

364

366
District 7
CLIENT
Tulane Hospital for
Children
AGENCY
Tulane University
Medical Center
Marketing
Department
New Orleans, LA

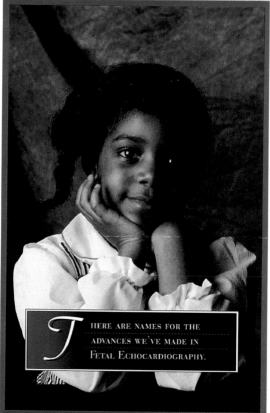

THERE ARE NAMES FOR THE ADVANCES WE'VE MADE IN FETAL ECHOCARDIOGRAPHY.

| Tonya Washington |

TONYA WAS DIAGNOSED WITH A SERIOUS HEART DEFECT BEFORE SHE WAS EVEN BORN. THROUGH FETAL ECHOCARDIOGRAPHY, TULANE'S PEDIATRIC CARDIOLOGY TEAM LEARNED THAT SHE HAD ONLY ONE PUMPING CHAMBER TO HER HEART AND A SEVERE CONDUCTION PROBLEM. AN ACCURATE PRENATAL DIAGNOSIS ENABLED US TO CARE FOR TONYA PROMPTLY AFTER BIRTH. A PACEMAKER WAS IMPLANTED, AND SHE BEGAN A CAREFULLY PLANNED SERIES OF HEART OPERATIONS. SHE IS NOW GROWING AND DEVELOPING NORMALLY. TONYA'S IS JUST ONE CASE WHERE ADVANCED DIAGNOSTIC AND SURGICAL TECHNIQUES ALLOWED US TO TREAT A CONDITION ONCE CONSIDERED 100 PERCENT FATAL. AND IT'S ONE MORE REASON TULANE HAS BECOME AN UNDISPUTED LEADER IN PEDIATRIC CARDIAC RESEARCH AND CARE.

Tulane Hospital
for Children
1415 Tulane Avenue · New Orleans, LA 70112
1-800-588-5300

DIRECT MARKETING

367
District 2

CLIENT
The Shooters

AGENCY
The Berry Company
Ambler, PA

CREATIVE DIRECTOR
David T. McCarty

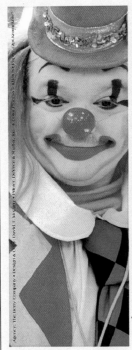

CLOWNS. WHAT ARE THEY ANYWAY? BADLY DRESSED BALD MEN WITH RED NOSES AND SHOES THAT DON'T FIT. HELL...THAT PRETTY MUCH DESCRIBES LAIRD'S UNCLE HANK BUT WE DON'T DRAG HIM OUT EVERY TIME SOMEONE POPS A TENT OR TURNS FOUR YEARS OLD. ACTUALLY THAT'S NOT TRUE — LAIRD INVITED HIM TO HIS SON'S BIRTHDAY PARTY LAST YEAR, BUT HANK SCARED THE KIDS AND ATE ALL THE CHEESE PUFFS. THE POINT BEING, HAVING A RED NOSE AND BIG SHOES DOESN'T MAKE YOU A CLOWN ANYMORE THAN OWNING A CAMERA MAKES YOU A PHOTOGRAPHER.

the SHOOTERS
PHOTOGRAPHY
PHILADELPHIA • NEW YORK • WASHINGTON
1.800.557.4668

THE OLD #2 PENCIL. THE MOST BASIC TOOL OF COMMUNICATION KNOWN TO MODERN MAN. THEY'RE CHEAP. NO MOVING PARTS. WON'T LEAK ON YOUR SHIRT. COMES WITH ITS OWN EDITING DEVICE AND WILL EVEN WRITE UPSIDE DOWN IN SPACE. JOE & LAIRD SHOT THIS PICTURE WHEN JOE'S CRAZY AUNT VERN WAS VISITING FROM TOLEDO. JOE SAYS #2 PENCILS REMIND HIM OF VERN AND HER GAUDY HATS. IT JUST GOES TO SHOW, BEING CHEAP, THIN AND HAVING A PINK RUBBER HAT DOESN'T MAKE YOU A PENCIL ANY MORE THAN OWNING A CAMERA MAKES YOU A PHOTOGRAPHER.

the SHOOTERS
PHOTOGRAPHY
PHILADELPHIA • NEW YORK • WASHINGTON
1.800.557.4668

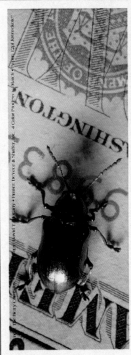

JOE & LAIRD WERE SHOOTING SOME DOLLAR BILLS WHEN THIS BEETLE LANDED ON THE LAYOUT. RATHER THAN DISTURB THE CAREFULLY LAID OUT SET, LAIRD TRIED TO SCARE THE BEETLE OFF WITH LITTLE SUCCESS. IT SEEMS THAT THE BEETLE, WHILE SITTING STILL AND BEING ROUGHLY THE SAME COLOR AS THE MONEY, FIGURED WE DIDN'T NOTICE IT. JOE'S DOG, ROO, FINALLY SOLVED THE PROBLEM BY SWIFTLY EATING HIM. IT JUST GOES TO SHOW, SITTING STILL AND BEING GREEN DOESN'T MAKE YOU A DOLLAR ANY MORE THAN OWNING A CAMERA MAKES YOU A PHOTOGRAPHER.

the SHOOTERS
PHOTOGRAPHY
PHILADELPHIA • NEW YORK • WASHINGTON
1.800.557.4668

WHILE ON ASSIGNMENT TO PHOTOGRAPH NEW JERSEY'S BEACHES, JOE & LAIRD DISGUISED THEMSELVES AS LIFEGUARDS IN AN ATTEMPT TO BE AS INCONSPICUOUS AS POSSIBLE. ABOUT THE ONLY ONES THEY WERE ABLE TO FOOL WERE A FEW SMALL CHILDREN AND THREE OLDER LADIES FROM NEWARK. JOE SWORE HE ONLY NARROWLY ESCAPED JAWS AND LAIRD ENDED UP WITH A 2ND DEGREE SUNBURN. IT JUST GOES TO SHOW, A WHISTLE AND RED SHORTS DOESN'T MAKE YOU A LIFEGUARD ANYMORE THAN OWNING A CAMERA MAKES YOU A PHOTOGRAPHER.

the SHOOTERS
PHOTOGRAPHY
PHILADELPHIA • NEW YORK • WASHINGTON
1.800.557.4668

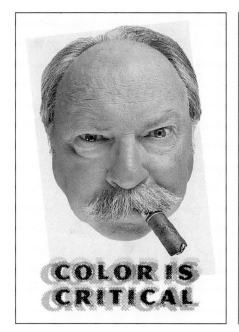

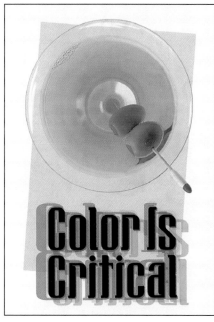

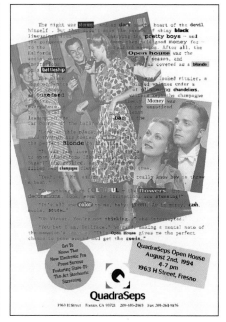

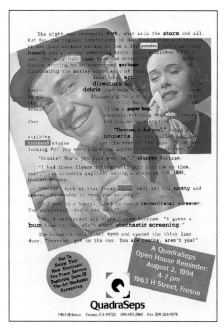

368
District 14

CLIENT
Quadra Seps

AGENCY
Shields Design
Fresno, CA

COPYWRITING
Mueller Creative

PHOTOGRAPHER
Keith Seaman

DESIGNER
Charles Shields

369
District 14
CLIENT
Dave Misconish
Illustrations
AGENCY
McCann-Erickson,
Inc.
San Francisco, CA

"It's simple. See, this old lady is vacuuming the rug with a cat in the foreground swishing his tail around like, "La-di-da-di-da, I'm Mr. Cat, La-di-da-di-da." The old lady moves the vacuum cleaner real near the cat when, Wham! The screen goes black. You hear the vacuum cleaner get close and the cat goes, "Ye-e-e-ow!" Voice-over says, "Maybe you need a longer-lasting bulb. Phillips, longer-lasting bulbs." It'll be great, don't you think?"

DAVE MISCONISH, STORY BOARD ARTIST

You got to see it to believe it. Phone and Fax:(404) 231-9711

"Okay, this guy is making a peanut butter sandwich. He's weird, so when the camera pans you see he's got like all this Alexander Hamilton stuff. On the walls. The desk. Everywhere. Then as he eats the peanut butter sandwich he's made, the phone rings and this DJ asks, "For $10,000 do you know who shot Alexander Hamilton in a duel?" Of course, he knows, but the peanut butter sandwich has him all gummed up. So he reaches for a milk carton. And it's empty. Hilarious, right? Cut to, "got milk?" Whaddaya think?"

DAVE MISCONISH, STORY BOARD ARTIST

You got to see it to believe it. Phone and Fax:(404) 231-9711

"Alright, there's this guy you never see on this cold day. We follow him as he trudges through the snow, focusing only on his feet. You know, his boots crunch through the snow until he gets in this car. Cut to a Volkswagon going down a snowy road to a snowplow. Then the guy gets out and gets into the big plow. "Ever wonder what the man who drives the snowplow drives to the snowplow?" Brilliant, huh? Can't you see it?"

DAVE MISCONISH, STORY BOARD ARTIST

You got to see it to believe it. Phone and Fax: (404) 231-9711

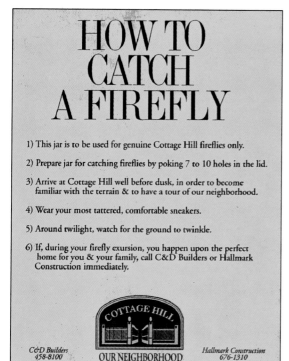

HOW TO CATCH A FIREFLY

1) This jar is to be used for genuine Cottage Hill fireflies only.

2) Prepare jar for catching fireflies by poking 7 to 10 holes in the lid.

3) Arrive at Cottage Hill well before dusk, in order to become familiar with the terrain & to have a tour of our neighborhood.

4) Wear your most tattered, comfortable sneakers.

5) Around twilight, watch for the ground to twinkle.

6) If, during your firefly exursion, you happen upon the perfect home for you & your family, call C&D Builders or Hallmark Construction immediately.

COTTAGE HILL.
OUR NEIGHBORHOOD

C&D Builders
458-8100

Hallmark Construction
676-1310

370

370
District 3

CLIENT
C-D Builders

AGENCY
Kimberley Westbury
Graphic Design
Simpsonville, SC

ART DIRECTOR
Kimberley Westbury

COPYWRITER
James Gibbons

ILLUSTRATOR
Bruce Ink

DESIGNER
Kimberley Westbury

371
District 10

CLIENT
WilTel

AGENCY
WilTel
Tulsa, OK

ART DIRECTOR
Harold Tackett

COPYWRITER
Matt O'Meilia

ILLUSTRATORS
Tom Curry
Ken Westphal
Gil Adams
Tim Jessell

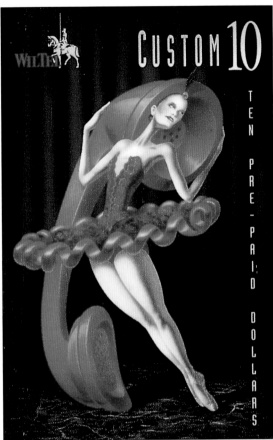
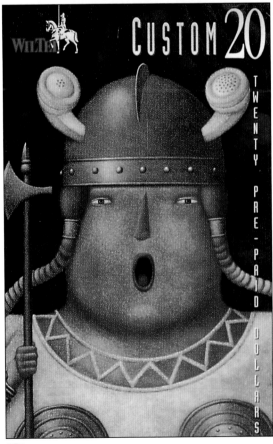
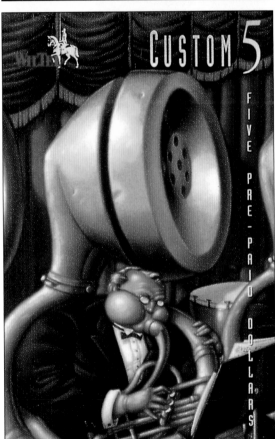

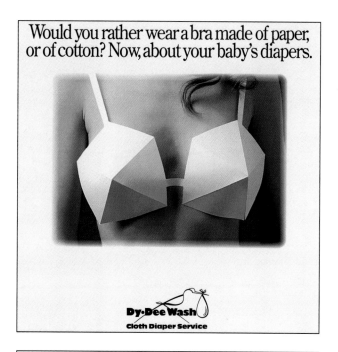

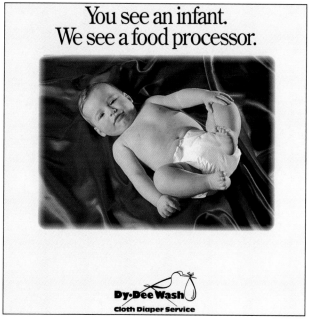

372
District 8

CLIENT
Dy-Dee Wash Diaper
Service

AGENCY
Meyer & Wallis, Inc.
Milwaukee, WI

CREATIVE DIRECTOR
Tim Wallis

ART DIRECTOR
Jim Brooks

COPYWRITERS
George Brumis
Tim Wallis

PHOTOGRAPHY
Bercker, Brice and
Davenport

PRODUCER
Julie Miller

373
District 8
CLIENT
Image Studios
AGENCY
Grey Sunder
Prescher
Cedarburg, WI
ART DIRECTOR
Blaine Huber
COPYWRITER
Blaine Huber
PHOTOGRAPHY
Image Studios
DESIGNER
Susan Griffiths

374
District 7
CLIENT
International Papers,
Hammermill Division
AGENCY
X Design, Inc.
Baton Rouge, LA
CREATIVE DIRECTOR
Martin Flanagan
ART DIRECTOR
Martin Flanagan
COPYWRITER
Martin Flanagan
DESIGNER
David Worrell
PRINTER
McCarthy Press
PRE-PRESS
Image 4

375
District 3
CLIENT
Weavexx
Corporation
AGENCY
Ralph Johnson
Associates
Raleigh, NC
CREATIVE DIRECTOR
Stan Beacham
ART DIRECTOR
Stan Beacham
COPYWRITER
Jan Karon
ILLUSTRATOR
Mark Pace
DESIGNER
Stan Beacham

376
District 5
CLIENT
Procter & Gamble
Company
AGENCY
Wolf Blumberg Krody
Cincinnati, OH
CREATIVE DIRECTOR
Vern Hughes
ART DIRECTOR
Diana Westendorf
COPYWRITER
Debbie Davidson
PHOTOGRAPHER
Jason Hathcock
ACCOUNT EXECUTIVE
Michelle Weech

373

374

375

376

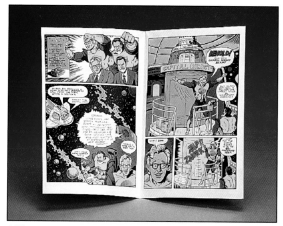

377

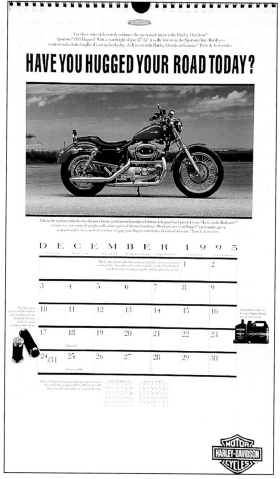

379

378

380

377
District 8
CLIENT
Capital City
Distribution
AGENCY
The Hiebing Group
Madison, WI
CREATIVE DIRECTORS
Barry Callen
Dick Kallstrom
ART DIRECTORS
Dick Kallstom
Tom Lowes
ARTIST
Mark Zingarlli

378
District 3
CLIENT
Redbone Alley
Restaurant
AGENCY
Gil Shuler Graphic
Design
Florence, SC
ILLUSTRATOR
Gil Shuler
DESIGNER
Steve Lepre

379
District 8
CLIENT
Harley-Davidson, Inc.
AGENCY
Jacobson Rost
Sheboygan, WI
CREATIVE DIRECTOR
Reed Allen
ART DIRECTORS
Paul Zwief
Frank Melf
COPYWRITER
Dan Ames
PHOTOGRAPHERS
Clint Clemens
Andrew Rosentah
SEPARATOR
ProGraphics
PRINTER
H-M Graphics
KEYLINE
Laura Fewerer
ACCOUNT EXECUTIVE
Peter Curran

380
District 3
CLIENT
Plain Clothes
AGENCY
SlaughterHanson
Birmingham, AL
CREATIVE DIRECTOR
Terry Slaughter
ART DIRECTOR
Marion English
COPYWRITERS
Laura Holmes
Marion English
PHOTOGRAPHER
Liz Von Hoene
SEPARATOR
Techtron
PRINTER
American Printing
TYPOGRAPHY
Communication Arts
ACCOUNT EXECUTIVE
Terry Slaughter

381

District 14

CLIENT
Norwegian Cruise
Line

AGENCY
Goodby, Silverstein
& Partners
San Francisco, CA

CREATIVE DIRECTORS
Paul Curtin
Rob Price

ART DIRECTORS
Paul Curtin
Damon Duree

COPYWRITER
Rob Price

PHOTOGRAPHERS
Jim Erickson
Herb Ritts
Devi Sandord
Pete Seaward

DESIGNER
Damon Duree

PRODUCER
Jim King

ACCOUNT EXECUTIVES
Marty Wenzell
Timothy Ellis

382

District 13

CLIENT
Princeville

AGENCY
Starr Seigle McCombs
Honolulu, HI

ART DIRECTOR
Charles Valoroso

DESIGNER
Charles Valoroso

383

District 4

CLIENT
Woodstock Inn and
Resort

AGENCY
Robinson, Yesawich
& Pepperdine
Orlando , FL

CREATIVE DIRECTOR
Michael Moynihan

ART DIRECTOR
Jeff Dahlberg

COPYWRITER
Ed Cobb

ILLUSTRATOR
Christian Milch

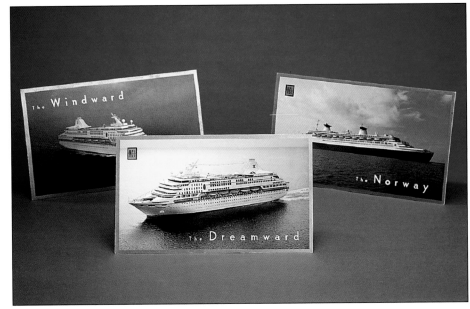

381

382

383

384

385

386

384
District 4
CLIENT
Interior Design
Services
AGENCY
Winner Keonig &
Associates
Tampa, FL
CREATIVE DIRECTOR
Joni Spencer
COPYWRITER
Joni Spencer
PHOTOGRAPHER
Gary Resnick
DESIGNER
Julie Daris
PRODUCTION
April Cummings

385
District 9
CLIENT
Inacom
AGENCY
Bozell Worldwide
Omaha, NE
CREATIVE DIRECTORS
Ellen Moran
David Moore
ART DIRECTOR
Bill Ervin
COPYWRITER
Jeanette Bendtsen
ACCOUNT EXECUTIVE
Olivia Poggenpohl

386
District 3
CLIENT
MTV Networks
AGENCY
Bazil-Victory
Advertising
Greenville, SC
CREATIVE DIRECTOR
Mark Bazil
ART DIRECTOR
Richard Salais
PRESIDENT
Patrick Victory

DIRECT MARKETING

387
District 3
CLIENT
Shenandoah Life
Insurance Company
AGENCY
The Packett Group
Roanoke, VA
CREATIVE DIRECTOR
Sandy Murray
ART DIRECTOR
Shawn Murray
COPYWRITERS
Robin Chalkley
Randy Walker
PHOTOGRAPHER
Greg Vaughn

388
District 4
CLIENT
Escambia County
Youth Orchestra
AGENCY
Sacred Heart
Hospital
Pensacola, FL
COPYWRITER
Becky Clark
DESIGNER
Becky Clark

389
District 10
CLIENT
Austin Angler
AGENCY
TateAustin
Austin, TX
CREATIVE DIRECTOR
Greg Barton
ART DIRECTOR
Greg Barton
COPYWRITER
Greg Barton
PHOTOGRAPHY
Cooke
Photographics
DIGITAL IMAGING
David Claunch
ACCOUNT EXECUTIVE
Laura Scott

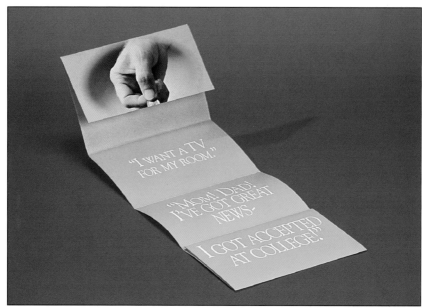

387

388

389

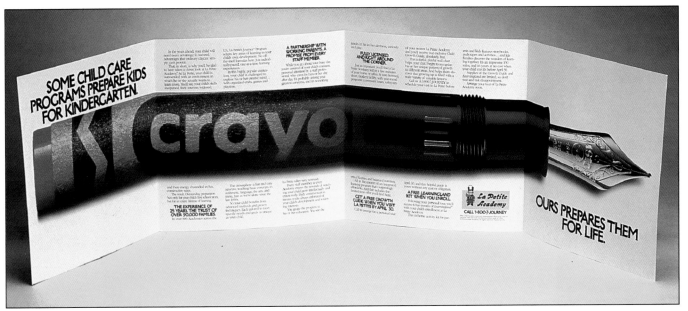

390

391

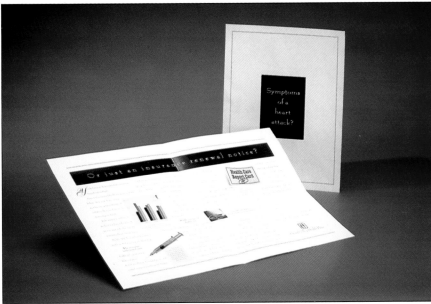

392

390
District 9
CLIENT
La Petite Academy
AGENCY
Valentine Radford
Kansas City, MO
CREATIVE DIRECTOR
Mark Weninger
ART DIRECTOR
Scott Kane
COPYWRITER
Mark Weninger
PHOTOGRAPHER
Darryll Bernstein

391
District 9
CLIENT
Cessna Aircraft
Company
AGENCY
Sullivan Higdon
& Sink
Wichita, KS
CREATIVE DIRECTOR
Joe Norris
ART DIRECTOR
James Kandt
COPYWRITERS
Joe Norris
Greg Hobson
PRODUCTION
Rod Bolay

392
District 6
CLIENT
Grand Valley Health
Plan
AGENCY
Burgler Advertising
Grand Rapids, MI
ART DIRECTORS
Art Webb
Carol Wagen
COPYWRITER
Judy Bean
PHOTOGRAPHER
Jim Powell

393
District 14
CLIENT
British Steel
AGENCY
Turner Duckworth
San Francisco, CA
DESIGNERS
David Turner
Bruce Duckworth
Janice Davidson

394
District 10
CLIENT
Harold's
AGENCY
Harold's
Norman, OK
CREATIVE DIRECTION
Team Harold's
PHOTOGRAPHER
S. Williams

395
District 6
CLIENT
Illinois Preservation
Society
AGENCY
Squires Advertising
Springfield, IL
DESIGN
Kevin Booton
ACCOUNT EXECUTIVE
Stan Squires

393

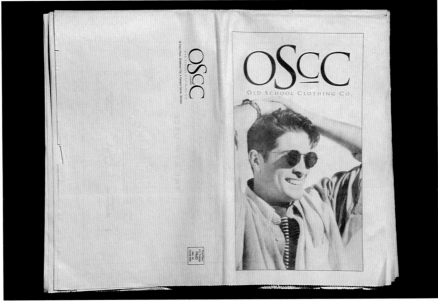

394

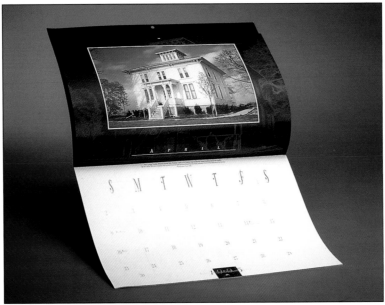

395

TRANSIT

NEW YORK
LOTTO Hey, you never know.

396

396
District 2

CLIENT
New York State
Lottery

AGENCY
DDB Needham
Worldwide
New York, NY

CREATIVE DIRECTORS
Jack Mariucci
Bob Mackall

ART DIRECTORS
Lara Gilmore
Steve Miller

COPYWRITER
Paul Spencer

PHOTOGRAPHER
Howard Berman

RETOUCHING
Side 1 at Horan
Engraving

ABSOLUT BROOKLYN.

399

400

401

399
District 3

CLIENT
Mint Museum of Art

AGENCY
Lapham/Miller
Associates
Charlotte, NC

DESIGNERS
Jeff Sutthott
Ralph Lapham

400
District 5

CLIENT
Jeff Wyler Dealer
Group

AGENCY
Jeff Wyler Dealer
Group Ad Design
Cincinnati, OH

CREATIVE DIRECTION
Jeff Wyler Dealer
Group

401
District 5

CLIENT
Louisville Zoo

AGENCY
Doe-Anderson
Advertising Agency
Louisville, KY

CREATIVE DIRECTOR
Gary Sloboda

ART DIRECTOR
Kevin Lippy

COPYWRITER
Rankin Mapother

402
District 2

CLIENT
Big Key Self Storage

AGENCY
J. Walter Thompson-
New York
New York, NY

CREATIVE DIRECTORS
Michael Hart
Richard Dilallo

ART DIRECTOR
James Offenhartz

COPYWRITER
Richard Yelland

403
District 4

CLIENT
Downtown
Development Board

AGENCY
Lynx Creative Service
Orlando, FL

CREATIVE DIRECTOR
Deborah Cooper

DESIGNER
Raul Balda

PAINTER
Doug Bloodworth

402

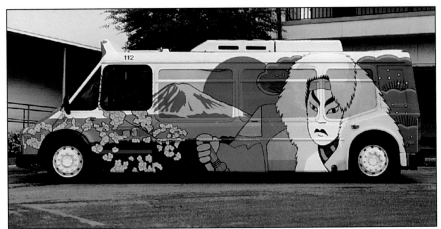

403

MULTIMEDIA
CAMPAIGN

404

District 2

CLIENT
House of Seagrams

AGENCY
TBWA
New York, NY

CREATIVE DIRECTORS
Arnie Arlow
Peter Lubalin

ART DIRECTORS
Maria Kostyk-Petro
Alix Botwin
Lisa Kay

COPYWRITERS
Lisa Lipkin
Alix Botwin

PHOTOGRAPHER
Steve Bronstein

District 7

CLIENT
Community Coffee

AGENCY
X Design
Baton Rouge, LA

CREATIVE DIRECTION
X Design

PHOTOGRAPHER
David Humphreys

ILLUSTRATOR
Karen Evans

PRINTER
Moran/Fres Company

PREPRESS
Image 4

406
District 9

CLIENT
Bum Steer

AGENCY
Bailey Lauerman
& Associates
Lincoln, NE

CREATIVE DIRECTOR
Rich Bailey

ART DIRECTOR
Carter Weitz

COPYWRITER
Laura Crawford

PRODUCER
Laura Crawford

ACCOUNT EXECUTIVE
Dan Levy

406

RADIO SCRIPT
Green Peace
SFX: *(Typewriter tune)*
COW: Dear Green Peace, I've got a little problem here. It's called Bum Steer. A great steak house. There lies the problem here. I'm a cow. Anyway, heard you saved a few whales. Well how bout us cows? Don't we count? It's not like you need to charter a boat. Just get on some bikes and start swervin' like maniacs in front of people headed for the Bum Steer. Anyway, the more I worry, the more I eat, which means time's running out. Signed, Cow.
ANNCR: The Bum Steer. Great steaks at sixty-fourth and O.
COW: Bummer.

RADIO SCRIPT
Veggie Club
MUSIC: *(Typewriter tune)*
COW *(Reading out loud as he's typing)*: Dear Vegetarians Club of America, You don't know me, but we have a lot in common. You like vegetables. I like vegetables. You don't eat meat. I don't eat meat. But here's where we differ. You wouldn't be caught dead in the Bum Steer steak house, and I would. I'm a cow. So please, go to the Bum Steer with your sprout-eating friends and order some of their non beef-related items. Thanks...Your veggie pal, Cow.
ANNCR: The Bum Steer. Great steaks at sixty-four and O.
COW: Bummer.

RADIO SCRIPT
Dear Mr. Prez
SFX: *(Typewriter tune)*
COW *(Reading out loud as he's typing)*: Dear Mr. President, Heard you're a Razorback fan. You know, "Go hogs and all that." Well, how bout us cows? How bout supporting us? You see, we've got this restaurant called the Bum Steer giving away free steak dinners for birthdays. Talk about a losing season for cows. Anyway, I could use your help. Not that I have anything against folks having a happy birthday, but this deal means happy trails for you know who. Signed...Cow.
ANNCR: The Bum Steer. Great steaks at sixty-fourth and O.
COW: Bummer.

407
District 5
CLIENT
Ohio Lottery
Commission
AGENCY
Marcus Advertising
Beachwood, OH
ART DIRECTORS
Brian Roach
Joel Karabinus
COPYWRITERS
Jim Sollisch
Mike Hudock

407

408

District 8

CLIENT
Sioux Valey Hospital

AGENCY
Lawrence & Schiller
Sioux Falls, SD

CREATIVE DIRECTION
Paul Schiller
Michelle Stotz
Scott Ostman
Mark Hansen
Mark Glissendorf
Jeff Zeuger
Darwin Heikes
Soug Lee
Rod Bergeson
Kyle Ruhland
Mary Lampy
Cindy Morrison

409

District 5

CLIENT
Great Financial Bank

AGENCY
The Buntin Group
Nashville, TN

CREATIVE DIRECTOR
Steve Fechtor

ART DIRECTOR
Bob Jensen

PRODUCER
Anne V. Birke

Sioux Valley Hospital Trauma Center. When time is limited, it's nice to know your hospital isn't.

You can never be ready for an emergency. But we are. It's all part of being one of America's Top 100 Hospitals.

We're ready with dedicated emergency physicians, critical care nurses and more trauma surgeons than any hospital in the region. All activated from the scene so they can begin caring for you even before you arrive.

We're ready with an experienced air transport team, recognized as South Dakota's only nationally accredited flight program.

And just as important as our medical attention is the personal attention given to families during this time of healing.

All the experience of the area's leading trauma center stands ready for you, around the clock. Because when time is limited, it's nice to know your hospital isn't.

SIOUX VALLEY HOSPITAL TRAUMA CENTER

408

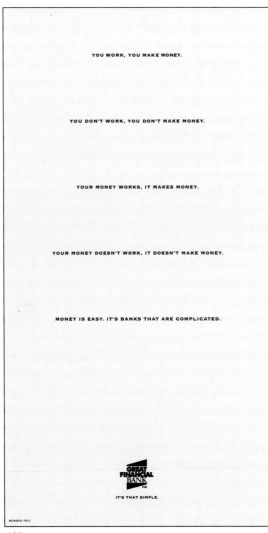

YOU WORK, YOU MAKE MONEY.

YOU DON'T WORK, YOU DON'T MAKE MONEY.

YOUR MONEY WORKS, IT MAKES MONEY.

YOUR MONEY DOESN'T WORK, IT DOESN'T MAKE MONEY.

MONEY IS EASY. IT'S BANKS THAT ARE COMPLICATED.

GREAT FINANCIAL BANK

IT'S THAT SIMPLE.

MEMBER FDIC

409

MONEY IS EASY.
IT'S BANKS THAT ARE COMPLICATED.

GUY: You know... I've been thinkin'... There's nothin' complicated about money. You work. You make money. You don't work, you don't make money. Your money works, it makes money. Your money doesn't work, it doesn't make money. Hey... Money is easy.
SUPER: Money is easy. It's banks that are complicated.
GUY: And, of course, because your money is workin' for you, you want to find it a very good job... in a very good bank.
SUPER: Our 6-month CD at 4.26%.
GREAT FINANCIAL BANK. It's that simple.

Photo courtesy of First Hawaiian Bank/Myers Corporation.

410

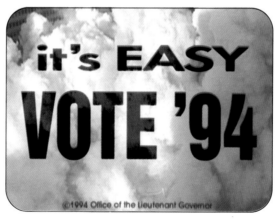

410
District 13
CLIENT
Office of the
Lieutenant Governor
AGENCY
Peck Sims Mueller
Honolulu, HI
CREATIVE DIRECTORS
Stan Moy
Jim Horiuchi
ART DIRECTOR
Vickie Kozuki
COPYWRITER
Anne McColl
PRODUCER
Natalie Wingert

SFX: *Blasts of TNT. Falling of building.*
VO: Hey, your old polling place might not be there this year. So refer to your Voter Registration Notice or call.
SUPER: Voter Hotline Oahu: 453-VOTE. Neighbor Islands 1-800-422-VOTE.
SFX: *Cheering of the crowd.*
SUPER: It's easy. Vote '94© 1994, Office of the Lieutenant Governor.

411
District 7

CLIENT
Columbia/HCA
Audubon

AGENCY
The Buntin Group
Nashville, TN

CREATIVE DIRECTOR
Steve Fechtor

ART DIRECTOR
Bob Jensen

COPYWRITER
Kerry Oliver

PRODUCER
Anne V. Birke

411

MAN: Every breath was very painful... I couldn't breath.
SUPER: It wasn't a heart attack
SUPER: blood clot in lung
MAN: Just like a weight was down on my chest... Just a weight pushing in.
SUPER: It wasn't a heart attack
SUPER: rupturing aneurysm
WOMAN: Had these terrible pains going down my arm.
SUPER: It was a heart attack
SUPER: 3 out of 4 times it's not a heart attack
SUPER: 4 out of 4 times we can help
MAN: I thought I was having a heart attack.
SUPER: Don't assume it's a heart attack
WOMAN: It scared me.
SUPER: Don't assume it's not. Audubon Chest Pain Center at Audubon Regional Medical Center.

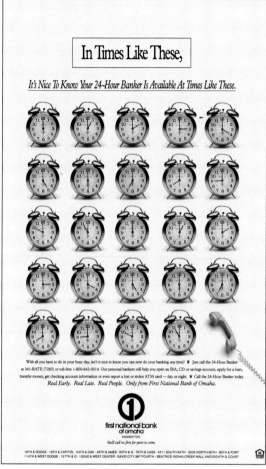

412

CLIENT
First National Bank

AGENCY
Bozell Worldwide
Omaha, NE

CREATIVE DIRECTOR
Ellen Moran

ART DIRECTOR
Chris Buhrman

COPYWRITER
Catherine Findley

PRODUCER
Nan Pike

PRODUCTION
Great Plains

MUSIC
Steve Horner

PHOTOGRAPHER
Mike Kleveeter

ANNCR: In times like these...
SFX: *Busy life noises*
ANNCR: It's nice to know your personal banker is available at times like these...
SFX: *Crickets chirping*
CAM CARD: The 24-Hour Banker. Real Early. Real Late. Real People. Only from First National Bank of Omaha.

413

District 9

CLIENT
Nike Ozarks Open

AGENCY
Brainstorm Creative
Service
Springfield, MO

CREATIVE DIRECTION
Steve Witt
Joe Totten
Korey Ireland
Steve Doddleston
Keith Stafford

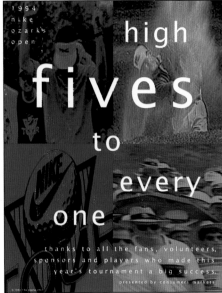

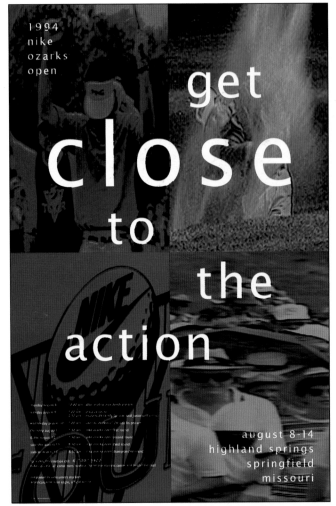

413

AT THIS RATE YOU CAN BRING SOMEONE YOU PASSIONATELY AND UNCONDITIONALLY LOVE. YOU CAN EVEN BRING SOMEONE YOU JUST KINDA-SORTA LIKE.

$109

You said you couldn't live without them. So why vacation without them? Particularly when there's a place as romantic as this one. The Grand Hotel. Where a staff, well versed in the matters of love, stands by to satisfy your whims and freshen your mint juleps. Call 800-544-9933 and ask about our 550-acre spread. We'll tell you everything you need to know. Except, of course, who to bring.

MARRIOTT'S
Grand Hotel
A BAYSIDE GOLF RESORT
Marriott Resorts Mobil★★★★ AAA◇◇◇◇

SCENIC HIGHWAY 98 • POINT CLEAR, ALABAMA 36564 • 205•928•9201
*FROM $109 PER NIGHT, PER ROOM. SUN-THURS ONLY. ASK ABOUT OUR WEEKEND RATES. INCLUDES BREAKFAST FOR TWO. AVAILABILITY AT THIS PRICE IS LIMITED. 3/20/94-10/27/94.

414
District 4
CLIENT
Marriott's Grand
AGENCY
The Zimmerman Agency
Tallahassee, FL
CREATIVE DIRECTOR
Daniel Russ
ART DIRECTOR
Rob Courtenay
COPYWRITER
Diane Dubose

SISSIES PLAY CROQUET.

$97.50*

The intent of this ad is not to entirely take away from our neatly manicured croquet lawn or its fans. But rather it's designed to illustrate the challenge of our 36 holes of championship golf. Call 800-544-9933 for the nitty-gritty. And if when you call you also happen to ask about the croquet, we'll never tell.

MARRIOTT'S
Grand Hotel
A BAYSIDE GOLF RESORT
Marriott Resorts Mobil★★★★ AAA◇◇◇◇

SCENIC HIGHWAY 98 • POINT CLEAR, ALABAMA 36564 • 205•928•9201
*$97.50 PER PERSON, PER NIGHT, DOUBLE OCCUPANCY. INCLUDES BREAKFAST BUFFET, UNLIMITED GREEN FEES AND CART RENTAL. AVAILABILITY AT THIS PRICE IS LIMITED. VALID 10/30/94 - 3/18/95.

WHALE-BONE CORSETS. BUSTLES. HOOP SKIRTS. IT'S NO WONDER WE DIDN'T OFFER A ROMANTIC PACKAGE IN 1847.

$89

Finding romance in the 1800s was about as easy as getting dressed. Today it's much simpler. You can slip into something comfortable and enjoy a comfortably priced romantic package. Call 800-544-9933 for reservations or information. It'll be the most fun you have with your basic black Donna Karan on.

MARRIOTT'S
Grand Hotel
A BAYSIDE GOLF RESORT
Marriott Resorts Mobil★★★★ AAA◇◇◇◇

SCENIC HIGHWAY 98 • POINT CLEAR, ALABAMA 36564 • 205•928•9201
*FROM $89 PER NIGHT, PER ROOM. SUN-THURS. ONLY. ASK ABOUT OUR WEEKEND RATES. INCLUDES BREAKFAST FOR TWO. AVAILABILITY AT THIS PRICE IS LIMITED. 10/28/94-3/16/95. CONTACT YOUR TRAVEL PROFESSIONAL.

415

CLIENT
Enzian
AGENCY
Gouchenour
Advertising
Orlando, FL
CREATIVE DIRECTOR
Chris Robb
ART DIRECTOR
Chris Robb
COPYWRITER
Mark Ronquillo
PRODUCTION
Craig Gouchenour

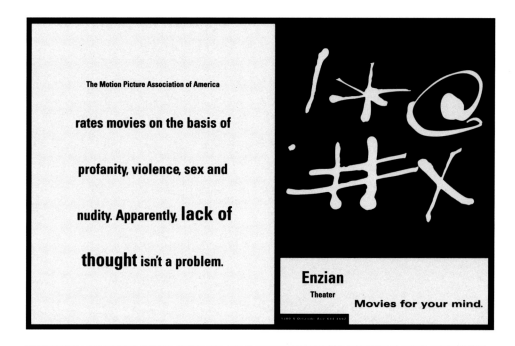

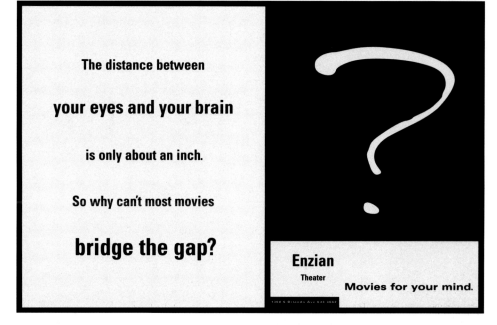

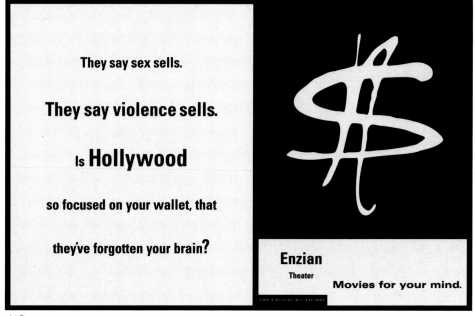

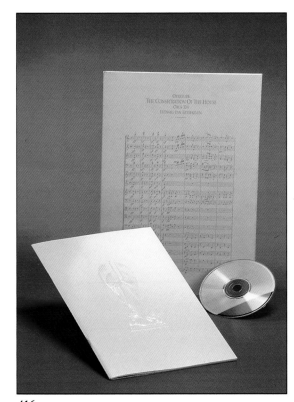

416

416
District 10
CLIENT
Performing Arts
Fort Worth
AGENCY
Witherspoon &
Associates
Fort Worth, TX
CREATIVE DIRECTOR
Debra Morrow
ART DIRECTOR
Randy Padorr-Black
COPYWRITERS
Debra Morrow
Preston Figley
ILLUSTRATOR
Phil Boatwright
SEPARATOR
RS Graphic Services
PRINTER
Motheral/Process
Engraving
PRODUCER
Debra Morrow
PRODUCTION
Aries Producion
TRAFFIC
Laura Pipkin
ACCOUNT EXECUTIVE
Susan Watt

417
District 8
CLIENT
Web Way
AGENCY
Hatling &
Thomas Ltd
St. Cloud, MN
ART DIRECTOR
Randy Thomas
PHOTOGRAPHER
John Ratzloff
ACCOUNT EXECUTIVE
William Hatling

418
District 8
CLIENT
Caradco
AGENCY
Lindsay, Stone &
Briggs Advertising
Madison, WI
CREATIVE DIRECTION
Lindsay, Stone &
Briggs

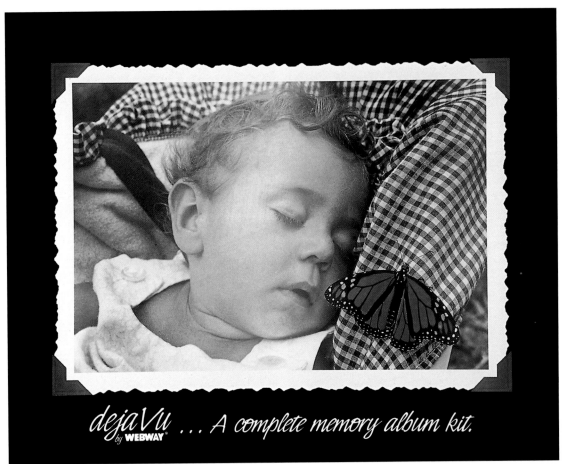

417

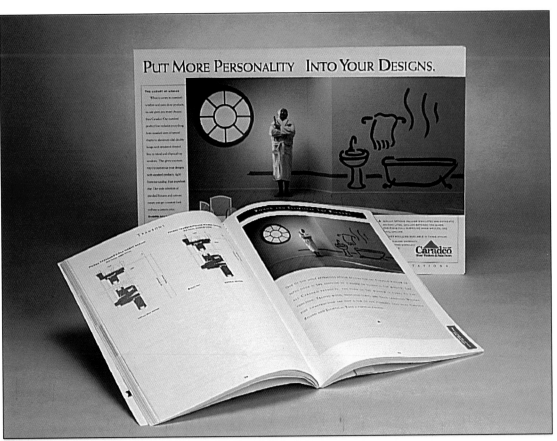

418

THE ORIGINAL SIX MILLION DOLLAR MAN.

At the tender age of 26, George Vanderbilt made six million dollars the old-fashioned way. He inherited it.

Unlike other wealthy men of his time, George had no interest in playing golf or watching the stock market.

He was an intellectual. He spoke eight languages. And was an avid student of the arts and architecture.

So George didn't just sit on his fortune. He put his money where his mind was. He built Biltmore House. A stately 255-room French chateau nestled in the heart of the Blue Ridge Mountains. To this day, it is the largest private residence in America.

Just recently there's been an addition to this palatial home. Hidden away for nearly a century, some of George's most prized and valued possessions are being revealed for the first time.

A rare painting, "Roches a Belle Isle" by Monet. Five etchings by Whistler. Historical autographs of Lafayette, Napoleon and Queen Elizabeth I. A priceless silver collection. And a lock of Lord Byron's hair (obviously an impulse purchase).

Today six million won't buy you a decent first baseman. To see how far it used to go, don't miss "George Vanderbilt: The Man And His Treasures."

An intimate look at George Vanderbilt. The man. The collector. The philanthropist. The devoted husband and father.

Just a part of the Centennial Celebration at Biltmore Estate, Asheville, NC. For more details, call 1-800-413-9786.

The Missing Monet. On display for the first time.

This elaborate ewer is part of George's priceless silver collection. A must see.

The 21 lb. Silver Charger by DeLamerie. Worth more than its weight in gold.

At christening, many children would receive a single Apostle Spoon. George's daughter received a complete set of thirteen.

The same artist who painted "Whistler's Mother" also painted George's daughter.

Biltmore Estate
1895 · CENTENNIAL · 1995

GEORGE VANDERBILT: THE MAN AND HIS TREASURES
➤ An Extraordinary Exhibit Opening May 27 ➤

419

419
District 3
CLIENT
Biltmore Estates
AGENCY
Price/McNabb
Charlotte, NC
CREATIVE DIRECTOR
John Boone
ART DIRECTOR
John Boone
COPYWRITER
David Oakley

ANNCR: Long before baseball cards were invented, George Vanderbilt collected Royalty Cards.
GEORGE'S VO: Honey, have you seen my King Louis XIV?
SFX: *The sound a trading card makes when it is put into the spokes of a tricycle.*
SUPER: The Royalty Cards.
ANNCR: See the Royalty Cards. Revealed for the first time in nearly a century. At Biltmore Estate.

RADIO SCRIPT
Locksmith Radio
SFX: *Clicking of a combination lock.*
LOCKSMITH: Right 10... left16... right 61? That's not it. Or was it left 10... right 16... left 61? No.
ANNCR: The secret vault of George Vanderbilt.
LOCKSMITH: ...right 10... left 16... right 62? Huff.
ANNCR: Locked for almost a century.
LOCKSMITH: ... left 10 ...right 16 ...left 63. Pfff.
ANNCR: Reportedly it contains a painting by Monet, a priceless silver collection,
LOCKSMITH: ...10...15...right 90. Dang.
ANNCR: ...a lock of Lord Byron's hair, and many other never-before-seen treasures.
LOCKSMITH: ...11...right 7...
ANNCR: Unfortunately, it also contains the combination.
LOCKSMITH: ...left 93. Dooooh!
ANNCR: "George Vanderbilt. The Man and His Treasures." A once-in-a-lifetime exhibit. At Biltmore Estate, Asheville, North Carolina. Opening May 27th.
LOCKSMITH: ...2...8...69. Dadburnit!
ANNCR: Well, we certainly hope so.

420
District 6

CLIENT
Chrysler/Dodge

AGENCY
BBDO-Detroit
Southfield, MI

CREATIVE DIRECTOR
Dick Johnson

ART DIRECTORS
Gary Slomka
Mike Lowes

COPYWRITERS
Jerry Hunnicutt
Dick Johnson
Jim Nicoll
Lance Aldrich

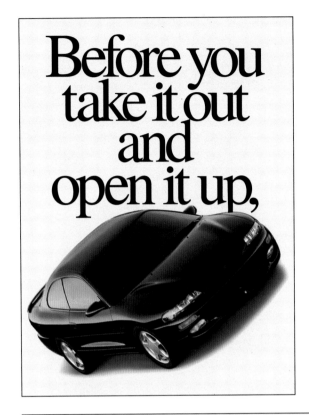

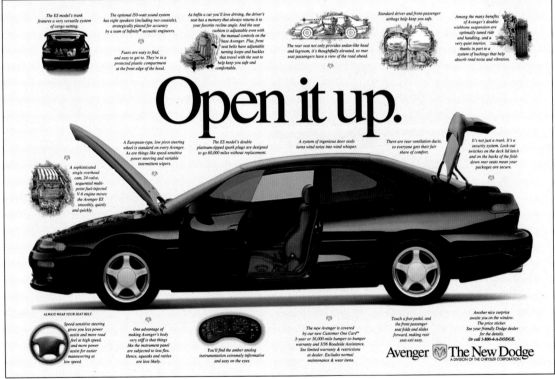

420

Open
ANNCR: Before you ask what's under the hood... look in the trunk.
SUPER: AVENGER ES
ANNCR: Before you sit behind the wheel... climb in back. Before you take a new Avenger out and open it up... open it up.
SUPER: Avenger *(Ram's head logo)* The new Dodge. A division of the Chrysler Corporation.

Elevator
ANNCR: Its double wishbone suspension elevates your feel of the road. Its multi-valve engine and speed sensitive steering elevate your sense of control. While its looks? Well, they will elevate your mood. Introducing the all new Dodge Avenger... It's more than just a car, it's an elevator.
SUPER: Avenger *(Ram's head logo)* The new Dodge. A division of the Chrysler Corporation.

Brain
ANNCR: Its multi-valve V-6 should appeal to all you right brain types... While its large trunk should please those of you on the left. Its double wishbone suspension... right brain. Its split fold-down rear seat... left brain. Dual airbags... decidedly left. Great stereo... definitely right. Introducing the all-new Dodge Avenger... a car for anyone with half a brain.
SUPER: Avenger *(Ram's head logo)* The new Dodge. A division of the Chrysler Corporation.

421
District 7

CLIENT
Audubon Institute

AGENCY
Audubon Institute
New Orleans, LA

COPYWRITERS
Josh Mayer
Lori Archer
Lundquist

PRODUCER
Marylynn Cahill

DIRECTOR
Brian Bain

PRODUCTION
Buckholtz
Production

MUSIC
Pelican Pictures

MUSIC: *Light and lively, up and under.*
VO: What is it with Sharks? Do you think they ever floss? Are they brushing between meals when no one's looking? I wonder if they lend money to the other fish.
ART CARD: The Aquarium of the Americas.
VO: Come to the Aquarium of the Americas and find out. Ooh, never borrow money from a sand tiger.

RADIO SCRIPT
MUSIC: *Surfer music up and under.*
ANNCR: Do white alligators turn pink when they blush? Do they use sunblock on the beach? And hey, do they only eat white meat? Come to the zoo and find out. Are the other ones green with envy?

COLLATERAL MATERIAL

422
District 9

CLIENT
Kid to Kid

AGENCY
Zipatoni Company
St. Louis, MO

CREATIVE DIRECTOR
Brad Fuller

ART DIRECTOR
Susan Chenot

COPYWRITER
Conne Pleimann

DESIGNER
Susan Chenot

PRODUCTION
Susan Binns-Roth

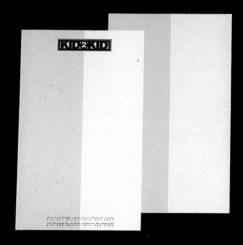

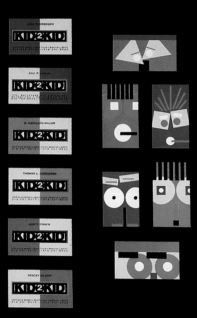

422

24
istrict 3
LIENT
/W Partners-Old
North State Club
GENCY
rice McNabb
harlotte, NC
REATIVE DIRECTOR
ohn Boone
RT DIRECTOR
onnie Hartman
OPYWRITER
atrick McLean
HOTOGRAPHER
onnie Hartman
ESIGNER
onnie Hartman

HOTEL
FORT DES MOINES
75TH
ANNIVERSARY
Hotel Fort Des Moines
Des Moines, Iowa
VALET LIST
CHECK SERVICE DESIRED
SOUVENIR VIEWS
20 VIEWS
DES MOINES, IOWA
Hotel Fort Des Moines,
Des Moines, Iowa.
HISTORY
OF
400 ROOMS
BATHS
CIRCULATING
ICE WATER
COFFEE ROOM
HOSPITALITY
Please go 'way and let me sleep
(Thank you)
HOTEL FORT DES MOINES Des Moines, Iowa

426
District 9

CLIENT
Hotel Fort
Des Moines

AGENCY
Sayles Graphic
Design
Des Moines, IA

ART DIRECTOR
John Sayles

COPYWRITER
Wendy Lyons

ILLUSTRATOR
John Sayles

DESIGNER
John Sayles

PRINTER
Artcraft, Inc.

427

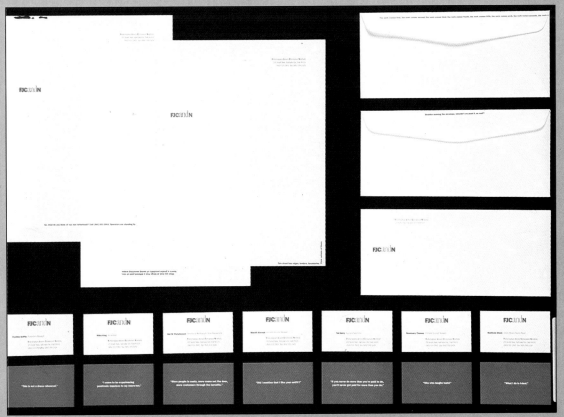

428

427
District 14

CLIENT
California Pear
Advisory Board

AGENCY
Solutions by Design
Fresno, CA

428
District 12

CLIENT
FJCandN

AGENCY
FJCandN
Salt Lake City, UT

CREATIVE DIRECTOR
Dave Newbold

ART DIRECTOR
Eric Bute

COPYWRITER
Dave Newbold

DESIGNER
Eric Bute

COLLATERAL

429

429
District 14
CLIENT
San Francisco
Advertising Club
AGENCY
Hal Riney & Partners
San Francisco, CA
CREATIVE DIRECTOR
Chris Chaffin
ART DIRECTOR
Chris Chaffin
COPYWRITER
Chris Chaffin
ILLUSTRATOR
Joe Spencer

430
District 7
CLIENT
American Red Cross
AGENCY
Martin, White and
Mickwee Advertising
Birmingham, AL
CREATIVE DIRECTOR
Susan Pickett
ART DIRECTOR
Phillip Smith
COPYWRITER
Susan Pickett
PHOTOGRAPHERS
Randy Mayor
Lee Harrelson
SEPARATOR
Communication Arts
PRINTER
American Printing
ACCOUNT EXECUTIVE
Susan Pickett

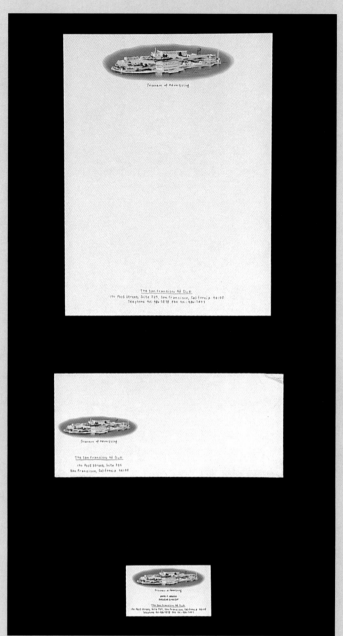

429

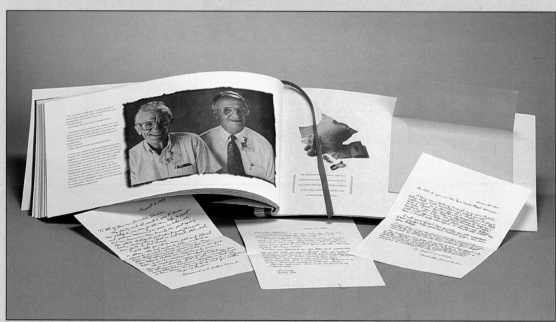

430

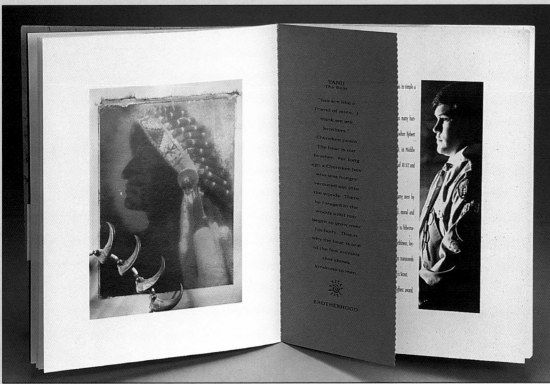

431

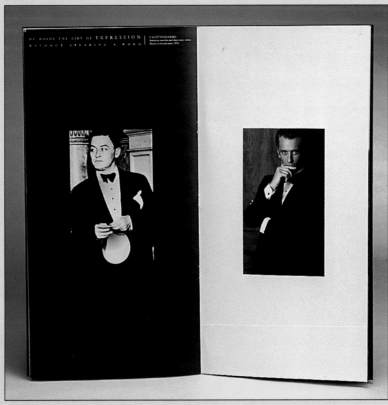

432

431
District 7
CLIENT
Middle TN Council -
Boy Scouts
AGENCY
Dye, Van Mol
& Lawrence
Nashville, TN
CREATIVE DIRECTOR
Chuck Creasy
ART DIRECTOR
Chuck Creasy
COPYWRITER
Nelson Eddy
PHOTOGRAPHER
Michael W.
Rutherford
DESIGNER
Chuck Creasy
ENGRAVER
Color Systems
PRINTER
Lithographics, Inc.
PRODUCTION
Kevin Hinson

432
District 2
CLIENT
Hartmarx
AGENCY
Grafik
Communications
Alexandria, VA
COPYWRITER
Alan Schulman
DESIGNERS
Melanie Bass
Gregg Glaviano
Judy Kirpich
PRINTER
Classic Color Litho

433
District 5

CLIENT
Christian & Timbers

AGENCY
**Wyse Cohen, Inc./
Artists Inc.**
Akron, OH

CREATIVE DIRECTOR
Larry Cohen

ART DIRECTOR
Laurel Kelleman

COPYWRITER
Larry Cohen

ILLUSTRATOR
Lawrence Churski

DESIGNER
David Buehler

434
District 2

CLIENT
Norwood School

AGENCY
Westland Printers
Burtonsville, MD

CREATIVE DIRECTOR
Leo Mullen

ART DIRECTOR
Mike Krain

PRINTER
**Westland Printers,
Inc.**

PRODUCER
Robin Winterrowd

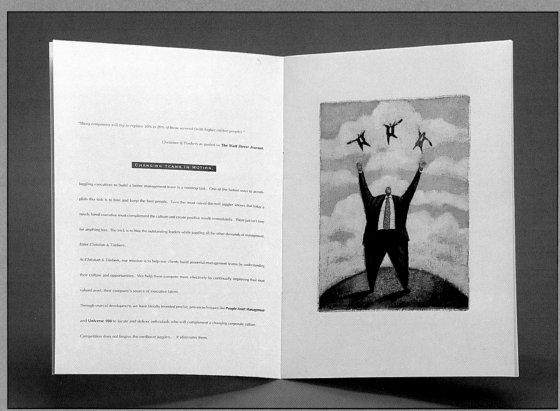

433

434

VCR&R.

BLOCKBUSTER VIDEO®

Make It A BLOCKBUSTER Night, Chicago.

435

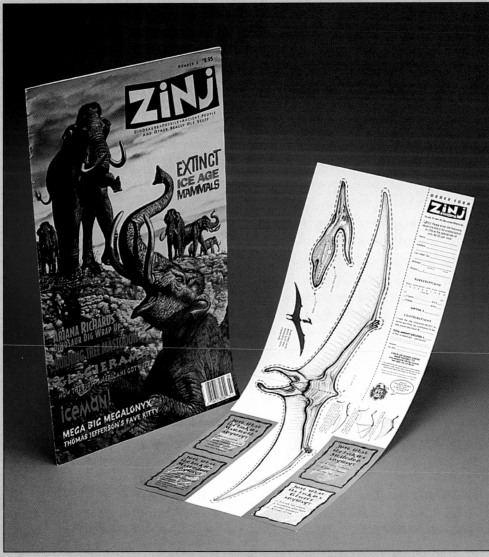

436

435
District 9
CLIENT
Blockbuster
Entertainment Group
AGENCY
DMB&B/St. Louis
St. Louis, MO
CREATIVE DIRECTORS
Charlie Claggett
Steve Good
ART DIRECTOR
Joe Gillman
COPYWRITER
Steve Good

436
District 12
CLIENT
Interagency Task
Force
AGENCY
Harris, Volsic Creative
Salt Lake City, UT
CREATIVE DIRECTORS
David Volsic
Debra Harris
ART DIRECTORS
David Volsic
Sheryl Lundgreen
COPYWRITERS
Debra Harris
Kevin Jones

Most Valuable Players Spend Time On The Bench.

THAT'S WHERE THEY
GAIN THE CONFIDENCE,
THE COORDINATION AND
THE CONCENTRATION
THAT HELPS MAKE
THEM WINNERS.
ON THE PLAYING FIELD.
AT SCHOOL.
IN LIFE.
GIVE A CHILD
THE GIFT OF MUSIC.
IT IS VALUABLE
BEYOND WORDS.

437

437
District 7
CLIENT
The Wurlitzer Company
AGENCY
Sossaman Bateman
McCuddy
Memphis, TN
CREATIVE DIRECTORS
Rikki Boyce
Eric Melkent
ART DIRECTOR
Billy Riley
COPYWRITER
Rikki Boyce
PHOTOGRAPHER
Nick Vedros
ENGRAVER
CCR
PRINTER
Pinnacle Press
TYPOGRAPHER
Billy Riley
PRODUCTION
Randall Hartzog
ACCOUNT EXECUTIVE
Ken Sossaman

438
District 11
CLIENT
Africola
AGENCY
Cole & Weber
Seattle, WA
CREATIVE DIRECTOR
Robert Brihn
ART DIRECTOR
Heidi Flora
COPYWRITER
Kevin Jones

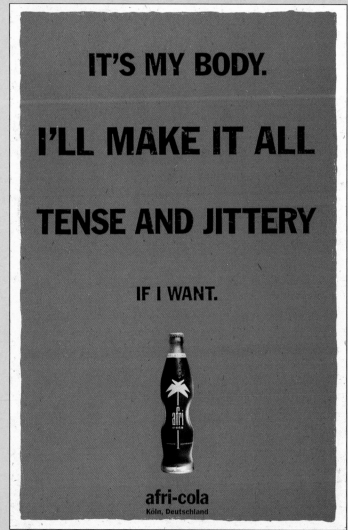

438

COLLATERAL

439

439
District 7
CLIENT
Un Ete Du Vin
AGENCY
Gish, Sherwood
& Friends
Nashville, TN
CREATIVE DIRECTOR
Roland Gibbons
ART DIRECTOR
Roland Gibbons
COPYWRITER
Tim Fish
PHOTOGRAPHER
John Guider
PRODUCTION
Mary Evans

440
District 6
CLIENT
Woodworks
AGENCY
Woodworks
Ann Arbor, MI
COPYWRITER
Mary Ann Verde-Bar
DESIGNER
Deborah Wood

441
District 14
CLIENT
BSS
AGENCY
Butler, Shine & Stern
Sausalito, CA
CREATIVE DIRECTORS
John Butler
Mike Shine
ART DIRECTOR
Geordie Stevens
COPYWRITER
Ryan Ebner

440

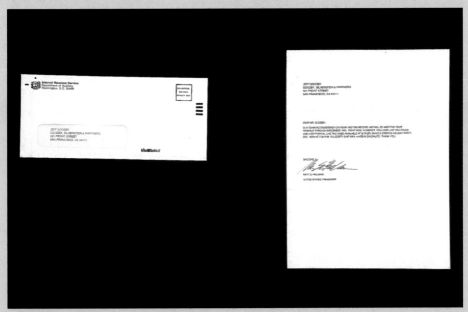

441

COLLATERAL

442
District 6

CLIENT
The Children's
Museum of
Indianapolis

AGENCY
FYI & Held Diedrich
Indianapolis, IN

CREATIVE DIRECTOR
Linda Lazler

ART DIRECTOR
David Snedigar

COPYWRITER
Linda Lazler

443
District 7

CLIENT
Ship Shape Cleaning

AGENCY
Davis & Associates
Communication
Nashville, TN

CREATIVE DIRECTOR
Mike Purswell

ART DIRECTOR
Rick Douglas

ILLUSTRATOR
Albert Roberts
Rick Douglas

ENGRAVER
Robinson Graphics

PRINTER
Classic Printing

444
District 4

CLIENT
Pelican Marsh

AGENCY
R.J. Gibson
Advertising Inc.
Palm Beach, FL

CREATIVE DIRECTOR
Ken Roscoe

ART DIRECTOR
Ken Roscoe

PRINTER
Fast Graphics

442

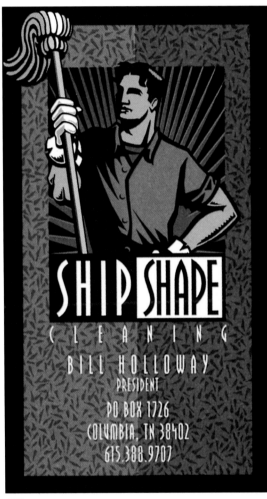

443

444

COLLATERAL

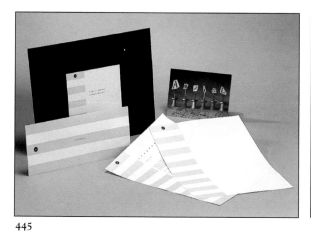

445

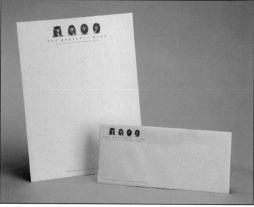

446

447

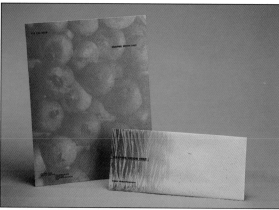

448

445
District 14
CLIENT
Aerial
AGENCY
Aerial
San Francisco, CA
CREATIVE DIRECTOR
Tracy Moon
PHOTOGRAPHER
R.J. Muna
DESIGNER
Tracy Moon

446
District 10
CLIENT
The Crockett Park
Association
AGENCY
The Roberts Group
San Antonio, TX
CREATIVE DIRECTOR
Claude Roberts
COPYWRITER
Kathy Roberts
DESIGNER
Claude Roberts
PRODUCTION
Wayne Eckhardt
ACCOUNT EXECUTIVES
Kathy Roberts
Linda Morse

447
District 7
CLIENT
Contrails
AGENCY
Oden & Associates
Memphis, TN
CREATIVE DIRECTOR
Bret Terwelliger
ART DIRECTOR
Bret Terwelliger
PRINTER
B&B Printing
PRODUCTION
George Peeler
ACCOUNT EXECUTIVE
Bill Carkeet

448
District 5
CLIENT
Graphik ON!ON
Corp.
AGENCY
Graphik ON!ON
Corp.
Columbus, OH
ART DIRECTOR
Thomas Slayton
PHOTOGRAPHY
Hickson & Associates
DESIGNERS
Thomas Slayton
David Cuccio

449
District 3

CLIENT
The Creative Market

AGENCY
The Creative Market
Greenville, SC

CREATIVE DIRECTOR
James Gibbons

ART DIRECTOR
Anne Peck

DESIGNER
Ellyson Kalagayan

450
District 8

CLIENT
Madison
International Youth
Arts Festival

AGENCY
Lindsay, Stone &
Briggs Advertising
Madison, WI

CREATIVE DIRECTION
Lindsay, Stone
& Briggs

451
District 3

CLIENT
Fundraisers

AGENCY
In-Line Creative
Asheville, NC

ART DIRECTOR
Scott Smith

452
District 9

CLIENT
Edward Whelan

AGENCY
Alex Paradowski
Graphic Design
St. Louis, MO

CREATIVE DIRECTORS
Alex Paradowski
Steve Cox

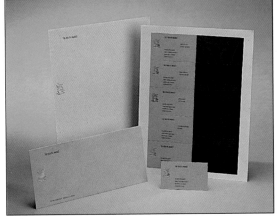

449

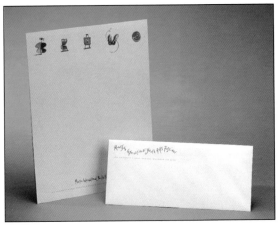

450

451

452

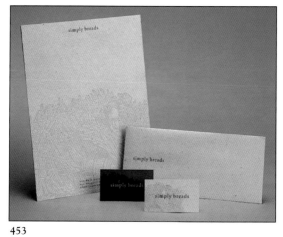

453

454

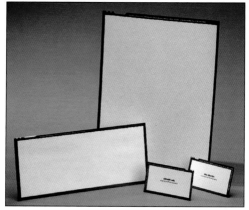

455

456

453
District 14

CLIENT
Simply Breads

AGENCY
Momentum Design
San Francisco, CA

DESIGNERS
Sandy Lee
Tom Hunt

454
District 3

CLIENT
Bolt

AGENCY
Bolt
Charlotte, NC

ART DIRECTOR
James Boiter

DESIGNER
Tim Bogert

PRODUCTION ASSISTANTS
Robert Gibson
Edmund Machen
Ed Montague

455
District 5

CLIENT
Studio Martin Inc.

AGENCY
Louis & Partners
Akron, OH

456
District 13

CLIENT
Kohala Spa

AGENCY
Kirk Pummill Design
Honolulu, HI

CREATIVE DIRECTOR
Kirk Pummill

ART DIRECTOR
Kirk Pummill

COPYWRITER
Sig Kramer

457

District 6

CLIENT
Autocam

AGENCY
Square One Design, Inc.
Grand Rapids, MI

ART DIRECTOR
Leslie Black

COPYWRITER
Polly Hewitt

PHOTOGRAPHER
Graig Vanderlende

DESIGNER
Leslie Black

PRINTER
Etheridge

TYPOGRAPHER
Leslie Black

457

458

District 10

CLIENT
Houston Firemen's Fund

AGENCY
Steven Sessions, Inc.
Houston, TX

CREATIVE DIRECTOR
Steven Sessions

ART DIRECTOR
Steven Sessions

COPYWRITING
Steve Barnhill & Associates

PHOTOGRAPHER
Bryan Kuntz

DESIGNERS
Phil Schmitt
Steven Sessions

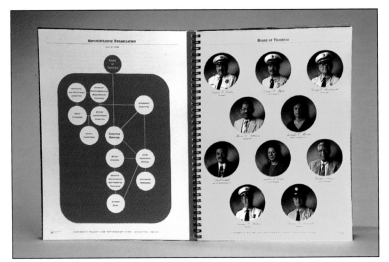

458

459

District 2

CLIENT
Andersen Consulting

AGENCY
Burson-Marsteller
New York, NY

DESIGNER
Julie Klein

PRODUCTION
D.L. Terwilliger

ORIGAMI
Gary Merill Gross

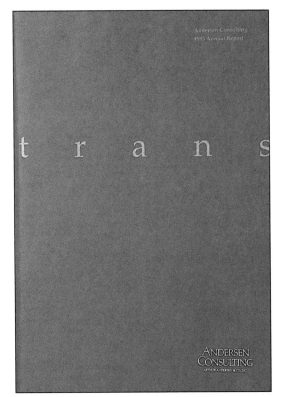

459

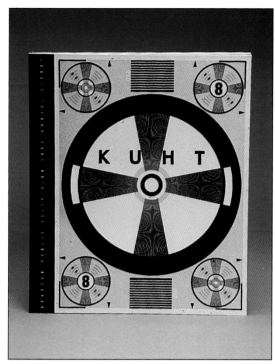

460

460
District 10
CLIENT
KUHT/Houston Public Television
AGENCY
KUHT
Houston, TX
COPYWRITER
Joe Militello
DESIGNER
Mark Geer

461
District 4
CLIENT
1884 Oakhurst Links
AGENCY
Boner and Associates Advertising
Palm Beach, FL
CREATIVE DIRECTORS
Gina Boner
Margaret Wilesmith
COPYWRITER
Margaret Wilesmith
DESIGNER
Fran Parente

461

462
District 4
CLIENT
R'Club
AGENCY
Paradigm Communications
Tampa, FL
CREATIVE DIRECTOR
Dick Leonard
ART DIRECTOR
Justin Leonard
COPYWRITER
Mary Jorn

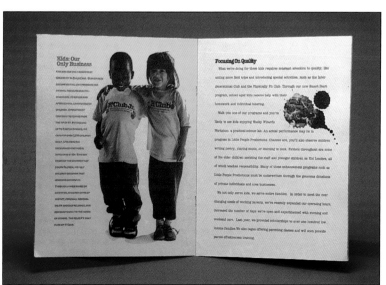

462

463
District 10

CLIENT
Sports Designs

AGENCY
Steven Sessions, Inc.
Houston, TX

CREATIVE DIRECTOR
Steven Sessions

ART DIRECTOR
Steven Sessions

COPYWRITER
John Kutch

PHOTOGRAPHER
Bryan Kuntz

ILLUSTRATOR
Phil Schmitt

DESIGNER
Steven Sessions

464
District 4

CLIENT
Florida Municipal
Power Agency

AGENCY
Larry Moore
Illustration Design
Orlando, FL

COPYWRITER
Mark McCain

ILLUSTRATOR
Larry Moore

DESIGNER
Larry Moore

PRODUCTION
Peggy Homrich

465
District 2

CLIENT
Norwood School

AGENCY
Westland Printers
Burtonsville, MD

CREATIVE DIRECTOR
Leo Mullen

ART DIRECTOR
Mike Kraine

PRINTER
Westland Printers

PRODUCTION
Robin Winterrowd

463

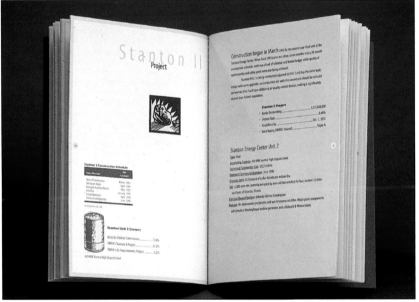

464

465

COLLATERAL

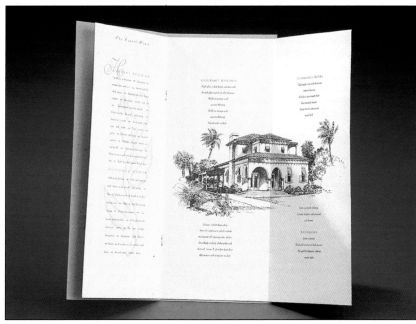

466

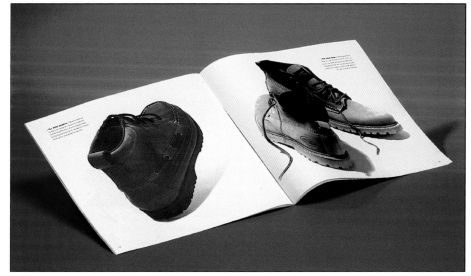

467

468

466
District 4
CLIENT
Diamond Craft Homes
AGENCY
Sunsplash Graphics
Santa Rosa Beach, FL
COPYWRITER
William Pope
DESIGNER
Pamela Breaux
ARTIST
Tom McCartney

467
District 10
CLIENT
Harold's
AGENCY
Harold's
Norman, OK
CREATIVE DIRECTION
Team Harold's
PHOTOGRAPHER
S. Williams
PRINTER
Heritage Press

468
District 13
CLIENT
Rain Song Graphite Guitars
AGENCY
Tongg Printing Company
Honolulu, HI
CREATIVE DIRECTOR
Dale Vermeer
ART DIRECTOR
Dale Vermeer

469
District 7
CLIENT
International Paper
AGENCY
Perdue Creative
Memphis, TN
CREATIVE DIRECTION
Perdue Creative
PRINTER
Graphic Arts Center
ENGRAVER
Graphic Arts Center
COLOR RETOUCHING
Charlie Reynolds

470
District 5
CLIENT
Financial Horizons
AGENCY
SBC Advertising
Westerville, OH
ART DIRECTOR
Gina Bennett
COPYWRITER
Gino Valli

471
District 9
CLIENT
Nebraska Book
Company
AGENCY
Bailey Lauerman
& Associates
Lincoln, NE
CREATIVE DIRECTOR
Rich Bailey
COPYWRITER
Mitch Koch
PHOTOGRAPHERS
Jon Nollendorfs
Don Farrall
DESIGNER
Carter Weitz
TYPOGRAPHER
Sean Faben
ACCOUNT EXECUTIVE
Rich Claussen

469

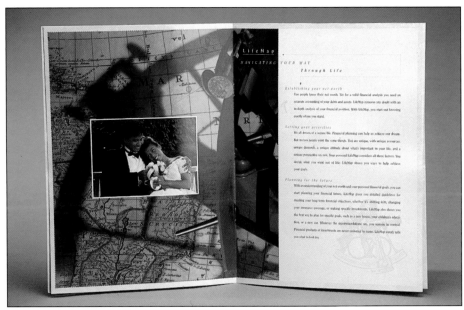

470

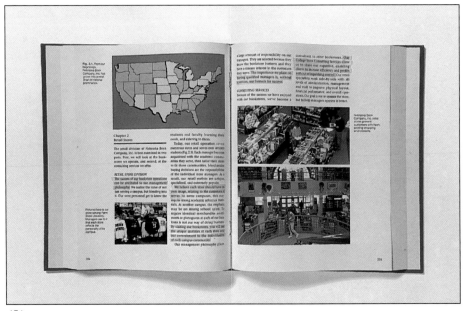

471

472

473

474

472
District 7
CLIENT
Sonics
AGENCY
WHM&G Advertising
Atlanta, GA

473
District 10
CLIENT
Gulf Printing
Company
AGENCY
Prism Design, Inc.
Houston, TX
CREATIVE DIRECTORS
Randy Nelson
Susan Reeves
DESIGNERS
Trish Rausch
Becky Prejean

474
District 3
CLIENT
Charlotte Ad Club
AGENCY
Price/McNabb
Charlotte, NC
CREATIVE DIRECTOR
John Boone
DESIGNER
Brandon Scharr

475
District 13

CLIENT
Maui Arts and
Cultural Center

AGENCY
Design Network
Honolulu, HI

COPYWRITER
Kari McCarthy

DESIGNERS
Patt Narrowe
Rita Goldman

476
District 3

CLIENT
Charlotte Ad Club

AGENCY
Price/McNabb
Charlotte, NC

CREATIVE DIRECTOR
John Boone

DESIGNER
Brandon Scharr

477
District 9

CLIENT
Sportscar Vintage
Racing Association

AGENCY
Muller + Company
Kansas City, MO

ART DIRECTOR
John Muller

PHOTOGRAPHER
Klemantaski

DESIGNER
Shana Eck

478
District 4

CLIENT
Children's Hospital

AGENCY
Sacred Heart
Hospital
Pensacola, FL

COPYWRITER
Becky Clark

DESIGNER
Becky Clark

475

476

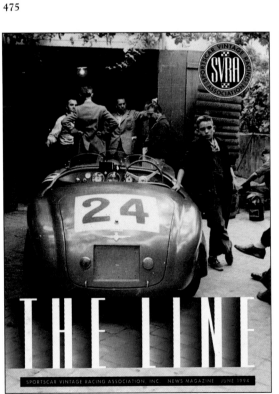

477

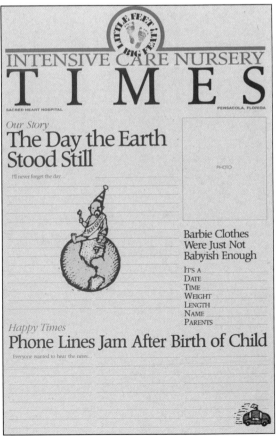

478

479

480

481

482

479
District 4
CLIENT
Morton Plant
Hospital
AGENCY
Altman Meder
Lawrence Hill
Tampa, FL
ART DIRECTOR
Lisa Hill
COPYWRITER
Robin Lawrence

480
District 10
CLIENT
Texas State Aquarium
AGENCY
Snyder & Associates
Corpus Christi, TX
DESIGNER
Brad Snyder
PRINTER
Grunwald Printing
EDITOR
Karen Wallace

481
District 8
CLIENT
KI
AGENCY
KI
Green Bay, WI
CREATIVE DIRECTOR
Mary Rass
COPYWRITING
KI Team
PHOTOGRAPHER
Image Studios
PRINTER
Post Printing

482
District 7
CLIENT
DeRoyal Industries
AGENCY
Shell Smith &
Associates
Knoxville, TN
ART DIRECTOR
John Reep

COLLATERAL

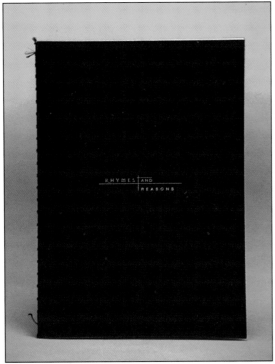

483

484

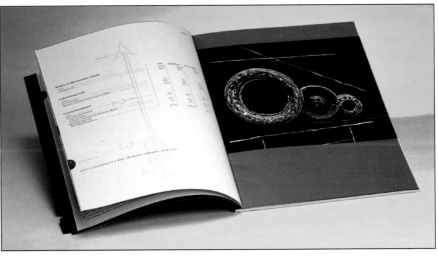

485

486

487

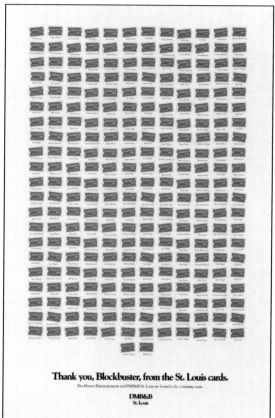

488

489

487
District 14
CLIENT
SF Video
AGENCY
Odiorne Wilde
Narraway Groome
San Francisco, CA
CREATIVE DIRECTORS
Michael Wilde
Jeff Odiorne
ART DIRECTOR
Mike Lewis
COPYWRITER
Oliver Albrecht
ILLUSTRATOR
Carl Buell
ACCOUNT EXECUTIVE
Harry Groome

488
District 9
CLIENT
Blockbuster
Entertainment Group
AGENCY
DMB&B/St. Louis
St. Louis, MO
CREATIVE DIRECTORS
Carole Christie
Ron Crooks
COPYWRITER
Arlo Oviatt
PRODUCTION
Don Griefenkamp

489
District 9
CLIENT
The Lincoln
Marathon
AGENCY
Bailey Lauerman
& Associates
Lincoln, NE
CREATIVE DIRECTOR
Carter Weitz
COPYWRITER
Mitch Koch
PHOTOGRAPHER
Don Farrall
DESIGNER
Carter Weitz
PRINTER
Jacob North
ACCOUNT EXECUTIVE
Rich Claussen

490
District 10

CLIENT
Friends of the Zoo

AGENCY
Stone & Ward
Little Rock, AR

CREATIVE DIRECTORS
Larry Stone
Jean Romano

ART DIRECTOR
Martin Wilford

COPYWRITER
Jean Romano

PRODUCTION
Brenda Fowler

ACCOUNT EXECUTIVE
Steve Jacuzzi

491
District 5

CLIENT
Hostess Brand,
Continental Baking
Company

AGENCY
Wolf Blumberg Krody
Cincinnati, OH

CREATIVE DIRECTOR
Vern Hughes

ART DIRECTOR
Kris Schwandner

COPYWRITER
John Sweney

PHOTOGRAPHER
Jason Hathcock

ACCOUNT EXECUTIVE
Lynn Shafer

492
District 2

CLIENT
Style of Man

AGENCY
Earle Palmer Brown/
Philadelphia
Philadelphia, PA

CREATIVE DIRECTOR
Mike Drazen

ART DIRECTOR
Robert Shaw West

COPYWRITER
Kelly Simmons

493
District 6

CLIENT
Skyknights Skydiving

AGENCY
5 to 9
Chicago, IL

ART DIRECTORS
Dan Weeks
Reid Holmes

490

491

492

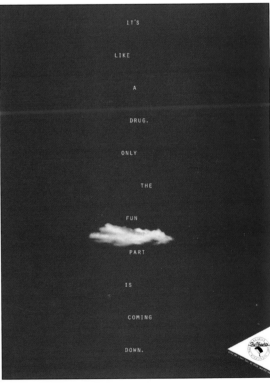

493

YOU MAY HAVE HEARD THAT THER
RE STARVING CHILDREN IN CHINA
MAYBE IT'S BECAUSE WE HIRED AWA
HEIR BEST CHEF.

HUNAN GARDEN 湖南園

11532 PAGE SERVICE RD. 314.432.7015

WHICH WOULD YOU RATHER HAV
T OUR RESTAURANT, GOOD ENGLIS
R GOOD CHINESE?

11532 PAGE SERVICE RD. 314.432.7015

ACCORDING TO THE CHINESE CALENDA
1995 IS THE YEAR OF THE PIG. SO IS
ANY COINCIDENCE WE'LL BE OFFERING A
LL-YOU-CAN-EAT BRUNCH?

11532 PAGE SERVICE RD. 314.432.7015

494
District 9
CLIENT
Hunan Garden
Restaurant
AGENCY
The Puckett Group
St Louis, MO
ART DIRECTOR
David Nien-Li Yang
COPYWRITER
David Nien-Li-Yang
Eric Weltner

COLLATERAL

495
District 4
CLIENT
Enzian
AGENCY
Gouchenour
Advertising
Orlando, FL
CREATIVE DIRECTOR
Chris Robb
ART DIRECTOR
Chris Robb
COPYWRITER
Mark Ronquillo
PRODUCTION
Craig Gouchenour

496
District 10
CLIENT
Rootin Ridge
AGENCY
GSD&M Advertising
Austin, TX
CREATIVE DIRECTORS
Brent Ladd
Brian Brooker
ART DIRECTOR
Brent Ladd
COPYWRITER
Brian Brooker
PHOTOGRAPHER
Dennis Fagan

497
District 5
CLIENT
The Murray Ohio
Manufacturing
Company
AGENCY
Sive/Young
& Rubicam
Cincinnati, OH
CREATIVE DIRECTORS
Mark Giambrone
Mike Kitei
ART DIRECTOR
Tom Anneken
COPYWRITER
Leanne Bryant
PRODUCTION
Chris Stegner

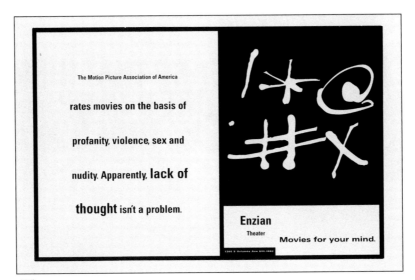

495

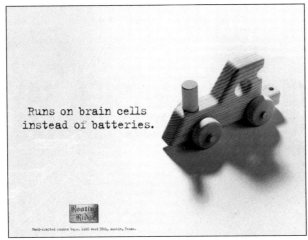

496

497

GRAY SUIT. GRAY SUIT. GRAY SUIT. GRAY
SUIT. GRAY SUIT. GRAY SUIT. GRAY SUIT.
GRAY SUIT. GRAY SUIT. GRAY SUIT. GRAY
SUIT. GRAY SUIT. GRAY SUIT. GRAY SUIT.
GRAY SUIT. GRAY SUIT. GRAY SUIT. GRAY
SUIT. GRAY SUIT. GRAY SUIT. GRAY SUIT.
GRAY SUIT. GRAY SUIT. GRAY SUIT. GRAY
SUIT. BIG BAGGY JACKET. GRAY SUIT.
GRAY SUIT. GRAY SUIT. GRAY SUIT. GRAY
SUIT. GRAY SUIT. GRAY SUIT. GRAY SUIT.
GRAY SUIT. GRAY SUIT. GRAY SUIT. GRAY
SUIT. GRAY SUIT.GRAY SUIT.GRAY SUIT.
GRAY SUIT. GRAY SUIT. GRAY SUIT. GRAY
SUIT. GRAY SUIT. GRAY SUIT. GRAY SUIT.
GRAY THE DROP SHOP. NOT A MAJORITY
DECISION. 114 S. COURT AVENUE. 839-6050.

498

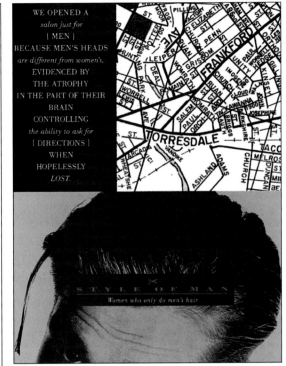

WE OPENED A *salon just for* { MEN } BECAUSE MEN'S HEADS *are different from women's,* EVIDENCED BY THE ATROPHY IN THE PART OF THEIR BRAIN CONTROLLING *the ability to ask for* { DIRECTIONS } WHEN HOPELESSLY *LOST.*

STYLE OF MAN
Women who only do men's hair

499

IN THE SAME

POLITICAL CIRCLES

AS

CIGARETTES, BEER, AND RED MEAT.

afri-cola
Koln, Deutschland

500

What Would Christmas Be Without The Appropriate Reds and Whites?

A. Bommarito Wines

501

502
District 6
CLIENT
Skyknights Skydiving
AGENCY
5 to 9
Chicago, IL
ART DIRECTORS
Dan Weeks
Reid Holmes

503
District 8
CLIENT
Bach Dancing
& Dynamite Society
AGENCY
Lindsay, Stone
& Briggs Advertising
Madison, WI
CREATIVE DIRECTION
Lindsay, Stone
& Briggs

504
District 7
CLIENT
Germantown
Community Theatre
AGENCY
Disciple
Memphis, TN
CREATIVE DIRECTOR
Craig Thompson
ART DIRECTORS
Craig Thompson
David Terry
PHOTOGRAPHER
Phillip Parker
ILLUSTRATORS
Craig Thompson
David Terry
ENGRAVER
Seamless Graphics
PRINTER
Jaco-Bryant Printers
PRODUCTION
Craig Thompson
ACCOUNT EXECUTIVE
Craig Thompson

505
District 6
CLIENT
Northern Plains
AGENCY
Weeks Epstein
Chicago, IL
ART DIRECTOR
Dan Weeks
COPYWRITER
Jeff Epstein

502

503

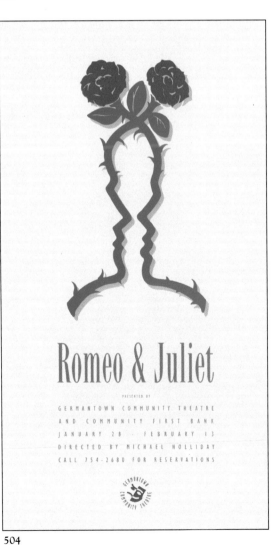

504

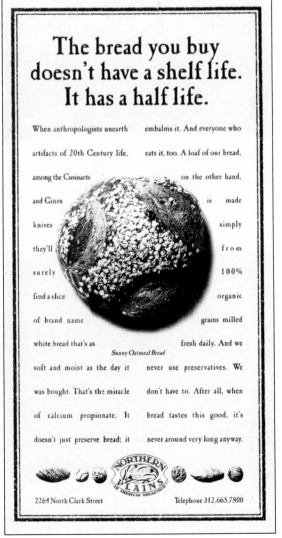

505

506

District 3

CLIENT
The Lighthouse
Project

AGENCY
Blackbird Creative,
McLeod/Register
Productions
Raleigh, NC

CREATIVE DIRECTORS
Todd Mcleod
Charles Register

ART DIRECTORS
Todd Mcleod
Charles Register

PHOTOGRAPHERS
Todd Mcleod
Charles Register

DESIGNER
Patrick Short

COLLATERAL

507

District 12

CLIENT
Marie Jackson

AGENCY
Dahlin Smith White
Salt Lake City, UT

ART DIRECTOR
Steve Cardon

COPYWRITER
John Kinkead

PHOTOGRAPHER
Ed Rosenberger

ILLUSTRATOR
Clint Hansen

508

District 10

CLIENT
Shelly Beck

AGENCY
Beck & Co. Design
San Antonio, TX

CREATIVE DIRECTOR
Terry Beck

COPYWRITER
Terry Beck

DESIGNER
Terry Beck

CONCEPT
Michael Karshis

509

District 10

CLIENT
The Atkins Agency

AGENCY
The Atkins Agency
San Antonio, TX

CREATIVE DIRECTOR
Tom Norman

ART DIRECTOR
Denise Degen

COPYWRITER
Michael Payer

PRINTER
Padgett Printing

PRODUCTION
Jana Abel

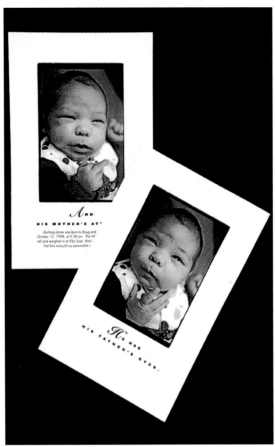

507

508

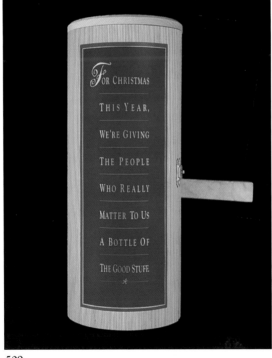

509

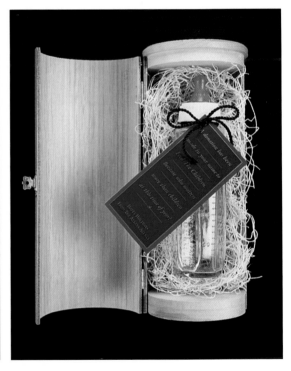

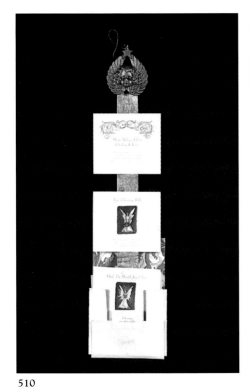

510

511

512

510
District 7
CLIENT
Calzone and
Associates
AGENCY
Calzone and
Associates
Lafayette, LA
ART DIRECTORS
Beth Sarradet
Laurie Landry
COPYWRITER
Kim Bergeron
ILLUSTRATOR
Ann Dubois
DESIGNERS
Beth Sarradet
Holly Jackson

511
District 4
CLIENT
The
Foundation/Winter
Haven Hospital
AGENCY
Gregory & Wahl
Limited
Winter Haven, FL
ART DIRECTOR
Ron Boucher
COPYWRITER
Ron Boucher

512
District 8
CLIENT
John Michael Kohler
Arts Center
AGENCY
Jacobson Rost
Sheboygan, WI
CREATIVE DIRECTOR
Reed Allen
ART DIRECTORS
Paul Zwief
Cheryl Anthony
COPYWRITER
Judith Garson
ILLUSTRATOR
Byron Zimmerman
DESIGNERS
Paul Zwief
Cheryl Anthony
PRINTER
Universal Lihographer
ACCOUNT EXECUTIVE
Judith Garson

513
District 3
CLIENT
Lewis Advertising
AGENCY
Lewis Advertising, Inc.
Rocky Mount, NC
CREATIVE DIRECTOR
John Poulos
ART DIRECTOR
Marty Hardman
COPYWRITERS
John Poulos
Marty Hardman

514
District 4
CLIENT
Florida Power Corporation
AGENCY
Groom Design Inc.
Orlando, FL
COPYWRITER
Mike Heidtman
PHOTOGRAPHER
John Bateman
DESIGNER
Joe Groom

515
District 8
CLIENT
Harley-Davidson, Inc.
AGENCY
Jacobson Rost
Sheboygan, WI
CREATIVE DIRECTOR
Reed Allen
ART DIRECTOR
Paul Zwief
COPYWRITER
Dan Ames
PHOTOGRAPHERS
Clint Clemens
Dave Gilo
SEPARATOR
ProGraphics
PRINTER
Inland Press
ACCOUNT EXECUTIVE
Peter Curran

513

514

515

516

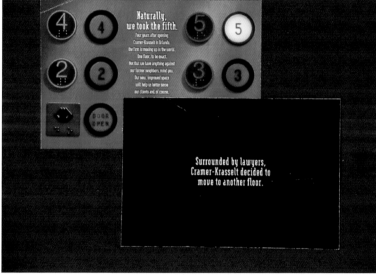

517

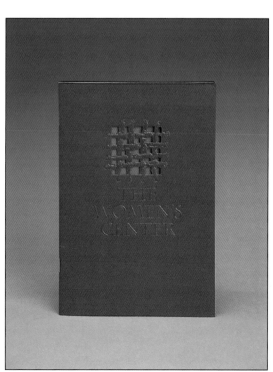

518

516
District 2
CLIENT
McAdams Richman
& Ong
AGENCY
McAdams Richman
& Ong
Bala Cynwyd, PA
CREATIVE DIRECTOR
Steve Martino
COPYWRITER
Peter Jones
DESIGNER
Randall Jones

517
District 4
CLIENT
Cramer-Krasselt
AGENCY
Cramer-Krasselt
Orlando, FL
CREATIVE DIRECTORS
Mitch Boyd
Bill Nosan
ART DIRECTOR
Mitch Boyd
COPYWRITER
Tom Woodward
PHOTOGRAPHER
John Bateman

518
District 8
CLIENT
Marshfield Clinic
AGENCY
Marshfield Clinic
Marshfield, WI
ART DIRECTOR
Andrea Picard
COPYWRITING
Corporate
Communications
PHOTOGRAPHER
Bill Paulson

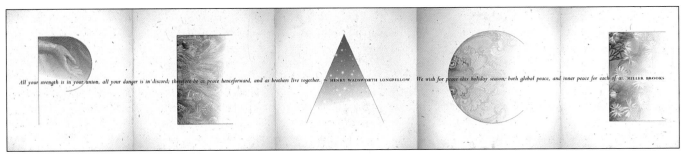

520

520
District 6
CLIENT
Miller Brooks, Inc.
AGENCY
Miller Brooks, Inc.
Zionsville, IN
ART DIRECTOR
Darryl Brown
COPYWRITER
Darryl Brown

521
District 9
CLIENT
McCullough Graphics
Inc.
AGENCY
McCullough Graphics
Inc.
Dubuque, IA
CREATIVE DIRECTION
McCullough Design
PHOTOGRAPHY
Design Photography
SEPARATOR
AGS
PRINTER
Union-Hoerman

522
District 5
CLIENT
Cindy Kessler
AGENCY
Wolf Blumberg Krody
Cincinnati, OH
CREATIVE DIRECTOR
Vern Hughes
ART DIRECTOR
Kris Schwandner
COPYWRITER
John Sweney

521

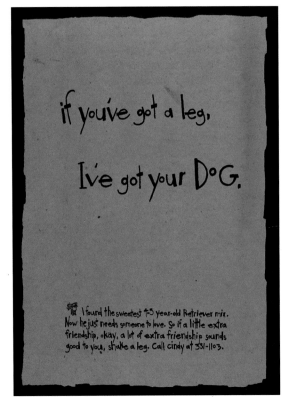

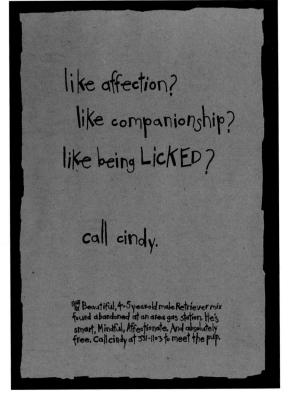

522

523

524

526

523
District 6
CLIENT
The Becker House
AGENCY
RileySimmons Inc.
Fort Wayne, IN
CREATIVE DIRECTOR
Audrey Riley
ART DIRECTOR
Mark Russett
COPYWRITER
Dan Schroeter
ILLUSTRATOR
Dan Schroeter

524
District 13
CLIENT
Hawaii International
Film Festival
AGENCY
Ogilvy & Mather
Hawaii
Honolulu, HI
ART DIRECTOR
April Rutherford
COPYWRITER
Richard Tillotson
PHOTOGRAPHER
Tuice Gibson
DESIGNER
April Rutherford

525
District 9
CLIENT
Doskocil Companies
AGENCY
Greteman Group
Wichita, KS
CREATIVE DIRECTOR
James Strange
ART DIRECTOR
James Strange
COPYWRITERS
Paul Hansen
Greg Menefee
DESIGNER
James Strange

526
District 13
CLIENT
Clarence Lee Design
AGENCY
Clarence Lee Design
Honolulu, HI
DESIGNER
Clarence Lee

COLLATERAL

527
District 12

CLIENT
PACT/Boelts Bros.

AGENCY
Boelts Bros. Visual
Communications
Tucson, AZ

DESIGNERS
Jackson Boelts
Eric Boelts

PRINTER
Fabe Litho

PRODUCTION
Michelle Ramirez

528
District 3

CLIENT
Pascale & Associates

AGENCY
Pascale & Associates
Greensboro, NC

CREATIVE DIRECTOR
Hugo Pascale

ART DIRECTORS
Kimberly Daniels Hun
Regina Barnhill

COPYWRITERS
Donna West Stokes
Kristin Williams

DESIGNERS
Rebecca Timberlake
Kelli Brookshire

529
District 10

CLIENT
Lynn Eskridge
Illustration

AGENCY
Meyer & Johnson
Irving, TX

CREATIVE DIRECTOR
Lynn Eskridge

COPYWRITER
Tom Wirt

ILLUSTRATOR
Lynn Eskridge

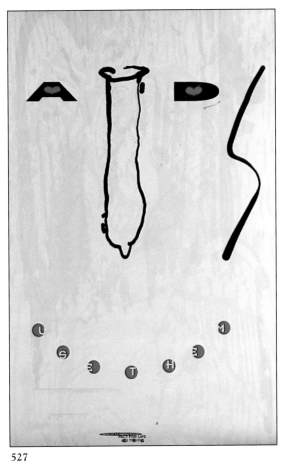

527

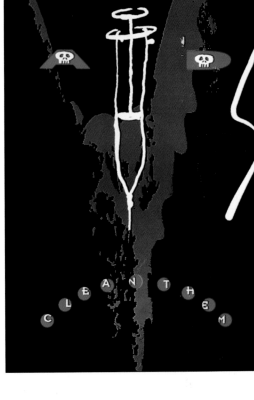

529

528

530

531

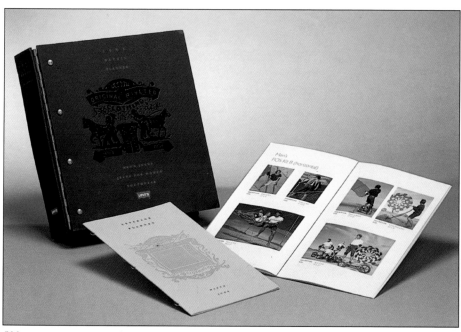

532

530
District 9

CLIENT
Wehrman &
Company

AGENCY
Garlich Printing
Company
Fenton, MO

DESIGN
Wehrman &
Company

531
District 6

CLIENT
Riley Hospital for
Children

AGENCY
Keller-Doll Design,
Inc.
Indianapolis, IN

CREATIVE DIRECTOR
Dawn Keller-Doll

ART DIRECTOR
Dawn Keller-Doll

COPYWRITERS
Karen Campbell
Lynda Neal

PHOTOGRAPHER
Dick Spahr

DESIGNER
Dawn Keller-Doll

SEPARATOR
Rheitone Inc.

PRINTER
Shepard Poorman
Communications

532
District 14

CLIENT
Levi Strauss &
Company

AGENCY
Foote, Cone &
Belding
San Francisco, CA

CREATIVE DIRECTOR
Mike Koelker

ART DIRECTOR
Stephen Wille

COPYWRITER
Mike Jurkovac

ACCOUNT EXECUTIVE
Anna Compaglia

COLLATERAL

533
District 9
CLIENT
Ruth Beggs
AGENCY
The Greatest Agency
in the World
Lincoln, NE
ART DIRECTOR
Ron Sack
COPYWRITER
Pat Piper
PHOTOGRAPHERS
Bob and Steve Ervin
PRINTER
Setells

534
District 9
CLIENT
Sheldon and Kathy
Coleman
AGENCY
Sherrie's
Wichita, KS
CREATIVE DIRECTORS
Sherrie Holdeman
Tracy Holdeman
ART DIRECTORS
Sherrie Holdeman
Tracy Holdeman
ILLUSTRATORS
Sherrie Holdeman
Tracy Holdeman
DESIGNERS
Sherrie Holdeman
Tracy Holdeman

535
District 7
CLIENT
South Central Bell
AGENCY
Dye, Van Mol &
Lawrence
Nashville, TN
CREATIVE DIRECTOR
Chuck Creasy
ART DIRECTOR
Chuck Creasy
COPYWRITER
Tracy Johnson
PHOTOGRAPHERS
Dean Dickson
Jim McGuire
DESIGNER
Bill Brunt
PRODUCTION
Bill Brunt

536
District 8
CLIENT
Image Studios
AGENCY
Grey Sunder Prescher
Cedarburg, WI
ART DIRECTOR
Blaine Huber
COPYWRITER
Blaine Huber
PHOTOGRAPHER
Image Studios
DESIGNER
Susan Griffiths

533

534

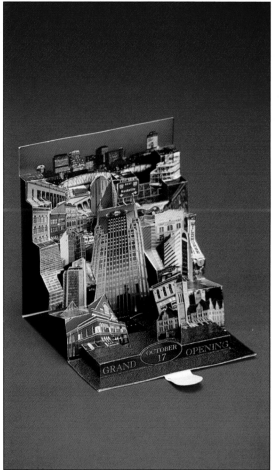

535

536

SALES
PROMOTION

AGENCY
Edison Brothers
Stores
St. Louis, MO

CREATIVE DIRECTOR
Flint Finlinson

ART DIRECTOR
Paul Jarvis

OAKTREE

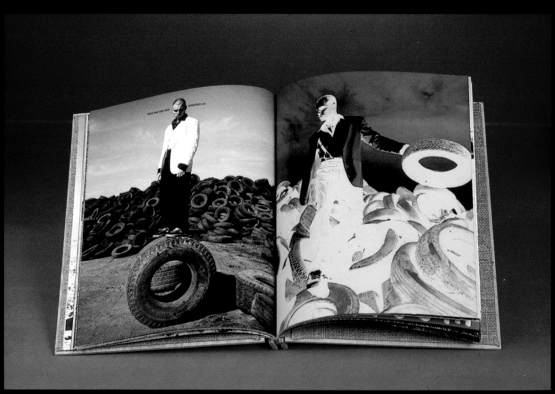

Company

AGENCY
Goodby Silverstein
& Partners
San Francisco, CA

CREATIVE DIRECTORS
Paul Curtin
Rob Price

ART DIRECTORS
Paul Curtin
Keith Anderson

COPYWRITER
Rob Price

PHOTOGRAPHERS
Jim Erickson
James Wojack
Bruce Debour

DESIGNER
Keith Anderson

PRODUCER
Anne Bodel

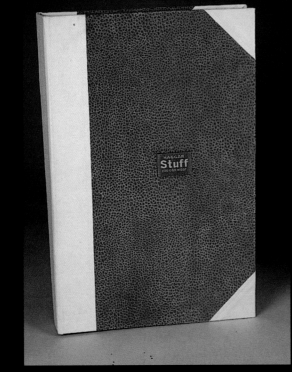

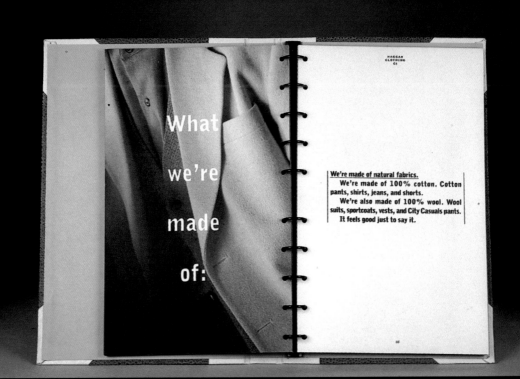

540

540
District 11
CLIENT
Smith Sport Optics
AGENCY
Hornal Anderson
Design Works
Seattle, WA
ART DIRECTOR
Jack Anderson
DESIGNERS
David Bates
Jack Anderson

541
District 4

CLIENT
Gary Lambert Salon

AGENCY
Anson-Stoner
Winter Park, FL

CREATIVE DIRECTOR
Joe Anson

ART DIRECTOR
Bernard Urban

PHOTOGRAPHER
Bernard Urban

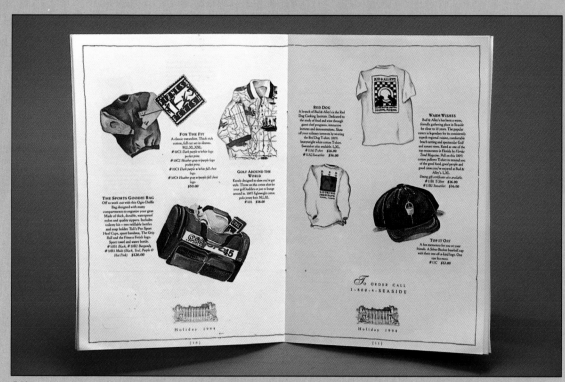

542

543

542
District 7

CLIENT
Seaside Community
Development

AGENCY
Litho-Krome
Columbus, GA

DESIGNER
Pam Breaux

543
District 6

CLIENT
Town & Country
Cedar Homes

AGENCY
Communi-Graphics
Petoskey, MI

ART DIRECTOR
Lori Step

COPYWRITER
Gary Buffington

SALES PROMOTION

544
District 14

CLIENT
Kenwood USA

AGENCY
Citron Haligman
Bedecarre
San Francisco, CA

CREATIVE DIRECTORS
Matt Haligman
Kirk Citron

ART DIRECTOR
Roz Tomney

COPYWRITER
Bryan Behar

ACCOUNT EXECUTIVE
Doug Sweeny

545
District 3

CLIENT
Cone Mills

AGENCY
Broach & Company
Greensboro, NC

CREATIVE DIRECTION
The Broach Team

PHOTOGRAPHER
Thaddeus Watkins

544

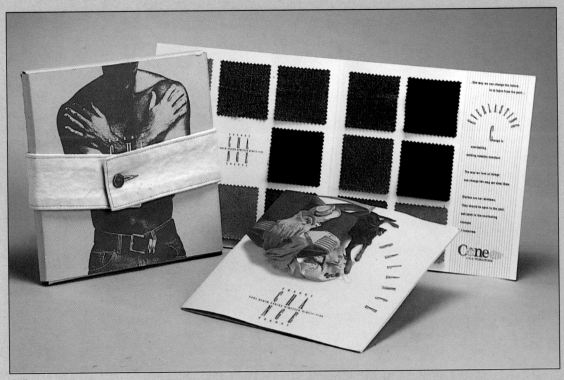

545

546

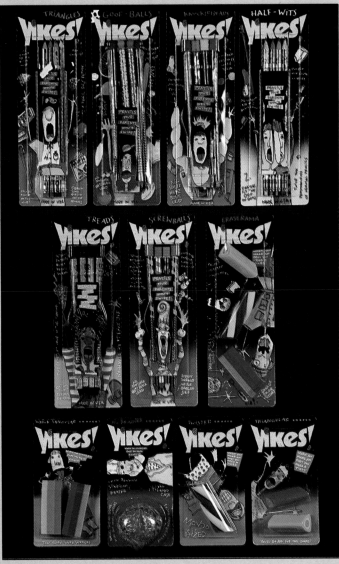

547

546
District 11
CLIENT
Talking Rain
AGENCY
Hornall Anderson
Design Works
Seattle, WA
ART DIRECTOR
Jack Anderson
ILLUSTRATOR
Julie LaPine
DESIGNERS
Heidi Favour
Leo Raymundo
Jana Nishi
Julie LaPine
Jack Anderson

547
District 7
CLIENT
Empire Berol
AGENCY
Jackson Design
Nashville, TN
CREATIVE DIRECTOR
Buddy Jackson
ART DIRECTOR
Buddy Jackson
ILLUSTRATOR
Beth Middleworth
DESIGNERS
Sam Knight
Beth Middleworth
ENGRAVER
Precision Color
PRODUCTION
Patty Dondeville

548
District 12
CLIENT
The Haircutter
AGENCY
Hurst Group
Salt Lake City, UT
CREATIVE DIRECTOR
Grant Phelps
COPYWRITER
Gary Sume
PHOTOGRAPHER
Michael Roberts
DESIGNER
Shawn Stoyle

549
District 7
CLIENT
Barq's Inc.
AGENCY
X Design
Baton Rouge, LA
CREATIVE DIRECTION
X Design
ART DIRECTION
X Design
PHOTOGRAPHER
David Humphreys
DESIGNER
David Worrell
PRINTER
Ivy Hill/Delta Conta
PREPRESS
Image 4

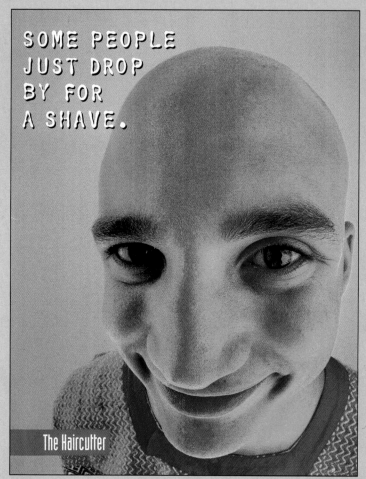

548

549

SALES PROMOTION

550
District 7
CLIENT
Arista/Nashville
AGENCY
High Five
Entertainment
Nashville, TN
EXECUTIVE PRODUCERS
Bud Schaetzle
Martin Fischer
PRODUCER
Susan O'Leary
DIRECTOR
Michael Salomon

551
District 7
CLIENT
ABC Sports
AGENCY
Deaton Flanigen
Productions
Nashville, TN
CREATIVE DIRECTOR
Bob Toms
ART DIRECTOR
Greg Horne
COPYWRITER
Bob Toms
PHOTOGRAPHER
Robert Gantz
EXECUTIVE PRODUCER
Tom Remiszewski
PRODUCER
Peter Zavadil
DIRECTORS
Robert Deaton
George J. Flanigen
MUSIC
Scott Hendricks

550   551

SUMMARY (Music Video for "Baby Likes to Rock It" by The Tractors) A pizza delivery boy walks down a dark, scary alley with half a dozen boxes. There are strange noises and shadows all around him. He is seriously considering a career change. He follows the directions on the crumpled piece of paper in his hand to a weathered door set deep in a brick building. Hung on the door is a handwritten sign, "CLOSED SESSION." He knocks. The door seems to creak open almost on its own. He cautiously steps through dark doorway and enters... the Tractor Zone.

552

District 5

CLIENT
Hush Puppies
Company

AGENCY
Fitch Inc.
Worthington, OH

ART DIRECTOR
Jaimie Alexander

PHOTOGRAPHER
Richard Bailey

DESIGNER
Paul Westrick

DOCUMENTATION
Mark Steele

553
District 2

CLIENT
Marriott Ranch

AGENCY
Enten and
Associates
Rockville, MD

CREATIVE DIRECTOR
Sharyn Panagides

ART DIRECTOR
Pat Cunningham

COPYWRITER
Sharyn Panagides

PHOTOGRAPHER
Debi Fox

PRINTER
Rockville Printing

PRODUCTION
Michele Mancuso

553

554
District 9
CLIENT
The Hayes Company
AGENCY
Love Packaging
Group
Wichita, KS
CREATIVE DIRECTOR
Tracy Holdeman
ART DIRECTOR
Tracy Holdeman
COPYWRITER
Clark Jackson
PHOTOGRAPHY
Rock Island Studios
ILLUSTRATOR
Tracy Holdeman
DESIGNERS
Tracy Holdeman
Daryl Hearne
PRINTER
P.I.
PRE-PRESS
E.T.S.
DIECUTTING
Love Box

555
District 4
CLIENT
Beef O'Brady's
AGENCY
King Matson
Advertising
Tampa, FL
CREATIVE DIRECTOR
Jeff King
COPYWRITER
Mike Matson
PHOTOGRAPHER
Chris Stickney

556
District 9
CLIENT
The Hayes Company
AGENCY
Love Packaging
Group
Wichita, KS
CREATIVE DIRECTOR
Tracy Holdeman
ART DIRECTOR
Tracy Holdeman
COPYWRITER
Clark Jackson
PHOTOGRAPHY
Rock Island Studios
ILLUSTRATOR
Tracy Holdeman
DESIGNERS
Tracy Holdeman
Daryl Hearne

557
District 2
CLIENT
Style of Man
AGENCY
Earle Palmer Brown/
Philadelphia
Philadelphia, PA
CREATIVE DIRECTOR
Mike Drazen
ART DIRECTOR
Robert Shaw West
COPYWRITER
Kelly Simmons

554

556

555

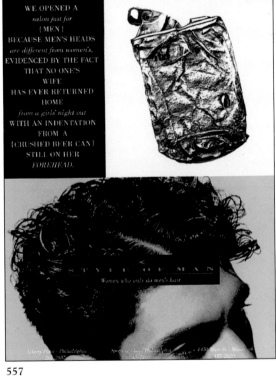

557

558

559

560

561

562

558
District 4
CLIENT
Brasmerica Inc.
AGENCY
King Matson Advertising
Tampa, FL
CREATIVE DIRECTOR
Jeff King
ART DIRECTORS
Eric Swanson
Stella Moore
COPYWRITER
Mike Matson

559
District 8
CLIENT
G. Heileman Brewing
Company
AGENCY
Culver Design
Milwaukee, WI
CREATIVE DIRECTOR
Wells Culver
ART DIRECTOR
Mark Drewek
DESIGNER
John Pfeiffer

560
District 9
CLIENT
Utilicorp
AGENCY
Muller + Company
Kansas City, MO
DESIGNERS
Jon Simonsen
Amy Dawson
Angela Coleman

561
District 6
CLIENT
Country Grown Foods
AGENCY
Perich & Partners
Ann Arbor, MI
CREATIVE DIRECTOR
Ernie Perich
DESIGNER
Scott Pryor

562
District 9
CLIENT
The Hayes Company
AGENCY
Love Packaging Group
Wichita, KS
CREATIVE DIRECTOR
Tracy Holdeman
ART DIRECTOR
Tracy Holdeman
COPYWRITER
Clark Jackson
PHOTOGRAPHY
Rock Island Studios
ILLUSTRATOR
Tracy Holdeman
DESIGNERS
Tracy Holdeman
Daryl Hearne
PRE-PRESS
E.T.S.
DIECUTTING
Love Box

SALES PROMOTION

563

District 8

CLIENT
RTJ Novelties

AGENCY
Imaginasium Design
Green Bay, WI

CREATIVE DIRECTOR
Joe Bergner

COPYWRITER
Joe Bergner

ILLUSTRATOR
Joe Bergner

DESIGNER
Joe Bergner

564

District 4

CLIENT
Barnies Coffee & Tea

AGENCY
Clarke Advertising
and Public Relations
Sarasota, FL

ILLUSTRATOR
Lynn Hirsch

565

District 2

CLIENT
Style of Man

AGENCY
Earle Palmer Brown/
Philadelphia
Philadelphia, PA

CREATIVE DIRECTOR
Mike Drazen

ART DIRECTOR
Robert Shaw West

COPYWRITER
Kelly Simmons

566

District 8

CLIENT
Johnsonville Foods Co.

AGENCY
Johnsonville Foods Co.
Kohler, WI

CREATIVE DIRECTOR
Mark Fischer

ART DIRECTOR
Anthony R. Rammer

PHOTOGRAPHER
Christopher Gould

DESIGNER
Ron Pike

PRODUCER
Anthony R. Rammer

567

District 8

CLIENT
Johnsonville Foods Co.

AGENCY
Johnsonville Foods Co.
Kohler, WI

CREATIVE DIRECTORS
Mark Fischer
Kim Barden

ART DIRECTOR
Anthony R. Rammer

COPYWRITING
Noble & Associates

PHOTOGRAPHER
Christopher Gould

DESIGNERS
Anthony R. Rammer
Ron Pike

564

563

566

565

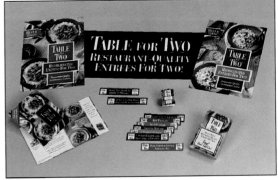

567

Pray that they shop here.

568

DO WHAT BUFFALO CAN'T.

WIN A COWBOY GAME.

Win tickets for two to the Dallas/Cleveland game at Texas Stadium, December 10, 1994. Includes airfare and hotel accommodations. Five lucky Cowboy fans will win.

YOUR HOMETOWN GMC TRUCK DEALERS

569

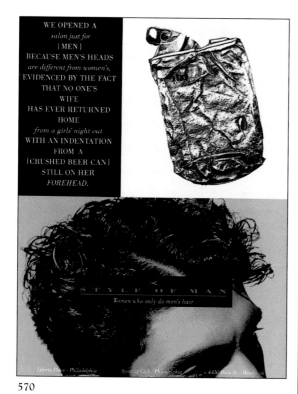

WE OPENED A *salon just for* { MEN } BECAUSE MEN'S HEADS *are different from women's,* EVIDENCED BY THE FACT THAT NO ONE'S WIFE HAS EVER RETURNED HOME *from a girls' night out* WITH AN INDENTATION FROM A { CRUSHED BEER CAN } STILL ON HER *FOREHEAD.*

STYLE OF MAN
Women who only do men's hair

570

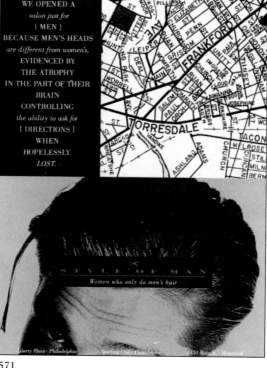

WE OPENED A *salon just for* { MEN } BECAUSE MEN'S HEADS *are different from women's,* EVIDENCED BY THE ATROPHY IN THE PART OF THEIR BRAIN CONTROLLING *the ability to ask for* { DIRECTIONS } WHEN HOPELESSLY *LOST.*

STYLE OF MAN
Women who only do men's hair

571

568
District 7
CLIENT
Condom Art
AGENCY
Tausche Martin Lonsdorf
Atlanta, GA
CREATIVE DIRECTORS
Kurt Tausche
Patrick Seullin
ART DIRECTOR
Ralph Watson
COPYWRITER
Carey Moore

569
District 10
CLIENT
Hometown GMC Truck Dealers
AGENCY
Anderson Advertising
San Antonio, TX
CREATIVE DIRECTOR
Stan McElrath
ART DIRECTOR
James Howe
COPYWRITER
Kevin Paetzel
PRODUCTION
Melissa Garcia
Jerry Lindemann
ACCOUNT EXECUTIVE
Allen Barrett

570
District 2
CLIENT
Style of Man
AGENCY
Earle Palmer Brown/ Philadelphia
Philadelphia, PA
CREATIVE DIRECTOR
Mike Drazen
ART DIRECTOR
Robert Shaw West
COPYWRITER
Kelly Simmons

571
District 2
CLIENT
Style of Man
AGENCY
Earle Palmer Brown/ Philadelphia
Philadelphia, PA
CREATIVE DIRECTOR
Mike Drazen
ART DIRECTOR
Robert Shaw West
COPYWRITER
Kelly Simmons

SALES PROMOTION

572
District 7
CLIENT
University Art
Museum / University
of Southwestern
Louisiana
AGENCY
Trinty Design &
Advertising for the
Creative Spirit
Acadiana, LA
ART DIRECTOR
Megan Barra
COPYWRITERS
Herman Mhire
William Moreland
PHOTOGRAPHERS
Robley Dupleix
John Chiasson
DESIGNER
Megan Barra
PRINTER
Print Service, Inc.
SCULPTOR
John Geldersma

573
District 7
CLIENT
Duck Head Apparel
Company
AGENCY
The Buntin Group
Nashville, TN
CREATIVE DIRECTOR
S.A. Habib
ART DIRECTOR
R.J. Lyons
COPYWRITERS
Tom Cocke
Karry Oliver
DESIGNER
Tonya Presley
ENGRAVER
GPI
PRINTER
Douglas Printing
PRODUCTION
Chris Carroll

574
District 12
CLIENT
Milk & Honey
AGENCY
Hine & Stock
Associates
Santa Fe, NM
CREATIVE DIRECTOR
Peter Stock
ILLUSTRATOR
Gregory Trivet Smith
PRODUCTION
Peter Scholz

575
District 8
CLIENT
Aurora Candlers
AGENCY
Wenger-Marsh
& Meier
Madison, WI
ART DIRECTOR
Frank Meier
ILLUSTRATOR
Kristy Hoffman

572

573

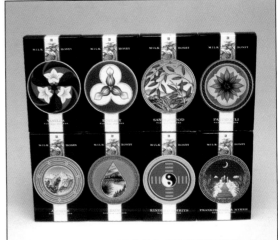
574

575

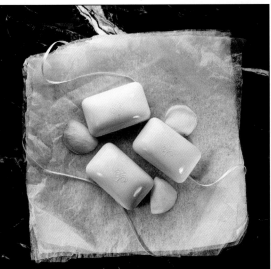

576

576
District 5
CLIENT
The Yardley Limited
Company
AGENCY
Price Weber
Marketing
Communications, Inc.
Louisville, KY
CREATIVE DIRECTOR
Larry Profancik
DESIGNER
Juliet Robertson
ACCOUNT EXECUTIVE
Henrietta Pepper

577
District 9

CLIENT
Chance Rides Inc.

AGENCY
Associated
Advertising Agency
Wichita, KS

CREATIVE DIRECTOR
Marsha Cromwell

PRODUCTION
Patrick Dreiling

ACCOUNT SUPERVISOR
Preston Huston

ACCOUNT EXECUTIVE
Susan Leasure

578
District 9
CLIENT
Pagoda Trading
Company
AGENCY
The Puckett Group
St. Louis, MO
CREATIVE DIRECTOR
Steve Puckett
ART DIRECTOR
David Young
PHOTOGRAPHER
Peter Sheplet
ACCOUNT SUPERVISOR
Todd Imming

579

District 7

CLIENT
United Chair

AGENCY
SlaughterHanson
Advertising
Birmingham, AL

CREATIVE DIRECTOR
Terry Slaughter

ART DIRECTORS
Marion English
Rebecca Fulmer
Maya Metz

COPYWRITER
Laura Holmes

TYPOGRAPHY
Communication Arts

PRODUCER
Diamond Display

ACCOUNT EXECUTIVE
Gail Cosby

579

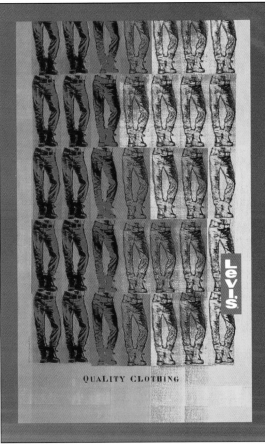

580

580
District 14
CLIENT
Levi Strauss
& Company
AGENCY
Foote, Cone
& Belding
San Francisco, CA
CREATIVE DIRECTOR
Mike Koelker
ART DIRECTOR
Stephen Wille
COPYWRITER
Mike Jurkovac
PHOTOGRAPHER
Randall Mesdon
ILLUSTRATOR
Richard Turtletaub
PRODUCER
Mary Jo Kollman
DIGITAL ARTISTS
Sue McIntire
Ellen Fortier
ACCOUNT EXECUTIVE
Anna Compaglia

581
District 4

CLIENT
Anheuser-Busch, Inc.

AGENCY
Innes Price Jones, Inc.
Tampa, FL

ART DIRECTOR
Wendy Sherman
Hiraok

PRODUCTION
Susan Mosley

ACCOUNT EXECUTIVE
Jill Kirkendall

581

SALES PROMOTION

582

583
District 10

CLIENT
Today's Kids

AGENCY
The Marketing
Company
Little Rock, AR

CREATIVE DIRECTOR
Susan Maddox

SCULPTURE
Joseph Melancon

FABRICATORS
Focus 2

PRODUCTION
Laser Tech

ACCOUNT EXECUTIVE
Stephanie Roberts

(Thanks Eve)

584
District 13
CLIENT
Delete Clothing
AGENCY
Ronnda Heinrich
Photography
Honolulu, HI
ART DIRECTOR
Arnie Yew
PHOTOGRAPHER
Ronnda Heinrich

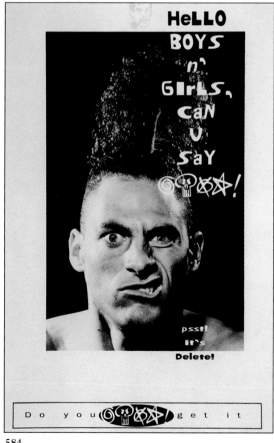

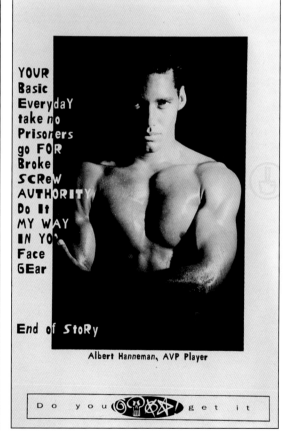

Albert Hanneman, AVP Player

585
District 8
CLIENT
Kimberly-Clark
Corporation
AGENCY
Jacobson Rost
Sheboygan, WI
CREATIVE DIRECTOR
Reed Allen
ART DIRECTOR
Bob MacDonald
COPYWRITER
Judith Garson
PHOTOGRAPHY
Image Studios
ILLUSTRATION
Nachreiner-Boie Art
Factory
ACCOUNT EXECUTIVES
Eileen Hutchison
Jenifer Kemper

586
District 3
CLIENT
Bassett-Walker
AGENCY
The Holt Group
Greensboro, NC
CREATIVE DIRECTOR
Vickie Canada
PHOTOGRAPHER
John Tesh
DESIGNER
Kristin Moore

587
District 3
CLIENT
College of
Engineering,
Virginia Tech
AGENCY
Virginia Tech
Blacksburg, VA
CREATIVE DIRECTOR
Michele Molden
Haver
ART DIRECTORS
Bob Veltri
Rick Griffith
Gary Colbert
COPYWRITER
Mark Nystrom
PHOTOGRAPHERS
Michele Molden
Haver
Bob Veltri
Rick Griffith
Mark Nystrom
Gary Colbert
DESIGNER
Michele Molden
Haver
EDITOR
Lynn A. Nystrom
CONTRIBUTING EDITOR
Harry Yeatts

585

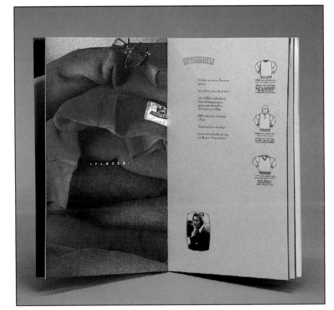

586

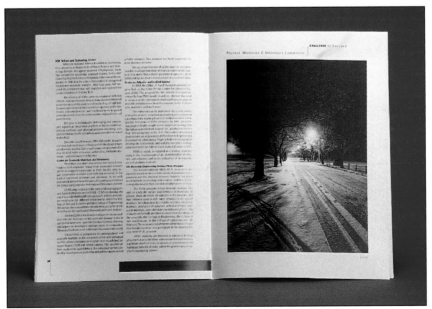

587

SALES PROMOTION

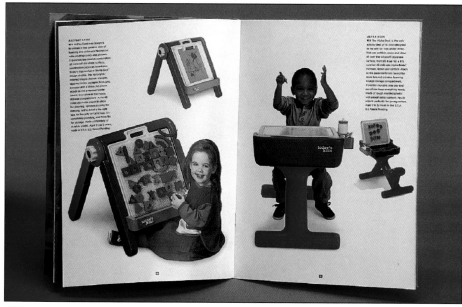

588

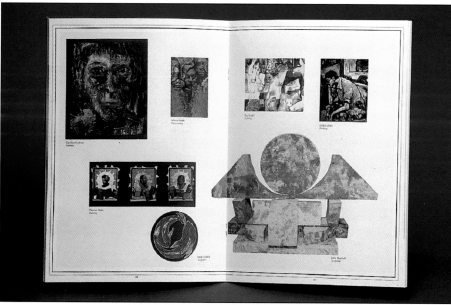

589

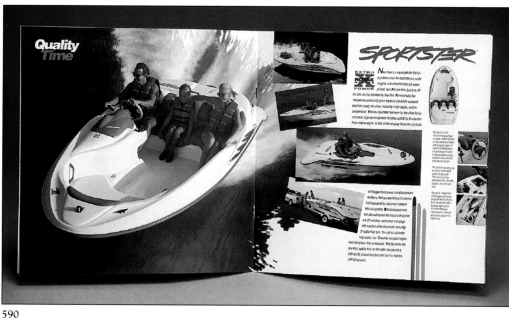

590

588
District 10
CLIENT
Today's Kids
AGENCY
The Marketing Company
Little Rock, AR
CREATIVE DIRECTOR
Susan Maddox
COPYWRITER
Shawn Solloway
PHOTOGRAPHER
Bobby Badger
SEPARATOR
Laser Tech
PRINTER
Padgett
STYLIST
Stacie Smith

589
District 7
CLIENT
Memphis College of Art
AGENCY
Patterson Design Works
Memphis, TN
CREATIVE DIRECTOR
Pat Patterson
ART DIRECTOR
Pat Patterson
ENGRAVER
Graphic Arts
PRINTER
Pinnacle Press
TYPOGRAPHY
Garphic Arts
PRODUCTION
Pat Patterson
ACCOUNT EXECUTIVE
Pat Patterson

590
District 4
CLIENT
Sea Doo Jet Boats
AGENCY
Tuzee Associates
Cape Coral, FL
CREATIVE DIRECTOR
David Belling
ART DIRECTOR
David Belling
COPYWRITER
Renee Shahinian
ACCOUNT EXECUTIVE
Renee Shahinian

591
District 8
CLIENT
Great Plains
Software, Inc.
AGENCY
Great Plains
Software, Inc.
Fargo, ND
CREATIVE DIRECTION
Mark Olson
Jay Richardson
Luann French
Knight Printing
Company

592
District 9
CLIENT
Precis-Edison
Brothers Stores
AGENCY
Cube Advertising
and Design
Clayton, MO
COPYWRITER
Steve Unger
PHOTOGRAPHER
Scott Smith
DESIGNER
David Chiow

593
District 7
CLIENT
StarSong
Communications
AGENCY
Jackson Design
Nashville, TN
CREATIVE DIRECTOR
Buddy Jackson
ART DIRECTOR
Buddy Jackson
COPYWRITER
Kevin May Smith
PHOTOGRAPHERS
Peter Nash
Ben Pearson
Mark Tucker
ILLUSTRATOR
Jimmy Abegg
DESIGNER
Buddy Jackson
ENGRAVER
Colourworks
PRINTER
Berryville Graphics

591

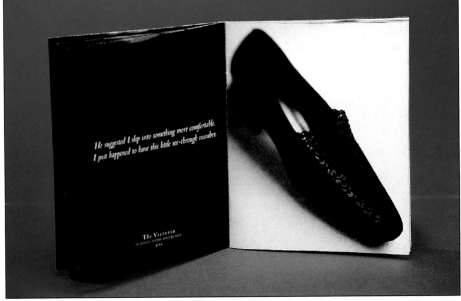

592

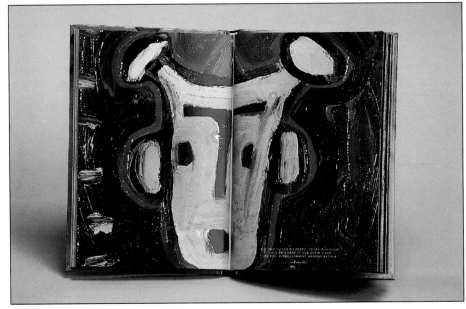

593

594

595

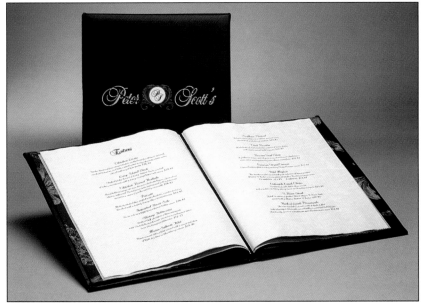

596

594
District 8
CLIENT
Berkley & Company
AGENCY
Lawrence & Schiller
Sioux Falls, SD
CREATIVE DIRECTION
Scott Lawrence
Kim Heidinger
Dan Edmonds
Nancy Lund
Shelley Vogel
Scott Ostman
Keith Hansen
Ben Alspach
Linda Rubis
Lennon Bausman
Fitzgerald
Photography
R&S Litho
The John Roberts
Company

595
District 10
CLIENT
Harold's
AGENCY
Harold's
Norman, OK
CREATIVE DIRECTION
Team Harold's

596
District 4
CLIENT
Peter Scott's
AGENCY
Derek Dugan
Advertising Design
Orlando, FL
ART DIRECTOR
Derek Dugan
DESIGNER
Derek Dugan
PRINTERS
Compton Press
Steve Welch

597
District 14
CLIENT
Specialized Bicycles
AGENCY
Goodby, Silverstein
& Partners
San Francisco, CA
CREATIVE DIRECTORS
Paul Curtin
Rob Price
ART DIRECTORS
Paul Curtin
Peter DiGrazia
COPYWRITER
Eric Osterhaus
PHOTOGRAPHERS
David Campbell
Julian Zgoda
Jim Erickson
Keith Silva
ILLUSTRATORS
Ed Roth
Doug Becker
DESIGNERS
Jon Weber
Paul Curtin
Peter Locke
PRODUCER
Jim King
ACCOUNT EXECUTIVE
Kitty Brunswick

598
District 10
CLIENT
United Design
Corporation
AGENCY
United Design
Corporation
Noble, OK
CREATIVE DIRECTOR
Gayla Goodell
ART DIRECTOR
Deana Parsons
ILLUSTRATOR
Jon Goodell
PRINTER
T.J. Smith
PRODUCTION
Cathy Hersom

599
District 5
CLIENT
Allo Spiedo
AGENCY
Packaging Unlimited
Louisville, KY
ILLUSTRATOR
Bud Hixon
DESIGN
Walter McCord
Mary Cawein
Chop Logic

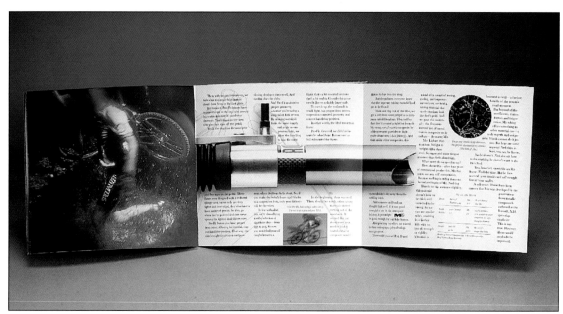

597

598

599

600

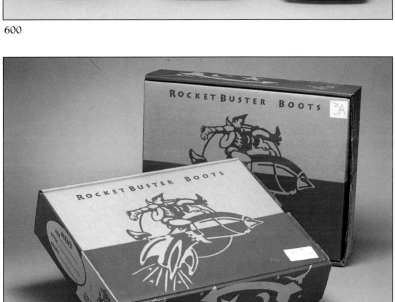

601

602

600
District 3
CLIENT
Brown Wooten
AGENCY
The Holt Group
Greensboro, NC
CREATIVE DIRECTOR
Vickie Canada
PHOTOGRAPHER
John Tesh
DESIGNER
Kristin Moore

601
District 12
CLIENT
Rocketbuster Boots
AGENCY
Snortum Studios
El Paso, TX
ART DIRECTOR
Marty Snortum

602
District 2
CLIENT
BLF, Inc.
AGENCY
Lavelle-Miller Murray
Scranton, PA
CREATIVE DIRECTION
Lavelle-Miller Murray

603
District 2

CLIENT
Planet Called Earth
Company

AGENCY
Supon Design Group,
Inc.
Washington, DC

CREATIVE DIRECTOR
Supon Phornirunlit

ART DIRECTOR
Andrew Dolan

ILLUSTRATOR
Debbie Savitt
Andrew Dolan

PRINTER
Anchor Promotions

604
District 7

CLIENT
Community Coffee
Company, Inc.

AGENCY
X Design, Inc.
Baton Rouge, LA

CREATIVE DIRECTION
X Design

ART DIRECTION
X Design

COPYWRITER
David Worrell

DESIGN
X Design

PRINTER
Fresco/International

PRE-PRESS
Image 4

605
District 12

CLIENT
Santa Fe Convention
and Visitors Bureau

AGENCY
Impressions
Advertising
Santa Fe, NM

ART DIRECTOR
Thomas Rodriguez

COPYWRITERS
Steve Lewis
Russ Raintree
Jay Leipzig

PHOTOGRAPHERS
Michel Monteaux
John McLean
Chris Cornie

ILLUSTRATOR
Jose Cisneros

DESIGNER
Thomas Rodriguez

603

604

605

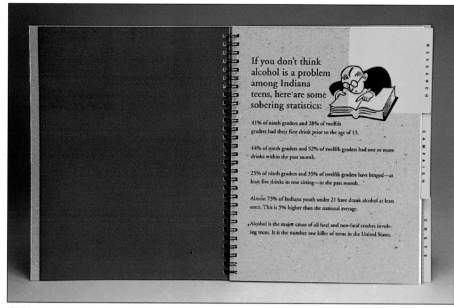

606

607

608

606
District 6
CLIENT
National Family
Partnership
AGENCY
Caldwell VanRiper
Indianapolis, IN
ART DIRECTOR
Jeff P. Morris
COPYWRITER
Jeff S. Morris
ACCOUNT SERVICE
Carrie Phelps

607
District 14
CLIENT
Specialized Bicycles
AGENCY
Goodby, Silverstein
& Partners
San Francisco, CA
CREATIVE DIRECTORS
Paul Curtin
Rob Price
ART DIRECTORS
Paul Curtin
Peter DiGrazia
COPYWRITER
Eric Osterhaus
PHOTOGRAPHERS
David Campbell
Julian Zgoda
Jim Erickson
Keith Silva
ILLUSTRATOR
Doug Becker
DESIGNERS
Paul Curtin
Peter Locke
PRODUCER
Jim King
ACCOUNT EXECUTIVE
Kitty Brunswick

608
District 14
CLIENT
Specialized Bicycles
AGENCY
Goodby, Silverstein
& Partners
San Francisco, CA
CREATIVE DIRECTORS
Paul Curtin
Rob Price
ART DIRECTORS
Paul Curtin
Peter DiGrazia
COPYWRITER
Eric Osterhaus
PHOTOGRAPHERS
David Campbell
Julian Zgoda
Jim Erickson
Keith Silva
ILLUSTRATOR
Doug Becker
DESIGNER
Paul Curtin
Jon Weber
PRODUCER
Jim King
ACCOUNT EXECUTIVE
Kitty Brunswick

609
District 14
CLIENT
IDO
AGENCY
Tsang Proop &
Guerin
San Francisco, CA

610
District 10
CLIENT
Sports Designs
AGENCY
Steven Sessions, Inc.
Houston, TX
CREATIVE DIRECTOR
Steven Sessions
ART DIRECTOR
Steven Sessions
COPYWRITER
John Kutch
PHOTOGRAPHER
Bryan Kuntz
ILLUSTRATOR
Phil Schmitt
DESIGNER
Steven Sessions

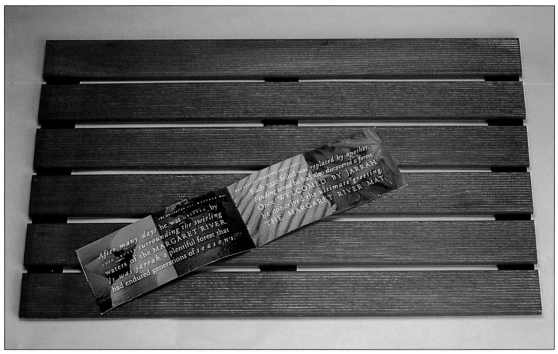

609

610

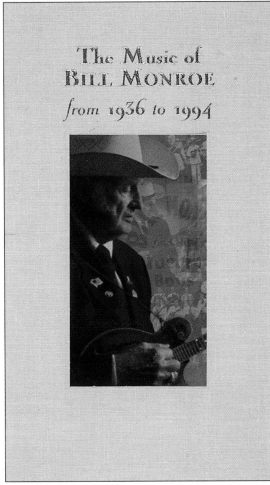

612

611
District 10
CLIENT
Performing Arts
Fort Worth
AGENCY
Witherspoon &
Associates
Fort Worth, TX
CREATIVE DIRECTOR
Debra Morrow
COPYWRITER
Debra Morrow
PRODUCER
Debra Morrow
PRODUCTION
Aries Productions
DIRECTOR
Steve Dunning
ACCOUNT EXECUTIVE
Susan Watt

612
District 7
CLIENT
MCA
AGENCY
Barnes & Company
Nashville, TN
ART DIRECTOR
Bill Barnes
COPYWRITER
John Rumble
PHOTOGRAPHERS
Les Leverett
Jim McGuire
Glenn Hall
Jim Devault
ILLUSTRATOR
Jerry Keeter
DESIGNER
Bill Tyler
ENGRAVER
Harris Graphics
PRINTER
The Queens Group
PRODUCTION
Bill Tyler

611

OPENING SUPERS: It is the promise of something special about to happen. The glow of lights. Hearts beating. The meeting of man, music and space. It is the shaping of cultural destiny. In the traditions of the great halls of Europe and Fort Worth's own individual spirit, A Great Hall will rise in 1998.

CLOSING SUPERS: There will be players both on and off stage at Fort Worth's Performance Hall. There are parts for all of us. In four short years, we will be the audience in a world-class hall. But first, we must all play a crucial role in making it a reality. This Great Hall deserves more than a gift of a lifetime. It calls for our contribution of many lifetimes. Not only for our generation, but also for our children's generation, and for their children's children.

SALES PROMOTION

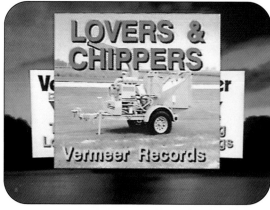

613

ANNCR: New from Vermeer Records, the makers of Favorite Trenching Love Songs, comes a brand new assortment of old favorites for you and yours. It's Lovers & Chippers.

I can see clearly now the brush has gone...

A-a-an, how can you mend a broken branch...

ANNCR: Remember these timeless classics?

It was a bru-ush chipper hydraulic driver, yeah...

ANNCR: Who could forget...

Mmmm. That's the time... I feel like clearing brush with you.

Lookin' for brush in all the wrong places...

ANNCR: It's the greatest collection of wood reducing love songs ever assembled!

Hey Mr. Diggin' Dutchman grind a twig for me. No more branches can I see. And my pruning operation has been flourishing.

ANNCR: Order yours today and receive as a bonus, Spade For Each Other - including hits like...

Spade Lady Spade. Uprooting yourself from a green grass bed.

ANNCR: You won't find this collection in any store. To order Lovers & Chippers call 1-800-C-H-I-P-P-E-R-S. You call now!

Oh darlin'... save the last branch for me.

614

SUMMARY: "What Color Am I?" was created after Denny's became the subject of a racial discrimination class action lawsuit. In response to the need for sensitivity training for all employees, Denny's, via its parent company Flagstar, launched an intensive, ongoing diversity appreciation training program for all employees.

SALES PROMOTION

615
District 7
CLIENT
MS Department of
Ecomomic and
Community
Development
AGENCY
Imageworks, Inc.
Jackson, MS
CAMERAMAN
Jim Dollarhide
EDITOR
Jim Dollarhide
PRODUCER
Lida Gibson
DIRECTOR
Jim Dollarhide
MUSICAL SCORE
Sergio Fernandez

616
District 12
CLIENT
Iomega
AGENCY
Dahlin Smith White
Salt Lake City, UT
CREATIVE DIRECTOR
Jeff Bagley
ART DIRECTOR
Steve Newman
COPYWRITER
Jeff Bagley
PRODUCER
Neal Tardio
DIRECTOR
Neal Tardio

615

616

ANNCR: Let's talk about data. And not that pasty-faced, smarty-pants from Star Trek. Data as in what goes into your PC. Only who calls it that? The same people that come up with things like "eight out of ten people who suffer from hemorrhoids." What, do the other two enjoy it? It's not your data, it's your stuff. Look, we're all just a bunch of pack rats. Yeah, you know what I mean. I think you can feel your big, pack-rat tail twitching. Your office is a mess. You haven't seen the top of your desk since Ronald Reagan was president. Nah... don't give me that "not me" look. Come on.. quick, what's the color of the top of your desk? Yeah... I thought so. And I think you'll like my answer. Iomega. It's a place to put your stuff. It's one big humongous warehouse for your stuff: Letters, reports, files, pictures, music, inventory, manuals, ads. Heck, the whole phone book for all I care. Whatever information you want to collect, it'll capture and keep safe. It's not like giving something to your kid brother. Mine's a moron. He lost everything. Iomega keeps it safe and organized. Here's a mental image: a bank vault with neat and tidy stacks of money. You know, I wish I could have some of that money. I think you would too. Maybe if I organize and protect all my stuff with Iomega I could make more money. Maybe you could too. Or maybe you'll be one of those eight of ten people who suffer from an embarrassing and irritating case of just too much data. Iomega. Because it's your stuff.

SALES PROMOTION

617
District 6

CLIENT
Off the Street Club

AGENCY
J. Walter Thompson
Chicago, IL

CREATIVE DIRECTORS
Kevin Houlihan
Bob Potesky

ART DIRECTOR
John Siebert

COPYWRITER
Paul Tilley

PRODUCER
Carolyn Van Driesen

PRODUCTION
Bob Ebel
Productions

POST PRODUCTION
Ruth Efrati-Epstein
Steve Morrison

DIRECTOR
Bob Ebel

MUSIC
Com/Track

618
District 4

CLIENT
Bolles School

AGENCY
Sound O'Rama/
Myrick
Entertainment/
Florida Production
Center
Orlando, FL

PHOTOGRAPHER
Dan Myrick

DESIGNER
K.C. Ladnier

PRODUCER
Ted Johnson

MUSIC COMPOSER
Kays Al Atrakchi

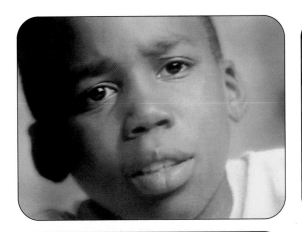

618

It matters not that decades have come and gone, my windows still open to the same river.

A shimmering sky, repeating sun, who's light pours through familiar hallways, into the rooms of my interior, where memories shape my destiny, of what I was, hotel, academy, school.

I call my spirit, I give it breath, and what I may be in the next sixty years, I listen for in the voices of the past.

617

SUPER: Just 5 miles west of this room lies West of Garfield. Home to hundreds of drug corners. Chicago's most troubled schools. 7 active gangs. And 3,000 kids with only one safe haven.

TYRONE: You have to use your imagination or else like will be boring.

SUPER: In the Club's art and crafts room, Tyrone sees his ideas come to life.

TYRONE: They bring out Spring to me, all the colors, all the different colors. The green, it brings out the color of the grass, and..., the brown brings out the color of tree trunks.

SUPER: At home, he's seen police chase drug dealers through his living room.

TYRONE: I like to build stuff. I guess it's part of my nature. You can use your imagination to pretend someone is by you, to pretend... you have a friend.

SUPER: When he was 9, he saw his uncle try to break up a gang fight. The gang beat his uncle to death with a baseball bat.

TYRONE: And use your imagination to pretend you have something that you don't really have.

SUPER: Feed a mind. Make a heart race. Share a victory. Let a kid be a kid. Give to the Off The Street Club. And give childhood a chance.

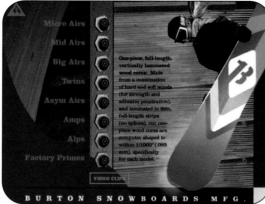

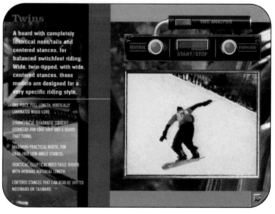

619

(Excerpt)

VO: There is still a place... Where blue skies are both a daily occurrence and a business condition; ...where the most abundant natural resources are also the most productive. It's a place bounded by a great ocean and blue mountains; yet growth and achievement are limited only by the imagination. There is still a place... Where ideas take flight; where people work together, and share a common vision; where the fire of success burns brightly, and the search for brilliance is shining strong.

SUPER: Call 1(800) 554-4373. Or Write: The Carolinas Partnership.

VO: Discover your place in the sun... The Charlotte Region... America's new business horizon.

620

619

District 3

CLIENT
Carolinas Partnership

AGENCY
Luquire George
Andrews
Charlotte, NC

CREATIVE DIRECTORS
Skip Grimes
Clay Andrews

ART DIRECTOR
Clay Andrews

COPYWRITER
Skip Grimes

PRODUCER
Skip Grimes

PRODUCTION
J. Martin Production

DIRECTOR
John Litschke

ASSISTANT DIRECTOR
Chuck Shedd

620

District 5

CLIENT
Burton Snowboards
MFG.

AGENCY
Resource
Columbus, OH

CREATIVE DIRECTOR
Dan Shust

COPYWRITER
David Schriber

DESIGNERS
Dennis Bajec
James Towning

INTERACTIVE PROGRAMMER
Michael Polivka

TECHNICAL SERVICES
Paul Rothrock
Ron Hackathon

3D MODELING
Joe Mack

621
District 4

CLIENT
Barnies Coffee & Tea

AGENCY
Clarke Advertising
and Public Relations
Sarasota, FL

ILLUSTRATOR
Lynn Hirsch

622
District 14

CLIENT
KTVU

AGENCY
KTVU
Oakland, CA

CREATIVE DIRECTION
KTVU
Chris Mack

623
District 10

CLIENT
Capitol-EMI

AGENCY
Summit Productions,
Inc.
McAllen, TX

ART DIRECTOR
Erren Seale

PRODUCER
Diego Aguilar

DIRECTOR
Sean Roberts

CINEMATOGRAPHER
Jack Morgan

(no art available)

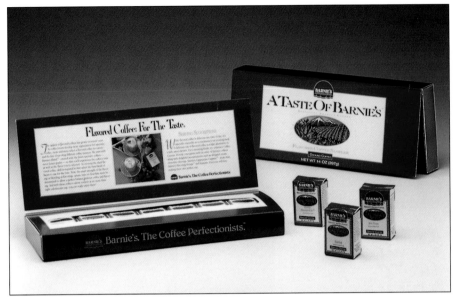

621

622

CRYSTAL: The first game I went to — May 30th, 1956 ... We
had these seats between third and home — really close ... You
can't imagine what it's like ... this grass went on forever, and
the clay, the dirt of the infield was so brown, the bases so white
... there was that excitement ... you just sat there and screamed
at people you loved, and ate things you never thought you
would ... I'm sorry I'm like this — but it's baseball shoeless —
Man did I love this game.

SCOTT: Part history, part folk-tale, the game that lives forever
returns again to KTVU with the historic San Francisco
Giants... returns again to KTVU with the historic San
Francisco Giants...

JONES: Unbelievable.

COSTNER: It's more than that, it's perfect.

SCOTT: ...And, the more things change, the more they stay
the same... always marked by their explosive offense and
thrilling defense in the past, Dusty Baker's lineup continued
that tradition in 1994... and in keeping with KTVU tradition,
our lineup of marketing, publicity and promotion always brings
'em home! As always, since 1951, it comes down to the Giants
and Dodgers... And recent history has been no exception... The
bay area never misses a good Giants show-down...

WIFE: Batter, batter, batter, batter

SCOTT: ...And KTVU brings 'em to ya!

COSTAS: Baseball is a beautiful thing... the way the field fans
out, the choreography, the pace and rhythm of it... baseball is
more fun than anything else, you can watch it and just enjoy it.
I don't think there's anything philosophical about it, I don't
think there's anything metaphysical, it's just so much fun to
watch.

CRYSTAL: It's the game my father taught me how to play

COSTAS: Although baseball has changed, its essence has
remained the same—we take some comfort in that.

ADVERTISING ARTS

624
District 9

CLIENT
Revolution

AGENCY
Revolution
Kansas City, MO

CREATIVE DIRECTORS
John Phillips, Eric Hartsock

ART DIRECTOR
Chris Foree-Williams

624

They're pawed all day by who knows how many retailers, all looking for the cream of the crop.

And too often, what's left for you is the bottom of the barrel. But what if the freshest,

best-looking selections came directly to you, week after week, untouched by anyone

except the growers? That's the advantage of our Flower Trading Corporation Marketing

HOW MANY PEOPLE HANDLE YOUR FLOWERS BEFORE YOU DO?

Partner program. Everything you order is grown exclusively for you.

[Goldtrends]

That means less time has passed between farm and florist. So your order will

[Tuchany]

last longer, with less shrinkage. Your customers will notice the difference. Get in

touch with your local Flower Trading Corporation Wholesale Marketing Partner today at (800)777-8866

And learn why untouchable quality means unbeatable profits. **Flower Trading Corporation**

625

District 4

CLIENT
Flower Trading Corporation

AGENCY
Beber Silverstein & Partners
Miami, FL

ART DIRECTOR
James Hale

ILLUSTRATOR
Stuart Bailey

626
District 9

CLIENT
Lincoln Marathon

AGENCY
Bailey Lauerman
Lincoln, NE

CREATIVE DIRECTOR
Carter Weitz

ART DIRECTOR
Carter Weitz

COPYWRITER
Mitch Koch

PHOTOGRAPHER
Don Farrall

PRINTER
Jacob North

ACCOUNT EXECUTIVE
Rich Claussen

626

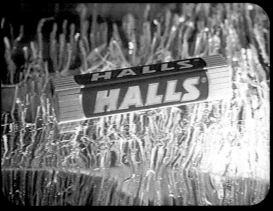

627

DISTRICT 2

CLIENT
Warner Lambert/Halls

AGENCY
J. Walter Thompson
New York, NY

CREATIVE DIRECTOR
Frank Costantini

ART DIRECTOR
Frank Costantini

COPYWRITER
J.J. Jordan

EXECUTIVE PRODUCER
Gary Bass

PRODUCTION
Palomar Pictures

ANIMATION
P.D.I.

628
District 2
CLIENT
American Red Cross
AGENCY
Wells Rich Greene
BDDP
New York, NY
CREATIVE DIRECTOR
Linda Kaplan Thaler
ART DIRECTOR
Patrick Sean Flahert
COPYWRITER
Linda Kaplan Thaler
VOCALS
Richie Havens
PRODUCERS
Evan Petty
Patrick Walsh

Don't Turn Away Jingle

Don't look away
Don't turn your back
Don't you pretend you cannot see
Don't shut your mind
To what you refuse to know
Don't you turn away from me.

Don't turn away
Open your heart
To a world that's not supposed to be
Do what you feel
Do what you can
But please don't turn away from me.

Do what you feel
Do what you can
But please don't turn away from me.
Please don't turn away from me.

628

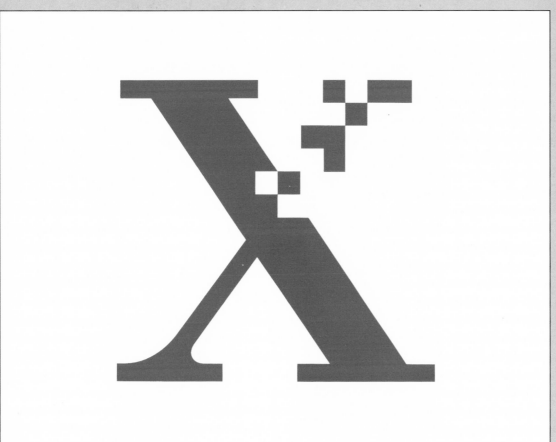

629
District 14

CLIENT
Xerox

AGENCY
Landor Associates
San Francisco, CA

CREATIVE DIRECTOR
Courtney Reeser

ART DIRECTOR
Margaret Youngblood

DESIGNER
Margo Zucker

ACCOUNT EXECUTIVE
David Ray

THE DOCUMENT COMPANY
XEROX

630
District 7

CLIENT
Dewin Tibbs

AGENCY
DogStar Design
Birmingham, AL

ILLUSTRATOR
Rodney Davidson

DESIGNER
Rodney Davidson

631
District 3

CLIENT
Santee Cooper

AGENCY
Eric Vincent
Illustration
Charleston, SC

CREATIVE DIRECTION
Advertising Service
Agency

630

631

633

It's Always Been True Jingle

As cool as your ragtop
your favorite hot spot
It's something with hometowns and
everyone's class clown
It's always been true, this Bud's for you
Oh yeah —
Familiar as blue jeans
Hollywood chase scenes
Its town misses pop fliers
And, you know who's the wise
It's always been true —
It's always been true —
It's always been true —

634

632

632
District 9
CLIENT
Anheuser-
Busch/Budweiser
AGENCY
DMB&B St. Louis
St. Louis, MO
CREATIVE DIRECTORS
Ric Anello
Michael Hutchinson
ART DIRECTOR
Michael Smith
COPYWRITER
Dave Swaine
PRODUCER
Chan Hatcher

633
District 7
CLIENT
NBAF
AGENCY
Fitzgerald &
Company
Atlanta, GA
CREATIVE DIRECTOR
Jim Paddock
ART DIRECTOR
Eddie Snyder
COPYWRITER
Jim Paddock
ACCOUNT EXECUTIVE
Katherine Way

634
District 9
CLIENT
Anheuser-
Busch/Budweiser
AGENCY
DMB&B St. Louis
St. Louis, MO
CREATIVE DIRECTORS
Ric Anello
Jim Borcherdt
Michael Hutchinson
ART DIRECTOR
Jim Borcherdt
COPYWRITERS
Tom Gow
Ric Anello
Larry Harris
David Swaine
Mark Choate
PRODUCER
Kevin VanFleet

635
District 5

CLIENT
Matrix Essentials

AGENCY
Matrix Essentials
Solon, OH

ART DIRECTOR
Susan Tate

ILLUSTRATION
Falcon Advertising
Art

DESIGNER
Susan Tate

636
District 8

CLIENT
Dr. Thomas
Trimberger, DDS

AGENCY
Griffiths Design
Sheboygan, WI

DESIGNER
Susan Griffiths

637
District 13

CLIENT
Carlson
Communications

AGENCY
Dale Vermeer Design
Honolulu, HI

ART DIRECTOR
Dale Vermeer

ILLUSTRATOR
Katie Doka

DESIGNERS
Dale Vermeer
Lowell Gellia

638
District 10

CLIENT
Armstrong Cricket
Farm

AGENCY
Newcomer, Morris
& Young, Inc.
Monroe, LA

ART DIRECTOR
Kristin Willis

636

635

637

638

WATER
MARK
COMMUNICATIONS

639

DESIGN EDGE
Industrial Design Firm

640

641

REIF CENTER DANCE

642

639
District 9
CLIENT
The Mark of Quad
Cities
AGENCY
Pederson Paetz
Davenport, IA

640
District 12
CLIENT
Design Edge
AGENCY
Kilmer, Kilmer
& James, Inc.
Albuquerque, NM
DESIGNERS
Richard Kilmer
Brenda Kilmer

641
District 13
CLIENT
Diamond Head
Theatre
AGENCY
Info Grafik
Honolulu, HI
CREATIVE DIRECTOR
Oren Schueman
ART DIRECTOR
Oren Schueman
ILLUSTRATOR
Katie Koka
DESIGNER
Oren Schueman

642
District 8
CLIENT
Reif Center Dance
AGENCY
Inc, Inc.
Grand Forks, ND
DESIGNER
Kelly Thompson

643
District 4
CLIENT
Bluebird Farms of
Indian River
AGENCY
Design Horizons
International, Inc.
Vero Beach, FL
CREATIVE DIRECTOR
Carl Miller
ILLUSTRATOR
Angela Hughes
DESIGNER
Angela Hughes

644
District 6
CLIENT
The Children's
Museum of
Indianapolis
AGENCY
FYI & Held Diedrich
Indianapolis, IN
CREATIVE DIRECTOR
Linda Lazler
ART DIRECTOR
David Snedigar
COPYWRITER
Linda Lazler

645
District 9
CLIENT
Traffic Cafe
AGENCY
Phoenix Creative
St. Louis, MO
CREATIVE DIRECTOR
Eric Thoelke
ART DIRECTOR
Kathy Wilkinson
ILLUSTRATOR
Kathy Wilkinson
DESIGNER
Kathy Wilkinson

646
District 3
CLIENT
Charlotte Ad Club
AGENCY
Price/McNabb
Charlotte, NC
CREATIVE DIRECTOR
John Boone
DESIGNER
Brandon Scharr

643

644

645

646

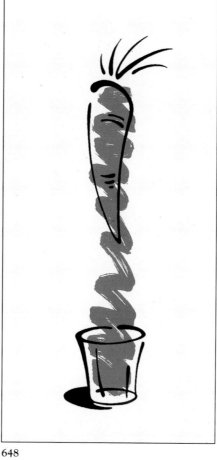

647

648

649

647

District 14

CLIENT
Federal Express

AGENCY
Landor Associates
San Francisco, CA

CREATIVE DIRECTOR
Courtney Reeser

ART DIRECTOR
Lindon Leader

DESIGNERS
Lindon Leader
Wally Krantz
Bruce McGovert

ACCOUNT EXECUTIVE
Charles Rashall

648

District 2

CLIENT
Omega Juicers

AGENCY
Knezic/Pavone
Advertisers
Harrisberg, PA

CREATIVE DIRECTORS
Joe Knezic
Michael Pavone

ART DIRECTOR
Robinson C. Smith

COPYWRITERS
Joe Knezic
Michael Pavone

ILLUSTRATOR
Robinson C. Smith

649

District 8

CLIENT
Aurora Candlers

AGENCY
Wenger-Marsch & Meier
Appleton, WI

ART DIRECTOR
Frank Meier

ILLUSTRATOR
Kristy Hoffman

ADVERTISING ARTS

650
District 3
CLIENT
Photovision
AGENCY
Photovision
Columbia, SC
CREATIVE DIRECTOR
Robin Smith

651
District 10
CLIENT
Deaf Action Center
AGENCY
Williams Graphic
Design/Smith
Photographic Service
Shreveport, LA
CREATIVE DIRECTOR
Michael Williams
ART DIRECTOR
Michael Williams
PRINTER
Associated Printing
**PHOTOGRAHIC DIGITAL
IMAGING**
Scot Smith
ACCOUNT EXECUTIVE
Michael Williams

652
District 13
CLIENT
Land Grab
AGENCY
XY Design
Kailua, HI
ART DIRECTOR
Teresa J. Black
ILLUSTRATOR
Christine Joy Pratt

653
District 9
CLIENT
David Radler Studio
Inc.
AGENCY
David Radler Studio
Inc.
Omaha, NE
PHOTOGRAPHER
David Radler

650

651

652

653

ADVERTISING ARTS

654

655

654
District 3
CLIENT
Photo Craftsman
AGENCY
Photo Craftsman
Norfolk, VA
PHOTOGRAPHER
Len Rothman
STYLIST
Veronica Donnelly

655
District 6
CLIENT
FBI/IHSAA
AGENCY
Cranfill & Company
Indianapolis, IN
CREATIVE DIRECTOR
Scott Willy
ART DIRECTOR
Scott Willy
PHOTOGRAPHER
Tom Casaliwi
DESIGNER
Kirk Nugent

656

656
District 4
CLIENT
Ellison Graphics
AGENCY
R. J. Gibson
Advertising Inc.
North Palm Beach, FL
CREATIVE DIRECTORS
Ken Roscoe
Steve Owens
PHOTOGRAPHER
Phillip Jon
PRODUCTION
Phyllis Maas

657
District 9
CLIENT
Vedros & Associates
AGENCY
Vedros & Associates
Kansas City, MO
PHOTOGRAPHER
Nick Vendros

657

ADVERTISING ARTS

658

659

660

ADVERTISING ARTS

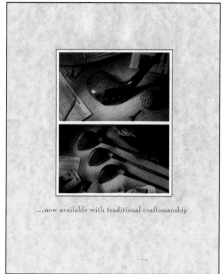

661

662

663

661
District 6
CLIENT
Sunshine Sports
AGENCY
OnSight Productions, Inc.
Dexter, MI
PHOTOGRAPHER
Mark Gregg
ILLUSTRATOR
Lisa Bush
DESIGNER
Sandy Ackerman
PRINTER
Goetzcraft
Kathy Marcum

662
District 2
CLIENT
Dupont
AGENCY
Earle Palmer Brown/ Philadelphia
Philadelphia, PA
CREATIVE DIRECTOR
Mike Drazen
ART DIRECTOR
Ted Tronnes
COPYWRITER
Michael Bense
PHOTOGRAPHER
Joe Mulligan

663
District 9
CLIENT
Parsons Technology
AGENCY
French Studios
Marion, IA
CREATIVE DIRECTOR
Marc Rhatigan
ART DIRECTOR
Randy Bohr
PHOTOGRAPHER
Douglas Benton

664
District 10

CLIENT
WilTel

AGENCY
WilTel
Tulsa, OK

ART DIRECTOR
Harold Tackett

COPYWRITER
Matt O'Meilia

ILLUSTRATORS
Tom Curry
Ken Westphal
Gil Adams
Tim Jessell

665
District 5

CLIENT
Cicigoi/Richards
AGENCY
Cicigoi/Richards
PHOTOGRAPHY
Cicigoi/Richards

666
District 7
CLIENT
Coca-Cola
AGENCY
McCann-Erickson
Atlanta, GA
CREATIVE DIRECTOR
Lloyd Fabri
ART DIRECTOR
David Stevenson
COPYWRITER
Jay Wallace
ACCOUNT EXECUTIVE
Anne Shoulders

666

667
District 14

CLIENT
Guess Inc.

AGENCY
Lambesis
San Francisco, CA

CREATIVE DIRECTOR
Paul Marciano

ART DIRECTOR
Chad Farmer

PHOTOGRAPHER
Michele Clement

667

668
District 8

CLIENT
Kerry Ingredients

AGENCY
The Hiebing Group
Madison, WI

ART DIRECTOR
Mike Freidel

ARTIST
Kirsten Booker

669
District 10

CLIENT
Gary Faye
Photography

AGENCY
Hill Group
Houston, TX

668

669

ADVERTISING ARTS

670
District 7
CLIENT
Plain Clothes
AGENCY
SlaughterHanson
Advertising
Birmingham, AL
CREATIVE DIRECTOR
Terry Slaughter
ART DIRECTOR
Marion English
PHOTOGRAPHER
Liz von Hoene
ACCOUNT EXECUTIVE
Terry Slaughter

670

671
District 5
CLIENT
Management
Recruiters
International
AGENCY
Nesnadny &
Schwartz
Cleveland, OH
DESIGN
Nesnadny &
Schwartz

672
District 5
CLIENT
The LTV Corporation
AGENCY
Nesnadny &
Schwartz
Cleveland, OH
ART DIRECTORS
Mark Schwartz
Tim Lachina
COPYWRITERS
Eric Evans
Mark Tomasch
PHOTOGRAPHY
Design Photography,
Inc.

673
District 7
CLIENT
High Five
Entertaiment
AGENCY
Jackson Design
Nashville, TN
CREATIVE DIRECTOR
Buddy Jackson
ART DIRECTOR
Buddy Jackson
PHOTOGRAPHER
Mark Tucker
SPECIAL EFFECTS
B. Middleworth

671

672

673

674

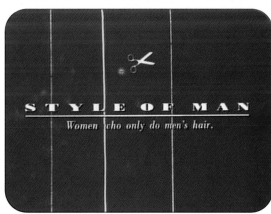

676

677

674
District 9
CLIENT
Ft. Dearborn Life
AGENCY
Sayles Graphic
Design
Des Moines, IA
ART DIRECTOR
John Sayles
ILLUSTRATOR
John Sayles
DESIGNER
John Sayles
PRINTER
Image Maker

676
District 2
CLIENT
Style of Man
AGENCY
Earle Palmer Brown/
Philadelphia
Philadelphia, PA
CREATIVE DIRECTOR
Mike Drazen
ART DIRECTOR
Robert Shaw West
COPYWRITER
Kelly Simmons

677
District 7
CLIENT
NBAF
AGENCY
Fitzgerald &
Company
Atlanta, GA
CREATIVE DIRECTOR
Jim Paddock
ART DIRECTOR
Eddie Snyder
COPYWRITER
Jim Paddock
ACCOUNT EXECUTIVE
Katherine Way

ADVERTISING ARTS

678
District 3

CLIENT
Centura

AGENCY
Price/McNabb
Charlotte, NC

CREATIVE DIRECTOR
Robin Konieczny

ART DIRECTOR
Carol Holsinger

COPYWRITER
Robin Konieczny

679
District 7

CLIENT
Kirk's Restaurant

AGENCY
Spenro Music
Productions
Knoxville, TN

COPYWRITER
Robert Spencer

PRODUCER
Robert Spencer

678

Down Home Meal Jingle

Don't want no burger
Don't give me no fries
Got a taste for some collards
and some sweet potato pie

I work everyday
baby just like you
if you want some "down home" cooking
then you know what you've gotta do

I'm going to Kirk's Restaurant
("Downhome meal", "Downhome meal")
for some cornbread, yams and beans
(Kirk's Restaurant for a "Downhome meal")
and some blackeyed peas

With just a little bit of "bread"
the whole family you can feed.

679

680

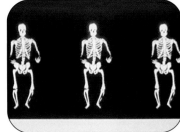

681

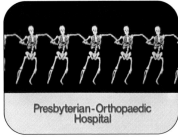

680

681

682

680
District 4
CLIENT
Andy Olsen Graphics
AGENCY
Communications
Concepts, Inc.
Cape Canaveral, FL
ANIMATOR
Andy Olsen
POST PRODUCTION
Rudy Gonzalez

681
District 6
CLIENT
GMAC
AGENCY
Lintas Campbell-
Ewald
Warren, MI
CREATIVE DIRECTION
Debbie Karnowsky
Cindy Sikorski
Terry Belitsos
Bill Biliti
Steve Platto
Stephen Pytel
David Haldeman

682
District 3
CLIENT
Presbyterian-
Orthopaedic
Hospital
AGENCY
The Reimler Agency
Charlotte, NC
CREATIVE DIRECTOR
Bill Owens
ART DIRECTOR
Bill Owens
COPYWRITER
Kay Reimler
PRODUCTION
Pinnacle Effects
DIRECTOR
Mark Claywell

683
District 10
CLIENT
Diamond Shamrock
AGENCY
Anderson
Advertising
San Antonio, TX
CREATIVE DIRECTOR
Stan McElrath
COPYWRITER
Stan McElrath
PRODUCTION
Jim Hodges Music
TALENT
Delbert McClinton
ACCOUNT EXECUTIVE
Chuck Leifeste

Diamond Shamrock Delbert McClinton Jingle

You're the gas in my tank
The lace in my shoe
The ice in my drink
You're my favorite brew
You're my coffee in the mornin'
Your my midnight snack
And every time I leave ya
I keep comin' back.

You're the aspirin for my headache
The jam on my toast
You're always around
When I need you the most

You're everything I want
The only one for me
Diamond Shamrock's all I need

Everything I want
The only one for me
Diamond Shamrock's all you need.

683

684

District 12

CLIENT
City of Tucson Water Department

AGENCY
City of Tucson
Tucson, AZ

PRODUCER
Terry Quinn

DIRECTOR
Thomas LaRochell

ANIMATION
Rhonda Graphics

SCORE
Louis Torres

685

District 9

CLIENT
Digital Cable Radio

AGENCY
Louis London
St. Louis, MO

ART DIRECTOR
Joe Ortmeyer

COPYWRITER
Anne Gartland

ANIMATION
Klasky Csupo

PRODUCTION
Klasky Csupo

DIRECTOR
Steve Kirklys

686

District 10

CLIENT
Casa Domecq

AGENCY
Match Frame
Computer
Graphics/Pedro
Torres & Associates
San Antonio, TX

ANIMATOR
David Benton

ANIMATION DIRECTOR
Steve Urbano

PRODUCER
Stephanie Schneider

684

685

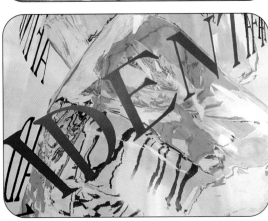

686

687
District 4
CLIENT
The Florida Lottery
AGENCY
Earle Palmer Brown
St. Petersburg, FL
CREATIVE DIRECTOR
Ted Nelson
ART DIRECTOR
Taras Wayner
COPYWRITER
Ted Nelson

688
District 10
CLIENT
Casa Domecq
AGENCY
Match Frame
Computer Graphics/
Pedro Torres &
Associates
San Antonio, TX
ANIMATOR
David Benton
ANIMATION DIRECTOR
Steve Urbano
PRODUCER
Stephanie Schneider
DIRECTOR
Pedro Torres

688

687

RADIO SCRIPT
Gospel Jingle

Wherever it happens, in every home town...
TV-5 will never let you down...
Friends you can trust, someone who will say...
We're proud to be a part of you everyday...
Together... forever... together with TV-5...
Together... forever... together with TV-5...

Sharing you world, day after day...
Making it happen in a special way...
Friends you can trust, someone who will say...
We're proud to be a part of your everyday...
Together... forever... together with TV-5...
Together... forever... together with TV-5...

689

689
District 6
CLIENT
WNEM TV-5
AGENCY
Parr Media
Flint, MI
CREATIVE DIRECTION
Reid Landis
Ian Richards
Michelle Kielitz

ADVERTISING ARTS

690
District 4
CLIENT
Developmental
Disabilities Council
AGENCY
Altman Meder
Lawrence Hill
Tampa, FL
CREATIVE DIRECTOR
Robin Lawrence
COPYWRITER
Robin Lawrence
MUSIC
Sweet Honey and
the Rock

691
District 7
CLIENT
Trustmark National
Bank
AGENCY
Godwin Group
Jackson, MS
CREATIVE DIRECTOR
Brenda Trigg
COPYWRITER
Jeff Pedigo
PRODUCER
Jeff Pedigo
COMPOSER
Rob Still
ACCOUNT EXECUTIVE
Marie Hartung

692
District 8
CLIENT
Cass County Elecric
Cooperative
AGENCY
Charpentier Hovland
Advertising
Fargo, ND
CREATIVE DIRECTION
Shannon Charpentier
Al Hovland
Mike & The Monsters
Audio Media
Corporation

693
District 14
CLIENT
Foster Farms Dairy
AGENCY
Maximus Recording
Studios
Fresno, CA
COPYWRITER
Jeff Hall
PRODUCTION
Maxiums
MUSIC
Jeff Hall
VOCALS
Sons of the San
Joaquin

Help Them Thrive, Birth to Five

Little ones need love and care
to keep them growing strong.
So give your all,
don't let them fall,
we need them to go on and on.

Help them thrive,
from birth to five.
We've gotta keep our children growing.
Help them thrive,
from birth to five.
We've gotta keep them growing.

Help them thrive,
we've gotta keep them growing.
Help them thrive,
we've gotta keep them going,
on and on,
we gotta keep them growing,
we gotta help them thrive,
we gotta keep them going.
Help them!

690

Rural Electric Cooperative Chill Jingle

The chill is gone;
The chill is gone away.
The chill is gone baby;
The chill is gone away.

You know you keep me warm baby;
All electric every day.

The chill is gone;
The chill is gone away from me.
The chill is gone baby;
The chill is gone away from me.

'Cause I'm warm and cozy baby
With total electricity.

692

Cash Management 101 Jingle

You're headin' off to college, not a care in
the world. Thinkin' 'bout nothin' but your
money and girls. Trustmark can't help you
with your female friends. But let me tell you
boy, we got a lot to lend.

Cash Management 101!

Student checking, credit cards and ATMs!
You may not have no money but you sure got
a friend in Trustmark... National Bank.

Cash Management 101!

Cash Management 101! Everything you need
for college and for fun... magic markers,
paper, music, tuition!

Cash Management 101! Pens and ink, stuff
to drink, skating rink...

Yo-yos... Bail! (Just kidding mom, heh! heh!)

691

Foster Farms Dairy Jingle

Foster, Foster, Foster Farms Dairy.

Taste the local freshness of Foster Farms,
Fresh dairy products from Foster Farms,
You've known our name for so long
as fresh as morning dew.

Real good stuff that comes from cows
We're really on the moooove.
Taste the local freshness of Foster Farms
Foster Farms Dairy.

A fresh and local milk drinker's dream
Plus non-fat yogurt and the richest cream.
Low fat, regular and buttermilk,
chocolate milk, too.

We're roundin' up them doogies
To milk 'em fresh for you.
Taste dairy freshness as fresh can be
Made from the cows of the San Joaquin.

Foster, Foster, Foster Farms Dairy.

693

ADVERTISING ARTS

695

694
District 5

CLIENT
Merry Go Round
Enterprises

AGENCY
Ron Foth Advertising
Columbus, OH

CREATIVE DIRECTORS
Ron Foth
Dana Beverly
David Hawthorne

GRAPHIC ARTIST
Gene Roy

PRODUCER
Ted Gordon

695
District 13

CLIENT
Maui Visitors Bureau

AGENCY
Peck Sims Mueller
Honolulu, HI

CREATIVE DIRECTOR
Jim Horiuchi

ART DIRECTORS
Richard Fraioli
Laura Mueller

COPYWRITER
Jim Horiuchi

ADVERTISING ARTS

INSTRUMENTAL SCORES

696
District 9
CLIENT
Pizza Hut
AGENCY
Valentine Radford
Kansas City, MO
CREATIVE DIRECTOR
Mark Weninger
COPYWRITER
John Godsey
PRODUCER
Justin White
PRODUCTION
Wheeler Audio/
Star Trax
MUSIC COMPANY
Walter Bryant
Productions

697
District 13
CLIENT
Kamehouncha
Schools
AGENCY
Laird Christianson
Honolulu, HI
CREATIVE DIRECTOR
Dennis Christianson
COPYWRITER
Dennis Christianson
AUDIO PRODUCER
Stan Wentzel
PRODUCER
Ann de Muerers

698
District 6
CLIENT
Indiana Department
of Tourism
AGENCY
McCaffrey & McCall
Advertising
Indianapolis, IN
COPYWRITER
Debi Keay
PRODUCER
Debi Keay
PRODUCTION
TRC Productions

699
District 5
CLIENT
Merry Go Round
Enterprises
AGENCY
Ron Foth Advertising
Columbus, OH
CREATIVE DIRECTORS
Ron Foth
Dana Beverly
PRODUCER
Ted Gordon

700
District 10
CLIENT
Doyle Wilson
Homebuilder
AGENCY
Barrett & Harwell
Music
Austin, TX
COMPOSERS
Barrett & Harwell
PRODUCER
Barrett & Harwell
RECORDING STUDIO
Production Block

701
District 13
CLIENT
Foodland
AGENCY
Peck Sims Mueller
Honolulu, HI
CREATIVE DIRECTOR
Stan Moy
ART DIRECTOR
Grant Miyasahi
COPYWRITER
Brad Shin
PRODUCER
Jo Suyeoka

702
District 12
CLIENT
City of Tucson Water
Department
AGENCY
City of Tucson
Tucson, AZ
PRODUCER
Terry Quinn
DIRECTOR
Thomas LaRochell
SCORE
Louis Torres

703
District 4
CLIENT
Ritz Carlton Hotels of
Florida/Mexico
AGENCY
Cole Henderson
Drake
Atlanta, GA
COMPOSER
Howard Kleinfeld
PRODUCER
Howard Kleinfeld
PRODUCTION
On the Air
Productions
DIRECTOR
David Nixon

704
District 7
CLIENT
Louisiana Lottery
Corporation
AGENCY
Bauerlein
New Orleans, LA
CREATIVE DIRECTOR
Robbie Vitrano
ART DIRECTOR
Pat McGuinness
COPYWRITER
Jim Houck
PRODUCER
Debbie Koppman
COMPOSER
Larry Peter/AdSound

705
District 5
CLIENT
OMNIMAX Theater at
Museum Center
AGENCY
Sound Images
Cincinnati, OH
CREATIVE DIRECTORS
Mike Kitei
John Nagy
ART DIRECTOR
John Nagy
COPYWRITER
Melanie Marnich
PRODUCER
Trish Bugitzedes
MUSIC PRODUCER
Jack Streitmarter
MUSIC ARRANGER
Jeff Bruner

706
District 5
CLIENT
Matrix Essentials
AGENCY
Matrix Essentials
Solon, OH
COPYWRITER
Kathy Miller
COMPOSER
Bill Duncan
PRODUCER
Kathy Miller

INDUSTRY SELF-PROMOTION

707
District 5

CLIENT
Williams McBride
Design, Inc.

AGENCY
Williams McBride
Design, Inc.
Lexington, KY

COPYWRITER
Amy Sharp

DESIGNER
Robin Williams Brown

**10 Thoughts on
Graphic Design**

#2. The Irish are known
for their enjoyment of
a good beer—but what
about that label? No
doubt a graphic designer
with a solid grasp of the
marketing objectives for
this particular brand
put pencil to tissue for a
few hours of sketching.
Results—a label
that catches the eye
of potential buyers.
No luck of the Irish
here—just some hard-
working design.

**Happy
St. Patrick's Day
from Williams
McBride Design, Inc.**

**10 Thoughts on
Graphic Design**

#4. Everybody's got one—
a mom that is. Are you
looking for a unique
way to honor your
maternal one this year?
What better way than a
one-of-a-kind tattoo.
Hey—we believe that
good design is good
design, wherever it shows
up, even on a bicep.

**Happy Mother's Day
from Williams
McBride Design, Inc.**

10 Thoughts on Graphic Design

#5. One of the most visible means of
showcasing exceptional graphic
design—the stamp. Remember this
one? Not just a great looking stamp,
but a famous logotype as well.
We thought it was particularly
appropriate for the marital month
of June.

**Happy Anniversary from
Williams McBride Design, Inc.**

10 Thoughts on Graphic Design

#6. Could Betsy Ross have
known her design for the
American flag would be
so celebrated? From
flagpoles to toothpicks,
its simplicity of shape,
color and layout make it
striking and memorable
—a flag worth flying—or
spearing olives!

**Happy Fourth of July
from Williams
McBride Design, Inc.**

708

709

708
District 7
CLIENT
Tom Cain
AGENCY
Tom Cain
Ridgeland, MS
COPYWRITER
Tom Cain
DESIGNER
Tom Cain

709
District 8
CLIENT
Independent Printing
Company
AGENCY
Insight Marketing
Communications
Green Bay, WI
CREATIVE DIRECTOR
Monica VonHoff
PHOTOGRAPHERS
Jim VonHoff
Jenny Roland
ILLUSTRATOR
Scott Cook
DESIGNERS
Monica VonHoff
Jon Stubb
PRINTER
Independent Printing

710
District 6

CLIENT
Ad Club of
Indianapolis

AGENCY
McCaffrey & McCall
Advertising
Indianapolis, IN

CREATIVE DIRECTORS
William Mick
Joseph Smith

COPYWRITERS
William Mick
Joseph Smith
Mark LeClerc

PHOTOGRAPHERS
Bob Fisher
Thom Kondas

DESIGNER
Angela Keortge

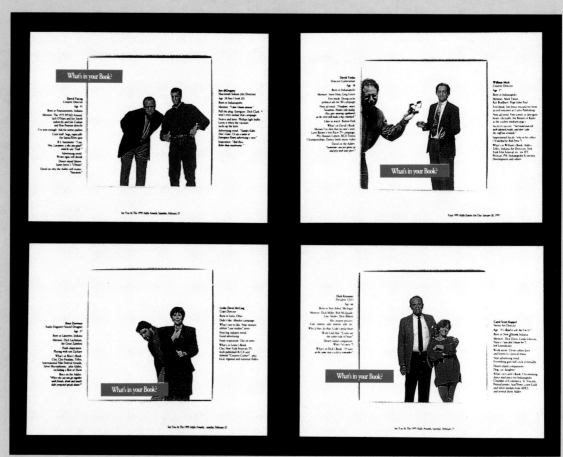

710

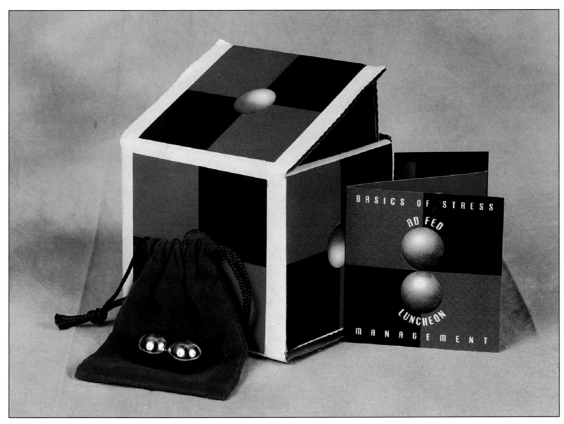

711

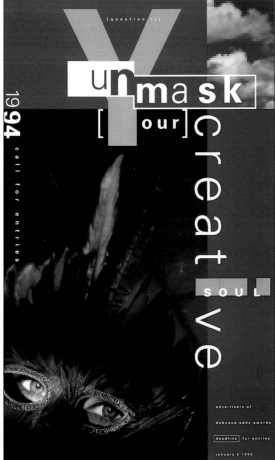

712

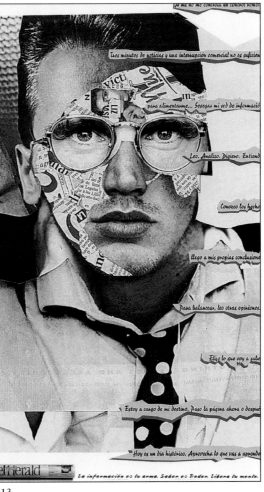

713

711
District 4
CLIENT
DBAF
AGENCY
DBAF/S2 Advertising
Daytona Beach, FL
CREATIVE DIRECTOR
Paul Sale
CONCEPT
Christopher Scali

712
District 9
CLIENT
Advertisers of
Dubuque
AGENCY
Advertisers of
Dubuque
Dubuque, IA
COPYWRITING
Get Smart Design
Company
PHOTOGRAPHER
Elite Images
DESIGN
Get Smart Design
Company
SEPARATOR
American Graphics
Services
PRINTER
Union-Hoermann
Press

713
District 4
CLIENT
El Nuevo Herald
AGENCY
The Miami Herald
Publishing Company
Miami, FL
CREATIVE DIRECTOR
Emmie Vazquez
ART DIRECTOR
Armando Garcia
COPYWRITER
Emmie Vazquez

714
District 14

CLIENT
Butler, Shine & Stern

AGENCY
Butler, Shine & Stern
Sausalito, CA

CREATIVE DIRECTORS
John Butler
Mike Shine

ART DIRECTOR
John Butler

COPYWRITER
Mike Shine

715
District 4

CLIENT
Ellison Graphics

AGENCY
R. J. Gibson
Advertising Inc.
North Palm Beach, FL

CREATIVE DIRECTORS
Ken Roscoe
Steve Owens

PHOTOGRAPHER
Phillip Jon

PRODUCTION
Phyllis Maas

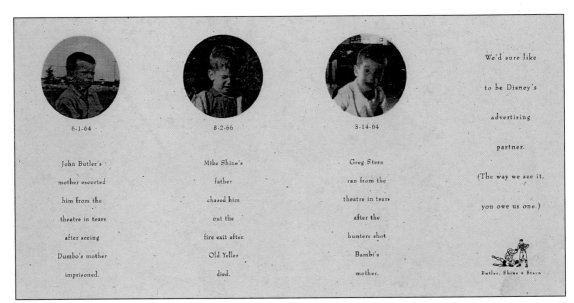

714

715

figure A, the common gopher

The Darwinian theory on advertising

states that most Account executives evolved from small burrowing mammals. See for yourself. Climb out of the primordial ooze and take your place on the agency evolutionary ladder. Sign up early, Class is subject to availability. One seat is available. O.K., it's not a class, it's an internship. Forget your other subjects. in our program you'll learn about: Physics: Relativity as it relates to the length of client meetings. Chemistry: Which brand of vermouth makes the best martinis. History: The 13th amendment does not apply to advertising interns. You'll Assist a real live account team with a variety of tasks including sorting, filing, and lunching. Participate in essential Marketing decisions. (Red tie or Paisley?) Learn the fundamentals of butt-kissing and compromise. Reconsider your major. More importantly you'll get real experience. donuts on Fridays, 3 credits, a few oh-so-important contacts, plus a meager paycheck. Hey, it's an internship. So unless you live in a cardboard box. ask your mommy to cover your rent 'cause your salary sure as hell won't. For details ask your Prof or call The Schiller Group/(808) 539-5720. Ask for Linda.

Applicants must have burning desire to learn the ad game and possess an average number of chromosomes. No deadheads or people named Marty need apply— one's enough in any agency.

Learn to appreciate freedom through a ten-week internment

in real life. Discover the difference between multi-media, multi-grain-media, and a real medium from New York named Madam Chuck. Sign up early, class is subject to availability. In fact, only one seat is available. And don't go thinking this is a class—it's an internship. There's no class involved. Of any kind. But you'll learn— oh, how you'll learn. Study the effects of sleep deprivation. Develop empathy for victims of slavery. Experience intense left-brain relations with filing cabinets. Learn how to DO lunch. Watch professionals grovel and compromise. Think about reconsidering your major. More importantly you'll get real experience, plus a meager paycheck. Hey, it's an internship. So unless you live in a cardboard box, ask your mommy to cover your rent 'cause your salary sure as hell won't. For details ask your prof or call The Schiller Group/(808) 539-5720. Ask for Noelani.

Applicants must have burning desire to learn the ad game and possess an average number of chromosomes. No deadheads or people named Medusa need apply.

ADVERTISING

101

In this hands-on ten week intensive study

you'll see what it's like to sell everything from enemas to dog biscuits.....from the inside. Sign up early, class is subject to availability. One seat is available. O.K., it's not exactly a class, it's an internship. Forget about your other subjects. in our special program you'll learn about: Biology: Sleep deprivation can produce seemingly hilarious headlines. Chemistry: Spray mount and stale coffee can give you a wicked buzz. History: The 13th amendment does not apply to advertising interns. You'll Assist a real live art director and copywriter with a variety of tasks including concepting, production, and light janitorial. Among other things, you'll participate in essential creative decision making. (Chili dogs or Thai?) Learn the fundamentals of butt-kissing and compromise. Reconsider your major. More importantly you'll get real experience. donuts on Fridays, 3 credits, a few oh-so-important contacts, plus a meager paycheck. Hey, it's an internship. So unless you live in a cardboard box, ask your mommy to cover your rent 'cause your salary sure as hell won't. For details ask your Prof or call The Schiller Group/(808) 539-5720. Ask for Tim or James.

Applicants must have burning desire to learn the ad game and possess an average number of chromosomes. No deadheads or people named Skippy need apply.

716

716
District 13
CLIENT
The Schiller Group
AGENCY
The Schiller Group
Honolulu, HI
ART DIRECTOR
James Ford
COPYWRITERS
James Ford
Trent Farr
Tim Anderson

717
District 14

CLIENT
San Francisco Ad
Club

AGENCY
Saatchi & Saatchi
Advertising/SF
San Francisco, CA

CREATIVE DIRECTOR
Rob Ingalls

ART DIRECTOR
Ernie Lageson

COPYWRITER
Adam Lau

PHOTOGRAPHERS
Andrew Vracin
Steve Conen

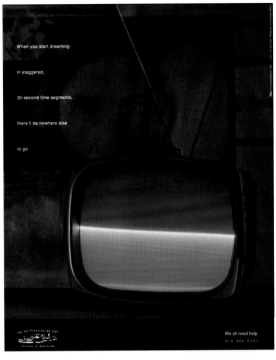

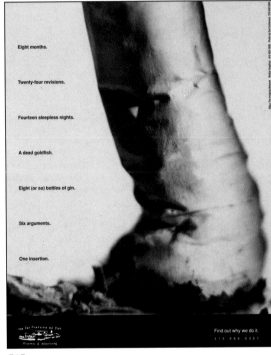

717

718

718
District 10

CLIENT
Arkansas Advertising
Federation

AGENCY
Stone & Ward
Little Rock, AR

CREATIVE DIRECTOR
Larry Stone

ART DIRECTOR
Martin Wilford

COPYWRITER
Trent Patterson

PRODUCER
Brenda Fowler

719
District 7

CLIENT
The Times-Picayune

AGENCY
Crewford Carroll
New Orleans, LA

719

INDUSTRY SELF-PROMOTION

720

District 12

CLIENT
A-Hill Design

AGENCY
A. Hill Design
Albuquerque, NM

COPYWRITER
Rhonda Little

DESIGNERS
Sandy Hill
Tom Antreasian
Elisabeth Spitalny

ILLUSTRATORS
Kevin Curry
Nancy Harvin
Heidi Merscher
Susan Roden
Diana Stetson
Kevin Tolman
Greg Tucker

PHOTOGRAPHERS
Michael Barley
Stephen Marks
Robert Reck
Jed Share
Eric Swanson
Don Werthmann

SEPARATORS
Digicolor/User
Friendly
Southwest Electronic
Prepress Services
The Printmaker

DIE CUTTING/EMBOSSING
Letter Press Services
Graphic Images

PRINTER
Cottonwood Printing

PRODUCTION
Judy Bowlin

721

District 4

CLIENT
Anson-Stoner

AGENCY
Anson-Stoner
Orlando, FL

CREATIVE DIRECTOR
Joe Anson

ART DIRECTORS
Brett Stiles
Bernard Urban

COPYWRITER
Joe Anson

722

District 14

CLIENT
Lithomania

AGENCY
Lithomania
San Francisco, CA

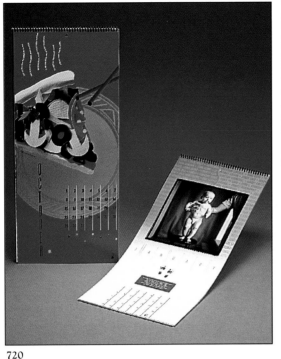

720

721

722

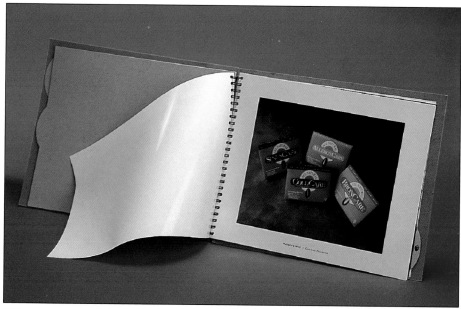

723

723
District 6
CLIENT
Perich & Partners,
Ltd.
AGENCY
Perich & Partners,
Ltd.
Ann Arbor, MI
CREATIVE DIRECTOR
Ernie Perich
ART DIRECTOR
Scott Pryor
COPYWRITERS
Dan Sygar
Ernie Perich

724
District 8
CLIENT
Image Studios
AGENCY
GreySunderPrescher
Cedarburg, WI
CREATIVE DIRECTOR
Blaine Huber
COPYWRITER
Blaine Huber
PHOTOGRAPHER
Image Studios
DESIGNER
Susan Griffiths
SEPARATOR
Image It
PRINTER
Post Printing

725
District 3
CLIENT
Adams Photography
AGENCY
Adams Photography
Charlotte, NC
COPYWRITER
Melissa Stone
PHOTOGRAPHER
Lisa R. Adams
DESIGNER
Merril M. Paylor
PRINTER
Classic Graphics

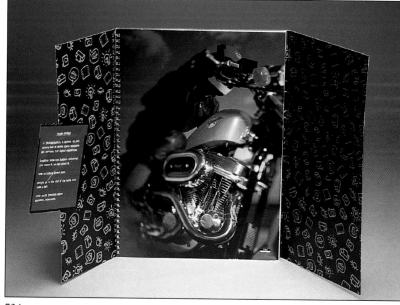

724

725

726

District 3

CLIENT
Erickson Productions

AGENCY
Erickson Productions
Raleigh, NC

CREATIVE DIRECTOR
Jeff Griffith

COPYWRITER
Larry Bennett

PHOTOGRAPHER
Jim Erickson

DESIGNER
Jeff Griffith

727

District 12

CLIENT
Cottonwood Printing

AGENCY
A. Hill Design
Albuquerque, NM

COPYWRITER
Rhonda Little

DESIGNERS
Sandy Hill
Tom Antreasian
Elisabeth Spitalny

ILLUSTRATORS
Kevin Curry
Nancy Harvin
Heidi Merscher
Susan Roden
Diana Stetson
Kevin Tolman
Greg Tucker

PHOTOGRAPHERS
Michael Barley
Stephen Marks
Robert Reck
Jed Share
Eric Swanson
Don Werthmann

SEPARATORS
Digicolor/User
Friendly
Southwest Electronic
Prepress Services
The Printmaker

DIE CUTTING/EMBOSSING
Letter Press Services
Graphic Images

PRINTER
Cottonwood Printing

PRODUCTION
Judy Bowlin

728

District 7

CLIENT
Armstrong State
College

AGENCY
Armstrong State
College
Savannah, GA

COPYWRITER
Bob Stronzier

PHOTOGRAPHER
Gail Brannen

PRODUCTION
Joan Lehon

EDITOR
Lauretta Hannon

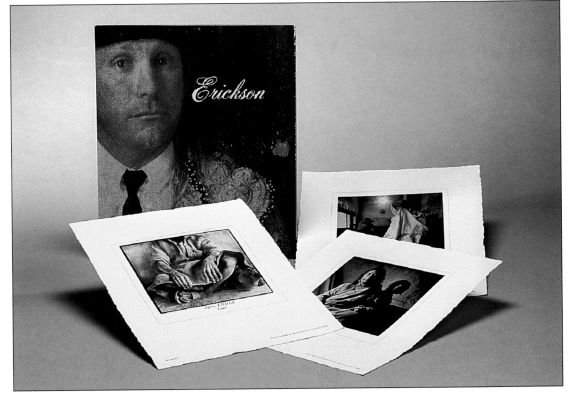

726

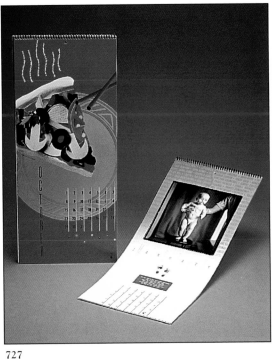

727

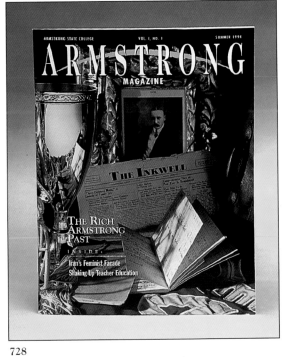

728

729

729
District 7
CLIENT
WIMZ Radio
AGENCY
WIMZ Radio
Knoxville, TN
CREATIVE DIRECTOR
April Sullivan
ART DIRECTOR
Todd Mills
COPYWRITER
Tripper Lewis
PHOTOGRAPHER
Charles Garvey
PRODUCER
Tripper Lewis
TALENT
Chris Corley
CONCEPT
Phil Williams

730

730
District 10
CLIENT
Dick Patrick Studios
AGENCY
Dick Patrick Studios
Dallas, TX
ART DIRECTORS
Mark Ford
Lori Walls
PHOTOGRAPHERS
Dick Patrick
John Hethorn

731
District 9
CLIENT
Reprox of St. Louis
AGENCY
Ferguson and
Katzman/Pfeiffer
& Co.
St. Louis, MO
PHOTOGRAPHERS
Scott Ferguson
Mark Katzman
DESIGNERS
Chris Mielke
Renee Walsh

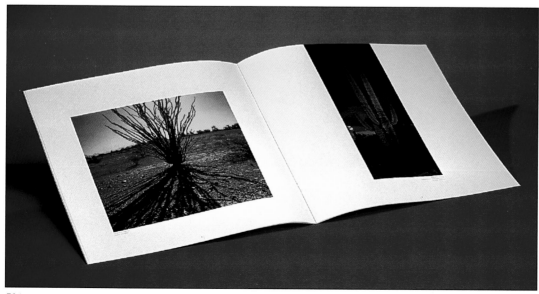

731

732

District 7

CLIENT
Graphic Arts

AGENCY
Disciple
Memphis, TN

CREATIVE DIRECTOR
Craig Thompson

ART DIRECTORS
Craig Thompson
Brad Henderson

COPYWRITERS
Brad Henderson
John Malmo

PHOTOGRAPHERS
Ben Fink
Terry Heffernan

ILLUSTRATORS
Robert Felker
Dan Brawner

ENGRAVER
Graphic Arts

PRINTER
Pinnacle Press

PRODUCTION
Craig Thompson
Brad Henderson

733

District 7

CLIENT
Nashville Advertising
Federation

AGENCY
The Buntin Group
Nashville, TN

CREATIVE DIRECTOR
Stephen Fechtor

ART DIRECTOR
Sharon Harms

COPYWRITER
Tony Cane

PHOTOGRAPHER
John Guider

ENGRAVER
Precision Color

PRINTER
TruColor

PRODUCTION
Betty Wayland

732

733

734

District 4

CLIENT
ABC 28 Tampa Bay
(WFTS)

AGENCY
ABC 28 Tampa Bay
(WFTS)
Tampa, FL

CREATIVE DIRECTOR
Chris Raynor

ART DIRECTOR
Mark Karlen

COPYWRITER
Ellery J. Aguayo

PRODUCER
Ellery J. Aguayo

EDITOR
Ellery J. Aguayo

735

District 10

CLIENT
Ramar Communi-
cations/KJTV34

AGENCY
Ramar Communi-
cations/KJTV34
Lubbock, TX

COPYWRITER
Erin Cauny

PRODUCERS
Dawndra Higgins
Bob Ebener

EDITORS
Sean Ryan
Bob Ebener

734

MUSIC: "Flip fantasia" by US 3
ANNCR#1: Think you're too cool for Andy Griffith?
ANNCR#2: Maybe Andy Griffith's too cool for you.

735

ANNCR: From the beginning you've demanded better... Now you've made us the best... You're watching the number one Fox station in the nation, Fox KJTV34.

736
District 9
CLIENT
KPTM Fox-42
AGENCY
KPTM Fox-42
Omaha, NE
ART DIRECTOR
Stodola
EDITOR
Mark Guzman
PRODUCER
Mark Guzman

737
District 4
CLIENT
WJNO
AGENCY
Fairbanks
Communications
West Palm Beach, FL
COPYWRITER
Jim Schuyler
PRODUCER
Jim Schuyler

738
District 8
CLIENT
WSN Radio
AGENCY
WSN Radio
Sioux Falls, SD
ANNOUNCERS
Jeff Gould
Michele Thury
TALENT
Mallory Gould

736

RADIO SCRIPT
Circus

JACK: Hello, Mary.

CALLER (*With Brooklyn accent*): Uh, Jack, I used to enjoy the program. Now, you made a "soicus" outta the station. They should call ya, you give 'em "shoits," you give 'em drinks, and it's a shame! (*Circus music under…*) … I swear to you. A soicus!

JACK: A soicus?

CALLER: Absolutely a soicus. This is not a station where you used to listen. You used to sing, you used to entertain, you used to speak nice, you used to have nice speakers, you used to have, uh, uh… (*Fade caller under tag*)

ANNCR: Jack Cole. Weekdays, 3 to 7, on WJNO.

CALLER: … Now, it's just a soicus!!

737

RADIO SCRIPT
Gould Promo

M: Well, see ya later. I've got to take this feeder to my dog, Alf.

W: See ya later. Say, that Alf feeder sure is zany!

M: There! Now use that visualization to say, "see ya later" in German.

W: Alf, feeder, zane?

M: Auf weder sehn!

W: Hey, German is easy!

M: Yes, you can learn all kinds of neat ways to learn German on Gould morning show.

W: I never knew German could be this easy.

M: Uh huh! Just dial in M 1230 WSN G-O-U-L-D.

W: G-O-U-L-D!

M: Mornings on WSN. See ya later.

BOTH: Auf weder sehn!

738

PUBLIC
SERVICE

739

District 2

CLIENT
Family Health Council

AGENCY
MARC Advertising
Pittsburgh, PA

ART DIRECTOR
John Swisher

COPYWRITERS
Laurie Habeeb
John Swisher

SEPARATOR
Electronic Images

PRINTER
GACC

PRODUCTION
Don McGreeby

ACCOUNT EXECUTIVE
Sharon Aulicino

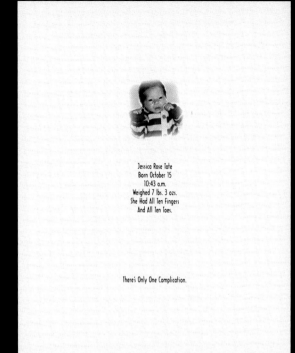

Jessica Rose Tate
Born October 15
10:43 a.m.
Weighed 7 lbs. 3 ozs.
She Had All Ten Fingers
And All Ten Toes.

There's Only One Complication.

This Is Her Mom.

CLIENT
National Family
Partnership

AGENCY
Greg & Greg Creative
Greenville, SC

CREATIVE DIRECTION
Greg & Greg Creative
John Lasne
Carol Reeves

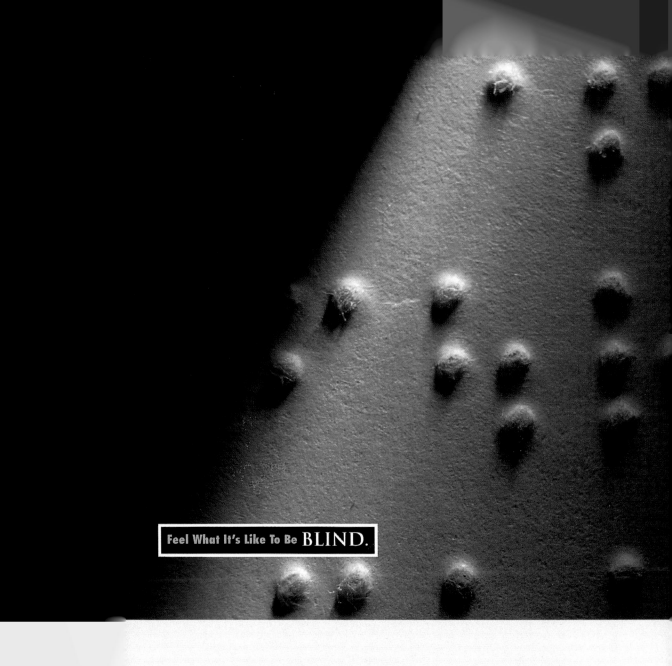

Feel What It's Like To Be BLIND.

What's it like to be blind, deaf or physically impaired? Come find out at the new Challenges exhibit at the Louisiana Children's Museum. Underwritten by Tulane Hospital for Children, Challenges is helping kids become sensitive to people with disabilities. It may just be the best exhibit you never saw.

Tulane Hospital
for Children

Photograph courtesy of Spectrum Photo

BURY YOUR DOG'S BONE.
SPAY/NEUTER YOUR PET.

A message from
MICHIGAN ANTI-CRUELTY SOCIETY

743
District 2

CLIENT
Partnership for a
Drug-Free America

AGENCY
Lord Dentsu
& Partners
New York, NY

CREATIVE DIRECTOR
Mark Hughes

COPYWRITERS
Steve St. Clair
Andrew Payton

PRODUCER
Phil Lee

PRODUCTION
Full House
Productions

RADIO SCRIPTS
To John

SFX: *Crackle of answering machine throughout*
SFX: *Beep.*
LUCRETIA: You know what, John? You kind of remind me of my brother. He was really cool. I know I never told you much about him, but you would have really liked him. He really loved to get high, just like you. I could tell you some sick stories. And he always, always made me laugh. But then he started doing coke, and some other stuff... and then I only saw him once in a while. Then I never saw him again. That could be you John. You could be as cool as my brother was.
SFX: *Phone hangs up.*
ANNCR: If someone you know is using drugs, you better talk to them. And if they won't listen, talk to us. Call 212-727-8502. Leave a recording and we'll get it on the air. 212-727-8502. Millions will hear it. Maybe one person out there will get the message.

To Michael

SFX: *Crackle of answering machine throughout*
SFX: *Beep.*
SANDY (crying throughout): This is to Michael. I love you more than anything in the world. And you destroyed your life... you destroyed our lives... you took away everything that we had and we loved... and you're going to kill yourself and you won't listen to nobody and I don't want to see that happen to you. So please wake up and go for help before something goes wrong and you'll never be able to take that... to make that step to go. I love you. Sandy.
SFX: *Phone hangs up.*
ANNCR: If someone you know is using drugs, you better talk to them. And if they won't listen, talk to us. Call 212-727-8502. Leave a recording and we'll get it on the air. 212-727-8502. Millions will hear it. Maybe one person out there will get the message.

To Jen

SFX: *Crackle of answering machine throughout*
SFX: *Beep.*
CHRISTIAN: What are you thinking, Jen? After everything we've been through, you're going to *beep* it up with drugs? You saw what they did to my body, what they did to my mind. I didn't even know who I was. I still don't know... sometimes.. Do you want that for yourself? Are you that stupid? No drug is worth it, or worth more you. Believe me, Jennifer. I know.
SFX: *Phone hangs up.*
ANNCR: If someone you know is using drugs, you better talk to them. And if they won't listen, talk to us. Call 212-727-8502. Leave a recording and we'll get it on the air. 212-727-8502. Millions will hear it. Maybe one person out there will get the message.

Rwanda Relief Fund
1-800-842-2200

✚

American Red Cross

744
District 2
CLIENT
American Red Cross
AGENCY
Wells Rich Greene
BDDP
New York, NY
CREATIVE DIRECTOR
Linda Kaplan Thaler
ART DIRECTOR
Patrick Sean Flahert
COPYWRITER
Linda Kaplan Thaler
PRODUCERS
Evan Petty
Patrick Walsh

744
ANNCR: Right now there are thousands of Rwandans dying of disease. The Red Cross is doing all it can, but they urgently need your help to support their relief operations. Don't turn away from this tragedy of human lives and the human spirit. Please give what you can. Thank you. 1-800-842-2200.

745
District 2

CLIENT
Ad Council

AGENCY
Wells Rich Greene
BDDP
New York, NY

CREATIVE DIRECTORS
Steven Landsberg
Carol DeMelio

ART DIRECTOR
Carol DeMelio

COPYWRITER
Steven Landsberg

PRODUCERS
Neal Bergman
Sally Hotchkiss

PRODUCTION
Red Car

**Alex Bishop.
Killed by a drunk driver
on November 8, 1992
on Kent-Kangley Road
in Kent, Washington.**

**Miranda Fay Standiford.
Killed by a drunk driver
on May 1, 1994 on Highway 60
in Borden, Indiana.**

**Paul Chambers.
Killed by a drunk driver
on Christmas Eve 1992
on Interstate 55
in Arnold, Missouri.**

745
Bishop
MOM: who is that swimming? Get your legs up!
ALEX: Like this?
MOM: That's the way.
FRIEND (*off camera*): What are you doing? Now you're kicking Al!
ALEX: I'm almost there.
MOM: OK
DISSOLVE TO SUPER: Alex Bishop. Killed by a drunk driver on November 8, 1992 on Kent-Kangley Road in Kent, Washington.
MOM: Whoa-you made it all the way.
ANNCR: If you don't stop your friend from driving drunk, who will?
MOM: Good job!
ANNCR: Do whatever it takes.
MOM: Are you having a good time?
ALEX: Yeah.
SUPER LOGO: Friends don't let friends drive drunk.

Standiford
PARTY GUESTS (*off camera*): Happy birthday to you. Happy Birthday to you. Happy Birthday dear Miranda, Happy Birthday to you.
GUESTS: Yea! What a fun birthday! Wow!
DISSOLVE TO SUPER: Miranda Fay Standiford.. Killed by a drunk driver on May 1, 1994 on Highway 60 in Borden, Indiana.
GUESTS: Do you need a scissors or something! Yea!
ANNCR: If you don't stop your friend from driving drunk, who will? Do whatever it takes.
GUESTS: Yea! Oh wow!
SUPER LOGO: Friends don't let friends drive drunk.

Chambers
DAD (*off camera*): Alright. You gonna win?
PAUL: I hope.
DAD: Are you scared of flying?
PAUL: No.
DAD: Good.
DISSOLVE TO SUPER: Paul Chambers. Killed by a drunk driver on Christmas eve, 1992 on interstate 55 in Arnold, Missouri.
DAD: 533
ANNCR: If you don't stop your friend from driving drunk, who will?
DAD: Ask that man which gate to Chicago?
ANNCR: Do whatever it takes.
SUPER LOGO: Friends don't let friends drive drunk.

PUBLIC SERVICE

746
District 15
CLIENT
Home Box Office/
Warner Music Grou
AGENCY
Home Box Office
New York, NY
EXECUTIVE PRODUCER
Shelby Stone

746
Et Tu Brutus
Inner city kids play basketball
KID #1: Right here, right here right here..
KID #2: It's like this, you know what I'm saying...
KID #3 (Doing a rap):..get a show...put on the pedal, damn...we comfortable with the ghetto
The kids, who appear to be gangmembers, gather together and talk amongst themselves. Two young men look towards an oncoming car. A hooded kid jumps out of the car with a gun, chasing after one member of the gang, in a striped shirt. The gangmember runs from him and throws his own gun in a nearby trash can. Hooded kid shoots at him. The boy jumps the railing. Another shot. Through a reflection of a puddle on the ground, we see the boy continue to run. Another shot. The boy leaps (in silhouette), trying to escape. He tries to climb a ladder but finds himself pinned against a fence with a gun in his face.
GANGMEMBER: Damn, you caught me.
HOODED KID: Shut up! Shut up!
CU of gangmember with sweat pouring down his face and the gun directly in front of him.
GANGMEMBER: So this is how it's gonna be?
HOODED KID: That's right. That's how it's gonna be.
CU of gangmember sweating, sighing desperately. CU of hooded kid. He slowly pulls the hood off to reveal that he is the gangmember. The gangmember has been running from himself, from the destiny he will face if he continues his life as a gangster.
HOODED KID: So there punk. Remember me?
CU of stunned gangmember, still sweating
HOODED KID (voice in slo-mo): Remember me? Remember me?
Dissolve to CU of the barrel of a gun.
ANNCR: Stop. You're only killing yourself.
CHYRON: Peace. Live It or Rest In It.

Stray Bullet
A kid sitting by a window is playing with a gun at home. He turns to see if anyone is around, then continues to play with it, cocking it and twirling it around his hand. He aims the gun toward the window.
BOY (making gun sounds): Bam. Pa Chu. Bam.
Involved with the moment, he pulls the trigger. The camera now follows the bullet. CU of an enormous bullet flying through the air. The bullet crashes through a car window, making a loud shattering sound. Shot of a man sitting comfortably in his armchair working the remote control. Bullet files through the air. CU of a man with his beer and remote. The bullet continues to fly. Man scratches his face with the remote. Bullet flies. CU of man listening to a sporting event. The bullet hits his tv, which explodes into flames. CU of the man's eyes as they shift. CU of explosion. Several quick cuts of the bullet piercing floral covered walls. CU of bullet flying towards a home down the street. Interior of a home. A mother talks to her baby eating breakfast in a highchair. CU of bullet. CU of baby hitting his toy against the highchair. Cu of bullet. CU of mother washing dishes. From bullet's pov, the camera speeds towards the kitchen window. CU of baby's legs. CU of bullet as it flies through the wall of the house. Music becomes eerie as the camera moves towards the baby in the highchair. The picture fades on the baby. In slo-mo, the baby's bowl, formula, and spoon drop on the floor and spatter.
CHYRON: Peace. Live It or Rest In It.

747
District 9

CLIENT
Lighthouse

AGENCY
Ad Federation
of Lincoln
Lincoln, NE

ART DIRECTOR
Ron Sack

COPYWRITER
Pat Piper

PHOTOGRAPHER
Bob Ervin

PRINTER
Graham Graphics

748
District 3

CLIENT
National Family
Partnership

AGENCY
Greg & Greg Creative
Greenville, SC

CREATIVE DIRECTION
Greg & Greg Creative
John Lasne
Carol Reeves

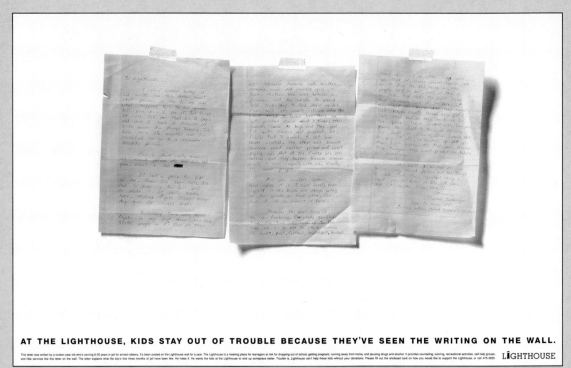

AT THE LIGHTHOUSE, KIDS STAY OUT OF TROUBLE BECAUSE THEY'VE SEEN THE WRITING ON THE WALL.

747

748

749

749
District 14
CLIENT
American Lung
Association
AGENCY
Mark Bell
San Francisco, CA
ART DIRECTOR
Mark Bell
COPYWRITER
Mark Bell

750
District 11
CLIENT
Seattle Times
AGENCY
Elgin Syferd DDB
Needham
Seattle, WA
CREATIVE DIRECTOR
Laurie Sinclair Fritts
ART DIRECTOR
Matt Myers
COPYWRITER
Cheryl Van Ooyen
PRODUCTION
Tracy Mullen

WOULD YOU HAVE BEEN THE PERSON WITH THE CLUB,

THE PERSON BEING HIT,

THE PERSON CHEERING,

OR THE PERSON LOOKING THE OTHER WAY?

Martin Luther King, Jr. Day is January 16th.

A DAY TO DREAM. A LIFETIME TO ACT.

750

751

District 2

CLIENT
House of Ruth

AGENCY
Profiles
Baltimore, MD

CREATIVE DIRECTOR
Sande Riesett

COPYWRITER
Sande Riesett

PRODUCER
Janet Mockard

ACCOUNT EXECUTIVE
Amy Elias

752

District 2

CLIENT
Family Violence
Prevention Fund

AGENCY
Altschiller
& Company
New York, NY

CREATIVE DIRECTOR
David Altschiller

ART DIRECTOR
John Gellos

COPYWRITERS
Kevin Mooney
David Altschiller

PRODUCER
Deanna Leodas

PRODUCTION
Sandbank/Kamen
& Partners

DIRECTOR
John Danza, Jr.

MUSIC
JSM

Venus Ann Shifflett got her answer four months later.

It was a bullet through the head.

IT IS YOUR BUSINESS.

751
TITLE CARD: Venus Ann Shifflett was 26 years old when she wrote this letter.
WOMAN VO: I'm writing you concerning a man you tried last year and released on probation.
TITLE CARD: She had only been seeing Neal for about six months when the beatings began.
WOMAN VO: This is a sick man who wants to hurt and kill me. He has already proven that he means it.
TITLE CARD: Like everything else in her life, she handled it by the rules.
WOMAN VO: So all I can do is sit here and wait. I've locked myself in my house and I'm scared for my life.
TITLE CARD: When he followed her to her office and attacked her, she charged him with assault.
WOMAN VO: This is why I am begging for your help.
TITLE CARD: When he started stalking her with threats, she reported it to his probation officer. When he told her he had a gun and was going to blow her away, she called the police. And when all else failed, she wrote the judge who put him on probation.
WOMAN VO: Does he have to kill me before I can finally be protected from him?
TITLE CARD: Venus Ann Shifflett got her answer four months later. It was a bullet through the head.
TITLE CARD: 10% of Baltimore's homicides each year are the result of domestic violence. Yet, there is less than a 1% chance that a man who beats his wife or girlfriend will serve any time in jail.
ANNCR: Isn't it time we let the victims walk free, instead of the abusers? Take a stand against violence. Attend harbor lights on September 7th and support the House of Ruth.

752
SFX: *Yelling, slapping, and crashing of furniture.*
SUPER: It is your business.
AVO: For Information On How You Can Help Stop Domestic Violence, Call 1-800-End-Abuse.
SUPER: There's no excuse for domestic violence.

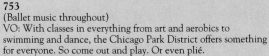

SUMMER

WITH THE YMCA

WITH THE YMCA

WITH THE YMCA

753
District 6
CLIENT
Chicago Park District
AGENCY
BBDO Chicago
Chicago, IL
CREATIVE DIRECTOR
Harold Woodridge
Phil Gant
ART DIRECTOR
Harold Woodridge
COPYWRITER
John Toth
DIRECTOR
John Komenich
PRODUCER
Jan Collins

754
District 10
CLIENT
YMCA of San
Antonio
AGENCY
Anderson
Advertising
San Antonio, TX
CREATIVE DIRECTOR
Stan McElrath
ART DIRECTOR
Bryan Edwards
COPYWRITER
Christopher Walther
EXECUTIVE PRODUCER
Mike Taylor
ACCOUNT EXECUTIVE
Loni Samet

753
(Ballet music throughout)
VO: With classes in everything from art and aerobics to swimming and dance, the Chicago Park District offers something for everyone. So come out and play. Or even plié.

754
Summer
OPEN ON: Summer with the YMCA. Summer bounces up and down like a basketball.
SFX: *Basketball dribbling*
Summer bounces off screen for a moment then comes back down.
SFX: *Dribbling then swish of basketball getting dunked through hoop. Buzzer sounds or kids cheering.*
ANNCR: Sounds like it's going to be a great summer.
SFX: *Kids cheering.*

Swimming
OPEN ON: Summer with the YMCA. Summer springs up into the air and dives back down.
SFX: *Sound of kid jumping off of a diving board. Ambient sounds of kids at pool in background.*
Summer dives into the bottom part of screen then comes up and floats around.
SFX: *Splash as summer dives back down. Ambient pool sounds.*
ANNCR: Sounds like it's going to be a great summer.
SFX: *Kids cheering.*

Archery
OPEN ON: Summer with the YMCA. With the YMCA pulls back and then zings through the air. Summer remains static.
SFX: *Sound of bow and arrow being pulled back.*
With the YMCA flies through the air and hits its target... the word summer.
SFX: *Arrow flying through the air followed by an arrow hitting its target.*
ANNCR: Sounds like it's going to be a great summer.
SFX: *Kids cheering.*

755
District 11

CLIENT
Seattle Times

AGENCY
Elgin Syferd DDB
Needham
Seattle, WA

CREATIVE DIRECTOR
Laurie Sinclair Fritts

ART DIRECTOR
Matt Myers

COPYWRITER
Cheryl Van Ooyen

PRODUCTION
Tracy Mullen

WOULD YOU HAVE BEEN THE PERSON WITH THE CLUB,

THE PERSON BEING HIT,

THE PERSON CHEERING,

OR THE PERSON LOOKING THE OTHER WAY?

Martin Luther King, Jr. Day is January 16th.

A DAY TO DREAM. A LIFETIME TO ACT.

THE VIEW OF FREEDOM

IS NEVER SO CLEAR

AS WHEN

IT HAS BEEN

OBSTRUCTED.

On January 16th, America honors Martin Luther King, Jr. and
the men and women he led in the cause of equal rights for all.
But in order to appreciate what these individuals stood for,
we must first remember what they had to stand against.

A DAY TO DREAM. A LIFETIME TO ACT.

AND ONE YEAR LATER,

BLACK CITIZENS WERE ALLOWED TO VOTE.

In 1965, our nation had pioneered a way to sustain a man in space. However
it wasn't until a year later, when President Johnson signed the Voters' Rights Act,
that we'd discovered how to sustain the constitutional rights of all its citizens—
within their own country. This Act, finally, abolished the "Jim Crow
Laws" used to prohibit blacks from exercising their right to vote.
On January 16th, join America in honoring Martin Luther King, Jr.
and the men and women he led in the cause of equal rights for all.

A DAY TO DREAM. A LIFETIME TO ACT.

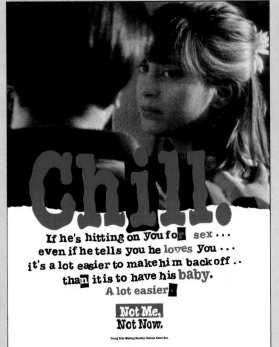

756
District 2
CLIENT
Monroe County
AGENCY
Jay Incorporated
Rochester, NY
CREATIVE DIRECTORS
John Brown
Duane Schweitz
COPYWRITER
John Brown
PHOTOGRAPHER
Mark Fogetti
DESIGNERS
Duane Schweitz
Ralph Newton
PRODUCER
Jeff Goff
PRODUCTION
Jay Incorporated

757
District 2

CLIENT
DC Rape Crisis Center

AGENCY
KSK Communications
Washington, DC

CREATIVE DIRECTORS
David Hadley
Chris Plumer

ART DIRECTORS
David Hadley
Chris Plumer

COPYWRITER
Chris Plumer

PHOTOGRAPHER
Debi Fox

PRINTER
Westland Enterprises

PRODUCTION
Claire Warwick

ACCOUNT EXECUTIVES
Karen Kenndey
Karla Chandler
Masters

758
District 10

CLIENT
Texas Prevention
Partnership

AGENCY
GSD&M
Austin, TX

CREATIVE DIRECTORS
Brent Ladd
Brian Brooker

ART DIRECTOR
Scott McAfee

COPYWRITER
Tim Bauer

PHOTOGRAPHER
Dennis Fagan

759
District 5

CLIENT
American Red Cross

AGENCY
Hameroff/Milenthal/
Spence
Columbus, OH

CREATIVE DIRECTOR
Wayne Hilinski

ART DIRECTOR
Jim McCabe

COPYWRITER
Dan Kendall

PRODUCTION
Betsy Cusick

757

758

759

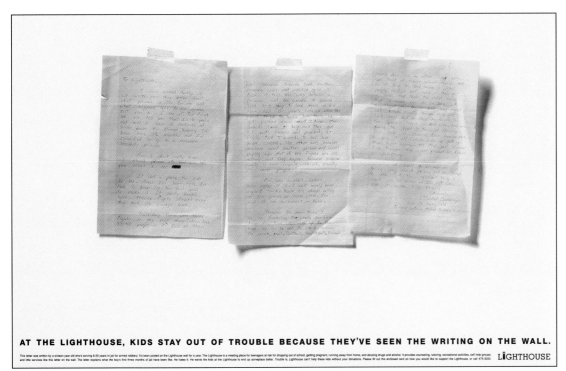

AT THE LIGHTHOUSE, KIDS STAY OUT OF TROUBLE BECAUSE THEY'VE SEEN THE WRITING ON THE WALL.

This letter was written by a sixteen year old who's serving 8-20 years in jail for armed robbery. It's been posted on the Lighthouse wall for a year. The Lighthouse is a meeting place for teenagers at risk for dropping out of school, getting pregnant, running away from home, and abusing drugs and alcohol. It provides counseling, tutoring, recreational activities, self help groups. and little services like this letter on the wall. The letter explains what the boy's first three months of jail have been like. He hates it. He wants the kids at the Lighthouse to end up someplace better. Trouble is, Lighthouse can't help these kids without your donations. Please fill out the enclosed card on how you would like to support the Lighthouse, or call 475-3220.   LIGHTHOUSE

760

I DON'T HAVE TO DO IT TO PROVE IT

A lot of my friends tell me that having sex is the only way to prove that I'm not a little girl any more. But for me, proving that I am growing up means making my own decisions about what is right for me.   **SEX CAN WAIT**

Brought to you by the Michigan Abstinence Partnership.

761

762

760
District 9
CLIENT
Lighthouse
AGENCY
Ad Federation
of Lincoln
Lincoln, NE
ART DIRECTOR
Ron Sack
COPYWRITER
Pat Piper
PHOTOGRAPHER
Bob Ervin
PRINTER
Graham Graphics

761
District 6
CLIENT
Michigan Dept. of
Public Health
AGENCY
BK&M Advertising
Ann Arbor, MI
CREATIVE DIRECTORS
Jon Gustafson
Debra Pregler
ART DIRECTOR
Debra Pregler
COPYWRITERS
Barbara Kalisewicz
Matt Fera

762
District 5
CLIENT
Portage County
Department of
Human Services
AGENCY
Tymcio Design
Associates
CREATIVE DIRECTOR
Annette Tymcio
COPYWRITER
Jenny Wilson
PHOTOGRAPHER
Dennis Sutton
DESIGNER
Annette Tymcio

763
District 11
CLIENT
Seattle Times
AGENCY
Elgin Syferd DDB
Needham
Seattle, WA
CREATIVE DIRECTOR
Laurie Sinclair Fritts
ART DIRECTOR
Matt Myers
COPYWRITER
Cheryl Van Ooyen
PRODUCTION
Tracy Mullen

764
District 5
CLIENT
Women for Women
Services
AGENCY
Doe-Anderson
Advertising Agency
Louisville, KY
CREATIVE DIRECTOR
Gary Sloboda
ART DIRECTOR
Stefanie Becker
COPYWRITER
Rankin Mapother
PHOTOGRAPHER
Geoffrey Carr

765
District 10
CLIENT
Houston Police
Department
AGENCY
Fogarty Klein
& Partners
Houston, TX
CREATIVE DIRECTOR
Tom Monroe
ART DIRECTOR
Marcus Wesson

766
District 6
CLIENT
Mel Trotter Ministries
AGENCY
Hanon McKendry
Grand Rapids, MI
CREATIVE DIRECTOR
Jim Hanon
ART DIRECTORS
Tom Crimp
Susan Johnston
COPYWRITER
Bill McKendry
PHOTOGRAPHER
Julie Line

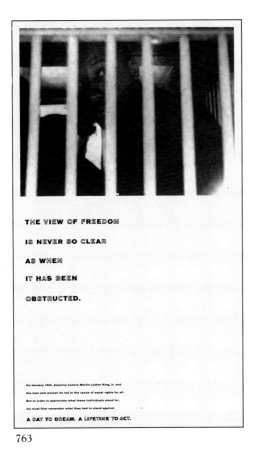

THE VIEW OF FREEDOM

IS NEVER SO CLEAR

AS WHEN

IT HAS BEEN

OBSTRUCTED.

763

764

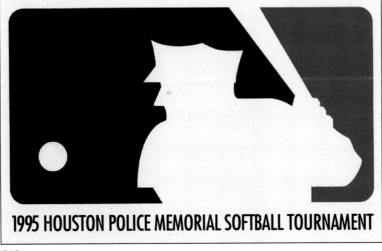

765

766

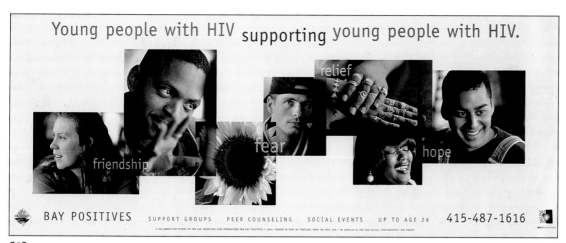

767

768

769

770

767
District 14
CLIENT
Bay Positives/SF AIDS
Foundation
AGENCY
Roz Romney & Kevin
Roberson
San Francisco, CA
ART DIRECTORS
Roz Romney
Kevin Roberson
PHOTOGRAPHER
Ken Probst
DESIGNERS
Roz Romney
Kevin Roberson

768
District 12
CLIENT
Humane Society
of Utah
AGENCY
Evans Group
Salt Lake City, UT
ART DIRECTOR
Steve Cardon
COPYWRITER
John Kinkead

769
District 6
CLIENT
Michigan Anti-Cruelty
Society
AGENCY
Lintas Campbell-
Ewald
Warren, MI
CREATIVE DIRECTION
Debbie Karnowsky
Cindy Sikorski
Terry Belitsos
Bill Biliti

770
District 7
CLIENT
City of New Orleans
AGENCY
The Montalbano
Group
New Orleans, LA
CREATIVE DIRECTION
Herb Montalbano

771
District 10

CLIENT
Junior Achievement

AGENCY
Rives Carlberg
Houston, TX

CREATIVE DIRECTOR
Ray Redding

ART DIRECTOR
Alan Babb

COPYWRITER
Cortny Jackson

PHOTOGRAPHER
Barry Fantich

772
District 2

CLIENT
Africare

AGENCY
Wells Rich Greene
BDDP Advertising,
Inc.
New York, NY

CREATIVE DIRECTORS
Michael Mark
Patrick Sean Flahert

ART DIRECTORS
Patrick Sean Flahert
Ray Davis

COPYWRITER
Michael Mark

773
District 7

CLIENT
Partners for Healthy
Babies

AGENCY
Van Galling-House
New Orleans, LA

774
District 6

CLIENT
Mel Trotter Ministries

AGENCY
Hanon McKendry
Grand Rapids, MI

CREATIVE DIRECTOR
Jim Hanon

ART DIRECTOR
Tom Crimp

COPYWRITER
Bill McKendry

PHOTOGRAPHER
Julie Line

775
District 6

CLIENT
Mel Trotter Ministries

AGENCY
Hanon McKendry
Grand Rapids, MI

CREATIVE DIRECTOR
Jim Hanon

ART DIRECTOR
Tom Crimp

COPYWRITER
Bill McKendry

PHOTOGRAPHER
Julie Line

771

772

773

774

775

Our plan was to show you a **bunch of teenagers** hanging out on a street corner looking for trouble, but they're busy **cleaning up a local park.**

Each year your donation allows United Way-funded agencies to help more than 160,000 young adults and teenagers in Greater Cincinnati and Northern Kentucky take part in activities that build independence and self-esteem.

MAKING A DIFFERENCE EVERY DAY. THE UNITED WAY.

You'll have to imagine a photo of an unemployed, single mother with three hungry kids because the children are in day care and their mother goes **back to school today.**

Each year your donation allows United Way-funded agencies to help more than 98,000 families throughout Greater Cincinnati and Northern Kentucky stay together and remain productive members of the community.

MAKING A DIFFERENCE EVERY DAY. THE UNITED WAY.

This was supposed to be a picture of a man who's been **living on the street** wondering where his next meal's going to come from. But he's **at work right now.**

Each year your donation allows United Way-funded agencies to help provide emergency food and shelter, job training and GED/literacy programs to more than 220,000 individuals and families in Greater Cincinnati and Northern Kentucky.

MAKING A DIFFERENCE EVERY DAY. THE UNITED WAY.

776
District 5
CLIENT
United Way
AGENCY
Wolf Blumberg Krody
Cincinnati, OH
CREATIVE DIRECTOR
Vern Hughes
ART DIRECTOR
Scott Morris
COPYWRITER
Terry Fletcher
PHOTOGRAPHER
Todd Joyce
ACCOUNT SERVICE
Sharon McCafferty
Lisa Hughes

777
District 6

CLIENT
Mel Trotter Ministries

AGENCY
Hanon McKendry
Grand Rapids, MI

CREATIVE DIRECTOR
Jim Hanon

ART DIRECTOR
Tom Crimp

COPYWRITERS
Bill McKendry
Jeff Kosloski

PHOTOGRAPHER
Julie Line

778
District 14

CLIENT
Coalition on
Homelessness

AGENCY
Odiorne Wilde
Narraway Groome
San Francisco, CA

CREATIVE DIRECTORS
Michael Wilde
Jeff Odiorne

ART DIRECTORS
John Aldrich
Jennifer Boyd

COPYWRITER
Paula Mangin

PHOTOGRAPHERS
Walt Denson
Dan Escober
Bob Mizono

ACCOUNT EXECUTIVE
Harry Groome

779
District 9

CLIENT
Izaak Walton League

AGENCY
DMB&B/St. Louis
St. Louis, MO

CREATIVE DIRECTORS
Tom Gow
Terry Yormark

ART DIRECTOR
Eric Revels

COPYWRITER
Brenda Bertts Long

DESIGNER
Eric Revels

PRODUCTION
Don Greifenkamp

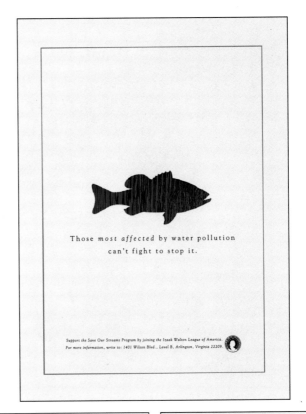

779

780
District 6

CLIENT
Michigan Department
of Public Health

AGENCY
BK&M Advertising
Ann Arbor, MI

CREATIVE DIRECTORS
Jon Gustafson
Debra Pregler

ART DIRECTOR
Debra Pregler

COPYWRITERS
Barbara Kalisewicz
Matt Fera
Andrea Collier

PHOTOGRAPHER
Lisa Spindler

781
District 5
CLIENT
Rock and Roll Hall of
Fame & Museum
AGENCY
Nesnadny &
Schwartz
Cleveland, OH
DESIGN
Nesnadny &
Schwartz

782
District 4
CLIENT
Sarasota Ballet
AGENCY
Coastal Printing
Sarasota, FL
ART DIRECTOR
Jennifer Mumford
PHOTOGRAPHERS
Nan Melville
Larry Vaughn
Jan Silverstein
DESIGNERS
Michael Long
Jody Haneke
PRINTER
Coastal Printing

781

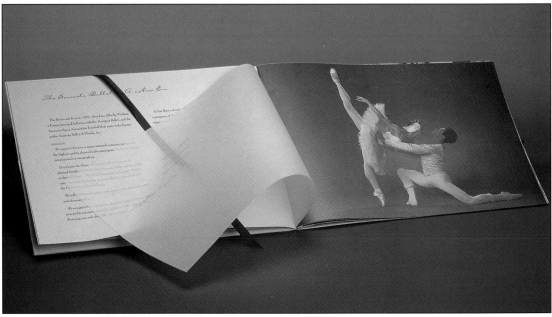

782

783

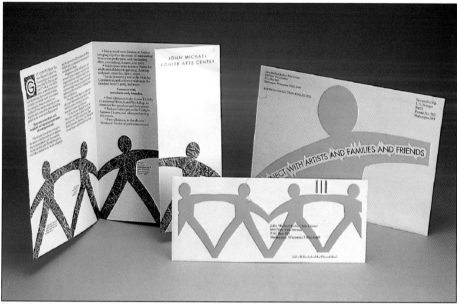

784

785

783
District 5

CLIENT
Cleveland Institute of Art

AGENCY
Nesnadny & Schwartz
Cleveland, OH

ART DIRECTORS
Joyce Nesnadny
Mark Schwartz

COPYWRITER
Anne Brooks Ranallo

PHOTOGRAPHERS
Mark Schwartz
Robert Muller

DESIGNERS
Brian Lavy
Joyce Nesnadny

784
District 8

CLIENT
John Michael Kohler Arts Center

AGENCY
Jacobson Rost
Sheboygan, WI

CREATIVE DIRECTOR
Reed Allen

ART DIRECTOR
Frank Melf

COPYWRITER
Judith Garson

ILLUSTRATOR
Frank Melf

DESIGNER
Frank Melf

PRINTER
Universal Lithograph

ACCOUNT EXECUTIVE
Eileen Hutchison

785
District 14

CLIENT
Fresno Metropolitan Museum

AGENCY
Charles Looney Advertising
Fresno, CA

786
District 7

CLIENT
The Andrews Agency

AGENCY
Robertson Design
Nashville, TN

ART DIRECTORS
Jeff Carroll
John Robertson

COPYWRITER
Susan Andrews

ILLUSTRATOR
Robert Felker

DESIGNER
Jeff Carroll

ENGRAVER
Color Systems

PRINTER
Lithographics
Anderson Studio

787
District 3

CLIENT
National Family
Partnership

AGENCY
Greg & Greg Creative
Greenville, SC

CREATIVE DIRECTION
Greg & Greg Creative

788
District 7

CLIENT
Istroumas Area
Council-BSA

AGENCY
X Design
Baton Rouge, LA

CREATIVE DIRECTOR
Martin Flanagan

ART DIRECTOR
Martin Flanagan

COPYWRITER
John Erickson

ILLUSTRATOR
Natalie Herndon

DESIGNER
Natalie Herndon

PRINTER
Franklin Press

PREPRESS
Image 4

789
District 14

CLIENT
The Poverello House

AGENCY
Saint Agnes Medical
Center
Communications
Department
Fresno, CA

DESIGNER
Douglas Hembd

PRINTER
Pacific Printing

PRODUCERS
Thomas Aller
Bonni Montevecchi

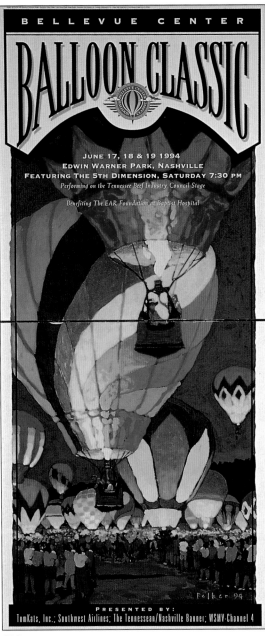

786

787

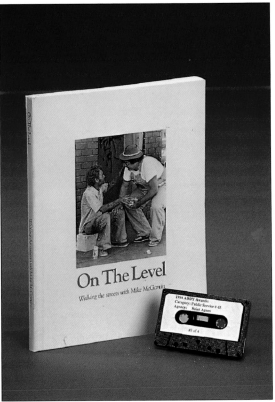

789

788

790

791

792

793
District 10

CLIENT
Circle Ten Council/
Boy Scouts of
America

AGENCY
DDB Needham
Worldwide Dallas
Group
Dallas, TX

CREATIVE DIRECTORS
Ted Barton
David Fowler

ART DIRECTOR
Christopher Gyorgy

COPYWRITER
Mark Cacciatore

PHOTOGRAPHER
John Katz

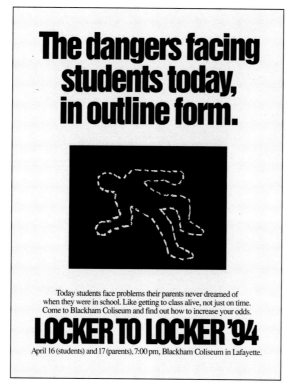

The dangers facing students today, in outline form.

Today students face problems their parents never dreamed of when they were in school. Like getting to class alive, not just on time. Come to Blackham Coliseum and find out how to increase your odds.

LOCKER TO LOCKER '94

April 16 (students) and 17 (parents), 7:00 pm, Blackham Coliseum in Lafayette.

794
District 7
CLIENT
Aranza Outreach
Ministries
AGENCY
Faith
Lafayette, LA
ART DIRECTOR
Glen Gauthier
COPYWRITER
Glen Gauthier
PHOTOGRAPHER
Doug Dugas
ILLUSTRATOR
Glen Gauthier

The newest weapon in the fight against drugs, violence and other student problems.

This clever device can do more for a troubled student than a week in detention. Or a slap on the wrist. Come and see who will be brave enough to use it.

LOCKER TO LOCKER '94

April 16 (students) and 17 (parents), 7:00 pm, Blackham Coliseum in Lafayette.

High school student, 1954:

"My teacher gave me an F, so I studied harder."

High school student, 1994:

"My teacher gave me an F, so I shot her."

If you think this only happens on TV or in inner city schools, think again. Violence of this kind happens right here in Acadiana. If you've got the guts to help change things, grab your friends and come to Blackham Coliseum.

LOCKER TO LOCKER '94

April 16 (students) and 17 (parents), 7:00 pm, Blackham Coliseum in Lafayette.

795
District 5

CLIENT
March of Dimes Birth
Defects Foundation

AGENCY
Olson and Gibbons,
Inc.
Cleveland, OH

CREATIVE DIRECTOR
Barry Olson

ART DIRECTOR
Sue Maczko

COPYWRITER
Barry Fiske

PRODUCER
Barry Smith

796
District 10

CLIENT
United Way of San
Antonio & Bexas
County

AGENCY
The Thompson
Agency
San Antonio, TX

ART DIRECTORS
Chris Colton
Jeff Jackson

COPYWRITER
Travis Waid

PHOTOGRAPHER
Oscar Williams

PRODUCER
Terry Osborne

POST PRODUCTION
Match Frame

DIRECTOR
Randy Rudd

EDITORS
Tom Strong
Jamie Norman
Tobin Holden

ACCOUNT EXECUTIVE
Donna Hinkelman

795
FEMALE VO: Over two million pregnant women in America are battered by their partners every year. If that makes you sick to your stomach... Just imagine what it's done to theirs.

796
SUPER: Different People. Different Stories. Different Needs.
SUPER: A loving home.
MALE VO: These sessions are helping me a lot. I think she's beginning to understand now that it was a problem with me, not her. I never wanted to hurt her.
SUPER: A hot meal.
DELAYED SUPER: And a friendly face.
SFX: *Doorbell and door opening.*
MALE VO: How are you doing, Mrs. Johnson? Got your lunch today.
FEMALE VO: Oh, thank you. You know, it's so nice to have a visitor...
SUPER: One Way that really works. By giving to United Way. Thank you.

PUBLIC SERVICE

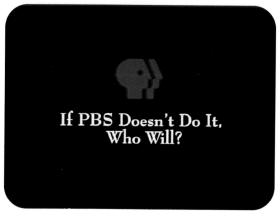

If PBS Doesn't Do It,
Who Will?

797
District 14

CLIENT
PBS

AGENCY
Hal Riney & Partners
San Francisco, CA

CREATIVE DIRECTOR
Marcus Kemp

ART DIRECTORS
Marcus Kemp

COPYWRITER
David Tessler

PRODUCER
Meegan Hanrahan
Tamsin Prigge

PRODUCTION
Sandbank Kamen
& Partners

ACCOUNT EXECUTIVE
Matt Ryan

798
District 2

CLIENT
Partnership for a
Drug Free America

AGENCY
Saatchi & Saatchi
New York, NY

CREATIVE DIRECTOR
Stanley Becker

ART DIRECTOR
Matthew Schwartz

COPYWRITER
David George

PRODUCER
Jerry Boyle

EDITOR
Alan Eisenberg

797
TITLE: PBS, JOURNALIST.
VO: Finally tonight the story - Sheik Muslims of Southern Iraq.
The Sheite tried to declare their independence from the Saddam
Husein regime in Baghdad.
TITLE: DATELINE: IRAQ, 1994.
VO: Saddam's republican guard and their tanks had been left
intact by the Allies and in the end the rebels were hopelessly
outgunned. There were no TV cameras here to record what
happened-only this extraordinary amateur video tape shot by two
brothers, one of whom was killed.
TITLE: THERE'S STILL A PLACE FOR SERIOUS NEWS.
VO: Desperate women and children can only call on God now to
help them. Most of these people are about to die.
TITLE: EVEN IN THE AGE OF TABLOID JOURNALISM
VO: This casual brutality has been justified by the Iraqi president
throughout his career in politics.
TITLE: "THE MCNEIL/LEHRER NEWS HOUR." IF PBS
DOESN'T DO IT, WHO WILL?

798
SFX: *Sound of projector followed by click of next slide.*
VO: In advertising,
SFX: *Click*
VO: they say one of the surest ways
SFX: *Click*
VO: to get your message across
SFX: *Click*
VO: is to put celebrities in your commercial.
(Dramatic pause)
SFX: *Click*
VO: We hope they're right.
SFX: *Click*

PUBLIC SERVICE

799
District 15
CLIENT
Home Box Office/
Warner Music Group
AGENCY
Home Box Office
New York, NY
CINEMATOGRAPHER
Bob Lechterman
EXECUTIVE PRODUCER
Shelby Stone

800
District 8
CLIENT
John Marshall
High School
AGENCY
SC Johnson & Son
Milwaukee, WI
CREATIVE DIRECTION
John Marshall
High School
Communications,
S.C. Johnson & Son

799
Inner city kids play basketball
KID #1: Right here, right here right here..
KID #2: It's like this, you know what I'm saying...
KID #3 *(Doing a rap)*:...get a show...put on the pedal, damn...we comfortable with the ghetto
The kids, who appear to be gangmembers, gather together and talk amongst themselves. Two young men look towards an oncoming car. A hooded kid jumps out of the car with a gun, chasing after one member of the gang, in a striped shirt. The gangmember runs from him and throws his own gun in a nearby trash can. Hooded kid shoots at him. The boy jumps the railing. Another shot. Through a reflection of a puddle on the ground, we see the boy continue to run. Another shot. The boy leaps (in silhouette), trying to escape. He tries to climb a ladder but finds himself pinned against a fence with a gun in his face.
GANGMEMBER: Damn, you caught me.
HOODED KID: Shut up! Shut up!
CU of gangmember with sweat pouring down his face and the gun directly in front of him.
GANGMEMBER: So this is how it's gonna be?
HOODED KID: That's right. That's how it's gonna be.
CU of gangmember sweating, sighing desperately. CU of hooded kid. He slowly pulls the hood off to reveal that he is the gangmember. The gangmember has been running from himself, from the destiny he will face if he continues his life as a gangster.
HOODED KID: So there punk. Remember me?
CU of stunned gangmember, still sweating
HOODED KID *(voice in slo-mo)*: Remember me? Remember me?
Dissolve to CU of the barrel of a gun.
ANNCR: Stop. You're only killing yourself.
CHYRON: Peace. Live It or Rest In It.

800
"Time & Time Again," a leading edge environmental education film about today's critical recycling issues, culminates the work of 29 John Marshall High School students in partnership with S.C. Johnson & Son, Inc. The film, developed for high school science students, illustrates the intricacies and importance of recycling as many empty containers as possible including steel aerosol cans.

801
District 9

CLIENT
Boy's Club of Omaha

AGENCY
Scott Anderson
Group
Omaha, NE

CREATIVE DIRECTOR
Mark Lanham

ART DIRECTOR
John Hardy

COPYWRITERS
Scott Anderson
Pat Piper

ACCOUNT EXECUTIVE
Ingrid Peridikis

801
CAMERA CARD: Violence at 12
BOY: One day, I was shooting hoops at the school and this kid came up to me and started calling me names and pushing me around. So I chased him all the way to his house and his brother came out and pulled a gun on me.
CAMERA CARD: 1 in 25 kids carries a gun to school
BOY: I told my mother and my mother told me to go to the Boys Clubs of Omaha. There, that influenced me with better friends and better people, instead of running the streets. I'd rather shoot a basketball than to shoot a gun.
CAMERA CARD: We give boys a better shot.
CAMERA CARD: Boys Clubs of Omaha

CAMERA CARD: Tonight's Story: Gangs
BOY: One night I went over to my friend's house to spend the night... and I got beat up pretty bad because I didn't want to help some Crips fight some Bloods.
CAMERA CARD: Estimated 1,000 boys in Omaha gangs
BOY: I learned a lesson because now I go to the Boys Clubs which is a safe place. They teach you the right things you need to know in life. It's a good place to be. I didn't want to be one of the gang, so I joined the club.
CAMERA CARD: Our club beats the gangs
CAMERA CARD: Boys Clubs of Omaha

CAMERA CARD: Drug story at 11
BOY: I used to sell all the time. I started dealing when I was 11. Mostly just bud. Nothing like crack or anything because it was too hard to get a hold of. When I started to get in trouble with the cops, my mom sent me to the Boys Clubs.
CAMERA CARD: 43% of high school students use drugs at least once
BOY: They have special classes like Smart Moves which helps me realize the dangers of drugs. I gave everything I had left to my Mom. She got rid of it. I haven't done anything else since.
CAMERA CARD: Boys are addicted to our club
CAMERA CARD: Boys Clubs of Omaha

802

District 14

CLIENT
PBS

AGENCY
Hal Riney & Partners
San Francisco, CA

CREATIVE DIRECTOR
Marcus Kemp

ART DIRECTOR
Marcus Kemp

COPYWRITER
David Tessler

PRODUCER
Meegan Hanrahan
Tamsin Prigge

PRODUCTION
Sandbank Kamen
& Partners

ACCOUNT EXECUTIVE
Matt Ryan

802

TITLE: PBS, STORYTELLER.
MALE: She was being pushed and pushed and pushed. I don't think she was eager to take that flight.
FEMALE: There was a lack of focus. She simply was not preparing for it.
TITLE: SHE WAS MISSING FOR OVER 50 YEARS.
MALE (MCCULLOUGH): There was her own puzzling disregard for such obvious professional necessities as knowing the Morse Code and the fact that the Queen of the air was not the best of pilots.
TITLE: Only PBS could bring her back, the way she really was.
FEMALE: To succeed, Earhart would need months of preparation and a lot of luck. In the end she had neither.
TITLE: "THE AMERICAN EXPERIENCE."
MALE: It was the disappearance of Amelia that created the legend.
TITLE: IF PBS DOESN'T DO IT, WHO WILL?

VO: I'm going to whip them here. Or they are going to whip me.
TITLE: PBS, HISTORIAN.
VO: Suddenly the Union artillery on Cemetery Ridge and Little Round Top opened fire and a great moan went up from the Confederate line.
TITLE: NO STARS. NO HAPPY ENDING.
VO: Almost a third of those engaged, 51,000 men were lost.
TITLE: WHAT TV NETWORK WOULD WANT IT? Nobody but PBS.
VO: As the rebels staggered back, Lee rode out to meet them. "All this has been my fault," he told them.
TITLE: "THE CIVIL WAR" BY KEN BURNS.
QUOTE: It was an incredible mistake and there's scarcely a trained soldier who didn't know it was a mistake.
VO: Lee's army would never again penetrate so far into northern territory.
TITLE: IF PBS DOESN'T DO IT, WHO WILL?

TITLE: PBS, OBSERVER OF THE AMERICAN SCENE.
VO: He had played in a record 2130 consecutive games. And earned himself the nickname "The Iron Horse."
TITLE: ANY TV STATION CAN SHOW YOU BASEBALL.
VO: But now something was terribly wrong. He was only 35, but had begun to play like an old man. Lou Gehrig took himself out of the lineup.
TITLE: ONLY PBS CAN SHOW YOU.
GEHRIG: "Today I consider myself the luckiest man on the face of the earth."
TITLE: WHY IT ISN'T JUST FOR BASEBALL FANS.
GEHRIG: I might have been given a bad break, but I have got an awful lot to live for. Thank you."
TITLE: "BASEBALL" BY KEN BURNS.
VO: He was benching himself, he said, for the good of the team.
TITLE: IF PBS DOESN'T DO IT, WHO WILL?

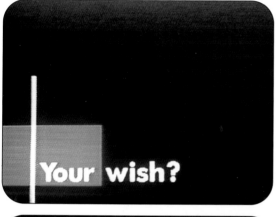

803
District 3
CLIENT
WRAL-TV
AGENCY
WRAL-TV
Raleigh, NC
COPYWRITER
David Creech
PRODUCER
David Creech
POST PRODUCTION
Steve Elizondo
DIRECTOR
David Creech
GRAPHICS
Stan Gilliland

804
District 6
CLIENT
Quatro Partners
AGENCY
The Production
Studio Inc
Fort Wayne, IN
CREATIVE DIRECTION
The Production
Studio

803
RACHEL: Almost like everyday, he's sitting on the couch, and just... watching football.
SUPER: Time with dad.
RACHEL: And when can I say can I watch, um, TV he always says just a minute, and he always says just a minute, just a minute.
SUPER: Your wish?
RACHEL: Play games with me, um, because there's one favorite game I like to play and I usually like Dad to play with me.
SUPER: Your child has something to say. Listen. It shows you care.

GINNY: Because I didn't understand it 'cause they divorced when I was about five years old. And I had never heard of that word before. So it took me a little time to figure out that word. And when I knew what they were doing it made me feel sad. 'Cause when I was with my mom I missed my dad, and when I was with my dad I missed my mom. So I wasn't really happy for a little bit until I got used to it.
SUPER: Your child has something to say. Listen. It shows you care.

TAMARA: That nobody would fight, nobody would get killed. 'Cause making people get dead.
STEPHEN: Nobody could boss anybody around. That there was nobody big, all of us were the same size, so couldn't really boss people around, and we were all the same age.
SUPER: Your child has something to say. Listen. It shows you care.

804
SUMMARY: The ocean and all that live in it call to a group of children, through a Michael Quatro instrumental, to come to the beach to save a dolphin who is caught in netting near the water's edge. During that rescue the children dance and reach to the sands and the waters to show their concern and hope for the oceans and those that inhabit it.

805
District 7

CLIENT
Augusta Symphony

AGENCY
Augusta Symphony
Augusta, GA

COPYWRITER
Judith Upchurch

CONCEPT
Judith Upchurch

806
District 12

CLIENT
Greg Kiefer
Productions

AGENCY
Greg Kiefer
Productions
Salt Lake City, UT

ART DIRECTOR
Rich Hansen

COPYWRITERS
Aria Vallejo
Stephen Spencer
Adam Smith

EXECUTIVE PRODUCER
Renee S. Beardsley

PRODUCERS
Adam Smith
Patt Kupka

DIRECTORS
Greg Kiefer
Gene Salvatori

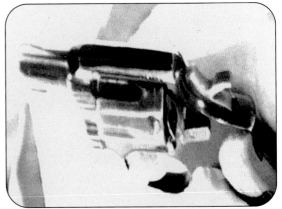

805
DR. PORTNOY: I'm Donald Portnoy, Music Director of the
Augusta Symphony with a challenge... you try my music, I'll try
yours.
SFX: *Country music throughout*
DR. PORTNOY *(miming)*: Look at me.
DR. PORTNOY *(miming)*: Whoomp there is
DR. PORTNOY: Everyone enjoys good music. So join us for an
Augusta Symphony Concert. You never know what might show
up on a program. So Join us for an Augusta Symphony Concert.

806
School bell rings. Music throughout
SCHOLAR *(Waving a test)*: You Guys! I got a 4.0 on my report
card.
ATHLETE: I can kick that. Check this out. Baam! Look at that
I got my football letter. You know I've got it made.
MUSTANG: My brother's out of town for the weekend and he
left me the keys to his Mustaaang!!!
BILLY: I can top all you guys. *(He lifts his shirt and pulls out a small
caliber handgun)* Check it out. I got it from my dad's closet. He
doesn't even know it's gone.
FRIENDS *(ad-lib)*: I gotta go. Later, man.
ATHLETE: I'm not gonna ruin my rep with that.
SCHOLAR: That's not even cool. In fact, it's stupid.
LAST FRIEND: Man, I've been kickin' it with you and all, man,
but I'm not down with that. Know what I'm sayin'? I'm out man.
SUPER: Speak Your Peace.

PUBLIC SERVICE

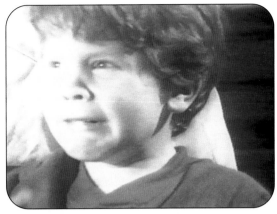

807

District 13

CLIENT
First Night Honolulu

AGENCY
Milici Valenti Ng Pack
Honolulu, HI

CREATIVE DIRECTOR
Walter Wanger

ART DIRECTOR
Tammy Ebert

COPYWRITERS
Jim Beyer
Trent Farr

808

District 5

CLIENT
Summit County
Children Services

AGENCY
The Reuben Group/
Brubaker &
Associates
Cleveland, OH

CREATIVE DIRECTORS
Lynn Jareb
Mickey Ulichney

ART DIRECTOR
Mickey Ulichney

COPYWRITER
Lynn Jareb

PRODUCER
Anita Ferris-Sears

DIRECTOR
Martin Reuben

807
MUSIC THROUGHOUT: Distorted "Auld Lang Syne"
TITLE: Sick of the same old New Year's Eve? This year, come to
First Night. It's Alcohol-free. With 35 city blocks of things to see
and do. It's Oahu's biggest New Year's Eve party. Without the
morning after.

808
HE: It's my money...I'll do what I want with it.
SUPER: Not all children
SHE: I'm tired of your drinking our money away.
SUPER: who need foster parents
HE: Don't start with me again...
SUPER: are drug addicts
SHE: Let go of me *(screams)* Help!!! I'm calling the police.
SUPER: or gang members. They're just kids
HE: Call the police...
SFX: *Phone smashing against wall.*
SHE: *(Crying)* I hate you. Get out of my life.
SUPER: who need a loving
HE: Get out of my house. And take that worthless kid with you.
Where is he anyway...
SUPER: home. Please... be a foster parent.
SHE: *(Screaming after him)* Nooooooo! Don't you touch him.
SUPER: And make a difference...
SFX: *Door slamming open.*
SUPER: one child at a time.

809
District 11
CLIENT
Seattle Times
AGENCY
Elgin Syferd/DDB
Needham
Seattle, WA
CREATIVE DIRECTOR
Laurie Sinclair Fritts
ART DIRECTOR
Matt Myers
COPYWRITER
Cheryl Van Ooyen
PRODUCER
Lynda Hammer

810
District 14
CLIENT
Rainforest Action
Network
AGENCY
Odiorne Wilde
Narraway Groome
San Francisco, CA
CREATIVE DIRECTORS
Michael Wilde
Jeff Odiorne
COPYWRITER
Oliver Albrecht
PRODUCER
Kathi Calef

811
District 5
CLIENT
Sprint/United
Telephone
AGENCY
Sprint/United
Telephone
Mansfield, OH
DIRECTOR
John Hewitt

812
District 2
CLIENT
UJA Federation
AGENCY
Wells Rich Greene
BDDP
New York, NY
CREATIVE DIRECTOR
Linda Kaplan Thaler
COPYWRITERS
Lynn Blumenfeld
Stephen Meyers
PRODUCERS
Stephen Meyers
Stuart Raffel
COMPOSER
Fred Thaler
Macrose Music

RADIO SCRIPT
Turkey Dinner

A man walks into a coffee shop around noon. He finds an empty stool at the counter and sits down. The woman seated to his right quickly moves 3 places away from him. "Can I have the turkey special?" he asks. "Maybe you didn't notice the sign," the man behind the counter says. Another customer in the diner begins to sniff the air, asking no one in particular, "Do you smell something in here? Because I smell something." At this point, another man dumps an entire sugar canister over the head of the man at the counter who tried to order the turkey special. Other customers cheer him on as spit flies from somewhere in the restaurant. Not long after that, a policeman is called to the diner... (pause) and arrests the man at the counter with the sugar on his head and the spit running down the back of this neck... for disturbing the peace.

This month America honors Martin Luther King, Jr. and the men and women he led in the cause of equal rights for all. But before we can truly appreciate what these individuals stood for, we must first remember... what they had to stand against.

809

RADIO SCRIPT
Extinct

(SFX: *Jungle sounds*)
ANNCR: Inhabitants of the rainforest. The kookaburra.
(SFX: *Bird squawk*)
The bengal tiger
(SFX: *Tiger growl*)
The Mitsubishi Corporation
(SFX: *Chainsaw throughout*).
Mitsubishi is the worst corporate destroyer of the worlds rainforests. Boycott their products. Call the Rainforest Action Network at 1-800-989-RAIN.
(SFX: *Tree crash*).

810

RADIO SCRIPT
Brad and Debbie

ANNCR#1: What you are about to hear is real
DISPATCHER: There's a hysterical child on line they need an ambulance at 8800 Munson Hill.
BRAD: I have no idea if she's dead or not.
ANNCR#1: Just seven years old, Brad is alone and desperately trying to save his mother's life.
DISPATCHER: Is there anybody out there with your mom?
BRAD: No we're the only one's here, I'm so scared.
DISPATCHER: I know you're scared.
ANNCR#1: In real life not every story has a happy ending. But thanks to 911 and Brad... This one does.
DISPATCHER: You did the right thing by calling 911.
BRAD: I think they're here, I think they're here.
ANNCR#1: 911 use it when you need it, need it when you use it.
ANNCR#2: A public service message brought to you by the national emergency number association and Sprint/United Telephone.

811

RADIO SCRIPT
Shirley

SHIRLEY: Watching the man you love deteriorate is so sad. We were married almost 48 years. I knew him from the age of 13. He lost his job when he was sixty and it was around that time when something went wrong. Terribly wrong. He just wasn't himself. At first we thought it was depression. Finally after endless tests we found our Alzheimer's.

The progression was rapid. He was totally dependent. I had to feed him, to bathe him... my entire life revolved around caring for him. I was emotionally and physically exhausted, and there was nowhere for me to turn.

Then my son found a senior-day care program sponsored by UJA Federation. My husband fit in beautifully. For the first time in months, I had peace of mind. And my husband, they gave him back his dignity.

ANNCR: UJA-Federation of New York. We help 4.5 million people a year. One At A Time. For more information or to make a donation, please call 1-800-UJA-FED7.

812

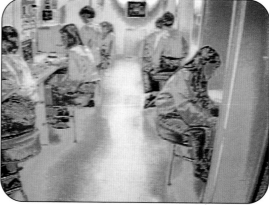

813
District 13
CLIENT
FCC Gun Control
AGENCY
Peck Sims Mueller
Honolulu, HI
CREATIVE DIRECTOR
Stan Moy
ART DIRECTOR
Grant Miyasahi
COPYWRITER
Brad Shin
PRODUCER
Natalie Wingert

814
District 8
CLIENT
Wausau school
AGENCY
Pamela Rucinski
& Associates
Mosinee, WI
COPYWRITER
Pamela Rucinski
EXECUTIVE PRODUCER
MaryEllen Marnholtz
PRODUCER
Pamela Rucinski
PRODUCTION
Greg Rasmussen
Joy Rasmussen

815
District 8
CLIENT
Wisconsin
Department of
Transportation
AGENCY
Zillman Advertising
& Marketing, Inc.
Madison, WI
CREATIVE DIRECTOR
Richard Zillman
MUSIC
Dave Hanson
TALENT
Emily Miller
(No frames or script
available)

813
MUSIC: Acid Guitar
SFX: *Gunfire mixed with voices*.
MAN #1: The animals must be dealt with.
MAN #2: Guns hold the freedom.
MAN #3: Guns are the solution.
ANNCR: Guns in the home kill 43 times more family members,
friends, neighbors than intruders. Call your legislator. Don't let
gun control die.

814
VO: Welcome to Space Station Quest. Quest is transporting
children into a new millennium of learning. Its functions are
similar to its mother ship, Space Station Freedom.
VO: Student astronauts will direct you through the ships learning
centers. Astronauts are responsible for all work on board.
VO: All adults remain seated for the remainder of this mission.

816
District 4
CLIENT
Monroe County
AGENCY
Jay Incorporated
Tampa, FL
CREATIVE DIRECTORS
Duane Schweitz
John Brown
COPYWRITER
John Brown
PHOTOGRAPHY
Mark Foggetti
PRODUCER
Jeffrey Peyton Goff

817
District 7
CLIENT
Knoxville Arts Council
AGENCY
Jester/Proud
Knoxville, TN
PHOTOGRAPHY
Scott Colthorp
MUSIC
Paul Jones

816
SUMMARY: The Monroe County Adolescent Pregnancy
Prevention Communications Program, using "Not Me, Not Now"
as the core message, communicates the consequences of teen
pregnancy to both kids and the community. It helps teens deal
with peer pressure that encourages sexual activity, promotes
parent-child communication about sexuality and relationships,
and raises community awareness as a whole.

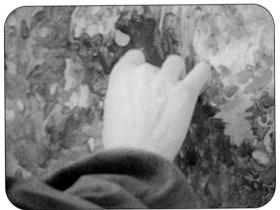

817

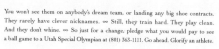

SOME ATHLETES ACTUALLY DO MAKE GOOD ROLE MODELS.

You won't see them on anybody's dream team, or landing any big shoe contracts. They rarely have clever nicknames. ∞ Still, they train hard. They play clean. And they don't whine. ∞ So just for a change, pledge what you would pay to see a ball game to a Utah Special Olympian at (801) 363-1111. Go ahead. Glorify an athlete.

818
District 12

CLIENT
Special Olympics

AGENCY
Dahlin Smith White
Salt Lake City, UT

CREATIVE DIRECTOR
Jon White

ART DIRECTOR
Shelly Schulthess

COPYWRITER
Eric White

DIRECTOR
Jeff France

PRODUCER
Diana Young

818
SUPER: Some athletes actually do make good role models.
Support a Special Olympian.

819
District 3

CLIENT
Free Medical Clinic

AGENCY
The Eison Goot
Group
Greenville, SC

ART DIRECTOR
Robbin Phillips

COPYWRITER
Scott Gould

PRODUCTION
TVP Productions

DIRECTOR
Scott Gould

 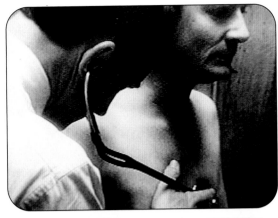

819

820
District 10

CLIENT
Tulsa Area United Way

AGENCY
Copy Cafe/Brander Creative
Tulsa, OK

ART DIRECTOR
Brent Brander

COPYWRITER
Shelley Brander

PRODUCERS
Tom Twomey
Shelley Brander

POST PRODUCTION
Winner Communications

MUSIC
Irving Productions

820
TITLE CARDS: Give a boy scout the tools to make a spark.
Spark a deaf child's interests.
Interest some disabled kids in a game of softball.
Soften an old man's hardened heart.
Give an asthma patient a chance to run a 10K.
Keep a tornado victim from going hungry.
Give a rape victim a chance to feel clean again.
Clean up a housing project.
Help a special athlete feel famous for a minute.
Help an arthritis patient hold her child's hand.
Hand a gang member a way out.
Outsmart a drug dealer.
Do your part.
Part the waters for a handicapped swimmer.
Give a flood victim aid.
Stop AIDS from spreading.
Spread the message of hope.
Find a home for someone who can't afford one.
Afford a crack baby the chance to grow.
Teach a grown man to write.
Right a wrong.
Write a check.
Give to the United Way.
Thanks.

821
District 9

CLIENT
Family Service of
Lincoln

AGENCY
Bailey Lauerman &
Associates
Lincoln, NE

CREATIVE DIRECTOR
Carter Weitz

ART DIRECTOR
Shelley Hanna

COPYWRITER
Laura Crawford

PHOTOGRAPHER
David Radler

FILM
Lincoln Graphics

ACCOUNT EXECUTIVE
Pam Hunzeker

821

RADIO

822

District 9

CLIENT
Bum Steer

AGENCY
Baily Lauerman &
Associates
Lincoln, NE

CREATIVE DIRECTOR
Rich Bailey

COPYWRITERS
Laura Crawford
Carter Weitz

PRODUCERS
Carter Weitz
Laura Crawford

PRODUCTION
Soundscapes

ACCOUNT EXECUTIVE
Dan Levy

823

District 9

CLIENT
Bum Steer

AGENCY
Baily Lauerman &
Associates
Lincoln, NE

CREATIVE DIRECTOR
Rich Bailey

COPYWRITERS
Laura Crawford
Carter Weitz

PRODUCERS
Carter Weitz
Laura Crawford

PRODUCTION
Soundscapes

ACCOUNT EXECUTIVE
Dan Levy

SFX: *(Typewriter tune)*

COW: Dear Green Peace, I've got a little problem here. It's called Bum Steer. A great steak house. There lies the problem here. I'm a cow. Anyway, heard you saved a few whales. Well how bout us cows? Don't we count? It's not like you need to charter a boat. Just get on some bikes and start swervin' like maniacs in front of people headed for the Bum Steer. Anyway, the more I worry, the more I eat, which means time's running out. Signed, Cow.

ANNCR: The Bum Steer. Great steaks at sixty-fourth and O.

COW: Bummer.

822

Dear Green Peace

SFX: *(Typewriter tune)*

COW: Dear Green Peace, I've got a little problem here. It's called Bum Steer. A great steak house. There lies the problem here. I'm a cow. Anyway, heard you saved a few whales. Well how bout us cows? Don't we count? It's not like you need to charter a boat. Just get on some bikes and start swervin' like maniacs in front of people headed for the Bum Steer. Anyway, the more I worry, the more I eat, which means time's running out. Signed, Cow.

ANNCR: The Bum Steer. Great steaks at sixty-fourth and O.

COW: Bummer.

Veggie Club

MUSIC: *(Typewriter tune)*

COW *(Reading out loud as he's typing)*: Dear Vegetarians Club of America, You don't know me, but we have a lot in common. You like vegetables. I like vegetables. You don't eat meat. I don't eat meat. But here's where we differ. You wouldn't be caught dead in the Bum Steer steak house, and I would. I'm a cow. So please, go to the Bum Steer with your sprout-eating friends and order some of their non beef-related items. Thanks...Your veggie pal, Cow.

ANNCR: The Bum Steer. Great steaks at sixty-four and O.

COW: Bummer.

Dear Mr. Prez

SFX: *(Typewriter tune)*

COW *(Reading out loud as he's typing)*: Dear Mr. President, heard you're a Razorback fan. You know, "Go hogs and all that." Well, how bout us cows? How bout supporting us? You see, we've got this restaurant called the Bum Steer giving away free steak dinners for birthdays. Talk about a losing season for cows. Anyway, I could use your help. Not that I have anything against folks having a happy birthday, but this deal means happy trails for you know who. Signed...Cow.

ANNCR: The Bum Steer. Great steaks at sixty-fourth and O.

COW: Bummer.

823

RADIO

(Man's voice has Eastern European accent. Delivery is slow and deliberate)

SFX: *Man's footsteps on concrete floor - pacing.*

MAN: I was there when it all happened. I was one of the last to see Rudolph Hess alive at Spandau. He hanged himself in his cell you know - the famous prisoner number seven.

They were all just waiting for the old man to die. Then the bulldozers came, and Spandau Prison was no more.

MUSIC: *Enters with ominous, sustained tone - builds over remainder of spot.*

MAN: But then, they found it. A few sheets of paper in the rubble. A diary. I don't know what it said, but everyone wanted it. The Americans. The Germans. The Israelis. The Russians. It was as if he rose from the ashes - like the phoenix. And the horror began again...

MUSIC: *Sting, then continues.*

ANNCR: Spandau Phoenix by Greg Iles. A long-buried Nazi secret erupts into an international nightmare as fact meets fiction in this electrifying novel. Spandau Phoenix. John Grisham calls it, "A scorching read." Spandau Phoenix by Greg Iles. Now a Signet paperback.

824

Three Theories

ANNCR: Dan Post Boots offers a few theories on why Western boots are historically very uncomfortable. One: The people who made cowboy boots were a bunch of lily-livered citified dandies who envied the cowboy his courage and freedom, and made cowboy boots painful out of sheer, pure-D spite. Two: Boots were just another hardship for cowpokes to endure. Along with stampedes. Saddlesores. Beef jerky. Three: Somehow, the Oriental tradition of binding women's feet to stop them from growing made it across the Pacific and into the psyche of cowboy boot manufactures. Go figure. Most boot makers carry on that painful tradition. But Dan Post Boots are made for comfort. If they're not the most comfortable boots you've ever worn, you have 30 days to bring them back. Get comfortable. Get Dan Post boots. The best break with cowboy tradition since padded riding breeches. Yee ha.

The Saddlehorn Thing

ANNCR: To explain why Western boots are typically so uncomfortable, Dan Post Boots has developed the theory that cowboys loved hardship. Why else would they eat food cooked in bear grease. Or ride spine-jarring, whiplash-inducing bucking broncos which as often as not threw you crashing against a large boulder so typical of the Wild West landscape. Then the cowboy was back in the saddle with that saddlehorn thing right there, ready to get him where it counts whenever his horse bucked. I tell you, their boots were just one symptom of this fascination with pain. But today's cowboy doesn't like pain so much anymore. That's why Dan Post boots are made for comfort. If they're not the most comfortable boots you've ever worn, take them back within 30 days for a full refund. Get comfortable. Get Dan Post Boots. The best break with cowboy tradition since, well, the cowgirl. Yee-ha.

825

824
District 2
CLIENT
Penguin, USA
AGENCY
Ziccardi & Partners
New York, NY
CREATIVE DIRECTOR
Joe Fontana
COPYWRITER
Joe Fontana
AUDIO ENGINEER
Mitch Rayboy

825
District 7
CLIENT
Dan Post Boots/Acme
Boot Company
AGENCY
Gillis Advertising & PR
Birmingham, AL
CREATIVE DIRECTORS
Charles Black
Henry Levkoff
COPYWRITER
Virginia Miller
PRODUCTION
Airwave
Craig Wiese & Co
ACCOUNT EXECUTIVE
Mike Laraway

RADIO

ANNCR: A bag of popcorn now has as much fat as ten big mac hamburgers. Not everyone who attends will be wearing deodorant. You might run into someone you used to beat up in junior high. It probably won't do justice to the book. Not all endings are happy. You can't smoke. It might make you cry. In a year or so you can probably rent it. It might make you late for supper. Soon there'll be over 500 channels on cable TV. You might miss a beautiful sunset. There are a lot of valid reasons not to attend the 20th Seattle International Film Festival running from May 20th through June 12th. But from now on...not knowing about it...isn't one of them. Cinema Seattle presents the 20th anniversary of the Seattle International Film Festival. See what the world is coming to May 20th through June 12th. Now you know.

826

MUSIC: (*Typewriter tune*)
COW (*Reading out loud as he's typing*): Dear Vegetarians Club of America, You don't know me, but we have a lot in common. You like vegetables. I like vegetables. You don't eat meat. I don't eat meat. But here's where we differ. You wouldn't be caught dead in the Bum Steer steak house, and I would. I'm a cow. So please, go to the Bum Steer with your sprout-eating friends and order some of their non beef-related items.

Thanks...Your veggie pal, Cow.
ANNCR: The Bum Steer. Great steaks at sixty-four and O.
COW: Bummer.

828

SFX: (*Typewriter tune*)
COW (*Reading out loud as he's typing*): Dear Mr. President, heard you're a Razorback fan. You know, "Go hogs and all that." Well, how bout us cows? How bout supporting us? You see, we've got this restaurant called the Bum Steer giving away free steak dinners for birthdays. Talk about a losing season for cows. Anyway, I could use your help. Not that I have anything against folks having a happy birthday, but this deal means happy trails for you know who. Signed...Cow.
ANNCR: The Bum Steer. Great steaks at sixty-fourth and O.
COW: Bummer.

827

ANNCR: And now, Mr. Robert Goulet reads from "The Writings of Bart"... the collected after-school blackboard writings of young Bart Simpson. Mr. Goulet...
MUSIC: *Dignified, classical*
ROBERT GOULET: I will not trade pants with others. I will not do that thing with my tongue. I will not Xerox my butt. A burp is not an answer. I will not pledge allegiance to Bart. I will not eat things for money. I will not bring sheep to class. I will not instigate revolution. My name is not Doctor Death.
ANNCR: To experience all of Bart's blackboard writings, watch every classic episode of "The Simpsons."
ROBERT GOULET: I will not call the principal Spud Head.
ANNCR: "The Simpsons," now five times a week.
MUSIC: *Music up, under and out.*

829

RADIO

From Now On

ANNCR: A bag of popcorn now has as much fat as ten big mac hamburgers. Not everyone who attends will be wearing deodorant. You might run into someone you used to beat up in junior high. It probably won't do justice to the book. Not all endings are happy. You can't smoke. It might make you cry. In a year or so you can probably rent it. It might make you late for supper. Soon there'll be over 500 channels on cable TV. You might miss a beautiful sunset. There are a lot of valid reasons not to attend the 20th Seattle International Film Festival running from May 20th through June 12th. But from now on...not knowing about it...isn't one of them. Cinema Seattle presents the 20th anniversary of the Seattle International Film Festival. See what the world is coming to May 20th through June 12th. Now you know.

Mental Note

VO: I will feel satisfied at the end of the day. I will introduce myself to strangers. I will enter unfamiliar situations with confidence. I am a worthy person. People value my opinion. I have something to give to the world. I will learn a new word each day. I will volunteer my services one hour a week. I will learn a foreign language. I will be more forgiving. I will not let the weather get me down. I will only press the crosswalk button once. I will stop eating cereal straight out of the box. I will stop harassing TV Guide for not offering a more up to the minute programming schedule for the home shopping network. I will stop spitting off tall bridges.

ANNCR: Cinema Seattle presents the 20th anniversary of the Seattle International Film Festival from May 20th through June 12th. If you feel the need, go ahead and make a mental note.

VO: I will stop sacrificing small farm animals. I will stop hiding the keys from my other personalities. I will never again be caught out in the rain without my umbrella.

ANNCR: See what the world is coming to.

Life

ANNCR: Life is about dirty dishes and doing laundry. Toe stubs and smoke in your eye. It's about poop scoops and lawn mowing. Allergies and 24-hour flues. Work and grocery stores. Broken hearts and tetanus shots. It's about poison oak and trachea holes. Disease and death. It's about anxiety and depression. Drug addiction and cheating on loved ones. And it's about divorce and abuse. The 20th Seattle International Film Festival, running from May 20th through June 12th is also about all of these things, but here you can count on it all - to happen - to somebody else. Cinema Seattle presents the 20th anniversary of the Seattle International Film Festival. See what the world is coming to May 20th through June 12th.

SFX: (Phone ringing, click)

JAY: Hello, you're on the line with Jay Buhner, Radio Answer Man.

MAN: Yeah, Jay, I'm having trouble with my neighbor.

JAY: Yeah.

MAN: He keeps putting his grass clippings in my compost heap.

JAY: If I were you, I'd walk over there and put him in a headlock until he picked 'em up.

SFX: (Click)

JAY: Line two.

WOMAN: Hello, Mr. Buhner. My girlfriend borrowed some earrings.

JAY: So.

WOMAN: Now she says they're hers!

JAY: Here's what you do. Ask her nicely to come over to you house.

WOMAN: Uh-huh.

JAY: Then when she shows up, boom! You put her in a headlock.

SFX: (Click)

JAY: Line three. This is Jay Buhner, Radio Answer Man.

MAN2: Jay, I'm having trouble wiring my dryer. You see, I need to run 220 down to the basement...

JAY: (Disgusted) Ehh.

SFX: (Click)

JAY: Line one. (Fade under)

ANNCR: Aren't you glad he plays right field for the Mariners instead?

JAY: (Fade up) So you got this cable guy in a headlock, see...

ANNCR: The Seattle Mariners.

831

830
District 11
CLIENT
Seattle International
Film Festival
AGENCY
Cole & Weber
Seattle, WA
CREATIVE DIRECTOR
Robert Brihn
COPYWRITER
Kevin Jones
PRODUCER
Sam Walsh

831
District 11
CLIENT
Mariners
AGENCY
McCann-Erickson
Seattle
Seattle, WA
CREATIVE DIRECTOR
Jim Walker
COPYWRITER
John Schofield
ACCOUNT EXECUTIVE
Eric Prock

RADIO

832
District 10
CLIENT
The Dallas Morning News
AGENCY
DDB Needham Worldwide Dallas Group
Dallas, TX
CREATIVE DIRECTOR
Lou Allison
COPYWRITER
Clay Hudson
PRODUCER
Dick Orkin's Ranch
PRODUCTION
Bert Berdis & Co.
EDITOR
Stewart Sloke

833
District 9
CLIENT
Southwestern Bell Mobile Systems
AGENCY
Simmons, Durham & Associates
St. Louis, MO
CREATIVE DIRECTORS
Ted Simmons
Brad Fels
COPYWRITER
Beth Dzengolewski

834
District 9
CLIENT
Record Wear House
AGENCY
Chris Fleck
St. Joseph, MO
COPYWRITER
Chris Fleck
VOCALS
Chris Fleck
HARMONICA
Chris Fleck
PRODUCER
Bob Heater

SFX: *Ding-dong. Door opens*
MAN: Yeah? Can I help you?
SELLER: Hello, sir or madam. My that is a lovely tie or dress you're wearing. If I might just take a moment out of your busy schedule -
MAN: What do you want?
SELLER: What?
MAN: What do you want?
SELLER: Hello, sir or madam. My that is a lovely tie or dress -
MAN: What are you selling?
SELLER: Magazines.
MAN: I don't need any.
SELLER: Not even Compost Connoisseur? Chock full or earthy recipes for the discriminating composter?
MAN: No, no, no. Look: Dallas Life is the only magazine I need, okay? It's got stuff on Texas gardening, computers, remodeling tips from Dallas experts. It's got local shopping, food, wine, Dallas fashion, fitness... You know, it's Dallas Life.
SELLER: What about Modern Bagpipe?
MAN: I get everything I need from Dallas Life. Every Sunday in The Dallas Morning News.
SELLER: Wait. Stormdrains Illustrated with their gala year end issue: The year in gutters.
MAN: I only read Dallas Life.
SELLER: Pearl Divers' Home Journal?
MAN: Dallas Life.
SELLER: Fondue Times.
MAN: Dallas Life.
SELLER: Uh...what about Hedgehog Confidential?
SFX: *DOOR SLAM*
SELLER: So that would be a no, sir or madam?
ANNCR: For life in Dallas, all you need is Dallas Life, the Sunday magazine of The Dallas Morning News. The story of all of us.

832

SFX: *Wedding music*
MINISTER: (*Voice echoes as if in large church*) Do you Robert, take this woman to be you lawful wedded wife? In sickness and in health, till death do you part, from now until the end of time, till you're blue in the face, till hell freezes over, till forever and a day...
ANNCR: At Southwestern Bell Mobile Systems we realize making a commitment isn't always easy.
MINISTER: Till the cows come home, till chickens grow lips, till the crack of doom... (*Continues under*)
ANNCR: That's why Southwestern Bell Mobile Systems is offering its exclusive 30-Day Test Drive. Just sign up and get a free Motorola Tote phone. Try it for a month and if doesn't make your life easier to manage bring it back.
MINISTER: Till pigs learn to fly, till time runs out, till you can barely stand the sight of one another...(*Continues under*)
ANNCR: So, take a Motorola Tote for a 30-Day Test Drive. Only from Southwestern Bell Mobile Systems.
MINISTER: Till shrimps learn to whistle, till the fat lady sings...(*Continues under*)
ANNCR: No commitment required.
MINISTER: Till the kitty litter is changed, till I can think of something else to say...

833

Bob Dilllon impersonator singing to acoustic guitar and harmonica accompaniment:
New and pre-owned cassettes and CDs
Lots of cool clothes and wild jewelry
Where else can you find sunglasses like these
'cept Record Wear House

St. Joe's largest selection of sweatshirts and Tees
Over a thousand designs we can print if you please
Or gag gifts and greeting cards for adults only at Record Wear House

Chiefs souvenirs and clothing galore
posters and toys a great place to explore
A whole lot more than just another record store
Record Wear House
ANNCR: Your groovy one-stop record shop at the corner of Belt and Mitchell, open 7 days a week, yeah.

834

RADIO

(*Lawn is a chorus of several voices all reacting as one but not in the same words. They almost overlap in their delivery, yet each is understood.*)

MUSIC: *Dawn from the William Tell Overture.*

ANNCR: It's the morning of an early spring day, your lawn is just beginning to awake...

LAWN: 1: Come on time to get up!

2: (*Yawning*) Spring already?

3: Let me sleep!

4: Yawns

ANNCR: When suddenly, crabgrass rears it's ugly head.

CRABBY: Wha-d'ya mean spring already?

LAWN: (*in background*) 1: O-o-oh, no-o-o!

2: There goes the neighborhood.

3: It's the crabby!!!

4: What a grouch!

CRABBY: I thought winter would never end.

LAWN: (*Overlapping with crabby under anncr*) 1: What are you doing?

2: Screams

3: Leave him alone!

4: Get outta here.

CRABBY: This yard ain't big enough for all of us, so I'm taking over. Got it?

ANNCR: Not to mention foxtail, and all those broad leaf weeds.

FOX/WEEDS: General monsters ravishing terrain with menacing remarks and gobbling sounds.

LAWN: (*Gasping as if being choked*) 1: Help!

2: Can't breathe!

3: Yo! Ref! Watch the choke here!

4: Choke! Choke!

ANNCR: This is a job for Lawn Pros!

LAWN: 1: Yeah!

2: All right!

3: Lawn Pros!

4: My hero!

ANNCR: Lawn Pros terminate crabgrass.

PRO: Asta la vista crabby.

SFX: *Application sound effect.*

CRABBY: Aaargh!

ANNCR: Along with foxtail and broadleaf weeds.

PRO: Remember when I said I'd save you for last?

SFX: *Application sound effect.*

FOX: Oh no!

BROADS: We're outta here.

ANNCR: And Lawn Pros' used safe, granular fertilizer with micro-nutrients to help your lawn grow.

LAWN: (*Happy now*) 1: This tastes great.

2. Mmmm!

3. Micro-nutrients!

4: Party time!

ANNCR: And Lawn Pros saves you money over other lawn services. No matter what size your lawn!

LAWN: 1: But broadleaf and the others will return later in the year.

2: yea!

3: Right on!

4: They always do!

PRO: I'll be back!

ANNCR: Lawn Pros year round lawn care. Call 277-1420 for a free estimate.

LAWN: (*Not overlapping*) 1: Because the grass should be greener on your side of the fence.

2: Wish I'd've said that.

835
District 10
CLIENT
Arkansas First Committee
AGENCY
Cranford Johnson Robinson Woods
Little Rock, AR
CREATIVE DIRECTOR
Boyd Blackwood
COPYWRITER
Tracy Munro
PRODUCER
Debbie Wilson
PRODUCTION
Soundscapes
ACCOUNT EXECUTIVE
Gary Arnold

836
District 9
CLIENT
Lawn Pros
AGENCY
Rochester Rossiter & Wall
Sioux City, IA
CREATIVE DIRECTOR
Tim Poppen
COPYWRITER
Ron Dobbs
PRODUCER
Tim Poppen
TALENT
Tim Poppen
Steve Ford
Ron Dobbs

837
District 7
CLIENT
Birmingham News
AGENCY
Lawler Ballard Van Durand
Birmingham, AL
CREATIVE DIRECTOR
Jeff Martin
COPYWRITER
Jack Becker
PRODUCTION
Craig Wiesse & Co.
ACCOUNT EXECUTIVE
Tinsley Van Durand

838
District 9
CLIENT
Bob Jones Shoes
AGENCY
Nelson Creative Works!
Kansas City, MO
CREATIVE DIRECTOR
Scott Nelson
PRODUCERS
Jim Shrader
Scott Nelson
PRODUCTION
Wheeler Audio Association

839
District 10
CLIENT
Ft. Worth Zoo
AGENCY
Regian & Wilson
Ft. Worth, TX
COPYWRITERS
Brian Pierce
D. Kasey
PRODUCER
Brian Pierce
PRODUCTION
Eagel Audio
VOICEOVER
Joel Murray
ACCOUNT EXECUTIVE
Margot Haller

840
District 2
CLIENT
Hotel Bar Butter
AGENCY
Greene & Company
Allentown, PA
COPYWRITER
Nick Katsarelas
PRODUCTION
Modern Audio Production

RED: Welcome to Legion Field, where Alabama is about to meet Auburn. I'm Red Riley, and with me is future Hall of Famer "Bobcat" Carruthers. Bobcat, you were at every practice last week talking with the players and coaches. What will their game plans be?
BOBCAT: Huh?
RED: I said, what will their game plans be?
BOBCAT: (*Obviously reading*) The - Tide- and - the - Tigers - are - both- trying - to - establish - young - offenses...
RED: What are you doing?
BOBCAT: What?
RED: You're obviously just reading that out of the paper in front of you.
BOBCAT: Yeah, but it's the Birmingham News. Their sports section has complete coverage of college and pro football, basketball, hockey...
RED: You weren't at any of the practices, were you?
BOBCAT: No, but the News was.
RED: And you didn't talk to any of the players or coaches, did you?
BOBCAT: Well, no. But the News did.
SFX: *Crowd cheering*
RED: What was that?
BOBCAT: Sounded like a touchdown. Don't worry, we can read about it in the News.
RED: Bobcat?
BOBCAT: What?
RED: Did you ever consider wearing a helmet while you were playing?
ANNCR: The Birmingham News. When you're not sure, someone is. It's 35 cents an issue, even less if we bring it to you. Call 325-2251 for home delivery.

837

VO: Chester Cheetah here, asking for your undivided ear. Ain't no lie, I've got a tip that's hotta than July. Get a clue to what's new at the Fort Worth Zoo. Live cheetahs. Now, lots of zoos have a cheetah or two. But no other exhibit's equipped this hip. Dig. Fort Worth is fixin' to bring six in. And that wild cat habitat is the real deal. Decked out to the max with tall trees, hills, and grass. There's just no place sweeta to be a cheetah. Man oh man, they've even got a breeding program. So don't balk, hit the boardwalk that extends far into the cheetah yard. Because you got to dig the show when these go-cats go. If feelin' the need for speed, these wheel-peelin' cats can blow zero to seventy in no time flat. Visit the Fort Worth Zoo for the Cheetos Cheetah Debut. Six of the coolest cats to ever prowl Fort Worth. The Cheetos Cheetahs. Now at the Fort Worth Zoo.

839

SFX: *A diverse series of different footsteps: a woman walking on pavement in high heels...Man going up stairs...Running on grass...A cowboy with spurs... Walking on snow...Etc.*
MUSIC: *Walking bass begins under footsteps after about :10 and continues to end under tag.*
SFX: *Different footsteps keep coming, one after the other. Ending with crowded corridor. Single set of footsteps emerge. Kill crowded corridor.*
TAG: Bob Jones Shoes. Nineteenth and Grand. We give everybody fits.
MUSIC: *Walking bass ends with distinctive flair.*

838

ENGINEER: (*Slight echo; he's speaking from the control room*) Hotel Bar Butter history. Take one.
SFX: *Sentimental music*
NARRATOR: Hotel Bar Butter was introduced in 1885, when it was sold door to door in hotel bars in New York City. People loved it so much the Brooklyn Bridge was built to carry Hotel Bar Butter from one borough...
ENGINEER: Uh, just stick to the script.
NARRATOR: Sorry. Ahem. Soon, the finest restaurants and hotels were serving Hotel Bar Butter. Napoleon was so impressed he built the Statue of Liberty to honor Hotel Bar Butter...
ENGINEER: I don't think so.
NARRATOR: Many of us grew up with Hotel Bar Butter. I remember the first time I saw the Hotel Bar Butter monument, its steel spire reaching toward the heavens.
ENGINEER: Uh, that's the Empire State Building.
NARRATOR: And who could forget the time Mayor LaGuardia promised "A pound of delicious Hotel Bar Butter in every refrigerator..."
ENGINEER: He never said that.
NARRATOR: Delicious Hotel Bar Butter. New York's choice for generations. Look for the new Hotel Bar Butter package. Brand new box, same great flavor.

840

RADIO

LARRY: My good friend Ortega Sanchez...

ORTEGA: Buenos Diaz Harry...I'm back again as the official professional pronouncer for Delta Martin Auto Parts.

LARRY: Where have you been?

ORTEGA: Well Harry, I was the top used parts salesman of the year here at Delta Martin Auto Parts for 5 straight years. I sold more used parts than anybody on this whole peninsula. I was a happy man and then it happened.

LARRY: What happened?

ORTEGA: Ulema Jones...that's what happened, Harry.

LARRY: Ulema Jones?

ORTEGA: That's right, Ulema Pasquale Diaz Jones. A black headed 24 year old beauty with a bad tail light assembly.

LARRY: A bad tail light assembly??

ORTEGA: She came in one day looking goood. Her taillights were just flickering...it was love at first sight right here at Delta Martin Auto Parts. So, I've been on a long honeymoon.

LARRY: Ortega, you are a remarkable man...but she's less than half your age...that could be fatal...

ORTEGA: Well Harry, all I can say is...if she dies...she dies.

ANNCR: Delta Martin Auto Parts...3949 Greenwood Road...guaranteed used parts, but no guaranteed romances.

841

SFX: *Hallway echo, footsteps*

BANKER: Tom, your grandfather must have loved you. He left you quite a bit.

TOM: He was really rich, right?

BANKER: He was rich in many ways, Tom.

TOM: Was he rich in money?

BANKER: Oh, he saved quite a bit over the years, thanks to the Sunday Dallas Morning News.

TOM: Great. Stock tips?

BANKER: No, coupons, Tom.

SFX: *Vault door opens*

TOM: Cou-Coupons?

BANKER: Here are all the coupons he was never able to redeem.

TOM: Coupons.

BANKER: There is some bad news, Tom.

TOM: Really?

BANKER: Like your grandfather these coupons have expired.

ANNCR: Sales, classifieds and coupons in the Sunday Dallas Morning News, the story of all of us.

843

ANNCR: (*Rapid delivery*) When you think tackle

SFX: *Football hit, grunt*

ANNCR: No, not that kind of tackle, this kind of tackle...

SFX: *Fishing cast, drops in water*

ANNCR: think Kokomon's!

MUSIC: *"Way Down To Kokomo!"*

SFX: *Record needle rip*

ANNCR: Not Kokomo...Kokomon! Mon! Mon! Mon!

JAMAICAN VOICE: Welcome to Jamaica, Mon!

ANNCR: No, it's in Port Charlotte...

SFX: *Drum roll*

ANNCR: And it's been world famous since June of...

SFX: *Record needle rip*

ANNCR: ah, 1993...as southwest Florida's unique fishing outlet. Outlet. Like the thing your mother warned you never to stick your finger into.

SFX: *Electrical explosion*

VOICE: Ouch!

ANNCR: So what does all this have to do with Kokomon's? Absoutely nothing! So let's quickly tell you what Kokomon's has to offer.

UNINTELLIGIBLY FAST VOICE: Star rods, live bait, licenses, fly fishing tackle, all star rods, free fishing info, clothing, gift certificates, guide service available

ANNCR: And if you think that's impressive, you should hear it in slow motion...

UNINTELLIGIBLY SLOW VOICE: Star rods, live bait, licenses, fly fishing tackle

ANNCR: But if you remember nothing else, drill this into your brain...

SFX: *Drill*

ANNCR: At Kokomon's, fishing is their business and they'll get you hooked.

SFX: *Hook boing*

ANNCR: Open seven days a week at 11-82 C Tamiami Trail in Port Charlotte. Phone 255-5873 for the biggest baddest store with the best prices. Now if this were a breakfast cereal commercial we might say something like...

CARTOON VOICE: I'm Kookoo for Kokomon's

ANNCR: But it's not, so we won't.

842

841
District 10
CLIENT
Delta Martin Auto Parts
AGENCY
LeGrand & Associates
Shreveport, LA
COPYWRITER
Al LeGrand
TALENT
Larry Ryan
Rich Grael
ACCOUNT EXECUTIVE
Al LeGrand

842
District 4
CLIENT
Kokomon's Tackle Outlet
AGENCY
WRXK
Estero, FL
CREATIVE DIRECTION
Rick Peterson
Maureen Buschkamper
PRODUCER
Rick Peterson
ACCOUNT EXECUTIVE
Maureen Buschkamper

843
District 2
CLIENT
The Dallas Morning News
AGENCY
Tracy-Locke/Dallas
Dallas, TX
COPYWRITERS
Jim Hord
Clay Hudson
PRODUCERS
Dan Price
Lisa Macchiesi
PRODUCTION
Oink Ink Inc.

844
District 4
CLIENT
Dennis' Store
for Men
AGENCY
WRZN
Hernando, FL
CREATIVE DIRECTION
Mark Varney
Linda Tilley
PSA DIRECTOR
Mark Varney
STATION MANAGER
Linda Tilley

845
District 6
CLIENT
Chicagoland
Chevrolet
AGENCY
Eisaman, Johns &
Laws, Inc.
Chicago, IL
CREATIVE DIRECTOR
Mike Waterkotte
COPYWRITER
Craig Shparago
PRODUCER
Stacey Verdon
SOUND EDIT
Jeff Van Steen

846
District 9
CLIENT
Intrust Bank
AGENCY
Associated
Advertising Agency
Wichita, KS
CREATIVE DIRECTOR
Marsha Cromwell
COPYWRITER
Deborah Brauser
PRODUCER
Deborah Brauser
PRODUCTION
KKRD, Studio
TALENT
Wayne Bryan
ACCOUNT SUPERVISOR
Kerry Gray

847
District 5
CLIENT
R&R Drain and Septic
Tank Service
AGENCY
Marion Radio
Company-WMRN
AM/FM
Marion, OH
CREATIVE DIRECTOR
Kurt S. Kaniewski
TALENT
Joe Suarez

WOMAN: I'm looking for a man.
CLERK: Well, I, I...
WOMAN: This is Dennis' Store for Men isn't it?
CLERK: Yes, but I don't think you understand.
WOMAN: Yes I do. This is a store for men and I want a man.
CLERK: Well, you see, we don't actually sell men. We sell fine clothing for men.
WOMAN: Oh, so I can't get a man here?
CLERK: No, but you can get suits, silk shirts and sport coats, custom casual slacks for 19.99 or two pair for 30 dollars... and if you mention WRZN, you'll get a free tie with your suit or sport coat purchase.
WOMAN: But, I really wanted a man. Say, what time do you get off work?
CLERK: Well, I, I, I...
ANNCR: Dennis' Store for Men in the Citrus Center, highway 44, Inverness.

844

SFX: *Musical theme songs from corresponding musicals play in background as narrator speaks.*
ANNCR: This is Wayne Bryan of Music Theatre of Wichita inviting you to spend the evening of May 9 with five talented ladies from the Musical Theatre. Ladies like...(*Narrator sings lines from each musical*) "Gigi, am I a fool without..." Ah, and the other little girl with the red hair with the dog and the optimism. You know, Annie... "Tomorrow, tomorrow, so ya gotta hang on till..." But not just the little girls. Big girls too. Like the one from Damn Yankees... "Whatever Lola wants, Lola..." Those Latin rhythms remind me of West Side Story, and that nice girl "Maria, I just met a girl named Maria..." Then finally..."Hello, Dolly." Hear selections from all five shows at the Festival of Broadway, sponsored by Intrust Bank and Music Theatre, free with a Wichita River Festival button. Bring the entire family to the West Bank stage Monday, May 9, 7:30 p.m. for The Festival of Broadway, sponsored by Intrust Bank. Member FDIC.

846

VO: When I was a kid, I thought by the time I grew up, lunch would consist of a single energy pill, the planet Mars would be a popular vacation spot and I'd drive a rocket ship to work, where every six months I'd ask a robot for a raise. Well as of today, lunch consists of pressed turkey on rye, pleasure cruise to Mars is about as likely as a junket to Jupiter, and though he's often cold and indifferent, Mr. Deering is much too fleshy to be an android. However, I do ride a rocket to work. It's the all new '95 Chevy Monte Carlo, loaded with great standard features like air, ABS, dual airbags and a V6 with more horsepower than Ford Thunderbird or Honda Accord. And boy, is it futuristic. One glance at the sleek lines, one ride in the richly-appointed cockpit and I see the world of tomorrow, right through to the part where everyone's cranium expands to gargantuan size to compensate for the added brain matter. Good thing the Monte Carlo has lots of headroom. The new Monte Carlo. Now at you local Chevy/GEO dealer.

845

VOICE 1: And now this word from R&R Drain and Septic Tank Service
VOICE 2: (*Sung*) My septic tank was overloaded... it caused me a terrible fit... but the thing that I found most disgusting... that the darn thing was loaded with shhh...
SFX: *Record Torn Off Turntable*
VOICE 1: From "shaving cream" - to whatever's clogging your drain and septic tank systems, call the professionals to do the job right at R&R Drain and Septic Tank... Call 382-3004.

847

Barney

ANNCR: A while back, I read in the paper that a bunch of kids in Florida beat up that big purple dinosaur during a mall opening. Roughed him up pretty bad, too. And I thought to myself, at this rate these kids will never grow up to work for Heinen's. See, Heinen's employs some of the nicest people in the grocery business. People who in their formative years would never have even considered assaulting a large costumed animal figure. Be it dinosaur. Be it bear. Be it moose. Heinen's employees are the eagle scouts of the supermarket world. Whipping up a custom deli tray just for that special occasion you're having. Carrying those heavy bags out to the car for you. Or cutting up a rack of lamb and putting those little chef's hats on the ends of them. Yes, in their youth, Heinen's employees were probably crossing guard kids, the four-h-ers, the volunteer tutors; but not the hall monitors. Let's face it, hall monitors were just snitches with a badge. Ah, if only the rest of the world was as good as Heinen's.

Government

ANNCR: There's a lot of talk these days about how the government doesn't work. And I thought, boy if only the government was more like a Heinen's supermarket, it would be great. And that's not just because the capitol building would have automatic doors. You know how senators and congressmen are always answering questions with, "I have no knowledge of that." or "I'll study that." or "I didn't know she was eighteen." Well, no more of that. They'd have to know what they're talking about just like Heinen's employees do. There'd be no more Gridlock, either. Things would move easily through congress. Just like everyone moves easily through Heinen's thanks to the extra wide aisles. Government would cost less, too. In fact, the IRS would have to accept coupons. Finally, the Supreme Court would have a really great deli counter like Heinen's. With both high quality deli meats and delicious prepared foods. Because, let's face it, who hasn't heard the phrase "Order in the court" and not thought of repeating that old joke, I'll take a ham and Swiss on rye. (Chuckles) Ah, if only the rest of the world was as good as Heinen's.

Airlines

AL: I took a flight recently. And frankly, I was really disappointed. I thought, wouldn't it be great if the airlines ran themselves more like a Heinen's supermarket. I mean, if airline meals were more like the wonderful eggplant parmesan and other prepared foods at Heinen's...maybe they wouldn't need those special little bags that are in the seat pocket in front of you. Behind the in-flight magazines. The aisles would be extra wide, too. Wide enough so that you, three members of your family, and the beverage cart, could all pass each other. And when the captain came on the speaker, he wouldn't talk about boring things like the altitude. He'd say, (Does static) this is your captain, if you look to your left, you'll see a spectacular sale on flank steak. On your right, marinades are on special. (Does static) Finally, all flights would be direct. If you ask someone at Heinen's how to get to the pimientos, they'll send you straight to them. They won't make you stop over at the trash bags and frozen foods. Ah, if only the rest of the world were as good as Heinen's.

850

MUSIC: *Spacy, ethereal, majestic, building*
GODLIKE ANNCR: The Universe... The Milky Way... The Solar System... The Planet Earth... North America... The United States... Springfield Elementary School... Room 218... Row 4, seat 3...
MUSIC: *Stops*
BART: Hey man! Get outa my face!!
GODLIKE ANNCR: Sorry.
MUSIC: *Simpsons theme*
ORDINARY ANNCR: The Simpsons. Now in your face five times a week.

851

848
District 14
CLIENT
CalTrain
AGENCY
Jamison Cawdrey Benjamin
San Francisco, CA
CREATIVE DIRECTOR
Dean Charlton
COPYWRITER
Scott Maney
PRODUCER
Scott Maney
PRODUCTION
TransMedia
ACCOUNT EXECUTIVE
Rich Lenant

849
District 7
CLIENT
Pasta de Pulcinella
AGENCY
Tausche Martin Lonsdorf
Atlanta, GA
CREATIVE DIRECTOR
Kurt Tausche
COPYWRITER
Carey Moore

850
District 5
CLIENT
Heinen's Supermarkets
AGENCY
W.B. Doner & Company
Cleveland, OH
COPYWRITERS
John Parlato
Mark Borcherding
ACCOUNT EXECUTIVE
Brian Povinelli

851
District 9
CLIENT
The Simpsons
AGENCY
Paul & Walt Worldwide
St. Louis, MO
COPYWRITER
Walt Jaschek
PRODUCER
Paul Fey
ENGINEER
Brent Hahn

RADIO

852
District 2
CLIENT
SEPTA Switches
AGENCY
Al Paul Lefton
Company
Philadelphia, PA
CREATIVE DIRECTOR
Lou Brandsdorfer
COPYWRITER
Bruce Waters

853
District 7
CLIENT
Tim Whitehead
Chrysler
AGENCY
Farnham & Galey
Advertising
Enterprise, AL
COPYWRITER
Eddie Galey
PRODUCERS
Tim Whitehead
Sam Farnham

Married

SFX: *Commuter train sounds, pulling into station*

ANNCR: I'm talking to Larry the Lawyer at Jenkintown...you stopped driving and you started taking SEPTA Becausssssse...

LARRY: I thought I could meet women. And I met my wife on the train.

ANNCR: Yeaah! I wanna hear every detail! What happened?

LARRY: We were introduced by a mutual passenger. The rest is history. We now have two children, thanks to SEPTA.

ANNCR: Did you get married on the train?

LARRY: Thought about it, but actually did propose at the train station where we met. She did say yes.

ANNCR: Where did you honeymoon?

LARRY: Hawaii. Did not take the train.

ANNCR: Hah! There you have it. Another true love story of romance on SEPTA. A romance that would have never happened if they had taken their car.

SFX: *Train horn beeps twice, switch to another station location*

ANNCR: I'm talking to newlyweds Doug and Trish who ride the train together. It's more time that you can spend together, don't you think?

DOUG: Yes it is.

TRISH: It also cuts down on arguments. He thinks I'm a bad driver. 'Course he's wrong!

DOUG: I know she's a bad driver!

ANNCR: See all those people stuck on the Schuykil Expressway? If you had any advice for the married people who are having a big fight, what would you say?

TRISH: Save yourself some stress.

DOUG: It's a lot easier to take the train than to drive.

TRISH: SEPTA is helping our marriage.

ANNCR: Oh my God! They're kissing! SEPTA is better than driving. Way better!

Convenience

SFX: *Rider intercepts - live city sounds, buses, subways, trains*

ANNCR: We're talking to SEPTA riders who used to take their cars to work. I'm talking to Barbara at 17th and Kennedy Boulevard. Barbara, you switched to taking SEPTA becaussssssse...

BARBARA: Because I don't like driving into the city. SEPTA stops right in front of my house. How more convenient can you be?

ANNCR: I'm talking to John who used to drive his car and now he takes SEPTA. Why did you switch?

JOHN: Cause it's easy and comfortable. And all around, it's the better way to go.

ANNCR: Plus, you meet people on the train.

JOHN: Especially beautiful women.

ANNCR: Well, heh, heh,... it's your lucky day.

WOMAN: I love SEPTA. SEPTA is marvelous. The convenience is outstanding.

ANNCR: We're talking to Tom, who used to drive, but now he takes SEPTA.

TOM: I take the bus mainly because it's too much aggravation to drive. Taking SEPTA is much better than driving. Life is less stressful, more pleasant. I've been driving for the last 22 years, and I decided that not only is SEPTA convenient, but it's economical for me.

ANNCR: You know what's really inspiring?

TOM: What?

ANNCR: That a man can change after 22 years.

TOM: Ha ha ha ha!

ANNCR: SEPTA. Better than driving.

Occupations

SFX: *Live street sounds, buses, trolleys, train, under all interviews*

ANNCR: I'm talking with Andrew who works for a bank. You used to drive your car...

ANDREW: Everywhere.

ANNCR: Why did you switch from driving to taking SEPTA?

ANDREW: Saves on gas, saves on parking. Do what smart people do. Take SEPTA. It pays.

(CONTINUED ON NEXT PAGE)

RADIO

(852 CONTINUED)

ANNCR: I'm talking to Louisa at 15th and JFK. And she switched. Now she takes SEPTA. What kind of work to you do?

LOUISA: I'm a cytologist.

ANNCR: What's a cytologist?

LOUISA: Someone who looks at cells.

ANNCR: I was gonna say "people who sigh a lot."

MAN: I switched because of the traffic.

ANNCR: What kid of work do you do?

MAN: I'm a lawyer.

ANNCR: So you never want to keep you clients waiting.

MAN: Clients and judges!

ANNCR: I'm talking to Lisa, on her way to Berwyn. Don't you find you get everything done on the train?

LISA: I've studied for exams on the train and I read for enjoyment.

ANNCR: What kind of exams?

LISA: The CPA exam.

ANNCR: And did you pass?

LISA: Yes!

ANNCR: So SEPTA helped you become an accountant!!!!

LISA: That's right!

ANNCR: I'm talking to Jack who works at the post office. So does taking the train sometimes keep down that stress?

JACK: Yes it does. It's a very comfortable ride. I enjoy it. SEPTA beats driving by 100%.

ANNCR: Perfect score! I'm talking to Charley, another postal worker who loves SEPTA. You used to drive your car and now you take the train...

CHARLEY: That's correct.

ANNCR: If SEPTA were a letter, what would it be?

CHARLEY: First class.

ANNCR: SEPTA. Better than driving.

852

VO: Accidents have a way of happening at the worst times. Seven year old Brad found that out first hand when his mother was the victim of a farm accident that left her in desperate need of medical care. Alone, afraid, and miles from help, Brad had only one place to turn: the 9-1-1 emergency number system. It's a life line for people in need of help. How do you put a price tag on that kind of life saving help? For Sprint/United Telephone the answer is clear: just pennies a day. Pennies per day, that's all 9-1-1 costs. But, as Brad found out, the real value of 9-1-1 isn't what it cost but what it saves. So, while Sprint/United Telephone hopes you'll never need 9-1-1, isn't it worth pennies a day to know that if you do, help will be there now?

854

SFX: *Squeak of faucet. Blast of water spray under throughout.*

WOMAN: (*Raw and unpolished rendition of Cole Porter's "I Love Paris"*) I love Paris in the springtime. I love Paris in the fall. I love Paris in winter when it drizzles. I love Paris in summer when it sizzles...

VO: (*Over singing*) This season, Leonard Slatkin and the Saint Louis Symphony are pleased to present everything from Cole Porter and Tony Bennett...

WOMAN: (*Changes to raw and unpolished version of Ravel's Bolero.*)

VO: To Ravel and Beethoven. So call 533-7888 for season tickets. It's great music that's sure to stay with you. Long after the performance...

WOMAN: More Bolero.

VO: Or at least until the hot water runs out.

WOMAN: (*With vigor*) I love Paris every moment...

855

854
District 5
CLIENT
Sprint/United Telephone
AGENCY
Sprint In-House Media
Mansfield, OH
DIRECTOR
John Hewitt

855
District 9
CLIENT
St. Louis Symphony
AGENCY
DMB&B/St. Louis
St. Louis, MO
CREATIVE DIRECTORS
Jim Fortune
Tom Townsend
ART DIRECTOR
Tony Gaudin
COPYWRITER
Anne Gartland
PRODUCERS
Tony Gaudin
Anne Gartland

RADIO

856

District 10

CLIENT
Bert Wheeler's Inc.

AGENCY
Radio Works, Inc.
Houston, TX

COPYWRITERS
Bill West
Jim Conlan

PRODUCERS
Bill West
Jim Conlan

Sticker Fixer

GAD: Boy, I'll tell ya, I've heard of specialization, but - what'd you say you do now?

BO: Well, I'm a sticker fixer.

GAD: A sticker fixer...

BO: Right. See, I take low-price stickers off things and I put high-price stickers on 'em.

GAD: And... this is a legitimate business, huh?

BO: I got a license and everything, pal.

GAD: Really?

BO: Sure! Look... whaddya got in the bag there?

GAD: Um, a single-malt scotch I just bought at Bert Wheeler's.

BO: Perfect! For your boss, right?

GAD: Well, yeah - how'd you...

BO: I know, OK? Now tell me - you really want to embarrass yourself by showing your boss how little you paid for this 12-year-old scotch?

GAD: Well, I...

BO: No. Instead, you want to come to Mr. Sticker Fixer, where I substitute a much higher price sticker for the Bert Wheeler's one.

GAD: Yeah, but it's smart to go to Bert Wheeler's, isn't it?

BO: It is! I just wouldn't broadcast the low price you're paying!

GAD: All right, so in other words, I could impress my girlfriend Betty with a really fine chardonnay...

BO: ...Or a super-premium beer...

GAD: ...Right... pay the low Bert Wheeler's price...

BO: ...And I'll swap out the sticker for ya.

GAD: Fantastic! So how much do you charge for the, uh, sticker fix?

BO: Nothin'! It's free!

GAD: Unbelievable!

BO: Of course I wouldn't turn my nose up at tip.

GAD: A tip?

BO: Yeah, otherwise I blab to Betty.

GAD: Bert Wheeler's. The best place for premium bottles, without the premium price.

Symphonette

SFX: *Bottle orchestra clinking and tuning up*

GAD: Well I have to admit, this is a pretty unusual venue for a concert...

BO: You mean 'cause it's a liquor store?

GAD: Right...

BO: Hey, not if you're the Bert Wheeler's Symphonette...

GAD: ...an orchestra that consists entirely of...

BO: Wine, beer, and liquor bottles from Bert Wheeler's.

GAD: I see, and why Bert Wheeler's?

BO: Well, c'mon, I mean where else are ya gonna find such a huge variety of premium brands?

GAD: And that's important...

BO: Are you kidding? Listen to this ordinary brandy bottle available at any ordinary liquor store:

SFX: *Weak toot*

BO: Now listen to this special imported brandy bottle from Bert Wheeler's:

SFX: *Beautiful French horn note*

BO: Huh? Huh?

GAD: Wow, I see what you mean!

BO: And this vintage wine ensemble - check this out:

SFX: *Gorgeous recorder quartet*

GAD: Gorgeous. Gorgeous...

BO: Aren't they? Y'know ya don't normally think of reds and white goin' together like that...

GAD: Uh-huh... well have you had any luck with any other unusual combinations?

BO: Well, we're experimenting with some single-malt Scotches and provincial German Beers.

GAD: Oh? I'd like to hear that!

SFX: *"Ach De Lieber Augustine" played by tubas with a bagpipe drone.*

GAD: Ooo, that' not too, uh...

BO: I know! Needs work, needs work...

GAD: Bert Wheelers. The best place to buy bottles - no matter, uh, what sounds good to you

RADIO

Taco Night

SFX: *Sultry music*

VO: It was a Monday. The wind was whining like a dame from Kahala heights. I was finishing up the bill on the Baker case... trying to figure out the going rate for a busted jaw when suddenly...

SFX: *Music stops-phone rings*

VO: Mike Stone, Private Eye.

SFX: *Music resumes, "Uh-Huh" begin & continue & fade*

VO: At first he seemed like just another Joe on a one-way trip to palookaville. Just back from a Vegas date with a pair of fixed dice and so broke he couldn't pay attention. Fortunately, it was a Monday, so I told him to get on down to Salsa Rita's at Restaurant Row or Salsa Kahala at Kahala Mall. They got all the delicious, mouth-watering beef, chicken or pork soft tacos you can eat for just $6.99. That's right, pay, $6.99. All you can eat. Every Monday and Tuesday night at Salsa Rita's at Restaurant Row or Salsa Kahala at Kahala Mall, next to McDonalds. Check it out... And tell 'em Mike sent you.

Fun Bar

SFX: *Sultry music*

VO: I think it was a Thursday. The moon looked like a cue ball on a black-felt table. I was contemplating one of the thornier questions of life:

SFX: *Beer being opened & poured*

VO: Less filling or tastes great? When suddenly...

SFX: *Music stops-phone rings*

VO: Mike Stone, Private Eye.

SFX: *Music resumes, "Uh-Huh" begin & continue & fade*

VO: It seems the little lady got herself mixed up with the wrong crowd. She was tired of hanging out at the same old joints with a bunch of stuffed shirts whose idea of a good time is an expensive watch. Now I've been around the block enough times to know danger when I see it, and in my book there's nothing more dangerous than a bored dame. So I told her to go on down to Salsa Rita's at Restaurant Row. They got great music, great drinks, and a lively atmosphere that'll chase anybody's blues away. Plus delicious Mexican food and a speedy staff with enough smiles to make a flatfoot suspicious. Salsa Rita's at Restaurant Row: they got you covered, with free covered parking, and lots of it. Check it out, and tell 'em Mike sent you.

Food/Dinner

SFX: *Sultry music*

VO: I think it was Friday. The night was hot as a dollar bill at the Club Tulips. I was taking a beating in a game of solitaire... cheating, and still losing, when suddenly..

SFX: *Music stops-phone rings*

VO: Mike Stone, Private Eye.

SFX: *Music resumes, "Uh-Huh" begin & continue & fade*

VO: He thought he was being cute, but to me he was just another wiseguy being played for a sap. He thought all Mexican restaurants were the same. I sad, "Look mac, go down to Salsa Rita's at Restaurant Row." Sure, they got the best Mexican food in town, with mouth-watering enchiladas, tacos and burritos; but they also serve up a tender New York steak and a Ahi filet so fresh the cook has to club 'em just to be sure they won't climb off the grill. Both are char-broiled to perfection and served with salad and fries. That's right, bub, fries. So don't be suckered into thinking all Mexican restaurants are the same. Check it out Salsa Rita's at Restaurant Row: And tell 'em Mike sent you.

857
District 10
CLIENT
Arby's
AGENCY
Y-106/Opus Group
Monroe, LA
CREATIVE DIRECTOR
Randi Guess

858
District 13
CLIENT
Salsa Noir
AGENCY
Rasmussen Communications
Honolulu, HI
CREATIVE DIRECTOR
Jon Rasmussen
COPYWRITER
Jon Rasmussen
VOICE
Jon Rasmussen

RADIO

859

District 9

CLIENT
Anheuser-Busch, Inc.

AGENCY
DMB&B/St. Louis
St. Louis, MO

CREATIVE DIRECTORS
Carole Christie
Kipp Monroe

ART DIRECTOR
Woody Boss

COPYWRITERS
Jeff Goetz
Gordon Robertson
Corinne Mitchell
Diane Greenhill

PRODUCERS
Kipp Monroe
Jeff Goetz
Gordon Robertson

After the Game

SFX: *Night sounds, wolves howling*

ANNCR: The Red Wolf and his pack. After the game.

WOLF #1: So, how'd you guys do today?

WOLF #2: Oh, I got a couple of birdies, and I just missed an eagle.

WOLF #3: I got a goat.

OTHER WOLVES: All right, yeah, way to go...

WOLF #1: Hey look, fellas, here comes the Red Wolf!

WOLF #3: Yeah, and check out what he bagged!

SFX: Bottles clinking as they are passed around

RED WOLF: Here you go boys! Pass 'em around.

SFX: *Beer pops all around*

OTHER WOLVES: Hey, this is great, thanks...

WOLF #1: Gentlemen, this could be the greatest day in pack history!

OTHER WOLVES: Cheers, wolf howls

WOLF #2: You know, we gotta run with this guy more often.

MUSIC: *Kicks in and continues under*

ANNCR: Introducing Red Wolf Lager. The full-bodied red beer that's a little adventurous. A little wild. But surprisingly smooth. Red Wolf is brewed with roasted malts for a taste and drinkability that stands alone. It can't be copied. It can't be tamed.

SFX: *Return to night sounds, echoing wolf howls*

RED WOLF: So, you guys ready for another one?

OTHER WOLVES: Sure thing, thanks, sounds great...

SFX: *Bottle clinks, beer pops*

WOLF #2: You know, I think my game was off today.

WOLF #3: Mine tasted fine!

OTHER WOLVES: Laughter

MUSIC: *BACK UP*

ANNCR: Real red, real smooth Red Wolf. Follow your instincts. From the Specialty Brewing Group of Anheuser-Busch, St. Louis, Missouri.

Big Eyes

SFX: *Party noises, maybe a "Happy Halloween"*

GIRL: Excuse me, I noticed you brought Red Wolf Lager to the costume party...and since I came as Little Red Riding Hood I thought...My what big eyes you have...

WOLF: The better to see you with my dear.

GIRL: And what big ears you have.

WOLF: Actually, big features run in my family.

GIRL: And what big teeth you have. What are they for?

SFX: *GRR (Two bottles open)*

ANNCR: Real red, real smooth. Red Wolf.

GIRL: By the way, I don't live with my grandmother.

ANNCR: Follow you instincts.

The Sheep are Nervous

ANNCR: There's a new beer in town. Red Wolf Lager. With roasted Malt for a full-bodied, smooth drinking taste that's anything but tame. So where does that leave other beers?

SFX: *Twist off cap, followed by sheep's baaaah, repeats several times: twist off, baaaah, twist off, baaaah, continues under as anncr comes back in*

ANNCR: Red Wolf. It's real red. It's real smooth. And the sheep are real nervous.

SFX: *Twist off, howl.*

SFX: *Baaah.*

ANNCR: Red Wolf. Follow you instincts.

RADIO

Shower

SFX: *Squeak of faucet. Blast of water spray under throughout.*

WOMAN: *(Raw and unpolished rendition of Cole Porter's "I Love Paris")* I love Paris in the springtime. I love Paris in the fall. I love Paris in winter when it drizzles. I love Paris in summer when it sizzles...

VO: *(Over singing)* This season, Leonard Slatkin and the Saint Louis Symphony are pleased to present everything from Cole Porter and Tony Bennett...

WOMAN: *(Changes to raw and unpolished version of Ravel's Bolero.)*

VO: To Ravel and Beethoven. So call 533-7888 for season tickets. It's great music that's sure to stay with you. Long after the performance...

WOMAN: More Bolero.

VO: Or at least until the hot water runs out.

WOMAN: *(With vigor)* I love Paris every moment...

Planets

SFX: *The Planets by Holst.*

VO: This season, Leonard Slatkin and the Saint Louis Symphony Orchestra didn't want to just give you the sun, the moon and the stars. We wanted to give you Jupiter.

SFX: *Jupiter up.*

VO: And Venus.

SFX: *Venus up.*

VO: And Mars.

SFX: *Mars up*

VO: And all the other planets composed by Gustav Holst. As well as everything from Beethoven to Tony Bennett. So be sure to come to our Open House at Powell Hall this Friday, August 19th. Anytime between 8 and 8. And choose your seat for the entire season. Because when the universe finally does come to a dramatically, abrupt, resoundingly powerful, climactic end...

SFX: *Dramatic conclusion of Mars.*

VO: Don't you want to know exactly where you'll be sitting?

Date

SFX: *Mendelssohn Wedding March.*

VO: For those of you not looking for a permanent, binding, long-term commitment...

SFX: *Mendelssohn abruptly stops.*

VO: How about just a date?

SFX: *Ravel's Bolero starts up.*

VO: With Leonard Slatkin and the Saint Louis Symphony Orchestra. Tickets for individual concerts go on sale September 6th. Performances include everything from Rachmaninoff's famous Rhapsody to of course, Ravel's Bolero. So call 534-1700 or MetroTix to order. Who knows? It could be the beginning of a long-lasting relationship.

SFX: *Mendelssohn March kicks in.*

VO: Then we can talk about season tickets.

860
District 9
CLIENT
St. Louis Symphony
AGENCY
DMB&B/St. Louis
St. Louis, MO
CREATIVE DIRECTORS
Jim Fortune
Tom Townsend
ART DIRECTOR
Tony Gaudin
COPYWRITER
Anne Gartland
PRODUCERS
Tony Gaudin
Anne Gartland

RADIO

861
District 9
CLIENT
Dubuque Fighting
Saints
AGENCY
WDBQ/KLYU 105
Dubuque, IA
COPYWRITER
Tommy Edwards
TALENT
Tommy Edwards

862
District 9
CLIENT
Kansas Lottery
AGENCY
Sullivan Higdon &
Sink
Wichita, KS
COPYWRITER
Greg Hobson
ENGINEER
Don Guidas
PRODUCER
Darryl Hagans
ACCOUNT EXECUTIVE
Kent Miracle

863
District 7
CLIENT
R.M.D. Hooters
AGENCY
Media Directions
Advertising/
Jester/Proud
Knoxville, TN
RECORDING ENGINEER
Curtis Parham
VOICE TALENT
Ben Campbell

Tennis Anyone?

SFX: *Heavy drum beat under*

VO: Okay. We're talking about hockey here. We're talking about a three inch piece of hard rubber flying at the speed of sound like a patriot missile aimed right at the goalie's skull. Shards of ice coming from under the left winger's skates when he goes from sixty to zero just before he slams a defenseman's face into the glass. We're talking hockey here, alright?

VO: *(Wimpy)* Anyone for tennis?

VO: Heh heh. No. I don't think so...

Na Na Hey Hey

VO: Okay. We're talking about hockey here. We're talking about fans that're yellin', screamin', and stomping their feet. People painting their faces and going "you-you-you" when the other guy gets two minutes in the box. Doin' the wave and singing' "na na hey hey good bye" as loud as their little lungs will let 'em. We're talking about hockey here.

SFX: *Polite applause and a "Pip Pip Good Show"*

VO: Heh heh. What are you pal, new to this planet?

Warp Nine

VO: Okay. We're talking about hockey here. We're talking about guys who move so fast on a pair of skates they make Mario Andretti look like he's going in slow mo. Speeds so gut wrenching that Chuck Yeager would loose his lunch. We're talking hockey here. So check your reflexes at the door, pal. 'Cause I'm bringing in the starship saints at warp nine!

SFX: *Slow and steady wins the race...*

VO: Heh heh. Don't make me laugh.

861

ANNCR: Felix Kane was just your typical Kansas Powerball player.

VO: For the past year, I bought one a week. Usually, I played the $5 ticket.

ANNCR: Then he handed a convenience store clerk his most recent ticket.

VO: I said, "Hey, put this sucker in that music box and see if it'll play a little music for me." So, she put it in there and that thing started playing music. She said "Oh my God! Oh my God!" I said, "What'd I do, win $2?" She said, "You just won 22 million!" I said "Oh my God!" Momma was out in the car waiting for me. And her toe had been hurting and she had one shoe off. And I said, "Babe, get in here!" And I said, "We won!" And here she come, one shoe off, one shoe on! I kept telling her, I said, "Now, one of these days we're gonna hit that baby."

ANNCR: Play Powerball from the Kansas Lottery. Millions of winners. Winners of millions.

VO: I've had a good life, worked hard. I don't know anything about money. I know it's hard to come by, until now.

862

SFX: *Presidential music up and under*

CLINTON: Follow Americans, I've taken this air time today to clear up a few misconceptions that have been in the press lately regarding my wife Hillary's involvement with Hooters. At no time prior to or since my having been elected President has Hillary invested in Hooters. Not that I have anything against Hooters. You may have heard lately that Hooters is one of the fastest growing restaurant chains in America. And that's good for the country. I think the good people of this country deserve as many Hooters as possible. But let me state, for the record, that my wife had no prior knowledge of all this Hooters activity, and furthermore did not make any investment based on that prior knowledge. My wife has made some investments from time to time and does have some stock holdings. She has some IBM and some General Motors, and some mutual funds. But she does not have any Hooters. I hope this has cleared things up. Thank you.

863

RADIO

ANNCR: Staples has everything you need to go back to school.
TEACHER: I'm Ms. Kupelmocker and I hope you're all prepared for math.
ANNCR: Notebooks.
TEACHER: Advanced Geometry.
ANNCR: Protractor, graph paper, notebooks
TEACHER: Here's your syllabus.
ANNCR: wastebasket.
TEACHER: And your textbooks.
ANNCR: 7-gallon wastebasket.
TEACHER: You're expected to read every word.
ANNCR: Highlighter.
TEACHER There will be homework.
ANNCR: Folders.
TEACHER: Lots of homework.
ANNCR: Book bag.
TEACHER: Tons of homework.
ANNCR: Hand truck.
TEACHER: And there will be pop quizzes.
ANNCR: Pencils.
TEACHER: Every week.
ANNCR: Pencil sharpener.
TEACHER: and a final examination.
ANNCR: calculator
TEACHER: There will be no calculators.
ANNCR: small calculator.
TEACHER: I expect your work to be neat.
ANNCR: White Out.
TEACHER: Organized.
ANNCR: Paper clips.
TEACHER: And legible.
ANNCR: 300 dot resolution laser printer.
TEACHER: I will not tolerate tardiness.
ANNCR: Alarm Clock.
TEACHER: And don't forget...
ANNCR: post it notes.
TEACHER: You can easily be removed from this class.
ANNCR: thank you notes. Staples has everything you need to go back to school. The guaranteed low price on over 5000 items. Staples, Yeah, we've got that.

864

ANNCR: OK. It's time to make more prank phone calls on shipping clerks that don't use DHL.
SFX: *Phone dialing/ringing*
CLERK: Shipping.
ANNCR: Hey, you guys send a lot of documents, right?
CLERK: That's right.
ANNCR: Do you ever, like, root through people's personal papers before you send them out?
CLERK: No.
ANNCR: Come on! Have you ever found out any juicy gossip, some inter-office romance stuff?
CLERK: Can I help you?
ANNCR: Actually you can. Do you know DHL now get documents from LA to London overnight?
CLERK: Should I care?
ANNCR: Well, should you care that there are two people in you office, right now, who are raised by rats?
SFX: *Nibbles, eek, eek*
CLERK: Get out of here!
SFX: *CLICK*
ANNCR: *(Laughs)* Hello?... Well, that was another prank call. With a real message. DHL's new service gets documents from LA to London overnight. So it's DHL. Or else.

865

864
District 2
CLIENT
Staples Office Supplies
AGENCY
Cliff Freeman & Partners
New York, NY
CREATIVE DIRECTOR
Arthur Bijur
COPYWRITERS
Jeff Watzman
Greg Bell
John Leu
PRODUCER
Maresa Wickham
PRODUCTION
Clack Sound Studio

865
District 14
CLIENT
DHL
AGENCY
Goodby, Silverstein & Partners
San Francisco, CA
CREATIVE DIRECTORS
Jeffrey Goodby
Rich Silverstein
ART DIRECTORS
Josh Denberg
Jeffrey Goodby
PRODUCER
Greg Martinez
PRODUCTION
TLA Productions

866
District 4
CLIENT
Blockbuster Entertainment Corporation
AGENCY
D'Arcy, Masius, Benton & Bowles
Ft. Lauderdale, FL
CREATIVE DIRECTORS
Carole Christie
Doug Potter
Lew Cohn
COPYWRITER
Lew Cohn

867

District 6

CLIENT
Anheuser-Busch
Bud Light

AGENCY
DDB Needham
Chicago
Chicago, IL

CREATIVE DIRECTORS
Dennis Ryan
Dave Merhar

COPYWRITER
Ann Coyle

MUSIC
Phil Glass

Song or Beer

SFX: *Music up*

HESTON: You know, there's been a lot of talk in this country about how today's "20 somethings" have no drive, no determination. Frankly, I beg to differ. Here's a story about the commitment ...one young woman showed when it came to making it a Bud Light.

GAL: Okay, me and my friends wanted to get tickets for this concert so we slept in line for like three days.

HESTON: They slept in line for three days!!! *(Pause)* Go on miss...

GAL: Oh...so we're at the concert and it's great. Except the beer guy keeps blowing me off.

HESTON: He's blowing her off!!!

GAL: I wanted to run after him, but I didn't want to miss the next song. Well I didn't know what to do...

HESTON: What to do? What... to... do?!!

GAL: So I chased him out into the hall and I got a Bud Light.

HESTON: She got the Bud Light!!!!!

GAL: Yeah... it was pretty cool.

HESTON: Pretty cool? I'd say you are very cool. A very cool cat indeed. So for great taste that won't fill you up and never lets you down, make it a Bud Light. Anheuser Busch, St. Louis, Missouri.

I'll Get It

SFX: *Music up*

HESTON: You know, it never ceases to amaze me...the sacrifices people will endure to make it a Bud Light...the personal hurdles they overcome when they reach deep into themselves...

SFX: *Music under*

MAN: Well, me and my wife are watching TV one night and I was really, really tired. I mean I was really tired. So I asked her to get me a Bud Light.

HESTON: He asked her for a Bud Light!!!

MAN: *(Pause)* ...And she said no, I'm not gonna get it...you get it. So now I realize I've got to get it.

HESTON: He realizes he's got to get it!!!

MAN: And you know, like I said, I'm really tired so I...I'm thinking I might not have one...

HESTON: He might not have one!!!

MAN: But, I'm really thirsty, so...so I got up and got one.

HESTON: He got up and got one!!!

MAN: Yup.

HESTON: Overcoming adversity and reaching your goal. You my friend, are an example to all Americans. So for the great taste that won't fill you up and never lets you down, make it a Bud Light. Anheuser Busch, St. Louis, Missouri.

Bar's Closed

HESTON: We've heard a veritable cornucopia of stories about what people will do to make it a Bud Light. And what strikes me is the sheer will, the determination...the human spirit that triumphs in these situations. To me it's nothing short of inspiring.

SFX: *Music under*

MAN: Well, I was on my way to this little bar on the corner. It's a really great place.

HESTON: It's a really great place!!!

MAN: But...it's closed. So now I was like...now what. Do I just go home or go to this bar down the street. So I figure...what the heck.

HESTON: He figures what the heck!!!

MAN: So, I go down the street and this bar's open. So I go in, and I order a Bud Light and I grab a seat.

HESTON: He grabs his seat!!!

MAN: Just for the record, I said I grabbed "a" seat.

HESTON: Whatever...just another example of the triumph of the human spirit...and people say this country is in trouble...so for great taste that won't fill you up and never lets you down, make it a Bud Light. Anheuser Busch, St. Louis, Missouri.

RADIO

Big

JOHN CULLUM: The makers of Mobil Delvac 1300 Super understand that truckers like to think big. Makes sense. You drive big trucks with big windshields and big engines. You tour a big country. You use big words like "viscosity." Naturally, you want an oil that thinks big too. And Delvac is as big as it gets out there on the road to happiness. Fact is, Delvac 1300 Super can take you a million miles without an overhaul. Think how big that is. A million's got that number one up front hauling six zeroes behind it - quite a payload. So when you big thinkers hop down from your big trucks and take big steps into a Pilot Travel Center, slam your big fist down on the counter and say: "I don't drive no itty bitty vehicle, gimme that big-thinking oil!" Or, you can ask for Delvac by name if you prefer.

Bugs

JOHN CULLUM: In a million miles of driving you'll see 324 folks cruising with part of their coat stuck out the door. You'll see 894 stuffed animals grinning at you from rear windows. You'll see 92 tourists taking pictures of cows. You'll see 26 stationwagons going 45 miles an hour in the right lane with their turn signal on. You'll also see 1,942 four wheelers cut you off. (The number of choice words you'll share with those four wheelers will vary.) Of course, what you won't see in that million miles is the need for an overhaul. Provided you're running with Mobil Delvac 1300 Super, "The Million Mile Oil." Delvac extends engine life. And Delvac's available right at the Pilot Travel Centers. By the way, we can't say exactly how many bugs you'll get on your grill in a million miles. Couldn't find a volunteer to count 'em.

Wear

JOHN CULLUM: If you'd been born with an odometer on you, what would the mileage read today? Would it match the wear and tear on your body and soul? Have you got a lot of wear on you? Well, the road of life treats everyone like a mud flap on occasion. But your engine, it's gots some help. In the form of Mobil Delvac 1300 Super, "The Million Mile Oil." See, Delvac reduces engine wear. Increases engine life. It's got more road in it. You can ramble a million miles without an overhaul. And you'll probably get more sunburn on your arm than wear on your engine. You'll find Mobil Delvac 1300 Super at Pilot Travel Centers. Or, if you're just dying to know something, call 1-800-662-4525. We'll be more than happy to improve your engine's life. Now as for your own wear and tear, well, that's outside our jurisdiction.

868

Robert Goulet

ANNCR: And now, Mr. Robert Goulet reads from "The Writings of Bart"... the collected after-school blackboard writings of young Bart Simpson. Mr. Goulet...

MUSIC: *Dignified, classical*

ROBERT GOULET: I will not trade pants with others. I will not do that thing with my tongue. I will not Xerox my butt. A burp is not an answer. I will not pledge allegiance to Bart. I will not eat things for money. I will not bring sheep to class. I will not instigate revolution. My name is not Doctor Death.

ANNCR: To experience all of Bart's blackboard writings, watch every classic episode of "The Simpsons."

ROBERT GOULET: I will not call the principal Spud Head.

ANNCR: "The Simpsons," now five times a week.

MUSIC: *Music up, under and out.*

Robert Goulet/Version I

ANNCR: Mr. Robert Goulet reads from the blackboard writings of young Bart Simpson. Mr. Goulet...

MUSIC: *Dignified, classical*

ROBERT GOULET: I will not trade pants with others. I will not do that thing with my tongue. I will not Xerox my butt. I will not bring sheep to class.

ANNCR: To see more of Bart's blackboard writings, watch every classic episode of "The Simpsons," five times a week.

MUSIC: *Music up, under and out.*

Robert Goulet/Version II

ANNCR: Mr. Robert Goulet reads from the blackboard writings of young Bart Simpson. Mr. Goulet...

MUSIC: Dignified, classical

ROBERT GOULET: I will not call the principal Spud Head. I will not pledge allegiance to Bart. I will not eat things for money. My name is not Doctor Death.

ANNCR: To see more of Bart's blackboard writings, watch every classic episode of "The Simpsons," five times a week.

MUSIC: *Music up, under and out.*

869

868
District 2
CLIENT
Mobil Delvac 1300 Super
AGENCY
Arnold Advertising
McLean, VA
CREATIVE DIRECTOR
Jim Kingsley
COPYWRITER
Francis Sullivan
PRODUCER
Francis Sullivan
PRODUCTION
The Music Source

869
District 9
CLIENT
The Simpsons
AGENCY
Paul & Walt Worldwide
St. Louis, MO
COPYWRITER
Walt Jaschek
PRODUCER
Paul Fey
ENGINEER
Brent Hahn

870
District 8
CLIENT
Express Communications
AGENCY
Lawrence & Schiller
Sioux Falls, SD
CREATIVE DIRECTION
Scott Lawrence
Kim Heidinger
Scott Ostman
Darwin Heikes
Greg Wollman

ABOUT THE
AMERICAN ADVERTISING FEDERATION
(AAF)

AAF STAFF

WALLACE SNYDER
President

RONALD ALLEN
Senior Vice President, Operations

JULIE A. DOLAN
Senior Vice President, Development and Communications

JANET KENNEDY
Senior Vice President, Western Region Services
San Francisco, CA

JEFFRY PERLMAN
Senior Vice President, Government Affairs

JOANNE WISEMAN
Senior Vice President, Club Services

CLARK RECTOR
Vice President, State Government Affairs

MARY ELLEN WOOLLEY
Vice President, Education Services

GAIL BOZEMAN
Director, Club Services

KAREN COHN
Director, Conference Services

JEFF CUSTER
Director, Media Relations

JENNY PHALZGRAFF
Director, Communications
Editor, American Advertising

MARYBETH CONNELLY
Senior Marketing Manager, Communications

AAF BOARD OF DIRECTORS 1995-1996

AAF BOARD OF DIRECTORS 1995-1996

WILLIAM C. SCHUMACHER
Director of Advertising
Kraft Foods

CLARENCE O. SMITH
President
Essence Communications, Inc.

WALLY SNYDER
President
American Advertising
Federation

LAWRENCE B. VARNES
Vice Chair & COO/
Western Division
Grey Advertising, Inc.

GUS WALES
Owner
Gus Wales Creative Services

ALAN WAXENBERG
SVP & Publisher
Hearst Magazines Division

DISTRICT GOVERNORS

ELIZABETH G. COOK
Executive Director
The Ad Club of Greater Boston

BARBARA WESTLAND
Vice President
Westland Printers

MICHAEL MAY
Account Executive
Sports Radio AM 910

ART ROWBOTHAM
President
WONN/WPCV

LISA DAVIS
President
One Alliance

MICHAEL N. RUGGIERO
Vice President
Perennial Pictures Film
Corporation

CECE HYLTON
Owner
CeCe Hylton & Company

JAY GOULD
President
The Gould Company

CLAUDIA MARTIN
Senior Media Director
Culver & Associates, Inc.

BILL LEA
General Manager
The Ouachita Citizen

PATTI CODY
Freelance

CONNIE CARVALHO
KLAQ/KROD Radio

BARBARA SCOTT
Account Executive
Krater 96.3

JIM MAGILL
President
Foley & Magill Advertising

JIM NYE
President
Designstream

COUNCIL OF GOVERNORS OFFICERS

Chairman
JIM MYERS
VP/Publisher
Honolulu Magazine

Vice Chairman
MIKE MILLER
Sales Representative
McCormick Armstrong

Secretary-Treasurer
LINDA SHERMAN
Local Sales Manager
WSMV-TV

Immediate Past Chairman
ED ACKERLY
Principal
Ackerly Advertising

CLUB REPRESENTATIVES

WENDA MILLARD
President/Group Publisher
SRDS, Inc.

TRENA PACKER-STREET
Vice President
Associates Promotion & Design

ALAN M. STEIN
Account Executive
WVLK Radio

WILLIAM HILL
Quality Printers

465

AAF NATIONAL ADDY AWARDS PROCESS COMMITTEE 1995-1996

The AAF ADDY Process Committee is a national body made up of local club members who are appointed each year by the AAF president. This committee reviews and revises the rules, entry procedures and categories of the ADDY Awards program. This committee is also charged with implementing standardization criteria and making recommendations regarding judging procedures and standards.

Committee Chair
STEPHEN P. ROGERS
Black, Rogers, Sullivan & Goodnight
Houston TX

AAF Staff Liaison
GAIL BOZEMAN
American Advertising Federation
Washington DC

Committee Members
ED ACKERLEY
Ackerley Advertising
Tucson AZ

JOHN AGUILLARD
Group 400 Advertising
San Antonio TX

STEVEN CURRAN
Harvest Productions
Lansing MI

CHIC DAVIS
Davis & Associates
Baltimore MD

JAY GOULD
Sietsma, Engle & Partners
Minneapolis MN

MIMI KIRSCH
Paradigm Press
Seattle, WA

JIM MAGILL
Foley & Magill Advertising
San Francisco CA

JOEL MORRIS
MediaMax
Salt Lake City UT

MICHAEL N. RUGGIERO
Perennial Pictures Film Corporation
Indianapolis IN

JUDY THOMPSON
Cincinnati Gas & Electric Company
Cincinnati OH

BETH A. WAGNER
Marketing Services
Valley Forge PA

MIKE WEBER
Creative Media Recording
St. Petersburg FL

GUS WALES
Gus Wales Creative Services
Baton Rouge LA

BARBARA WESTLAND
Westland Printers
Burtonsville MD

AAF ADVERTISING HALL OF FAME

Sparked by a proposal from the New York Ad Club's president, Andrew Haire, the Advertising Hall of Fame was begun in 1948. Since then, 129 advertising men and women have been elected to this highly distinguished honor.

Inductees into the Hall of Fame are determined annually by a panel of prominent advertising professionals. The Council of Judges, appointed by the president and the Chairman of the American Advertising Federation, includes respected leaders and executives from advertisers, agencies, media and academia around the country.

The charge to the Council of Judges is to review and consider all nominations to the Hall of Fame, and select those deemed most worthy of election.

Nominees to the Advertising Hall of Fame must have completed their primary business careers, and are judged on the following criteria:

PRIMARY:
The candidate's accomplishments evidenced by creative, media research or marketing excellence; innovations to advertising education, the advertising process and structure; or impact on brand and corporate success and leadership of his or her company.

SECONDARY:
The contribution the candidate made to enhancing the reputation of the advertising industry through volunteer efforts outside his or her company.

The Judges consider the election of both living and deceased individuals; however, the nominees' records of advertising and service must have been accomplished in the United States, or with an American company abroad. The number of annual inductees is determined by the Council of Judges.

Anyone who has been nominated, but not elected, remains a candidate for election for two additional years without the necessity of renomination. Nominations to the Hall of Fame may be made by any individual, group or firm. "Calls for Nominations" are issued by AAF each fall.

Upon induction, each electee receives a "Golden Ladder" trophy signifying membership in the Advertising Hall of Fame. Designed and created by Bill Bernbach and Tom Dillon, both members of the Hall of Fame, the trophy's inscription reads, "If we can see further, it is because we stand on the rungs of a ladder built by those who came before us."

MEMBERS OF THE ADVERTISING HALL OF FAME

1949
Rollin C. Ayres
Cyrus H. K. Curtis
Alfred W. Erickson
William H. Johns
Lewis B. Jones
Theodore F. MacManus
Edwin T. Meredith
John Irving Romer
Walter A. Strong
John Wanamaker

1950
F. Wayland Ayer
Stanley Clague
Benjamin Franklin
James H. McGraw
Merle Sidener

1951
William Cheever D'Arcy
E. St. Elmo Lewis

1952
Erma Perham Proetz
J. Earle Pearson

1953
Samuel C. Dobbs
Charles Coolidge Parlin
James O'Shaughnessy

1954
Frank Presbrey
John E. Powers

1955
Henry T. Ewald
George Burton Hotchkiss

1956
None elected

1957
Herbert S. Houston
Claude Clarence Hopkins

1958
Orlando Clinton Harn
Albert D. Lasker

1959
Merlin Hall Aylesworth
Kerwin Holmes Fulton

1960
Allen Loren Billingsly
James Randolph Adams

1961
Barney Link
Harley Procter

1962
Mac Martin
Donald W. Davis

1963
Gilbert T. Hodges
Paul B. West

1964
Homer J. Buckley
Edgar Kobak
Jesse H. Neal

1965
Robert M. Feemster
Samuel C. Gale
Harrison King McCann

1966
Lee Hastings Bristol
Walter Dill Scott

1967
Ernest Elmo Calkins
Stanley B. Resor
Mrs. Stanley B. Resor
George P. Rowell

1968
Russell T. Gray
Charles W. Mears
Alex F. Osborn

1969
Bruce Barton
Thomas D'Arcy Brophy

1970
Don Belding
Laurence W. Lane
Graham C. Patterson

1971
None elected

1972
Leo Burnett
Ralph Starr Butler
Philip Livingston Thomson

1973
John P. Cunningham
Bernard C. Duffy

1974
James Webb Young
Raymond Rubicam

1975
Fairfax M. Cone
G.D. Crain, Jr.
Artemas Ward

1976
William Bernbach
Victor Elting, Jr.
David Ogilvy

MEMBERS OF THE
ADVERTISING HALL OF FAME

1977
John Caples
George Gallup

1978
John H. Crichton
Barton A. Cummings
William A. Marsteller
J. Walter Thompson

1979
Atherton Wells Hobler
Neil Hosler McElroy

1980
Tom Dillon
Roy Larsen
Shirley Polykoff

1981
Ted Bates
Charlie Brower
Bernice Fitz-Gibbon

1982
Paul Foley
Alfred Seaman

1983
Clarence Eldridge
John Elliott, Jr.
Howard J. Morgens
Owen Burtch Winters

1984
Thomas B. Adams
James S. Fish
Charles H. Sandage

1985
Donald A. Macdonald
Samuel W. Meek
Arthur Harrison Motley

1986
Carl W. Nichols
Arthur C. Nielsen, Sr.
Raymond J. Petersen
Robert W. Woodruff

1987
Eugene H. Kummel
Edward N. Ney
Vance L. Stickell

1988
Sidney R. Bernstein
Robert V. Goldstein
Ray A. Kroc

1989
James E. Burke
Raymond O. Mithun
Jean Wade Rindlaub

1990
Carl J. Ally
Sam R. Bloom
Philip H. Dougherty

1991
Richard C. Christian
Theodore S. Repplier
Neil H. Borden

1992
John S. Bowen

1993
Ralph Carson
Charles T. Coiner
Rosser Reeves

1994
Ira C. Herbert
John E. O'Toole
Michael J. Roarty

1995
Edwin L. Artzt
William Backer
Howard H. Bell
Thomas Murphy

AAF ADVERTISING
HALL OF ACHIEVEMENT

In February 1993, members of the AAF Board of Directors proposed a companion awards program to add a new dimension to the existing Advertising Hall of Fame. The award was triggered by a suggestion that the AAF should recognize young people from across the country who are making enormous progress and positive contributions to the advertising industry, thereby generating great respect from their peers in the business.

Nominees to the Advertising Hall of Achievement must be 40 years old, or under, and employed in the advertising industry (agency, client, or media) in the United States, or with an American company abroad.

The Advertising Hall of Achievement is designed to encourage and recognize those individuals who have begun to make a significant impact on, or contribution to, the advertising business. Nominees are evaluated by an industry Council of Judges on the basis of the following criteria:

PRIMARY:
>   Outstanding career achievements, with measurable results, in the field of advertising, whether in publishing, marketing, sales or media.

SECONDARY:
>   Qualities that motivate others to excel, either by mentoring, inspiring, training or volunteering.

MEMBERS OF THE ADVERTISING HALL OF ACHIEVEMENT

1993	1994	1995
Mary Berner	Kirk Citron	Kimberly Bealle
Sheri Colonel	Lee Garfinkel	Edward R. Erhardt
Donny Deutsch	Scott Kurnit	Donna Kalajian Galotti
Bill Katz	William J. Ludwig	Michael Lotito
Ken Mandelbaum	Nora McAniff	Jon Steel
Jim Speros	Wenda Harris Millard	Anne Sweeney
	Glenn Smith	

INDEX OF COMPANIES AND INDIVIDUALS

INDEX OF INDIVIDUALS

KEY:
AD=Art Director
AE=Account Executive
CD=Creative Director
CDir=Creative Direction
CW=Copywriter
DI=Director
DS=Designer
ED=Editor
EN=Engraver/Retoucher/Pre-Press
GR=Graphics/Animation
IL=Illustrator
MU=Music
PC=Production
PD=Producer
PH=Photographer
PR=Printer
SE=Separator
TL=Talent
TP=Typographer

474

475

11

Alaska

11

14

12

15

Hawaii

13

The three regions
and fifteen districts of the
American Advertising Federation.

1

2

3

7

Virgin Islands
4

Puerto Rico